Northrop Frye

Northrop Frye

Religious Visionary and Architect of the Spiritual World

Robert D. Denham

University of Virginia Press
Charlottesville and London

University of Virginia Press
© 2004 by the Rector and Visitors of the University of Virginia
All rights reserved
Printed in the United States of America on acid-free paper
First published 2004

9 8 7 6 5 4 3 2 1

Library of Congress Cataloging-in-Publication Data

Denham, Robert D.
   Northrop Frye : religious visionary and architect of the spiritual world /
Robert D. Denham
        p.   cm.
   Includes bibliographic references and index.
   ISBN 0-8139-2299-2 (alk. paper)
   1. Frye, Northrop—Religion. I. Title.
   PN75.F7D46 2004
   801'.95'092—dc22
                                                        2004011625

RACHELAE UXORI

Contents

Preface

Almost thirty-five years ago I picked up *Anatomy of Criticism,* read it, and realized I was in the presence of an extraordinary mind. For a number of years I was convinced that this was the central work in the Frye canon, even though in the 1960s the canon was not all that large. I was attracted to the *Anatomy's* schematic ingenuity, its power as a teaching manual, and, as I had come under the sway of the new criticism, its claims for the autonomy of both literature and criticism. Had I come to Frye by way of *Fearful Symmetry,* I suspect that my view of his work would have caused me to take a different course. In any case, as I have followed the contours of Frye's career, I have become more and more convinced that what is fundamental to his work is not so much the principles outlined in the *Anatomy,* though that is surely a book that will remain with us, but the values that emerge from those works that serve as the bookends of his career, *Fearful Symmetry* at the beginning and fifty years later the two Bible books and *The Double Vision.* During the past two decades I have had a developing intuition that the central feature of the superstructure Frye built is its religious base. This intuition has been strengthened during the ten years I have been pondering Frye's notebooks, especially his late notebooks. The present book is an exploration of this intuition.

To examine fully Frye's religious views would require a much more expansive commentary than the present one. I have taken little account of Frye's writings on the Bible, contained primarily in *The Great Code, Words with Power,* and the essays in part 1 of *Northrop Frye on Religion* (which includes *The Double Vision*), although I have turned to these writings when they are apposite to my own exposition. Much has been written on Frye's biblical criticism already, including several hundred reviews, essays from three symposia, Alvin Lee's introduction to *Northrop Frye on Religion,* and two collections of essays (*Frye and the Word: Religious Contexts in the Criticism of Northrop Frye,* edited by Jeffrey Donaldson and Alan Mendelson, and *Northrop Frye and the Afterlife of the Word,* edited by James M. Kee). On the whole I have had to neglect as well Frye's remarkably mature student essays, many of which anticipate his later views.

The final cause of the present study is understanding, not judgment, and its efficient cause is primarily exposition. It seeks to make clear the religious ideas found in Frye. While I believe that many of these ideas are liberating and am sympathetic to his grand project, I make no effort to assess their powers and limitations. My intent has been to read Frye on his own terms. Accordingly I devote little attention to the religious, theological, and critical contexts of Frye's writing. Evaluating and contextualizing Frye are both important tasks, but they follow from understanding and are thus the subjects for subsequent study.

I have quoted liberally from Frye, especially from his notebooks, published and unpublished, and I have given some attention to the sources of Frye's ideas. In his published writings Frye was very stingy when it came to noting his sources, and his own endnotes, when they exist at all, are random, selective, and sketchy, if not sometimes a parody of acknowledgment. While we know a great deal from Frye's books and essays about his debts to, say, Spengler, Frazer, Freud, Jung, the Cambridge anthropologists, Plato, Aristotle, Hegel, Heidegger, nineteenth-century British thinkers, and a number of poets and novelists, we could not have known much at all before Frye's notebooks came to light about his reading of Robert Anton Wilson's *Cosmic Trigger,* Itzhak Bentov's *Stalking the Wild Pendulum,* Rudy Rucker's *Infinity and the Mind,* Ken Wilber's *The Holographic Paradigm,* Stanislav Grof's *Realms of Human Unconscious,* Michael Baigent, Richard Leigh, and Henry Lincoln's *Holy Blood, Holy Grail,* A. E. Waite's books on the grail and the Tarot, Marilyn Ferguson's *The Aquarian Conspiracy,* Gurdjieff and his pupil Ouspensky, and scores of other books in the Eastern, mystical, hermetic, and esoteric traditions. Part of my purpose, then, is to reveal a side of Frye not previously known or only dimly perceived, and while my intent is different from that of *The Road to Xanadu,* I have tried to document what Frye was reading and when (so far as it can be determined). This task has been made easier by the access we now have to the diaries, notebooks, and annotated books in Frye's personal library. Occasionally I refer to the number of times a topic is mentioned in Frye's notebooks. These data do not count as qualitative evidence in an argument, but they do indicate the degree to which Frye often addresses topics in his notebooks that are largely absent from his published work.

The two chapters devoted to Frye's interest in the esoteric traditions will make it clear, I hope, the meanings attached to "esoteric." Although I use the word "exoterica" as a heading for part 1, the word and its cognates seldom appear elsewhere. I do not define the term, using it simply to designate Frye's religious speculations that are not esoteric and that are broadly within the framework of Christianity, though I include Eastern religion within the category of exoterica. I do not mean, however, for exoteric to suggest institutional religion, much less doctrine.

I have not tried to define in any systematic way the nouns lying behind the adjectives "religious" and "spiritual" in my subtitle, both of which are what W. C. Gallie calls "essentially contested concepts"—words about whose meaning and use there is widespread debate. Jonathan Z. Smith maintains that "'religion' is not a native term; it is a term created by scholars for their intellectual purposes and therefore is theirs to define. It is a second-order generic concept that plays the same role in establishing a disciplinary horizon that a concept such as 'language' plays in linguistics or 'culture' plays in anthropology."[1] The different meanings that cluster around the words *religious* and *spiritual* as Frye uses them will emerge, it is hoped, as we proceed. A large part of what follows is devoted to uncovering the rich array of meanings that accumulate around other of Frye's key terms, and many of these terms are part of the semantic field of *religious* and *spiritual,* which I take to be "generic" terms in Smith's sense, not "native" ones.

I have borrowed from several essays I wrote during the past decade and from the introductions to two of the notebook volumes in the Collected Works of Northrop Frye, and I thank the editors and publishers of that material for letting me recirculate it in a revised and expanded form and in a wider context. The original sources of this appropriated material are "Interpenetration as a Key Concept in Frye's Critical Vision," in *Rereading Frye: The Published and Unpublished Works,* edited by David Boyd and Imre Salusinszky (Toronto: University of Toronto Press, 1999), 140–63; "Frye and the East: Buddhist and Hindu Translations," in *Northrop Frye: Eastern and Western Perspectives,* edited by Jean O'Grady and Wang Ning (Toronto: University of Toronto Press, 2003), 3–18; "The Religious Base of Northrop Frye's Criticism," *Christianity and Literature* 41 (Spring 1992): 241–54; "Northrop Frye's 'Kook Books' and the Esoteric Tradition," in *Frye and the Word: Religious Contexts in the Criticism of Northrop Frye,* edited by Alan Mendelson and Jeffery Donaldson (Toronto: University of Toronto Press, 2003), 329–56; introduction to *Northrop Frye's Late Notebooks, 1982–1990: Architect of the Spiritual World* (Toronto: University of Toronto Press, 2000), xix–xlv; "'Vision' as a Key Term in Frye's Criticism," *University of Toronto Quarterly* 73 (Summer 2004): 807–46; and introduction to *Northrop Frye's Notebooks and Lectures on the Bible and Other Religious Texts* (Toronto: University of Toronto Press, 2003), xxix–lv.

The citations to most of Frye's writings are in the text itself. These citations use the abbreviations that have become standard for the Collected Works, and a list of these abbreviations follows the preface. For the published notebooks the number that follows the cited volume (e.g., *RT,*

223) is to the page number. For the unpublished notebooks the two numbers separated by a period are to the notebook number and the paragraph
number (e.g., 31.24). This means that once the remaining notebooks are
published, readers so inclined can find the cited passage by paragraph
number.

I have, as usual, many debts. An important one is to my friend and
collaborator in editing Frye's unpublished work, Michael Dolzani, whose
wide knowledge of Frye runs deep and who remains for me Frye's best
commentator. A draft of the present manuscript benefited from his insights. Richard Outram, whose understanding of Frye is considerable, has
pointed me to a number of passages in Frye's work that I had forgotten or
passed over, and I am grateful to him for that and for other generosities.
Nicholas Graham has assisted me in meticulously combing through several dozen books in Frye's library and cataloguing marked passages and
annotations. He has worked without recompense, save his own love of
learning and, I trust, the knowledge of my gratitude for his help. My col-
leagues at the Northrop Frye Centre at Victoria University—Alvin Lee,
Jean O'Grady, and Margaret Burgess—deserve special recognition for
their cooperation and encouragement over the years and for other nameless, unremembered acts of kindness and of love. All of these friends give
testimony to Frye's contention that the individual crystallizes from a genuine community. I am grateful to Roanoke College for providing a publication grant, to the National Endowment for the Humanities for a
fellowship that once again gave me a year to write without other obligations, and to Victoria University, which holds the copyright for much of
Frye's writing, for permitting me to quote a large body of his words. My
greatest debt remains, as always, to my wife, Rachel, who forgives my
many trespasses.

Abbreviations

AC	*Anatomy of Criticism: Four Essays.* Princeton: Princeton University Press, 1957.
CP	*The Critical Path: An Essay on the Social Context of Literary Criticism.* Bloomington: Indiana University Press, 1971.
D	*The Diaries of Northrop Frye, 1942–1955.* Ed. Robert D. Denham. Collected Works of Northrop Frye, vol. 8. Toronto: University of Toronto Press, 2001.
DG	*Divisions on a Ground: Essays on Canadian Culture.* Ed. James Polk. Toronto: Anansi, 1982.
DV	*The Double Vision: Language and Meaning in Religion.* Toronto: United Church Publishing House, 1991.
FI	*Fables of Identity: Studies in Poetic Mythology.* New York: Harcourt, Brace and World, 1963.
FS	*Fearful Symmetry: A Study of William Blake.* Princeton, N.J.: Princeton University Press, 1947.
FT	*Fools of Time: Studies in Shakespearean Tragedy.* Toronto: University of Toronto Press, 1967.
GC	*The Great Code: The Bible and Literature.* New York: Harcourt Brace Jovanovich, 1982.
LN	*Northrop Frye's Late Notebooks, 1982–1990: Architecture of the Spiritual World.* Ed. Robert D. Denham. 2 vols. Collected Works of Northrop Frye, vols. 5 and 6. Toronto: University of Toronto Press, 2000.
LS	*Northrop Frye on Literature and Society, 1936–1989: Unpublished Papers.* Ed. Robert D. Denham. Collected Works of Northrop Frye, vol. 10. Toronto: University of Toronto Press, 2002.
MD	*The Myth of Deliverance: Reflections on Shakespeare's Problem Comedies.* Toronto: University of Toronto Press, 1983.
MM	*Myth and Metaphor: Selected Essays, 1974–1988.* Ed. Robert D. Denham. Charlottesville: University Press of Virginia, 1990.
NFC	*Northrop Frye in Conversation,* by David Cayley. Concord, Ont.: Anansi, 1992.
NFCL	*Northrop Frye on Culture and Literature: A Collection of Review Essays.* Ed. Robert D. Denham. Chicago: University of Chicago Press, 1978.

NFHK   *The Correspondence of Northrop Frye and Helen Kemp, 1932–1939*. Ed. Robert D. Denham. 2 vols. Collected Works of Northrop Frye, vols. 1 and 2. Toronto: University of Toronto Press, 1996.

NFR   *Northrop Frye on Religion*. Ed. Alvin A. Lee and Jean O'Grady. Collected Works of Northrop Frye, vol. 4. Toronto: University of Toronto Press, 2000.

RE   *The Return of Eden: Five Essays on Milton's Epics*. Toronto: University of Toronto Press, 1965.

RT   *Northrop Frye's Notebooks and Lectures on the Bible and Other Religious Texts*. Ed. Robert D. Denham. Collected Works of Northrop Frye, vol. 13. Toronto: University of Toronto Press, 2003.

RW   *Reading the World: Selected Writings, 1935–1976*. Ed. Robert D. Denham. New York: Peter Lang, 1990.

SE   *Northrop Frye's Student Essays, 1932–1938*. Ed. Robert D. Denham. Collected Works of Northrop Frye, vol. 3. Toronto: University of Toronto Press, 1997.

SeS   *The Secular Scripture: A Study of the Structure of Romance*. Cambridge, Mass.: Harvard University Press, 1976.

SM   *Spiritus Mundi: Essays on Literature, Myth, and Society*. Bloomington: Indiana University Press, 1976.

SR   *A Study of English Romanticism*. New York: Random House, 1968.

StS   *The Stubborn Structure: Essays on Criticism and Society*. Ithaca, N.Y.: Cornell University Press, 1970.

TBN   *The "Third Book" Notebooks of Northrop Frye, 1964–1972: The Critical Comedy*. Ed. Michael Dolzani. Collected Works of Northrop Frye, vol. 9. Toronto: University of Toronto Press, 2001.

WGS   *A World in a Grain of Sand: Twenty-Two Interviews with Northrop Frye*. Ed. Robert D. Denham. New York: Peter Lang, 1991.

WP   *Words with Power: Being a Second Study of "The Bible and Literature."* New York: Harcourt Brace Jovanovich, 1990.

WTC   *The Well-Tempered Critic*. Bloomington: Indiana University Press, 1963.

Northrop Frye

Introduction

I'm an architect of the spiritual world.
—*Late Notebooks*, 1:414

I think what mostly bothers [Harold Bloom] about my present books is that a religious position seems to be emerging, both in *The Critical Path* and *The Secular Scripture*.
—Northrop Frye, letter to Robert Denham, 21 June 1976

It has been almost a dozen years since Margaret Burgess, speaking at a conference devoted to the legacy of Northrop Frye, examined the anxieties surrounding the religious scope of Frye's thought, anxieties that produced in her view a widespread resistance to directly confronting things spiritual. Craig Stewart Walker, speaking at the same conference, observed in a similar vein that in the modern world it has become increasingly difficult to speak about religion because "the language of religion is widely regarded with suspicion and indifference."[1] A more recent conference entitled "Frye and the Word," which focused on the religious contexts of Frye's work, especially as they related to his studies of the Bible, suggests that this "resistance to religion" (Burgess's phrase) may be diminishing. If it is diminishing, perhaps those interested in Frye will be receptive to a fuller study than now exists on the role of religion in his work as a whole.[2] The present book takes a step in that direction. If the resistance is not diminishing, perhaps this study will offer sufficient evidence that it should.

Frye is one of the preeminent humanists of the last century, and his reputation derives chiefly from *Anatomy of Criticism,* which, twenty years after its publication, was the most frequently cited book in the arts and humanities by a writer born in the twentieth-century.[3] This expansive book about the conventions of literary structure is very much a product of the 1950s, when critical formalism reigned supreme, and Frye insists in the "Polemical Introduction" to the *Anatomy* that criticism must free itself from determinisms of all sorts—social, psychological, political, *and* religious. The fact that the *Anatomy* looms large in both Frye's career and the history of modern criticism is perhaps one reason that many of his readers have tended either to overlook or to neglect the thirty books that followed in its wake. But the scope of Frye's work as a whole is now coming into focus with the publication of the Collected Works. The chief assumption on which the present study is based is that we cannot properly understand that large body of work without considering the ways Frye's views on religion interpenetrate practically everything he wrote. His religious ideas emerge unmistakably, though often behind a Blakean mask, in *Fearful Symmetry* (1947); they are clearly present in his account of anagogy and elsewhere in *Anatomy of Criticism;* and the coda of the Frye canon, *The Double Vision* (1991), is subtitled "Language and Meaning in Religion," suggesting that in Frye's end is his beginning.

In the massive commentary on Frye only a relatively small portion has concerned itself at all with his visionary religious views. My own study is naturally indebted to a number of Frye's commentators, but it differs in what has come before because the subject it addresses has not been treated comprehensively before. In differs as well because it draws extensively on the large body of Frye's writing that was not published (and not written for publication) during his lifetime—his student essays, diaries, essays left in manuscript, and notebooks.[4] This material, an extraordinary record of Frye's critical and imaginative life and his religious reflections, is not so much a supplement to his books and essays as it is a major component of his oeuvre. The importance of this rich body of material, which often differs in tone and substance from his published work, will become evident as we proceed. One of the principal areas of difference is Frye's interest in what I am calling "esoteric spirituality," an umbrella phrase that includes mysticism, certain practices and concepts in Eastern religious traditions, astrology, alchemy, numerology, Kabbalism, hermeticism, New Age science and religion, occultism, channeling, synchronicity, fourth-force psychology, and a group of zany and eccentric texts that Frye refers to as his "kook books." The esoteric tradition appears repeatedly in Frye's notebooks, and this little-known aspect of his thinking deserves attention if we are to have a full understanding of the religious dimensions of his thought. Chapters 5 and 6 are a study of Frye's esoteric interests.

In 1948 Edith Sitwell, having read *Fearful Symmetry* and Frye's early essay "Yeats and the Language of Symbolism," wrote to Frye, "It is most exciting to me to know that at last we have a critic we have been waiting for. But it goes further than that. I think you will also prove to be the religious teacher we have been waiting for."[5] It is a testimony to Sitwell's prescience that she recognized more than fifty-five years ago that the religious base of Frye's thought is a defining feature. That base is what the present study seeks to elucidate. The weak claim for such an argument would be that, yes, of course, religion *was* important for Frye. He did, after all, serve as an ordained minister in the United Church of Canada for fifty-five years. Early in his career he wrote a trenchant essay on American civil religion and another one on the relation of the church to society.[6] He preached and married and buried and composed some exceptionally eloquent prayers, and he got rather testy with the church bureaucrats when they wrote to him suggesting, apparently because of his absence from the parish or his liberal views or his failure to attend church on Sunday mornings, that it might be time for him to surrender his holy orders. Frye replied, a bit irritably, that he had no intention of doing so.[7] And, yes, he wrote about Blake, who was a deeply religious poet; he wrote about and taught the Bible; and he addressed religious subjects on numerous occasions: *Northrop Frye on Religion,* volume 4 in the Collected Works, contains forty-three texts. Only the uninformed, then, would claim that religion was not important for Frye. But to say that religion was of interest to Frye the literary critic, or even of some consequence, would be the weak claim.

The strong claim would be that religion was central to practically everything Frye wrote, the foundation on which he built the massive superstructure that was his life's work. The strong claim, which is the one I want to make, would be to take Frye at his word when he says, "I'm an architect of the spiritual world" (*LN,* 1:414). I would not have made that argument twenty-five years ago, when I wrote a book that centered on the structure and method of *Anatomy of Criticism,* and I would not be able to make the claim now had I not been immersed in Frye's notebooks for the past decade. My focus in what follows is on the final cause of Frye's work. The structural poetics of *Anatomy of Criticism,* which is what placed Frye at the center of criticism in the 1960s, "moves toward a *telos*" (*TBN,* 54) but is not itself the *telos.* "Post-structuralists," Frye writes, "say that it's illusory to use the spatializing metaphor of structure, but that's just the idling machinery of negativism running on its own: to gain a simultaneous understanding of a poem as a unit is both possible and highly desirable. The only thing is that it isn't an ultimate goal: as soon as you've reached it you discard it like a snake's skin or a nautilus's shell" (*LN,* 2:507).[8] Structure, then, is a means toward the ultimate goal, which, according to the strong claim I am making, is spiritual vision. This, then, is another difference between my study and what has come before.

The chief challenge of the strong claim is to avoid reductionism. The more than two dozen books devoted solely to Frye and the hundreds of essays on his work have often isolated central features in the considerable body of criticism he produced over a period of sixty years—his formalism, his structural ingenuity, his links with the mythopoeic tradition, his poetics of process, his theoretical imagination, his vision of the new world, his Blakean Romanticism, and so on.[9] The scope of Frye's canon is large enough to accommodate the study of any number of key ingredients, and the anxiety associated with claiming that there is *a* key for unlocking the treasure in his oeuvre is a genuine one. Finding such a key is complicated by the fact that *Anatomy of Criticism,* as already said, has been taken by most readers as the central work in the Frye canon. It is the book that made him famous in America and, having been translated now into twelve languages, has given him a substantial reputation abroad.[10] But an understanding of Frye's works cannot overlook what followed the *Anatomy,* including the manuscripts that came to light following his death. Most of the essential material in the large body of unpublished writing has now made its way into print, and the present study takes advantage of my good fortune in having had access to all of this material, including those notebooks that still await publication and the unpublished typescripts. If I am mistaken in advancing the strong claim, I can take some comfort in the fact that Frye's work is like the net of Indra, each jewel mirroring the whole.

The Human Form Divine

The religious base in Frye's thought begins, as do most things in his work, with William Blake, who was the source, Frye said repeatedly, of all his critical ideas. Perhaps the most well-known statement of this influence is in the preface to the Beacon Press edition of *Fearful Symmetry,* written some seventeen years after Frye had last read the book: "I had not realized, before this last rereading, how completely the somewhat unusual form and structure of my commentary was derived from my absorption in the larger critical theory implicit in Blake's view of art. Whatever importance the book may have, beyond its merits as a guide to Blake, it owes its connection to the critical theories that I have ever since been trying to teach, in Blake's name and in my own."[11] Or again, as Frye remarked in two different interviews, "I've learned everything I know from Blake" (*WGS,* 275, 285). This is at best a half-truth, but to have learned half of what one knows from a single poet, if one's learning is as broad as Frye's, is still a substantial amount.

    A. C. Hamilton notes four "seminal" influences of Blake on Frye: Blake's lifestyle provided Frye a model for his own life; he taught Frye the importance of the literary context for literature; he showed Frye the centrality of the Bible in Western art; and he led Frye to see the importance of the schematic nature of poetry and therefore of criticism.[12] But perhaps the most important thing Blake taught Frye was the religious vision of radical immanence. Blake insists, says Frye, that "everything that God does comes through man—the consciousness and imagination of man. . . . God becomes man in order that we may be as he is" (*NFC*, 54). In his Laocoön aphorisms Blake says, "The Eternal Body of Man is The IMAG-INATION. That is, God himself."[13] Or again, in his annotations to Berkeley's *Siris,* Blake exclaims, "Man is All Imagination God is Man & exists in us & we in him."[14] These are different ways of putting what Blake calls "the human form divine" in the *Songs of Innocence.*[15] Here we have a doctrine of the radical immanence of the divine, as opposed to divine transcendence. When an interviewer once asked Frye what the word God means in the modern world, he replied: "The only thing that God can possibly mean is what he really does mean in Christianity, that is to say a suffering man. . . . [T]he only role that God can have in human life is that of a man who cares enough about society to go even to the extent of a hideous death for man's salvation" (*WGS*, 96).

But to speak of God as immanent or as transcendent is to rely on a theological language of subjects and objects. Such an approach is valid from Frye's point of view, though it is extremely limited; for language that assumes human beings are subjects and God is an object is an exclusive mode of verbal communication, one belonging to what Frye calls the secondary phase of language, its generally discursive mode, of which theology is one form. Among the classical theologians, Frye knew Augustine well. He knew less of the Reformation theologians, though early in his career he studied Calvin. Among modern theologians he read at least the first volume of Karl Barth's *Dogmatics* and had some familiarity with Paul Tillich and Rudolf Bultmann.[16] But on the whole Frye paid little attention to the theologians because he was not much interested in doctrine or systematic theology as modes of thought. The more inclusive and illuminating mode of consciousness, for Frye, is the imaginative or metaphorical one, and this will be a note sounded often in the chapters that follow. "The metaphorical approach," he says, "moves in the direction of the identity of God and man" (*NFC*, 183), which is his way of talking about the Incarnation. Or again, "I think the real conception 'God' must start in typological metaphor: God is the existential reality of the 'all one body we' metaphor" (*RT,* 350).[17]

Identity, as opposed to analogy, is the principle lying behind metaphor, which makes the paradoxical claim that two different things are the same thing: "Christ is a lamb" or "God is man" or, to use Frye's oft-quoted example from Genesis 49, "Joseph is a fruitful bough." Those who have difficulty with paradox will make little headway in Frye, because paradox lies at the heart of both religious and literary language, both of which stretch the mind, resist our habitual ways of thinking, and may represent the ultimate linguistic function: "Metaphors are paradoxical, and again we suspect that perhaps only in paradox are words doing the best they can for us" (DV, 17). Frye was fond of endorsing what he called the Tertullian paradox: "It is believable because it is absurd; it is certain because it is impossible."[18] The paradox appealed to Frye because Tertullian dissociated belief and credibility. Although the context here is belief, the principle applies to hypothetical or imaginative acceptance as well.

Identity is also a principle of myth: in our earliest stories, which are stories about gods, the gods are themselves identified with forces in nature. In such hyphenated words as *sky-god* or *river-god,* the hyphen really functions as an equal mark, identifying the sky or the river with the god. *Mythos* or narrative, moreover, has to do with the loss and regaining of identity, or recognition of self by both literary characters and readers, which is the general topic of *The Secular Scripture.* We will look more closely at the principle of identity in chapter 2.

Frye's lack of interest in theology notwithstanding, it is perhaps worth remarking that his poetics does have some parallels with Friedrich Schleiermacher's theology of feeling, which is a theology less encumbered with doctrine than most theologies. Frye encountered Schleiermacher as a theology student at Emmanuel College, and in several of his student essays he writes about Schleiermacher as the typical Romantic theologian—one who, with his intuitive religious aestheticism, represents the last effort to hold together the nature-and-spirit opposition of the zeitgeist.[19] In one of his papers the twenty-three-year-old Frye declares that his own approach to the relation of religion to art "is Arminian, via Schleiermacher."[20] Later Frye encountered Rudolf Otto's treatment of Schleiermacher in *Mysticism East and West.* Otto attempts to make the case that Schleiermacher's work represents the "two ways" of mysticism, the mysticism of introspection and the mysticism of unifying vision. "Vision" is one of Frye's key terms, and he always sought unity in diversity. But for all of Frye's emphasis on experience, the Romantic notion of introspective feeling had little appeal for him, for reasons that will become clear as we proceed, and Schleiermacher, at least in Otto's view, was never able to resolve the opposition between the "two ways."[21] The only other place Frye ever mentions Schleiermacher is in a sketchy outline, entitled "Summa," for the book he planned to write, or at least for one section of his unrealized third book, *The Critical Comedy,* having to do with various displacements of myth. One part of this project was to treat the conceptual displacements of myth in philosophy. In "Summa" he outlines the various philosophers he proposes to include, followed by the theological displacements, particularly those of Protestantism. In this outline he writes, "The three aspects of Blake's theology of imagination: Ritschl on the Kingdom of Heaven teaching of Jesus, Schleiermacher on the quasi-aesthetic response, [Thomas Hill] Green on the growth of Christianity as a proletarian religion."[22]

But beyond these meager references, there is no evidence that Frye paid much attention to Schleiermacher. Still, their positions are in some respects remarkably similar, especially with regard to aesthetic and religious experience. In the following passage by Schleiermacher on the imagination, Frye would have found the Arminianism and the almost Blakean ideas on creation congenial to his own way of thinking:

> The stages of religion depend on the sense, the idea of God on the direction of the imagination. If your imagination attach itself to the consciousness of freedom so that it cannot think of what originally operates on it, except as a free being, you will personify the Spirit of the Universe and have a God. If it attach itself to understanding, so that you always clearly perceive that freedom has only meaning in the individual and not for individuals, then you have a World and no God. You will not I trust consider it blasphemy that the belief in God should depend on the direction of the imagination. You will know that imagination is the highest and most original activity in man, and that all besides is only a reflection upon it. Your imagination creates the world, and you could have no God without the world.[23]

René Wellek defines Romanticism as the effort "to identify subject and object, to reconcile man and nature, consciousness and unconsciousness, by poetry which is 'the first and last of all knowledge.'"[24] According to one commentator, "Schleiermacher could well be taken as a textbook case of the definition, with the added stipulation that the word 'poetry'. . . would have meant something like Christian poetic theology or a Christian theological poetics, as the force that integrates the antithetical pairs of subject and object, man and nature, consciousness and unconsciousness."[25]

Romantic religious thought, with its emphasis on experience, may not issue in a theology of transcendence, but there is a strong current running throughout Frye's work which moves in a direction opposite from immanence. It is an idealizing tendency which wants to escape from the nightmare of history, which is attracted to those moments of intense consciousness that move us beyond time and space, and which wants to climb up the Platonic ladder to the world of pure spirit. Sometimes this may appear in Frye as a nostalgic longing for the mythical world of pure identity and a yearning for an altogether different order of experience:

> Continued study of literature and the arts brings us into an entirely new world, where creation and revelation have different meanings, where the experience of time and space is different. As its outlines take shape, our standards of reality and illusion get reversed. It is the illusions of literature that begin to seem real, and ordinary life, pervaded as it is with all the phony and lying myths that surround us, begins to look like the real hallucination, a parody of the genuine imaginative world. The glimpses that I have had of the imaginative world have kept me fascinated for nearly half a century. (*MM*, 77–78)

The key issue here is the experience of myth and metaphor. It is possible, Frye feels, to recapture the intensity of perception that was available to people in Vico's age of the gods. These are what he calls "moments of ecstatic union," or what we refer to as peak experiences—epiphanic moments that take us away from ordinary waking consciousness. Here are two typical accounts of such experience.

> The poem or painting is in some respects a "hallucination": it is summoned up out of the artist's mind and imposed on us, and is allied to delirium tremens or pretending that one is Napoleon. Blake would say that such creative hallucinations are spiritual visions, and that what they present is more detailed, more vivid, and more accurate than anything that normal eyesight affords. In other respects a work of art is like a dream, but it does not introduce us to the ordinary dream world, where we retreat from reality into our withdrawn selves. It takes us into the world of social vision that informs our waking life, where we see that most of what we call "reality" is the rubbish of leftover human constructs. It speaks with authority, but not the familiar authority of parental or social conditioning: there will always be, I expect, some mystery about the real source of its authority. (*MM*, 77)

> Moments of ecstatic union . . . may come and go, like flashes of lightning, but some moments are . . . the frozen or simultaneously grasped aspects of a *mythos* or continuous narrative. Within the limitations of human life, the most highly developed human types are those whose lives have become, as we say, a legend, that is lives no longer contemplating a vision of objective revelation or imprisoned within a subjective dream. The New Testament presents the ultimate human life as a divine and human Logos, but the Logos has transcended its relation to

logic and has expanded into *mythos,* a life which is, so to speak, a kind of self-narration, where action and awareness of action are no longer clashing with each other. (*MM,* 17)

Such ecstatic moments carry one into a symbolic world, and the French *symbolistes,* Rilke, and Pater, among others, are especially given to recording these "portents or auguries of what life could be." "It is worth any amount of commonplace life," Frye says, "to purchase one of them" (*MM,* 38). He remarks that we try to capture the intensity of experience involved in the identification of metaphor with such words as "magical" and "religious" (*MM,* 22–23). These moments of intense perception are what Blake calls seeing with a twofold vision. When such perception takes place, Frye says, "the whole world is humanized" (*DV,* 23). Or again,

> Metaphor, as a bridge between consciousness and nature, is in fact a microcosm of language itself. It is precisely the function of language to overcome what Blake calls the "cloven fiction" of a subject contemplating an object. . . . Language from this point of view becomes a single gigantic metaphor, the uniting of consciousness with what it is conscious of. This union is Ovid's metamorphosis in reverse, the transfiguring of consciousness as it merges with articulated meaning. In a more specifically religious area this third order would become Martin Buber's world of "Thou," which comes between the consciousness that is merely an "I" and a nature that is merely an "it." (*MM,* 115)

The continuous narrative or *mythos* that Frye speaks of is the universal human story from creation to apocalypse. He was always much more attracted to the forms of comedy and romance than to tragedy and irony because such stories represent the possibilities of a redeemed life. "Resurrection," for Frye, is "the symbol of man's self-transcendence into a larger framework of existence" (*MM,* 274). Our understanding of revelation or apocalypse is limited if we try to grasp it only in doctrinal terms. Apocalypse, he says, "is primarily a vision of a body of imagery, where the images of every category of being, divine, angelic, paradisal, human, animal, vegetable, and inorganic, are all identified with the body of Christ. That means that all the images are metaphorically related" (*MM,* 101).

Apocalyptic reality for Frye—however it may sometimes seem to be pure noumenon in Kant's sense—is, as we will see, never an escape from the phenomenological world. If it were, Frye's commitment to the Hegelian *Aufhebung,* about which we will have a great deal to say, would be beside the point. One recent study of Frye makes a case for describing his whole approach to myth as phenomenological, meaning that it is always rooted in the concrete, existential experience of the phenomenal world and that it requires participation in, not flight from, that world.[26] This view is confirmed by a number of Frye's central claims: the *axis mundi* points in two directions, and the calm and detached vision of what Frye calls the panoramic apocalypse is always followed, or should be, by the engagement of the participating one.

In the chapters that follow we will have occasion to investigate in some detail all the issues just broached—the imagination, ecstatic awareness, the anabatic impulse and its relation to katabasis, spiritual vision, the different uses of language, metaphorical identity, higher consciousness, spiritual vision, the panoramic and participating apocalypse, and the *Aufhebung* dialectic.

Apocalypse, the final event of *Heilsgeschichte,* raises the question of the end of things, and one of the places where the visionary side of Frye emerges most clearly is in his sense of an ending. He often wrote about the end of things, apocalypse being a central category for him in both literature and life. The sense of an ending, says Frank Kermode in his book of that title, reflects our "irreducibly intermediary preoccupations."[27] Frye's sense of an ending is a function of his religious vision, his own central intermediary preoccupation.

In *The Secular Scripture* Frye remarks that "not all of us will be satisfied with calling the central part of our mythological inheritance a revelation from God, and, though each chapter of this book closes on much the same cadence, I cannot claim to have found a more acceptable formulation" (60). The context of this perception is still another of Frye's many efforts to name the imagination's sense of otherness, but what is perhaps most revealing is the dependent clause tucked away in the middle. To speak of the cadence of closure calls our attention to the intimate relation between the rhythm of Frye's ideas and his sense of an ending. The conclusions to Frye's books, to chapters within his books, and to his essays seem more often than not to return to his own sense of what is fundamental—what he refers to as "the third order of experience" (*CP,* 170). This is imaginative experience, but it is also the experience of a religious vision, which is perhaps why Frye referred to his own written texts as "incarnational or prophetic" (*LN,* 1:248). Here are three typical endings:

> In the last plate [of Blake's Job illustrations], things are much as they were before, but Job's family have taken the instruments down from the tree and are playing them. In Blake, we recover our original state, not by returning to it, but by re-creating it. The act of creation, in its turn, is not producing something out of nothing, but the act of setting free what we already possess. (*StS,* 199)

If the human race were to destroy both itself and the planet it lives on, that would be the final triumph of illusion. But we have other myths, myths telling us that time and space and life have an end, but that the sense of identity with something other than these things will not, that there is a word which, whether flesh or not, is still dwelling with us. Also that our ability to respond to what it says is the only sensible reason yet proposed for our being here. (*MM*, 122–23)

There is nothing so unique about death as such, where we may be too distracted by illness or sunk in senility to have much identity at all. In the double vision of a spiritual and a physical world simultaneously present, every moment we have lived through we have also died out of into another order. Our life in the resurrection, then, is already here, and waiting to be recognized. (*DV*, 85)

There are for Frye recognition and self-recognition scenes in life as well as in literature. The latter, he says, have much to do with helping us in the journey toward our own identity. In *The Secular Scripture* he makes clear that the highest form of self-identity comes from one's vision of the apocalyptic world, the original world from which we have fallen, a world of revelation and full knowledge which exists between "is" and "is not" and in which divine and human creativity are merged into one. This matter of the relation between literary and personal identity is addressed in chapter 2.

The two tendencies in Frye's criticism we have glanced at—one moving in the direction of theological immanence, the other in the direction of transcendence—naturally raise the question: how are they to live together in some kind of concord? Frye is a dialectical thinker, and the effort to answer this question, in the various ways he introduces the opposing terms of the dialectic, will recur throughout the present study. One central form that the resolution takes is what Frye calls interpenetration, which is the subject of chapter 1. The process of resolution, to be examined in detail as we proceed, is an imaginative mode of Hegel's philosophical *Aufhebung,* a process of canceling, preserving, and lifting up to a higher level. This dialectic, which refers to both a retention and a transformation of the two opposites of the dialectic and which is related to Frye's sense of an ending, manifests itself at those points where Frye is confronted with an either-or opposition. As one of Hegel's commentators puts it: "Unity is therefore the *transcendence* of that which is unified, and transcendence is a *movement* from an initial state (e) to its negation (−e). In this unity each opposite is *aufgehoben,* i.e. (a) it is cancelled, yet (b) preserved *as* a negative presence and (c) raised to a higher or 'richer' level in that *as* a negative presence each element (e) can be conjoined with its opposite (−e) expressing a state of transition . . . without contradiction."[28]

Part of our purpose will be to trace this process: it reveals as much as anything else about the way Frye's mind works. One of the central dialectics Frye keeps coming back to is the human-divine one, the containing form of which is the Incarnation. Frye approaches the Incarnation not doctrinally but metaphorically, as in these passages:

> The Bible begins by showing on its first page that the reality of God manifests itself in creation, and on its last page that the same reality is manifested in a new creation in which man is a participant. He becomes a participant by being redeemed, or separated from the predatory and destructive element acquired from his origin in nature. In between these visions of creation comes the Incarnation, which presents God and man as indissolubly locked together in common enterprise. (*WP,* 135)

> Job begins with a spiritualized form of Genesis. It ends with a spiritual form of apocalypse or revelation. And in the middle comes this vertical contact between God and man. The New Testament has a different version of this: it sees the contact as existing in Jesus. (*NFC,* 201)

In *Myth and Metaphor* Frye speaks of the Incarnation as pointing to "an apocalypse, or ultimate vision of creation, the world-book with its seals taken off" (10). And in *The Double Vision* he writes, "As the New Testament begins with the myth of the Messiah, so it ends, in the Book of Revelation, with the metaphor of the Messiah, the vision of all things in their infinite variety united in the body of Christ" (17). The metaphors here of an indissoluble lock, of vertical contact united in a body, and of the vision of an unsealed world-book are as endlessly fascinating as others we will encounter. This brings us back to where we began this overview, with Blake's view of the Incarnation as fusing the human and the divine, as identifying subject and object, and as containing the timeless and the temporal.

In a note on Blake's mysticism at the end of *Fearful Symmetry,* Frye indicates that he is willing to call Blake a mystic but not in the sense of either "contemplative quietism" or "spiritual illumination expressing itself in a practical and . . . unspeculative pietism" (432). Rather, Blake is a mystic because of his visionary effort to realize in experience the identity of the divine and the human that radical metaphor tries to capture. "No one," Frye writes, "can read very widely in . . . mystical literature without feeling the urgency of the question of whether there is an identity of the kind that the verbal metaphor suggests but does not assert. In fact some sense of ultimate identity, of the kind implicit in the Hindu formula 'thou art that,' seems to lie behind nearly all of the profoundest religious feelings and experiences, whatever the actual religion, even when the ideological censor forbids its expression as doctrine" (*MM*, 106).

One final thing, by way of introduction, relates to Frye's own quest. Throughout the chapters that follow, we will see that for Frye there is a stage of the quest beyond *imaginative* identity and that language tends to fail him in trying to articulate the form and content of this stage. In an early notebook he muses, "The thing found isn't really communicable: it's the process of finding that is, & no one ever stops finding" (30r.6). Still, he struggles mightily to discover the proper verbal formulas by which to communicate, and in his quest—what Alvin Lee has called Frye's "personal quest for a humanized god"[29]—he mines the entire tradition of poets and historians, philosophical and religious thinkers, and not just in the Western tradition. After setting down a series of injunctions to himself about structuring his life, Frye writes in the same early notebook, "The path is before me, & it is always there: no God puts my application on file & makes me wait until I hear from him. Nor is there any magical spell on it: I may start out & turn back innumerable times, but the path is unaffected by that, though I'm not" (30r.12). The narrative pattern of Frye's grand imaginative journey can be likened to a quest romance. Its goal, which is spiritual vision, draws on a number of sources: some are mystical and esoteric, as we will see in chapters 5 and 6, others are decidedly Christian; some are imaginatively visionary, others are conceptual; some are rooted in the Everlasting Gospel, others in the *philosophia perennis*. Frye spent his whole life trying to find the right verbal formulas for representing the quest, searching for a proper rhetoric to say what he felt compelled to say. "My job in this world," he writes, "appears to be that of a mantra-gleaner, a picker up (inventor) of possibly useful verbal formulas. One set has to do with the role of art as a potential liberator of whatever gets liberated. Again, I suspect (and I hope, rather than at present believe) that Christianity has at least as much to be said for it as any other religion, & I'd like to keep this comparative aspect of my Bible book open. If I could suggest this I'd be very grateful" (*TBN*, 323). In this connection Frye says in a notebook from the late 1960s that he would "like to say something new about religion & nobody really succeeds in doing so" (*RT*, 76). Fifteen years later he writes, "I'm no evangelist or revivalist preacher, but I'd like to help out in a trend to make religion interesting and attractive to many people of good will who will have nothing to do with it now" (*LN*, 1:74). We will be in a better position to determine whether

Frye succeeds in saying something new about religion and making it interesting and attractive once we have explored in more depth the issues raised in this introductory overview.

Frye was naturally aware of the widespread perplexity in contemporary thought about whether we use language or language uses us,[30] and the case can be made that Frye's language—the material cause of his work—pulls him along one critical path rather than another. His central terms tend to expand beyond ordinary usage, taking on such a variety of subtexts and overtones that they actually become the formal cause of his work, linguistic matter transformed into conceptual substance. One can hardly grasp Frye's intent in *Anatomy of Criticism* without looking closely at the different meanings that cluster around such central words as "myth," "archetype," "displacement," *"dianoia,"* "allegory," "rhythm," "radical of presentation," among scores of other key words. In that book Frye refers to himself as a "terminological buccaneer" (362)—one who pirates words from here and there and adapts them for his own purposes—and he also says in the *Anatomy* that exploring the "range of . . . connotations" of individual words used by philosophers can provide a key to understanding their systems (335). The present study follows this procedure, probing a number of key words in Frye's poetics, including "interpenetration," "kerygma," "identity," "imaginative literalism," "revelation," "vision," "recognition," "consciousness," "dialectic," *"Aufhebung,"* "imagination," "vortex," "love," and even the preposition "beyond." Because the meanings of these words are not transparent, representing instead what W. C. Gallie calls "essentially contested concepts," it is important to examine the range of their connotations.[31] In this respect the present study, mutatis mutandis, is not unlike R. B. Onians's examination of Homer's vocabulary in *The Origins of European Thought* and Owen Barfield's of Coleridge's in *What Coleridge Thought,* both studies that Frye admired.

Frye was a holistic thinker, one who saw his separate books and essays as informing parts of a larger whole, like the net of Indra. His notebooks are especially important jewels in that net. They also illustrate not so much the product of Frye's quest as its process. Since they are central documents in the present study, a word needs to be said about the form and substance of these unusually rich documents, which have only recently come to light.

The Notebooks: Form

Among Frye's papers at the Victoria University Library are seventy-six holograph notebooks in various shapes and sizes (the longest is 253 pages), which he kept from the late 1930s, when he was a student at Oxford, until only a few months before his death in 1991. Although portions of some notebooks are drafts of Frye's various books, essays, reviews, and lectures, most of the material consists of neatly organized and syntactically complete paragraphs separated by blank lines. The entries are not the polished prose of Frye's published work, but they do reveal a genuine concern for the rhetorical unit that can stand alone. The holograph notebooks contain approximately 800,000 words, excluding the drafts. In the 1970s Frye began typing some of his notes. The experiment was not altogether successful in his mind (he even wrote of wanting to destroy his typed notes for *The Great Code*), but a large percentage of these notes is practically identical in form and scope to the holograph material. The typescripts, which have become known in Frye's Collected Works as "Notes" to distinguish them from the holograph "Notebooks," constitute another 350,000 words.

While Frye's notebooks do contain material that will be of considerable interest to his biographers, their form is altogether different from the diaries he kept in the 1940s and 1950s, and their intent is neither to record his personal life nor to explore his own psyche. The notebooks are first and foremost the workshop out of which Frye created his books. After *Anatomy of Criticism* he produced books at the rate of about one per year, giving the impression perhaps that writing for him was a facile enterprise. But while the shorter books that emerged from his lectures were often written quickly, the process was anything but quick for his four major books. *Fearful Symmetry* (1947) and the *Anatomy* (1957) were each more than ten years in the making; *The Great Code* (1982) was begun more than a decade before it appeared; and *Words with Power* (1990), as Frye notes in the introduction to *The Great Code*, was "in active preparation" in the early 1980s (xi). The notebooks record this deliberate and often labyrinthine process, and the process did not always issue in the product Frye had envisioned, the most obvious example being his inability to complete the major book that was to follow *Fearful Symmetry* and *Anatomy of Criticism*. At times the workshop function seems to fade away almost completely, for the notebooks contain entries on scores of topics that have no obvious connection to the project at hand. An entry will be triggered by a detective story Frye is reading, a newspaper article, a lecture or sermon he has to prepare, a Latin quotation, a glance at the books on his shelves, a quotation he remembers, a letter received, a memory from a trip, and occasional personal reflections—thoughts about his own status as a critic, about the difficulties of writing, about the bankruptcy of contemporary criticism, and the like.

Writing for Frye, of whatever form, was, if not an obsession, as indispensable a part of his life as eating and sleeping. He wrote because he could do no other, and the process was not always liberating. "I know from experience," he writes, "and I've read the statement often enough, that if one could turn off the incessant chatter in one's psyche one would be well on the way to freedom. In all my life I've never known an instant of real silence" (*LN,* 1:200).[32] Several times he expresses a deep desire for the apophatic and contemplative life, or at least for certain moments when he could "turn off the chatter in [his] mind, which is making more noise than a punk rock band ("drunken monkey," the Hindus call it) and relax into the divine knowledge of us which is one of the things meant by a cloud of unknowing" (*LN,* 1:161).[33] In one of his notebooks, written in the mid–1940s, Frye ruefully wonders "what it would really be like to get one's mind completely clear of the swirl of mental currents. It would be like walking across the Red Sea to the Promised Land, with walls of water standing up on each side" (*RT,* 71). The fact that Frye was never really able to turn off the "drunken monkey" is what accounts for both the sheer mass of material in the notebooks and the constant repetition of ideas, hunches, insights, poetic passages, and illustrations. Still, Frye approached the discipline of note making with Benedictine zeal: "[W]orking at what one can do is a sacrament," he writes at the beginning of Notebook 44 (*LN,* 1:102). Or again, "My whole life is words: nothing is of value in life except finding verbal formulations that make sense" (*LN,* 1:267).[34]

The process of writing the notebooks is as important as the product, one form of which we already have in the books that resulted. Frye is on a monumental quest. The quest is not toward Hegelian absolute knowledge, as he says several times,[35] but toward absolute vision. Its goal is a vision beyond both the kerygmatic and the poetic, a form of vision that Frye characterizes in dozens of ways but perhaps most revealingly, as we shall see, as interpenetration. The notebooks are a kind of labyrinth that Frye is both building and trying to extricate himself from: he sometimes ascends to moments of pure illumination; he sometimes descends into the dark abyss; he often gets lost in the maze; he is beleaguered by false starts and dead ends; he is haunted by a multitude of ghosts that keep flashing across his inward eye, which is very seldom the bliss of solitude. He describes the quest as taking a purgatorial shape:

> My whole conscious life has been purgatorial, a constant circling around the same thing, like a vine going up an elm. I note that I'm repeating even things from earlier pages of this notebook. And "purgatorial" is only a vague hope: maybe I'm not really going up to a final apocalyptic vision but just going in circles, like a senile old man who

thinks the two-hundredth repetition of the same old story is new. Perhaps the end is the choking of the host. Well, when it's vertigo to look down and despair to look up, one can only keep going. But there again I'm assuming an up and a down, and assuming I'm going somewhere. Actually I keep revolving around the same place until I've brought off a verbal formulation that I like. (*LN*, 1:89).

Here and there Frye speaks of the intent of his notebook writing, as in this remark about the relation between his obsessive note taking and the books that eventually emerge: "[A]ll my life I've had the notebook obsession manifested by what I'm doing at this moment. Writing in notebooks seems to help clarify my mind about the books I write, which are actually notebook entries arranged in a continuous form. At least, I've always told myself they were that" (*LN*, 1:172–73). In one of his marginalia to Coleridge, Frye observes that Coleridge's "mind moves in a series of crystallizations, like Homer trying to write an epic. We need a prose Poe to assert that a long prose structure is impossible."[36] The notebook entries can also be seen as a series of crystallizations, Frye's ideas suddenly emerging into discontinuous prose form. Continuity in Frye's published prose is sometimes difficult to discern, and when he is especially elliptical, one wonders if he does not believe about prose what Poe said about the long poem. But the notebook entries are kernels of what he hopes can be incorporated into longer forms: "I keep notebooks because all my writing is a translation into a narrative sequence of things that come to me aphoristically. The aphorisms in turn are preceded by 'inspirations' or potentially verbal *Gestalten*. So 'inspiration' is essentially a snarled sequence" (*LN*, 1:226). While the notebook entries are ordinarily not as brief as an aphorism (they contain on average about seventy-five words), they do consist on the whole of discontinuous reflections. But, as "snarled sequence" suggests, the entries are by no means unrelated to each other. Frye will often devote a succession of paragraphs to a single topic,[37] and he frequently refers to previous sections of the notebook in which he is writing at the time and occasionally to other notebooks.

Frye puts "inspiration" in quotation marks because the actual genesis of the notebook entries is often somewhat mysterious. "I think in cores or aphorisms, as these notebooks indicate, and all the *labor* in my writing comes from trying to find verbal formulas to connect them. I have to wait for the cores to emerge: they seem to be born and not made" (*LN*, 1:364). In one of his notebooks for *Anatomy of Criticism*, he speaks of these aphorisms as auditory epiphanies: they are, he says, "involuntarily acquired" and have "something to do with listening for a Word, the ear being the involuntary sense" (38.36). If the birth of the aphorisms comes from things "heard," the connections among them come from things "seen." Realizing the potential of "verbal *Gestalten*" or patterns of continuous argument, Frye says, has something to do "with the spread-out performance of the eye" (38.36). But as the notebooks unequivocally reveal, the pattern of continuity is never achieved without a mighty struggle: once Frye got hold of the building blocks, "the spread-out performance" was never necessary or even predictable. In his words, "Continuity, in writing as in physics, is probabilistic, and every sequence is a choice among possibilities. Inevitable sequence is illusory" (*LN*, 1:21). The sequence that Frye eventually achieved in his published work came only after revisions of numerous drafts, sometimes as many as eight or nine revisions. Some of the chapters in *Words with Power* were, in their early form, as long as a hundred pages, so Frye's revisions involved a great deal of cutting (*LN*, 1:369–70). He would typically type three or four drafts himself before giving them, often with holograph additions and corrections, to his secretary Jane Widdicombe to type or enter on a word processor.[38] Once he received the draft back, he would revise again, and this process would be repeated as many as five times. But the notebooks themselves are by no means drafts: they reveal a stage of Frye's writing before, sometimes years before, he began even to work on a first draft.

As for the rhetoric of the notebooks, one can naturally detect features of Frye's style on every page: the wit, the koan-like utterances that capture some paradox, the attention to the shape of the periodic sentence, the grace and elegance of the prose, the ironic tone. But the difference between Frye's notebook entries and his published work is readily apparent, for in the notebooks Frye is wearing everything on his sleeve. He feels no need for the detachment that was almost always a feature of what he presented to the public, no need to create that sense of assurance that comes with a distanced academic presence. Frye did insist that the antithesis between the scholarly and unscholarly, between the personal and impersonal was an antithesis that needed to be transcended. Still, the voice in the notebooks is not Frye's public voice. There is, on the one hand, the direct expression of convictions, often taking the form of beliefs. Frye's own beliefs were, of course, implicit in all his writing, from *Fearful Symmetry* on. But in the notebooks they are explicit, sometimes amounting almost to a confession of faith. On the other hand, at the level simply of diction, Frye's not infrequent use of coarse and indecent language may come as a surprise. But Frye's four-letter words are used fairly innocently, serving as a kind of shorthand for referring to sex, which is of course one of his "primary concerns" (as in the male and female principles in Genesis 1 and 2 that are the starting points for his account of the mountain and garden archetypes in *Words with Power*), and to bodily functions. Still, Frye's language often deflates the most sober of reflections. Thus, while there is not so much as a whisper of the mock-heroic in the notebooks, there is a good measure of the Swiftian burlesque, which is one of the ways that Frye, never without a sense of irony, brings his soaring speculations back down to earth.

If we cannot always with assurance follow the sequence of the arguments in Frye's published work or always understand clearly why one paragraph follows the next, we nevertheless have the impression that *he* knew where he was going. But this confident sense of direction is often absent from the notebooks. "God knows," he writes at one point, "I know how much of this is blither: it makes unrewarding reading for the most part. But I have to do it: it doesn't clarify my mind so much as lead to some point of clarification that (I hope) gets into the book. Hansel & Gretel's trail of crumbs." Or again, when speculating on the relation between the dialogues of Word and Spirit and the four levels of meaning, Frye remarks, "I don't know if this is anything but bald and arbitrary schematism." Or still again, "I'm again at the point in the book where I wonder if I know what the hell I'm talking about."[39] Remarks such as these are sprinkled throughout the notebooks, and there are entries in which Frye begins to explore an idea but, by the time he gets to the end of the paragraph, forgets the point he was going to make. Over and over we see the persona of a Frye who is human, all too human.

There is nothing particularly surprising in this: writing for Frye was a discovery procedure, and we should not expect that every aphorism that came to him should issue in "verbal *Gestalten*." In this respect Frye's notebooks are like Nietzsche's own book of aphorisms, *Human, All Too Human,* an exercise in free thinking; and free thought, by definition, is under no obligation always to issue in certitude. The persona of the writer is revealed too in the occasional intemperate epithets ("fool," "idiot," and the like) that Frye hurls at himself for overlooking the obvious or for a lapse in memory, and in the self-deprecating remarks ("By the standards of conventional scholarship, *The Great Code* was a silly and sloppy book," *LN,* 1:160). Still, Frye's most explicit reference to the use readers might make of his notebook aphorisms, which follows on a remark about the metaphor of *sparagmos* (tearing to pieces) that runs through his writing, helps to justify the extensive use made of these documents in the chapters that follow:

The way I begin a book is to write detached aphorisms in a notebook, and ninety-five percent of the work I do in completing a book is to fit these detached aphorisms together into a continuous narrative line. I think that Coleridge worked in the same way, though he seems to have had unusual difficulty when it came to the narrative stage, and so instead of completing his great treatise on the Logos he kept much of the best of what he had to say hugged to his bosom in the form of fifty-seven notebooks. Holism is not only not the end of the critical enterprise: it is an axiom pursued for its own rewards which at a certain point may turn inside out. I may work hard enough to weld my books into a narrative unity, but it is possible that many of my readers tend to find their way back to the original aphoristic form, finding me more useful for detached insights than for total structures. However, if bits and pieces of me float down to Lesbos with the head still singing, it doesn't matter to me if some of those pieces (I'm mixing metaphors violently here, but the mixing seems to fit the context) get swallowed by someone and grow up again from inside him.[40]

The Notebooks: Aphorism and Schema

We do not read very far in Frye before discovering that, for all his analytic gifts, he is an intuitive thinker. In Notebook 11f he writes, "In my speeches I often speak of earlier moments of intensity. They were usually not moments of intensity, but only look so when I remember them. In a sense, therefore, I'm simply lying" (*RT,* 109). A half-dozen of these moments, nevertheless, were important enough for Frye to continue to refer to them: an experience in high school when the albatross of Methodist fundamentalism fell from his neck, an illumination about Spengler during the summer of 1931 in Edmonton, a sudden intuition about Blake during his second year at Emmanuel College, a vision of the shape that *Fearful Symmetry* would finally take, and two epiphanies referred to more than twenty times in the notebooks—one in Seattle during the summer of 1951 and the other on St. Clair Avenue in Toronto.[41] Frye refers to these moments variously as intuitions, epiphanies, illuminations, and enlightenments. They were experiences of unity—experiences, as he says, "of things fitting together" in a momentary flash of insight (*NFC,* 48). Such experiences are best described, not as mystical or even religious, but as visionary or spiritual. "Above the soul," Frye writes,

> is the spirit, and when the "body" makes contact with that, man possesses for an instant a spiritual body, in which he moves into a world of life and light and understanding that seemed miraculous to him before,

as well as totally unreal. This world is usually called "timeless," which is a beggary of language: there ought to be some such word as "timeful" to express a present moment that includes immense vistas of past and future. I myself have spent the greater part of seventy-eight years in writing out the implications of insights that occupied at most only a few seconds of all that time. (*LN,* 2:663)

These insights are an important part of Frye's visionary poetics, and we will take a closer look at two of the experiences in chapter 3. The momentary epiphanies should be distinguished from what Frye calls the aphoristic "cores" that he sets down in the notebooks. The latter, which he often refers to as "hunches," are essentially discontinuous. They are not epiphanic wholes, but epiphanic parts which, Frye hopes, will find their proper whole. Frye's epiphanic hunches may be involuntarily acquired, but scores of them, once they have made their appearance, recur with regularity throughout the notebooks. The intuitions get repeated, reformulated, and refined as Frye returns to his "repetitive & endlessly recycled thoughts" in his search for the proper verbal formula to build what he calls his "palaces of criticism" (*LN,* 1:156, 123) and his "temples to . . . the 'gods'" (*LN,* 1:120).

If Frye is an intuitive thinker, he is also a schematic one. It would be misleading to think of what he calls "the spread-out performance"—his effort to arrive at a continuous argument—as occurring only when he began to organize his aphorisms for a first draft. The intuitive deductive framework for Frye is always prior.[42] While it is true that he thinks "in cores or aphorisms," it is no less true that he thinks geometrically, and such thinking is a feature of Frye's mental life that was with him from the beginning. Even in his student days he could hardly put pen to paper without a diagram in his head. He refers to his own work as possessed by "a mandala vision," the mandala being "a projection of the way one sees" (*SM,* 117). In Frye's grammar of the imagination the mental diagrams are what provide the syntax or ordering principle for the aphorisms. Or, to borrow another pair of Frye's terms, while the aphorisms belong to *mythos,* or experience in time, "the spread-out performance" is a matter of *dianoia,* or representation in space. He is nevertheless aware of the problems with the schematic way he tends to represent his ideas: "False symmetry is my worst enemy, because, founded as it is on arbitrary association, it is perpetually elaborating a total form too restricted to contain the pullulating swarm of ideas I get" (32.21).

"I have proceeded deductively," Frye announced in *Anatomy of Criticism* (29), and in the writing of his last major book, thirty years later, he is still proceeding deductively. "In the next few days," he writes with no sense of irony, "I must do a blitz on this infernal book, get its main construction lines blocked out, & then start reading" (*LN*, 1:126). Or again, "I've got stuck in my noddle the two names Prometheus and Hermes, and am beginning to feel that, apparently just for reasons of symmetry, there must be a second cycle incorporating the bulk of the imagery of modern poetry that doesn't get into the Eros-Adonis cycle. I'm putting it in the strongest terms a hostile critic would apply: because I've got a pretty pattern to apply, the facts have simply got to conform to it, and naturally with that attitude I'll succeed sooner or later." And then he adds, "You can't be original unless you work with hunches and treat them exactly as a paranoiac would do. Of course I find what I want to find in the texts themselves: what else does the double meaning of 'invention' mean?" (*LN*, 2:422).

This is the typical Frygian approach: first, to set up the organizing framework and then to look around for the myths and metaphors to give body to the structure. It is almost always possible to represent Frye's frameworks diagrammatically. One does not read far in his published work before encountering some spatial or linear form. In the notebooks this inveterate pattern making is raised to another power: the notebooks, as well as the books in Frye's own library that he annotated, contain scores of diagrams that form a part of what he called the Great Doodle, and the intricacy of the diagrams becomes no longer a scaffolding to be dismantled when criticism is in better shape, as Frye said in the *Anatomy* (29). Thirty years later, Frye writes: in that book I "said I attached no particular importance to the construct *qua* construct. I think I've got past that now, and that it's only by means of such dizzily complex constructs that one can ever get anything substantial out of criticism. Those who appear not to have such a construct, like Johnson, are attached to an ideology: those who do often don't get it worked out, like Coleridge" (*LN*, 1:121).

The notebooks also contain complex patterns of organization based on numbers—seven, twelve, fourteen, and twenty-eight appear with regularity—and on several occasions Frye projects a book with one hundred chapters. In Notebook 21 he labors over one of his seven-part schemes for some two hundred entries, trying to relate it to the Tarot pack but finally abandoning it in favor of another scheme that he calls the "spiral curriculum," a fourteen-chapter book, two chapters of which are to be on narrative and imagery. He then sketches, matter-of-factly, an arcane outline of the chapters: "The spirals are 1, 7, 11; 2, 8, 12; 3, 9, 13; 4, 10, 14. 2 & 4 make 22 & 28 respectively; 1 is the lucky numbers of the creature; 3 are the female lunar (Queen) numbers" (*RT*, 201). In this somewhat cryptic code, we would have, if we were to organize it as a chart, three columns of four chapters each. Adding the chapters on narrative and imagery to these twelve gives Frye his fourteen, and even though the Tarot has disappeared from the discussion, seven is still implicit in the three-by-four arrangement and in the doubling of seven.[43] In saying that "2 & 4 make 22 & 28 respectively," Frye is referring to the sum of the numbers in the second and fourth horizontal axes (2 + 8 + 12 and 4 + 10 + 14). The lucky numbers are those in the first horizontal matrix: 1, 7, 11; and the lunar numbers are those in the third matrix: 3, 9, 13.

All this numerological musing does not lead to anything ostensible, but Frye devotes an astonishing amount of energy to working through what he sees as contained in each of the twelve chapters. Sevens and twelves figure prominently in Frye's schemes,[44] and this is partially because of their connection with two temporal and two spatial categories: seven with the days of the week and the planets (in the ancient reckoning), and twelve with the months of the year and the signs of the zodiac. But the numerology is more complex than this, and we examine it in more detail in chapter 6. The point here is that Frye incessantly engages in this kind of schematic reverie as he wanders freely through the labyrinth of myth and archetype. "Sooner or later," he remarks, "a book of mine ought to fall into a traditional orbit, but I don't know which book or which orbit" (RT, 173). The "spiral curriculum" is just one of hundreds of Frye's notebook schemes. The most complicated and the most mysterious is the Great Doodle, the diagram of diagrams that Michael Dolzani continues to illuminate.[45] To his exposition I can only add a few footnotes.

Frye writes at one point that he's not revealing what the Great Doodle is because he does not really know (7.190), but his frequent references to it reveal that it is primarily his symbolic shorthand for the monomyth. Originally Frye conceived of the Great Doodle as "the cyclical quest of the hero" (TBN, 214) or "the underlying form of all epics" (TBN, 241). But as he began to move away from strictly literary terms toward both religious language and the language of Greek myth and philosophy, another pattern developed, one with an east-west axis of Nous-Nomos and a north-south axis of Logos-Thanatos. At this point the Great Doodle took on an added significance, becoming a symbolic shorthand for what he called the narrative form of the Logos vision: "the circular journey of the Logos from Father to Spirit" (TBN, 260) or "the *total* cyclical journey of the incarnate Logos" (TBN, 201). But the Great Doodle is never merely a cycle. Its shape requires also the vertical *axis mundi* and the horizontal axis separating the world of innocence and experience. These axes, with their numerous variations, produce the four quadrants that are omnipresent in Frye's diagrammatic way of thinking. In Notebook 7 he refers to the quadrants as part of the Lesser Doodle (7.190), meaning only that the quadrants themselves are insufficient to establish the larger geometric design of the Great Doodle.

But the Great Doodle has still further elaborations. In the extensive notes he made for his Norton Lectures at Harvard (*The Secular Scripture*) Frye remarks self-referentially that in book 14 of Longfellow's *Hiawatha* the heroine "invents picture-writing, including the Great Doodle of Frye's celebrated masterpieces" (56.455). The reference is to Hiawatha's painting on birch bark a series of symbolic and mystic images: the egg of the Great Spirit, the serpent of the Spirit of Evil, the circle of life and death, the straight line of the earth, and other ancestral totems in the great chain of being.[46] Frye elaborates his Great Doodle in a similar way, the Hiawathan "shapes and figures" becoming for him points of epiphany at the circumference of the circle—what he twice refers to as beads on a string (*TBN*, 241, 245). The beads are various topoi and loci along the circumferential string. They can be seen as stations where the questing hero stops in his journey (50.813) or as the cardinal points of a circle.[47] Frye even overlays one form of the Logos diagram with the eight trigrams of the *I Ching*, saying that they "can be connected with my Great Doodle" (*TBN*, 209), and one version of the Great Doodle recapitulates what he refers to throughout his notebooks as "the Revelation diagram," the intricately designed chart that he passed out in his course "Symbolism in the Bible."[48]

The Great Doodle, then, is a representation, though a hypothetical one, that contains the large schematic patterns in Frye's memory theater: the cyclical quest with its quadrants, cardinal points, and epiphanic sites; and the vertical ascent and descent movements along the chain of being or the *axis mundi*. It contains as well all the lesser doodles that Frye creates to represent the diagrammatic structure of myth and metaphor and that he frames in the geometric language of gyre and vortex, center and circumference.

There are other large frameworks that structure Frye's imaginative universe, such as the eight-book fantasy—the ogdoad—that he invokes repeatedly throughout his career, or the Hermes-Eros-Adonis-Prometheus (HEAP) scheme that begins in Notebook 7 (late 1940s) and dominates the notebook landscape of Frye's last decade. The ogdoad, which Michael Dolzani has definitively explained, is fundamentally a conceptual key to Frye's *own* work, though it is related in a slippery and often vague way to the Great Doodle.[49] The HEAP scheme in its half-dozen variations, which we will examine in chapter 7, is clearly used to define the quadrants of the Great Doodle, and there are countless other organizing devices, serving as lesser doodles, that Frye draws from alchemy, the zodiac, musical keys, colors, the chessboard, the omnipresent "four kernels" (commandment, aphorism, oracle, and epiphany), the shape of the human body, Blake's Zoas, Jung's personality types, Bacon's idols, the boxing of the compass by Plato and the Romantic poets, the Greater Arcana of the Tarot cards, the seven days of Creation, the three stages of religious awareness, numerological schemes, and so on. We will have occasion to look at several of these deductive frameworks in the chapters that follow.

The Notebooks: Free Play

In one of his early notebooks Frye expresses the fear that his speculations will not turn out to be definitive (*RT,* 70), but this is a fear he is soon able to vanquish. The pace of the writing initially seems to be almost frenetic—the drive of a man possessed to record every nuance of the "obstinate questionings" of his active mind. But when we stand back from the notebooks as a whole, the mood they convey is neither fear nor frenzy. It is rather a process of speculative free play, "of letting things come & not forcing or cramping or repressing them" (*RT,* 49). Frye is in no panic to bring things to closure, moving as he does at a leisurely pace, releasing himself from all inhibitions, and not worrying that his schemes "go bust immediately." "Perhaps that's the reason I have them," he muses (*RT,* 177). Sometimes anxieties about the efficacy of the incessant scribbling arise: "Why do I try to keep notes like this, when forty years of experience shows me they don't do me any good" (33.80). At other times boredom sets in "because so much of what I put into [the notebooks] is just a form of masturbation: an empty fantasy life making the scene with beckoning fair charmers who don't exist" (*TBN,* 332). But this sentence is followed by the single telling word "however," which signals, of course, that the doubts he might have about the value of recording his imaginative life do not deter him from moving on immediately.

In one of his notebooks from the 1960s Frye issues these tactical instructions to himself: "in beginning to plan a major work like the third book, *don't eliminate anything. Never* assume that some area of your speculations can't be included & has to be left over for another book. Things may get eliminated in the very last stage . . . but *never, never,* exclude anything when thinking about the book. It was strenuous having to cut down FS [*Fearful Symmetry*] from an encyclopaedia, but . . . major works are encyclopaedic & anatomic: everything I know must go into them—eye of bat & tongue of dog" (*TBN,* 74–75). Frye goes on to say that all his major books are essentially "the same book with different centres of gravity: interpenetrating universes. Give me a place to stand, and I will include the world" (*TBN*, 75). This "same book" theory means that we encounter many iterations and echoes of the same idea. Repetition was a feature of Frye's published work, which, as he said, assumed the shape of a spiral curriculum, "circling around the same issues" in a way that produced a gradual continuity over time.[50] He justifies the repetition in his books and essays by noting that the principles he keeps returning to are the only ones he knows. Like thematic returns in music, the same ideas can be presented in different contexts, and repetition can be a sign of a consistency of conviction: "[R]epetition charges the emotional batteries & suspends the critical faculties. What I tell you three times is true. What I tell you three hundred times is profoundly true" (*RT*, 198).[51]

The repetition in the notebooks, however, is of a different kind. Like Daedalus, who set his mind to unknown arts, Frye uses his notebooks for invention and discovery, returning again and again to the archetypes of his mental landscape in an effort to get the architecture and the verbal formulation right. The repetition can be vexing, but it is nonetheless an example of Frye's following the principle underlying his most important educational advice: develop the habit of Samuel Butler's practice-memory. "The repetitiousness of the Koran would drive a reader out of his mind if he were reading it as he would any other book" (*RT*, 195), and one could almost say the same thing about the discontinuity of Frye's notebooks: they contain little linear argument, even though there are many occasions where sequences of paragraphs focus on a single, obsessively pursued issue. Still, the entire notebook enterprise is based on a theory of verbal meaning that turns Aristotle's notion of causality upside down. Frye writes at one point that there is "a convergence causation founded on the analogy of space," as opposed to linear causation, which assumes that writing is a temporal sequence of effect following cause (*RT*, 255). Such convergent causation, which is close to the first-phase language of metaphor, is the kind that governs the notebooks.

If one abandons both linear causation and a concern for continuity, the principles of the figurative use of words become more important than conceptual meaning. Frye's fertile and energetic mind is always pursuing similarities or, as he is fond of calling them, links. Aristotle says that the ability to perceive likenesses is one of the marks of genius, and if that is true then the notebooks reveal the mental dance of a genius. Perceiving likenesses requires the free play, not of the imagination, but of fancy, as Frye writes in one revealing entry:

I am intensely superstitious; but there are two kinds of superstition, related as self-destructive melancholy is to penseroso melancholy. There is the superstition based on fear of the future: this is based also on my character as a coward & weakling, & is of course to be avoided. There is another kind which consists of removing all censors & inhibitions on speculation: it's almost exactly what Coleridge calls fancy. It may eventually be superseded by imagination: but if there's no fancy to start with there won't be any imagination to finish with. Let's call it creative superstition. It works with analogies[,] disregarding all differences & attending only to similarities. Here nothing is coincidence in the sense of unusable design; or, using the word more correctly, everything is potential coincidence—what Jung calls synchronistic. (*TBN,* 211)

Once the similarities Frye observes begin to organize themselves into patterns, the imagination has taken over: the schematic structures then take the form of the mental diagrams mentioned in the previous section, which are one of the signatures of Frye's thinking.

Why all this imaginative free play, with its incessant spatial projections and schematic doodling? As we have said, it is an uninhibited form of free writing that eventually distills itself into Frye's books and essays. But more important, it represents the many stages in his own religious quest. Frye remarks in Notebook 21 that his "particular interest has always been in mythology & in the imaginative aspect of religion. . . . The whole imaginative picture of the world which underlies both religion and the arts has been constant from the beginning" (*RT,* 157–58). Notebook 21 begins by Frye's announcing that while his immediate object is to collect ideas for his 1971 Birks Lectures at McGill University, his ultimate aim is to work through his "thoughts on religion" (*RT,* 140). Religion for Frye is not a matter of belief, though it stems from the conviction that life has a point. "All attempts to find out what that point is are religious quests" (*RT,* 177), which is reminiscent of what Frye wrote in a student essay forty years earlier: "[T]he most fundamental intellectual activity of the human race is . . . an attempt to find a pattern in existence" (*SE,* 403).

If the ubiquitous spatial projections of the notebooks form the *dianoia* of Frye's critical and imaginative universe, the forthrights and meanders of his quest are its *mythos*. But a quest for what? Well, for *The Great Code* and *Words with Power*. "For at least 25 years," Frye writes in the early 1970s, "I've been preoccupied by the notion of a key to all mythologies" (*RT,* 198), and what he really wants to discover, he writes at one point, is "the myth of God, which is a myth of identity" (*TBN,* 69). Identity is one of the central principles in Frye's universe, the principle he returns to again and again in his speculations on the paradoxes of literal meaning, metaphor, and the Incarnation. From the perspective of the imagination, the *telos* of knowledge comes from the ability to perceive not differences but identities. While knowledge is clearly not divorced from perception, Frye's quest has to do more with seeing than with knowing; hence, the centrality of light and sight, of recognition and vision and illumination— terms that we examine in some detail in chapter 3.[52]

Frye often organized his categories in cyclical patterns, the most familiar of these being the specific forms of drama and the thematic convention of *epos* and lyric in *Anatomy of Criticism,* along with the phases of the four *mythoi.* The quest for Frye, including his own, can be seen as cyclical, a matter addressed in our final chapter, but he distanced himself from some of the implications of the cycle. The treadmill of endless repetition, the dull sameness in the myth of the eternal return, the Druidic recurrences of natural religion, the doctrine of reincarnation—all these cyclic myths were antithetical to Frye's belief in the Resurrection, one of his firmest religious convictions. The cycle never permitted what he called the revolutionary *culbute* or overturn in individual and social life— the possibility for a genuine reversal and a new beginning. One of the most powerful verses of scripture for Frye is Revelation 22:17: "And the Spirit and the bride say, Come. And let him that heareth say, Come. And let him that is athirst come. And whosoever will, let him take the water of life freely." These words at the very end of the Bible signal for Frye a new beginning, a new creation, and this new beginning is in the mind of the reader. To be able to see the possibilities in such a new beginning is a way of formulating the goal of Frye's quest, but there are numerous other ways to phrase it: the Everlasting Gospel, Milton's Word of God in the heart, the interpenetration of Word and Spirit.

The quest movement in Frye more typically moves up and down a vertical axis. At the top is the point of epiphany of the Logos vision, the transcendent moment of pure illumination. There is a strong tendency for Frye, especially in his earlier work, to move up the *axis mundi* to the point where Word and Spirit are identical, a place where space and time interpenetrate. The answer for Frye is not to be found in history, which he saw mostly as a series of repeating nightmares. In the dialectic of his thought the search for the moment of pure illumination, the anagogic vision, represents his Platonic, Longinian, and Romantic inclinations. The movement is from Eros to Logos. But the katabatic movement down the ladder is equally important for Frye: in his later writings it appears to be even more important. "Everybody," Frye writes, "has a fixation. Mine has to do with meander-and-descent patterns. For years in my childhood I wanted to dig a cave & be the head of a society in it—this was before I read Tom Sawyer. All the things in literature that haunt me most have to do with katabasis. The movie that hit me hardest as a child was the Lon Chaney Phantom of the Opera. My main points of reference in literature are such things as The Tempest, P.R. [*Paradise Regained*], [Blake's] *Milton, the Ancient Mariner, Alice in Wonderland, the Waste Land*—every damn one a meander-&-katabasis work. I should have kept the only book Vera kept, *The Sleepy King*" (*TBN,* 76).[53] The study of archetypes in part 2 of *Words with Power* begins with the mountain and the garden, but it concludes with the cave and the furnace. Thus, the last part of the last book published in Frye's lifetime treats the archetypes on the lower half of the *axis mundi.*

We have spoken of Frye's notebook entries as speculations, as he himself does. The word has parallels to its use in Keats's letters, although Frye's speculations ordinarily have more shape than those that come tumbling out of Keats's fertile brain. Keats distances his speculations from what he calls "consecutive reasoning,"[54] and Frye would agree that if there is any truth in his speculations, it belongs to an order different from that of the "reflective" mode of truth in the descriptive writing that Keats has in mind. Underlying both "reflection" and "speculation" is, as Frye notes in *Words with Power* and elsewhere, the mirror metaphor.

> If we ask what the speculation is a mirror of, the traditional answer is being, a conceptual totality that transcends, not only individual beings, but the total aggregate of beings. Heidegger endorses the statement that the first question of philosophy is, "Why are there things rather than nothing?" But things are not what Heidegger means by being, and the question leads to another: "Why is there being beyond all beings?" (*WP,* 10)

The being beyond all beings lies in the background of Frye's own quest, although his search for it typically relies on language different from Heidegger's Greek vocabulary. We turn now to examine the language of Frye's speculations, beginning with interpenetration.

I   Exoterica

1 Interpenetration

In trying to understand the thought of a philosopher, one often starts by considering a single word, say nature in Aristotle, substance in Spinoza, or time in Bergson, in the total range of its connotations. One often feels that a full understanding of such a word would be a key to the understanding of the whole system.

—*Anatomy of Criticism,* 335

The "subject" swallows everything objective to it: hence the pan-historical critics of today, the Hegelian pan-philosophical absolute knowledge, the pan-literary universe which only three people understand: Blake, Mallarmé, and myself. The *final* answer, naturally, is interpenetration.

—*Late Notebooks,* 1:247

One does not read very far in Frye before realizing that he is a dialectical thinker, his mind repeatedly moving back and forth between opposing poles of reference: knowledge and experience, space and time, stasis and movement, the individual and society, tradition and innovation, Platonic synthesis and Aristotelian analysis, engagement and detachment, freedom and concern, *mythos* and *dianoia,* the world and the grain of sand, immanence and transcendence, and scores, no, hundreds of other oppositions.[1] A second self-evident feature of his expansive body of work is its drive toward unity—an effort to get beyond dialectic.[2] Frye always resists the Kierkegaardian either/or solution. But unity is not achieved at the expense of variety, and in his notebooks he never tires of insisting that opposites are never resolved by reconciliation, harmony, or agreement. Such terms relate to propositional language and are forms of what he calls "imperialistic compulsion" (*LN,* 2:653). In one of his notebooks from the mid–1960s Frye writes: "I have always distrusted what I call Reuben the Reconciler in thought: the syncretism that 'reconciles' Plato & Aristotle or St. Thomas & Marx. I think every great structure of thought or imagination is a universe in itself, identical with and interpenetrating every other, but not similar or harmonizable with any other" (*TBN,* 39).[3] And in one of his late notebooks he reiterates the point:

If it was Vico who began the philosophy of history, it was Hegel who saw that a philosophy of history had to include a history of philosophy. Philosophy begins in an assertion of territoriality; it grows and diversifies through criticism, dispute, "refutation," and so on; but its real being is in a tradition of consensus. Every poem is "unique," in the soft-headed phrase, and "archetype spotting" is a facile and futile procedure; but the traditions and conventions of poetry make a shape and a meaning. They move toward a future (emergence of primary concerns), and they expand into a wider present.

Criticism also has a tradition that gives a consensus to all the disagreement, including, not impossibly, all the blather and stock response. Because, as I've said from the beginning, even the bullshit documents a history of taste.

The bullshitters, of course, are always chasing donkeys' carrots (or bulls' tails), looking for a final reconciliation of all disagreements in the bosom of Marx, S. Thomas, the Great Mother, or what not. The correct form of this is the "God exists in us and we in him" formula of Blake, Juliana of Norwich, and many others. (*LN*, 2:641)

Later in the same notebook he writes:

Conversion is imperialism, reconciliation at the price of subjection. If a Jew tells me he can't accept Jesus as the Messiah, there isn't, in these days, any question of conversion on either side, merely a realization that we both see the same things from different points of view: in short, interpenetration. . . . Two levels of history: aggressive and cultural. The aggressive is imperialist and seeks the reconciliation of the pax Romana: agreement on the linguistically aggressive dogma. Cultural history interpenetrates: variety and unity, but no uniformity. (*LN*, 2: 650–51)

The key concept in these notebook entries is interpenetration. If opposites in a dialectic are not to be reconciled or harmonized in some way, what does it mean to say that they interpenetrate? Considering some of the ways Frye uses the word will provide an initial insight into his expansive religious quest. The word appears in different contexts, but whatever the context, interpenetration is one of the many verbal formulas Frye uses to push language toward expressing the ineffable or capturing the highest mode of thought. "I don't believe affirmations," Frye says in a notebook from the years he was writing *Words with Power,* "either my own or other people's. The motto I've chosen for the book (quique amavit cras amet) represents a hope but not a faith: I can't pin down my faith so precisely. What I believe are the verbal formulas I work out that seem to make sense on their own" (*LN*, 1:145).⁴ Or again, in a notebook from the early 1970s: "It is possible that I ought to write two short books. . . . The first book, which could conceivably be the Birks Lectures, would be on the three awarenesses of religion, that of the light-dark dialectic of the Father, of the journey of the Logos through the seven creative stages, and of the decentralized interpenetration of the Spirit. Caution: don't say 'solving the problem of,' which is projection: say 'finding the verbal formulas for'" (*TBN*, 282).⁵ Frye's writing is, among all of the other things it represents, an extended quest in search of such verbal formulas, interpenetration being only one of many, though a central one. He uses the word to help define a kind of experience, a way of understanding, a process of enlightenment, a religious final cause, and a visionary perception. Around the word "interpenetration" cluster a host of additional verbal formulas that help to define it, and interpenetration is a function of the Hegelian *Aufhebung*, which will recur throughout our study as a central element in Frye's dialectic. But, first, where did the idea of interpenetration originate for Frye?

The Birth of an Idea

Interpenetration, Frye says in an interview, is a "key idea that has always been on my mind" (*NFC*, 61). "Always" is certainly a hyperbole, but Frye did come to the intuition early. What helped crystallize the idea was, first of all, his reading as a teenager of Spengler. In 1930 Frye read *The Decline of the West* after he happened upon it in the library at Hart House, the student center at the University of Toronto, and he reread the book during the summer of 1931, remarking in one of his essays that he "practically slept with Spengler under [his] pillow for several years."⁶ What attracted Frye to Spengler was the latter's view of the organic growth of cultures and his meditation on the destiny of art forms. But Frye was always somewhat puzzled by his fascination with Spengler, and it was only years later, he reports in one of his notebooks, that he realized that his attraction was also "the result of divining in him the principle of historical interpenetration: everything that happens is a symbol of everything else that's contemporary with it. Such a perspective helps one to escape from the abstracting of culture, including the arts and sciences, from what I've called the dissolving phantasmagoria of political events" (*LN*, 2:617). He puts it almost the same way in another notebook: "The great intuition I got from Spengler, and later from Vico, was the sense of every historical phenomenon being symbolic of every other phenomenon contemporary with it" (*LN*, 1:219).⁷

If Spengler helped to crystallize the idea for Frye, Alfred North Whitehead's *Science and the Modern World* helped to articulate it. "I can still remember the exhilaration I felt," Frye recalls, "when I came to the passage" in Whitehead's book (*DV,* 40-41).[8] The word "interpenetration" does not actually appear in *Science and the Modern World,* which was the first book of philosophy that Frye "read purely on [his] own and purely for pleasure" (*DV,* 40), but the passage that so struck Frye came from Whitehead's chapter entitled "The Romantic Reaction": "In a certain sense everything is everywhere at all times. For every location involves an aspect of itself in every other location. Thus every spatio-temporal standpoint mirrors the world."[9] We will return to this philosophical riddle shortly.

At several places in the papers he wrote as a student at Victoria and Emmanuel Colleges Frye uses the word "interpenetration" in the sense of religious syncretism or assimilation, but in a paper on Calvin he presented at the Theological Society of Emmanuel College in 1935 he remarks, in what seems to be a clear reference to the passage in Whitehead, that "the centre of the universe is wherever one happens to be" (*SE,* 414). And he concludes that paper by contending that when our understanding of the Spenglerian rise and fall of civilizations and the Incarnation "interpenetrate and focus into one, we shall have a theology which can accommodate itself to twentieth-century requirements" (416). Interpenetration, then, was an idea that, in its Whiteheadean sense, Frye began to exploit at an early age: he was twenty-two when he wrote the paper on Calvin.

The Mahayana Buddhist sutras, especially the Avatamsaka and the Lankavatara, were a third defining source for interpenetration. In a notebook from the 1980s Frye recalls that learning about interpenetration from Whitehead "was followed by [Peter] Fisher's introducing to me the Lankavatara Sutra, where it [interpenetration] was said to be in the Avatamsaka Sutra" (*LN,* 2:713). Fisher was one of Frye's students who, after graduating from college, had approached Frye about doing an M.A. thesis on Blake. As Frye reports this episode in his preface to Fisher's book on Blake, Fisher "nearly walked out again when he discovered that I had not read the Bhagavadgita in Sanskrit, which he took for granted that any serious student of Blake would have done as a matter of course." Frye adds that he had earlier been misled in his reading of Oriental philosophy by bad translations, but that thereafter his and Fisher's "conversations took the form of a kind of symbolic shorthand in which terms from Blake and from Mahayana Buddhism were apt to be used interchangeably."[10] These conversations were frequent: in the late 1940s and early 1950s Frye and Fisher met every Monday to drink beer and talk about literature, philosophy, and religion. Frye was familiar with the Lankavatara Sutra through the edition that Fisher introduced him to—the 1932 translation by the well-known Buddhist scholar D. T. Suzuki.[11] In one of his notebooks from the 1940s Frye reports that Fisher had in fact given him a copy of the Lankavatara (*RT,* 45). Frye seems to have known as well Suzuki's commentary on the sutra, *Studies in the Lankavatara Sutra,* where Suzuki says that the Avatamsaka Sutra, "the consummation of Buddhist thought," represents "abstract truths so concretely, so symbolically . . . that one will finally come to the realisation of the truth that even in a particle of dust the whole universe is seen reflected—not this visible universe only, but the vast system of universes, by the highest minds only."[12] Here we have an echo of Blake's "world in a grain of sand." This is similar to the statement in the Lankavatara Sutra about the intuitive experience of the Tathagatas (enlightened Buddhas) being likened to holding a fruit in the palm of the hand, beside which passage, in fact, Frye wrote in his copy, "Seeing the world in a grain of sand."[13]

A few years later Frye seems less certain about the sequence of his early encounter with Whitehead and the Mahayana Buddhist texts. In a notebook devoted to his Emmanuel College lectures, "The Double Vision," he writes:

> The theme I want for the third lecture takes me into fields I'm ill prepared to enter, and unless I can connect it with something already central in me I don't know how I can complete it in time. The general idea is that harmony, reconciliation (whether of God and man or of two arguments) and agreement are all terms relating to propositional language. The poetic counterpart is what I've been calling interpenetration, the concrete order in which everything is everywhere at once. Whitehead's SMW [*Science and the Modern World*] says this in so many words: I must have got it from there originally, though I thought I got it from Suzuki's remarks about the Avatamsaka Sutra. (*LN,* 2:616)[14]

In trying to remember when he first encountered "Suzuki's remarks," Frye is doubtless referring to Suzuki's comment on the Lankavatara Sutra that interpenetration in the Avatamsaka Sutra "constitutes the central thought of the sutra."[15] Suzuki's book appeared about the time Frye came across the passage in Whitehead—the early 1930s; his detailed exposition of the Avatamsaka Sutra did not appear for another two decades.[16]

In any case, there are three primary contexts for Frye's early encounter with the idea of interpenetration—the historical by way of Spengler, the philosophical by way of Whitehead, and the religious by way of the Mahayana sutras. In Frye's late books the idea of interpretation, though found sparingly, usually appears in a religious context: it is found, as we shall see, in key passages in *The Great Code* and *The Double Vision*. In the notebooks, where the word "interpenetrate" or some form of it appears more than 150 times, the context is most often religious as well. There are also decidedly literary and political or cultural uses of the term. Before considering the fundamentally religious meaning of inter-penetration, we shall glance at the ways the word is used in these other contexts.

The Historical Context

As indicated, one of the principles that Frye learned from Spengler was the interpenetration of symbolism: "[E]verything that happens in the world symbolizes everything else that happens." "Nobody," Frye says, "had really established this before, though there are hints of it in Ruskin; today it's a staple of pop-kulch McLuhan-Carpenter stuff, but they (at least McLuhan) got it through Wyndham Lewis, whose Time and West-ern Man is a completely Spenglerian book" (54–3.10). What Lewis at-tacks in this book is what he calls "time-philosophy," and although he is thoroughly anti-Spenglerian, Lewis does show "how twentieth-century philosophy, literature, politics, popular entertainment, music and ballet, and half a dozen other social phenomena all form an interwoven texture of 'time-philosophy,' and are all interchangeable symbols of it" (*SM,* 189).[17] This means that the unity of culture is viewed organically, rather than in a linear or cyclical way. The various units of cultural history are of a piece, and within a given "culture," as Spengler uses the term, its philosophies and myths and metaphors mirror each other or, as Frye says in the notebook just quoted, they "are intertwined in a historical pro-gression" (54–3.10).[18] In short, they interpenetrate, thus providing Frye a way to move beyond the endless repetitions in the cyclical view of his-tory. "In the cyclical vision *everything,*" he says in a notebook from the late 1970s, "becomes historical, and there is no Other except the social mass. The impulse to plunge into that is strong but premature. Something here eludes me. The answers are in interpenetration and Thou Art That" (*RT,* 327).[19] Or again:

> With the Fall man lost good & got the knowledge of good & evil, a cyclical & interpenetrating knowledge in which evil is primary & good a secondary derivation from it. So much I've always got clear. Man also lost life, life which is the *opposite* of death, life where death is an alien & non-existent possibility like unicorns, and got the interpenetrating

cycle of life & death, where death is not only natural & inevitable, but implied in the very conception of life itself.

I'm intellectually a prisoner of my own profession: for me, to know anything is to find a verbal formula for it. Hence the above represents something I've always known but never really knew. I suppose the good-evil & life-death cycles are only aspects of a total pattern of double-gyre or antithesis which can "exist" only in that form, as CP [*The Critical Path*] says. Youth & age, male & female, master & slave, & so on. So the cycle is the demonic analogy of interpenetration. (*TBN,* 319)

The apocalyptic analogy of interpenetration, as we will see, is the Incarnation, because the Incarnation liberates one from the myth of eternal recurrence.

The Philosophical and Scientific Contexts

Philosophically, Frye sees interpenetration as synonymous with the identity of the one and the many, of particularity and totality. To return to *Science and the Modern World,* what does Whitehead mean by the cryptic utterance "In a certain sense everything is everywhere at all times"? In a certain sense, of course, everything is not everywhere at all times: if I am in Virginia, I am not in China, and the book you are now holding is not on Mars. The context of Whitehead's remark is his account of "the romantic reaction" to eighteenth-century scientific materialism, which holds the doctrine of simple location, the tendency to think of material things as located at a particular point in space and time. He has just given his reasons for distrusting the subjectivist position, which holds that "the nature of our immediate experience is the outcome of the perceptive peculiarities of the subject enjoying the experience."[20] Then Whitehead turns to the relationship between bodily experience and perception: "[W]e have to admit that the body is the organism whose states regulate our cognisance of the world. The unity of the perceptual field therefore must be a unity of the bodily experience. In being aware of the bodily experience, we must thereby be aware of the whole spatio-temporal world as mirrored within the bodily life. This is the solution of the problem I gave in my last lecture."[21] And the solution in his last lecture involves abandoning the idea of simple location, for nothing is an isolated bit of matter. To so conceive of things is to mistake the abstract for the concrete, what Whitehead has earlier called the fallacy of misplaced concreteness.[22] At this point he sets down his celebrated axiom that "everything is everywhere at all times." For Whitehead there is no paradox in such a view. The paradox lies rather in the position of simple location, and the fallacy of simple location can be seen in his illustration of the idea that "every spatio-temporal standpoint mirrors the world": "You are in a certain place perceiving things. Your perception takes place where you are, and is entirely dependent on how your body is functioning. But this functioning of the body in one place, exhibits for your cognisance an aspect of the distant environment, fading away into the general knowledge that there are things beyond. If this cognisance conveys knowledge of a transcendent world, it must be because the event which is the bodily life unifies in itself aspects of the universe."[23] Had Eliot's Prufrock been able to act on his question "Do I dare disturb the universe?" he would have illustrated Whitehead's principle, which is a version of John Donne's "No man is an island" thesis. Like Frye, Whitehead wanted to get beyond the dualisms that have traditionally confronted us: subject and object, mind and body, the individual and the community. In one of his late notebooks Frye writes, "Whitehead surrounds his principle of interpenetration by talking about the prehension of an event and its relation to other events: particularity and totality make nonsense without each other" (*LN*, 2:619). Whitehead's version of the principle can be found in *Religion in the Making*, a series of lectures in which he applied to religion what he had applied to science in *Science and the Modern World*:

> The actual temporal world can be analyzed into a multiplicity of occasions of actualization. These are the primary actual units of which the temporal world is composed. Call each such occasion an "epochal occasion." Then the actual world is a community of epochal occasions. In the physical world each epochal occasion is a definite limited physical event, limited both as to space and time, but with time-duration as well as with its full spatial dimensions.
>
> The epochal occasions are the primary units of the actual community, and the community is composed of the units. But each unit has in its nature a reference to every other member of the community, so that each unit is a microcosm representing in itself the entire all-inclusive universe.[24]

In his notes for a lecture on Blake's illustrations for the book of Job, Frye uses the Whiteheadean phrase in observing that the checkered pavement with intersecting circles in plate 20 is a "symbol of an interpenetrating world where everything is everywhere at once" (57.135). Another example is in Borges's story "The Aleph," where Carlos Argentino Daneri explains to the narrator that the Aleph in his cellar "is one of the points in space that contains all other points . . . the microcosm of the alchemists and Kabbalists, our true proverbial friend, the *multum in parvo!*"[25] This, Frye says, "illustrates the principle of interpenetration, everything everywhere at once" (*LN,* 2:448).

Whitehead's interpenetrative universe has philosophical analogues in Frye's reading of Hegel, Plotinus, and David Bohm, among others. Frye announces in a 1971 notebook that this identity of the one and the many is, in fact, the motto of the so-called third book, the elaborate, encyclopedic work that he planned to write after finishing *Anatomy of Criticism* (*TBN,* 326). And in a notebook entry written some fifteen years later, he remarks that there is a note in his edition of Hegel's *Phenomenology of Spirit* "that quotes Plotinus as saying that what is beyond is also here. So Plotinus has interpenetration, though the buggers don't give a reference, and Hegel doesn't allude to Plotinus" (*LN,* 2:631). Frye is referring to the quotation from Plotinus ("Everything that is yonder is also here") in J. N. Findlay's analysis of Hegel's *Phenomenology of Spirit.*[26] But Frye actually did know the Plotinus reference, or at least had known it earlier: in Notebook 34 he quotes the passage from the *Fifth Ennead,* 8 ("They see all not in process of becoming but in Being, and they see themselves in the other. Each Being contains within itself the whole intelligible world. Therefore all is everywhere. Each is there all and all is each.") and places it beside the more familiar passage from *Science and the Modern World,* which he also reproduces in the notebook.[27] And in his own edition of *Science and the Modern World* he has the following marginal notation for Whitehead's interpenetration formula: "[T]his doctrine of the universal mirror is a point for me, I think. The passage is almost identical to Plotinus, V, 8."[28] Moreover, in his edition of *The Enneads* Frye wrote "vision of interpenetration" beside the following passage: "To 'live at ease' is there; and to these divine beings verity is mother and nurse, existence and sustenance; all that is not of process but of authentic being they see, and themselves in all: for all is transparent, nothing dark, nothing resistant; every being is lucid to every other, in breadth and depth; light runs through light. And each of them contains all within itself, and at the same time sees all in every other, so that everywhere there is all, and infinite the glory" (*Enneads,* 5.8.4).

The original source of Frye's knowledge of the *Fifth Ennead* was almost certainly Rudolf Otto's *Mysticism East and West,* a book he had read about 1946 or 1947.[29] As we noted earlier, Otto argues that there are two approaches to mysticism, the way of introspection and the way of unifying vision. Frye is not convinced that such a division really exists: "Surely the discovery of the self and the unifying of vision are and always must be the same thing" (*RT,* 11). But Otto goes on to say that the two traditions actually converge in Eckhart and Sankara, whom he takes to be the greatest representatives of Western and Eastern mysticism, and he even uses the word "interpenetration" to describe the convergence.[30]

There were other philosophical formulas. Following the claim in one notebook that the whole-part antithesis is resolved by interpenetration, Frye inserts the parenthetical remark "Coleridge through Barfield" (*LN,* 1:179). The reference is to Owen Barfield's *What Coleridge Thought,* which provides a detailed exposition of Coleridge's understanding of interpenetration, a dynamic and generative process that does not reconcile polarities but re-creates a new entity from them.[31] Coleridge, in fact, uses the word itself, maintaining that only through the imagination can one see the power "of interpenetration, of total intussusception, of the existence of all in each as the condition of Nature's unity and substantiality, and of the latency under the predominance of some one power, wherein subsists her life and its endless variety."[32] Polarity, the two forces of one power, is, Coleridge says in the *Statesman's Manual,* "a living and generative interpenetration."[33] Barfield points to analogues of Coleridge's theory of polarity in Ramon Lull and Giordano Bruno, two thinkers to whom Frye was attracted.[34] Here is one of Frye's versions of polarity: "The revealed community would have to be based on some such conception as Christ, who is conceived metaphorically, as an interpenetrating force we're a part of and yet is also a part of us" (58-6.12).[35]

Frye was also drawn to the notion of the "implicate order" in the work of David Bohm, the eminent quantum physicist and protégé of Einstein. Bohm's early work is more scientific than philosophical, but after he met Krishnamurti in 1961 his interests expanded from pure science to larger questions about human nature and cosmology.[36] The extent of Frye's knowledge of Bohm's work is uncertain, and in one of his notebooks he indicates that he does not know enough mathematics to keep up with the arguments of the new physics. But he did read at least parts of Bohm's *Wholeness and the Implicate Order,* as we know from his annotations of that book, and he was familiar with a less-technical presentation of Bohm's argument in such popular accounts as Ken Wilber's *The Holographic Paradigm* and Fritjof Capra's *The Turning Point* and *The Tao of Physics.*[37] In *Wholeness and the Implicate Order* Bohm argues that all existence consists of a continuous wholeness, the order of which exists at some deeper level he calls the implicate order, "implicate" meaning "to fold inward." "In the implicate order," he says, "the totality of existence is enfolded within each region of space (and time)."[38] The implicate or enfolded order stands in opposition to the explicate (mechanistic) or unfolded order.[39] Bohm sees the hologram—three-dimensional images projected into space with a laser—as a metaphor of the implicate order, for in the hologram each part implicitly contains the whole.[40] That is, the important feature of the hologram is that any part of the photographic plate contains the image of the whole.[41] In the implicate order, in other words, the whole universe is enfolded into each part. This is close to Whitehead's idea that the conventional ways of conceiving space ("simple location" or the subjectivist perception of the explicate order) are undermined by the principle that "everything is everywhere at all times." In one notebook Frye translates the idea of the implicate order into these terms: "Where religion and science can still get together is on the conception of the objective world as an 'unfolding' of an 'enfolded' or unborn order, which is beyond time and space as we experience them" (*LN,* 1:105).[42] In another notebook, Frye writes, "Explicitly, the part is 'in' the whole; implicitly, the whole is 'in' the part. But the way that the chicken is in the egg is different: a world of interlocked energies. I suppose this is what the hologram-paradigm people are getting at" (*LN,* 1:324).

The "world of interlocked energies" is for both Frye and Bohm a more fundamental and important order than the explicate order of classical physics. As Bohm says, the new order "is not to be understood solely in terms of a regular arrangement of *objects* (e.g., in rows) or as a regular arrangement of *events* (e.g. in a series). Rather, a *total order* is contained, in some *implicit* sense, in each region of space and time. . . . in some sense each region contains a total structure 'enfolded' within it."[43] Frye sees criticism as the means for retrieving the original or undisplaced form of metaphor—its enfolded shape, which has become "unfolded" in the explicate order: "Criticism approaches a literary work which is a metaphor-cluster made explicit. Why do we need the critic? Because there's so much implicit in the metaphor-cluster that he didn't make explicit. Mainly, of course, the relation of context, to other cultures of words" (*LN,* 1:109).[44] The implicate form of work is play. All features of one of Spengler's culture-organisms are the explicate order of an implicate seed that he expresses as the symbols of those cultures (*LN,* 1:110).

In *The Turning Point* Fritjof Capra maintains, "Subatomic particles are not separate entities but interrelated energy patterns in an ongoing dynamic process. These patterns do not 'contain' one another but rather 'involve' one another in a way that can be given a precise mathematical meaning but cannot be expressed in words." Frye's marginal annotation for this passage is one word, "Interpenetration,"[45] and it appears that the Blakean idea of energy is in Frye's mind parallel to the energy that drives what Bohm calls the "holomovement" in his implicate-order paradigm. In one of his notebooks for *Words with Power,* Frye, projecting a conclusion for that book, writes, "The apocalyptic finale will have to take in the total-consciousness speculations of Schrodinger [Schrödinger] and (now) David Bohm" (*LN,* 1:26). Although Frye writes a great deal about consciousness, from ordinary to intensified, in *Words with Power,* he does not call on either Schrödinger or Bohm in that book.[46] But in his "apocalyptic finale" to *The Double Vision* he speaks of spiritual nature as "a nature of 'implicate order,' as it has been called, or interpenetrating energies" (84). Or, another version of the apocalyptic finale from one of the notebooks: "The end of the journey is interpenetration, or perhaps the hologram model. It's the recognition scene of proclaiming word & responding spirit" (*LN,* 1:395).

Bohm himself uses the word "interpenetration" to describe his enfolding universe,[47] and without interpenetration we have only discrete entities and events in the explicate order. The idea of wholeness in Bohm, about which Frye does not comment but which was surely appealing to him, entails the implicate order.[48] It is perhaps worth noting that Barfield was familiar with Bohm's work, and Frye may well have first encountered Bohm in *What Coleridge Thought.* Consider, finally, this passage, which sounds as if it comes from *Words with Power, The Double Vision,* or one of Frye's notebooks: "[W]e are often led to speak of the totality, of a wholeness which is both immanent and transcendent, and which, in a religious context, is often given the name of God. The immanence means that the totality of what is, is immanent in matter; the transcendence means that this wholeness is also beyond matter." While these words appear to be something Frye might have written, they actually belong to David Bohm.[49]

Another eminent scientist, the neurophysiologist Karl Pribram, working independently on the structure of the brain, arrived at a very similar conclusion about the holographic nature of brain cells and, by extension, consciousness, memory, and perception. He was attracted to Bohm's holographic model, proposing a theory that impulses received by the surface of the brain are enfolded and unfolded across it. There is no evidence that Frye had firsthand knowledge of Pribram's scientific studies, though he does refer to him as one of the "Tao of Physics people" (*LN,* 1:106). Frye's knowledge of Pribram may have come initially from Bohm or, what is more likely, from Wilber's *The Holographic Paradigm.*[50] Although Pribram's theory of the hologram began with his studies of the brain, in 1975 he made an effort to synthesize his theory with Bohm's, thereby linking his brain research to the philosophy of science.[51]

Finally, Frye suggests that there is a parallel between his belief in the unity and interconnectedness of things and Geoffrey Chew's bootstrap theory, which Frye mentions in passing in one notebook (*LN*, 1:416). According to the bootstrap theory, elementary particles (protons, neutrons, mesons) exist not independently but by virtue of the existence of all other particles. There are no elementary particles: lifting one particle by its own bootstraps enables one to determine all the other particles.[52] The bootstrap theory, according to Capra, one of Chew's chief devotees, conceives of the universe "as a dynamic web of interrelated events. None of the properties of any part of this web is fundamental; they all follow from the properties of the other parts, and the overall consistency of their interrelations determines the structure of the entire web."[53] Again, Frye appears to have been familiar with Chew's bootstrap hypothesis from his reading of Capra's *The Tao of Physics* and *The Turning Point*. In any event, Chew's bootstrap theory, like Coleridge's polarity, Bohm's implicate order, and Barfield's thesis about identity, is analogous to Whitehead's spatiotemporal standpoints mirroring the world. These are all different philosophic and scientific translations of the principle of interpenetration.

The speculations of Bohm, Pribram, Capra, Wilber, and Chew have had wide appeal among the popularizers of New Age science, philosophy, and religion, and we will note Frye's reading in these various New Age movements later. At this point we are interested in showing how Frye's notion of interpenetration is rooted in and partially defined by certain broadly philosophical currents of thought beginning with Whitehead. The idea that two things are the same thing (as in metaphor) is for Frye better captured by the word "interpenetration" than by the word "identity"; for interpenetration, whether of unity and variety, wholes and parts, totality and particularity, self and other, human and divine, suggests more strongly than does identity that each half of the dialectic retains its own distinctiveness while each is also present in the other. This idea of preservation is contained within the process of the Hegelian *Aufhebung*. Unity, as Frye is fond of insisting, does not mean uniformity. Moreover, interpenetration is a more dynamic concept than identity, the former implying a free flow back and forth between, in Coleridge's phrase, the "two forces of one power." Each of the philosophical speculations on interpenetration suggests that once we get beyond the assumptions of Cartesian coordinates and Aristotelian causality, the idea that "everything is everywhere at once" is not so inexplicable a paradox as it initially might seem.

Aufhebung

Sometimes Frye speaks as if interpenetration takes the form of a Hegelian synthesis, or at least the dialectical transition described by Hegel as an

Aufhebung, a term used to embody the idea that oppositions can be transcended without being abolished. The verb *aufheben* has a triple meaning: "to lift or raise," "to abolish or cancel," and "to keep or preserve." At the end of chapter 1 of his *Logic,* Hegel explicitly calls attention to at least the dual meaning:"To transcend (*aufheben*), and that which is transcended, are among the most important concepts of philosophy. . . . To transcend (*aufheben*) has this double meaning, that it signifies to keep or to preserve and also to make, to cease, to finish. To preserve includes this negative element, that something is removed from its immediacy and therefore from a Determinate Being exposed to external influences, in order that it may be preserved."[54] There is no evidence that Frye read the *Logic,* but *aufheben* and its cognates are scattered throughout *Phenomenology of Spirit,* where *Aufhebung* is usually translated as "sublation," "sublimation," or "supercession." Hegel writes, for example, that a negation "supersedes [*aufhebt*] in such a way as to preserve and maintain what is superseded, and consequently survives its own supercession [*Aufhebung*]."[55] In the Preface to the *Phenomenology* he says that reflection "overcomes the antithesis between the process of its becoming and the result," "overcomes" being A. V. Miller's translation of *aufheben.*[56] And in his discussion of perception, Hegel remarks, "*Supercession* [*Das Aufheben*] exhibits its true twofold meaning which we have seen in the negative: it is at once a *negating* and a *preserving.*"[57] Lurking in the background of the pun is the primary meaning of lifting or raising up, and Hegel goes on to say about the opposites of negating and preserving: "as a *simple* unity they therefore interpenetrate."[58] We have then in *Aufhebung* a triple meaning—a canceling, a preserving, and a lifting up—and it was this threefold meaning of the term that Frye appropriated for his own ends. The notion of preserving, which Hegel emphasizes in the final paragraph of *Phenomenology of Spirit,* means that the quest of Absolute Spirit is not an escape from history and human experience but is rooted in and arises out of the phenomenological world. Hegel concludes his immense speculative journey by quoting Schiller's *Die Freundschaft:* "from the chalice of this realm of spirits / foams forth for Him [God] his own infinitude," the "realm of spirits" being the phenomenological world of substance. What Hegel calls "the Calvary of absolute Spirit" is his own version of the Incarnation.[59] Frye's ends are directed more toward experience than knowledge: "Hegel showed how the thesis involved its own antithesis, although I think the 'synthesis' has been foisted on him by his followers. Anyway, the expansion to absolute knowledge is too close to what Blake calls the smile of a fool. My goal would be something like absolute experience rather than absolute knowledge: in experience the units are unique, and things don't agree with each other; they mirror each other" (*LN,* 2:616).[60]

In one of his *Great Code* notebooks, where Frye is trying to work out the structure of the second part of the book, he says, "Unity is a (relatively static) thesis; its negation is not so much the decentralized Bible as the recreation in which it becomes a historical process, and interpenetration, the real decentralized Bible, is the Aufhebung which follows" (*RT,* 296).[61] Here interpenetration emerges from the re-creation (process) that negates unity (stasis). The place where Frye most clearly discloses his understanding of the triple reference of *Aufhebung* is in *The Great Code:*

> Polysemous meaning, then, is the development of a single dialectical process, like the process described in Hegel's *Phenomenology.* I mention the *Phenomenology* because it seems to me that the ladder Hegel climbs in that book contains a theory of polysemous meaning as well, and that a new formulation of the old medieval four-level sequence can be discerned in it. The hero of Hegel's philosophical quest is the concept (*Begriff*), which, like Odysseus in the *Odyssey,* appears first in an unrecognized and almost invisible guise as the intermediary between subject and object, and ends by taking over the whole show, undisputed master of the house of being. But this "concept" can hardly exist apart from its own verbal formulation: that is, it is something verbal that expands in this way, so that the *Phenomenology* is, among other things, a general theory of how verbal meaning takes shape. Even the old metaphor of "levels" is preserved in Hegel's term *Aufhebung.* What Hegel means by dialectic is not anything reducible to a patented formula, like the "thesis-antithesis-synthesis" one so often attached to him, nor can it be anything predictive. It is a much more complex operation of a form of understanding combining with its own otherness or opposite, in a way that negates itself and yet passes through that negation into a new stage, preserving its essence in a broader context, and abandoning the one just completed like the chrysalis of a butterfly or a crustacean's outgrown shell. (*GC,* 222)

Aufhebung (or one of its related forms) does not make an appearance in Frye's writing until the two Bible books—three instances in the notebooks for *The Great Code* and six in the notebooks for *Words with Power.*[62] In the published work, *Aufhebung* appears only in *The Great Code,* once in the passage just quoted and again shortly after that where Frye suggests that the disinterested and engaged approaches to reading the Bible might just be transcended and preserved by an *Aufhebung* (*GC,* 223). But the dialectical transition represented by the word, even if the word itself is absent, is omnipresent in Frye's thought. Only the object of what is superseded changes. "Unity," Frye writes, "has to be negated to achieve its Aufhebung of interpenetration" (*RT,* 298), which is one example of supercession. We will encounter others as we proceed.

The Social Contexts

Interpenetration appears frequently in the notebooks in a social context. Frye maintains that "in proportion as we move away from secondary concern with its hierarchies to primary concern our cosmology will decentralize, become increasingly classless in its assumptions, and come to focus on the central idea of interpenetration" (*LN* 2:435). The centralizing tendency in human affairs is aggressive and authoritarian, and like his preceptor Blake, Frye always resists all forms of imperialism. "The crusade," he says, "is expanding empire, in Blake's terms, not decentralizing (interpenetrating) art. (Note that decentralizing is one stop on the way to interpenetration)" (*LN* 2:696). The movement toward interpenetration, then, is a movement away from power, ideology, and secondary concern, while the focus of the genuine community is dialogue. Dialogue, like decentralization, is not the same thing as interpenetration,[63] but the two ideas are related in many of the notebook entries.[64] At one point Frye says that authentic dialogue is interpenetrative, adding that "Plato, the inventor of dialogue, goes in an anti-dialogue direction. He begins what Aristotle, especially in his conception of *telos,* greatly develops: the *tendentious* argument, the writing cat-walk leading to an end, the end being really the justification of existing authority" (*RT,* 91). Ideology is monologic and exclusive, but in dialogue the opposites of different ideologies interpenetrate (*LN* 1:121). The ultimate revelation, Frye says in a 1969 notebook, is "through mysticism to dialogue—interpenetration of Word." And "the final sense of interpenetration," he adds, is "the key to dialogue as well as identity" (*RT,* 90, 91).

   In the one essay where interpenetration is headlined—"Culture as Interpenetration" (*DG,* 15–25)—Frye speaks less abstractly, using the concept to describe the synthesis of the indigenous and immigrant cultures in Canada. We see this synthesis realized, he observes in his notes for the essay, in Leonard Cohen's *Beautiful Losers,* a novel about "a Montreal Jew writing with genuine compassion about a seventeenth-century Algonquin woman turned Catholic saint, with twentieth-century themes mixed in" (54-15.12). "I speak of interpenetration," Frye adds, "because it seems to me that one decisive feature of high culture is cross-fertilization, something that's beyond the external influence of a mother country and the internal response to it" (54-15.29). Socially and culturally, then, interpenetration derives in part from Frye's own liberal politics, his utopian vision of a classless society in which differences are abolished not so much by acceptance or reconciliation as by identification. Community, communion, and commonwealth are ideas that cluster in the margins of Frye's comments on interpenetration, ideas not unrelated to his own personal identification with the principles of the Co-operative Commonwealth Federation.[65] "Centralizing and homogenizing versus interpenetration," Frye says in thinking about one of the themes of *The Double Vision*: "probably it's the germ of Utopia: nowhere becoming everywhere" (*LN,* 2:695).

While individuals can themselves interpenetrate with each other and with texts, individual egos cannot:

> I gather that Bakhtin's "dialogism" is gradually replacing "deconstruction" as a buzzword. Of course there's dialogue between writer & reader, but much more goes on than that: it's more like an interpenetrating of identities. Montaigne's "consubstantial" remark shows that the writer's ego and the reader's ego *can't* interpenetrate: they're like the old-style atoms, or, more accurately, like the Leibnitzian monads. In this century we have to forget that "atom" means the unsplittable (or did mean it) or that the individual is the "individable." Two egos identifying would be like two billiard balls copulating. (*LN,* 1:195–96)[66]

Or as Frye puts it in another entry: "[L]ove is interpenetration, but it has to extend beyond the sexual interpenetrating of intercourse. Every act of hostility is penetration with a threat, with a desire to dominate or acquire for oneself. Love means entering into and identifying with other people and things without threats or domination, in fact without retaining an ego-self" (*LN,* 1:209–10).

In the process of identity, individuality—which Frye says is "the ethical and political side of the principle of interpenetration" (*RT,* 326)—does not, on the principle of the *Aufhebung,* disappear.[67] There is one power, as Coleridge says, but still two forces. Or, as the idea gets expressed in another verbal formula, "Man is awake at night & sees that the moon & stars are orderly as well as the sun. He also sees the sun vanish into the dark world & reappear. The Logos & Thanatos visions, then, may begin as bordering haloes of one world; but each *is* the world, & they interpenetrate. The morning has come, and also the night" (*TBN,* 231). As mentioned in the previous chapter, the Logos and Thanatos visions are the upper and lower points on the circle-and-cross diagram that Frye used throughout his notebooks as a schematic shorthand for organizing his ideas. He associates scores of images, metaphors, and concepts with the northern and southern points of the Logos–Thanatos axis, but here the two points represent generally light and darkness, order and chaos.[68] Frye's point is that, to use Coleridge's aphorism, while we can distinguish between Logos and Thanatos, we cannot divide them because they interpenetrate.[69]

Other Contexts

Frye occasionally uses the word "interpenetration" in the context of metaphor, which is based on the principle of identity. "Imaginative literalism" (the metaphorical *is* the literal), he says in *The Double Vision,* "seeks what might be called interpenetration, the free flowing of spiritual life into and out of one another that communicates but never violates" (18). In *The Great Code* he uses the word to describe the kind of vision contained in metaphors of particularity, such as Blake's "To see the world in a grain of sand," as opposed to metaphors of unity and integration (*GC,* 166–67).[70] But identity, which we turn to in the next chapter, is a more fitting context than interpenetration for understanding Frye's views on metaphor.

On a higher level of generality, interpenetration underlies Frye's conception of the unity of the entire verbal cosmos. At the anagogic level of meaning, Frye says in the *Anatomy,* "the symbol is a monad, all symbols being united in a single infinite and eternal verbal symbol which is, as *dianoia,* the Logos, and, as mythos, total creative act" (121). Without such a hypothesis we are left, in Frye's view, with a countless series of minute particulars.[71] By assuming the unity of the consciousness and the cosmos—that is, the unity of all things—Frye could say, in reflecting on the products of human enterprise and trying to distance himself from Arnold, "As for the danger of poetry becoming a 'substitute' for religion, that again is merely bad metaphor: if both poetry and religion are functioning properly, their interpenetration will take care of itself" (*SM,* 121). Here interpenetration suggests complementarity, the idea being that literature cannot be properly possessed in the absence of its religious dimension, and vice versa. As Frye says in his "Letter to the English Institute," "Literature itself is not a field of conflicting arguments but of interpenetrating visions,"[72] religion being one such vision.

Frye's earliest use of the word "interpenetration" comes at a point in his first published essay where he is distinguishing among the forms of

Menippean satire: "But precisely because the Menippean satirist is not taking an idle delight in watching philosophers disagree but an artist's interest in the patterns their conflicts make, his dialogues need not be always satiric, in the narrow sense. The imaginary conversation, the *Totengesprach,* the cultural dialogue, are all species of the form, but the grave and rarefied beauty of Landor is as much a part of the tradition as the hair-pulling brawl of Lucian's *Symposium.* Ideas may clash or they may simply interpenetrate."[73] There are other contexts: specialized disciplines can interpenetrate; an individual's life can be interpenetrated by the sense of the slow passage of time in the face of time's winged chariot; a critic's principles can be interpenetrated by knowledge outside his or her field, as Frye's were by psychology, anthropology, comparative religion, esoteric traditions, and other bodies of thought; Frye's own books, each with its center of gravity, interpenetrate with each other; work and play, necessity and freedom interpenetrate; food and sex interpenetrate symbolically; the individual reader interpenetrates with the universal one; love itself is interpenetration; life and death, good and evil, creation and criticism interpenetrate.[74] In short, the idea is pervasive in Frye's writing, appearing in a host of contexts and with different shades of meaning.

Moreover, in his reading Frye always kept an eye out for the word "interpenetration," underlining or otherwise marking it when he came across it, or making marginal annotations when he encountered parallel or similar expressions of the idea. Such underlining is found, for example, in his copies of books by G. R. Levy, Francis Huxley, C. G. Jung, Alphonse Louis Constant, and others. And in a number of instances he would write in the margins of his books "interpenetration" or some phrase including the word ("vision of interpenetration," "point of interpenetration," "good sense of interpenetration").[75]

Frye was something of a fan of E. R. Eddison's fantasy novels, particularly his Zimiamvia trilogy and his epic adventure story *The Worm Ouroboros.*[76] In *The Worm Ouroboros,* Eddison has a scene between Lord Gro and Lady Merrian in which she asks him, pointing a sword at his throat, who and how many are in his company. Then Eddison writes: "He answered her like a dreamer, 'How shall I answer thee? How shall I number them that be beyond all count? Or how name unto your grace their habitation which are even now closer to me than hand or feet, yet o'er the next instant are able to transcend a main wilder belike than even a star-beam hath journeyed o'er.'" Frye's answer to the Lady Merrian's question, which he wrote in the margin, was "interpenetrating spiritual world."[77] To that world we now turn.

Interpenetration as Spiritual Vision

What emerges from the infinite variety of Frye's notebooks is the dialectic of a katabatic and anabatic journey: Frye's central mission is to descend and then ascend the imaginative ladder to the ultimate level of spiritual vision. The journey is similar to Hegel's quest in the *Phenomenology of Spirit* for the absolute ideal, except that the verbal formulas used to describe it are altogether different.

In a notebook from the late 1960s, when Frye was thinking through the intricate schema for the third of the eight major books he planned to write, he says, "I still have to work out the right verbal formulas for the similarity–identity business. All religions are one, not alike; 'that they may be one,' not that they should all think alike: community means people thinking along similar lines & motivated by similar drives; communion means that all men are the same man. The Hegelian-Marxist 'synthesis' is this identity projected as the end of a process, but that's illusory. These are of course only hunches, but the right formulas are there if I can find them. And identity is important because it's the key to the interpenetration climax" (*TBN*, 266). The passage on interpenetration from *Science and the Modern World* was, Frye said in 1990, "my initiation into what Christianity meant by spiritual vision" (*DV*, 41). Fifty-five years earlier, as we have also seen, Frye used interpenetration in a theological context in his Emmanuel College paper on Calvin. Although Frye was not entirely innocent of theology, he largely avoided the German theologians during his three years at Emmanuel College, choosing to focus instead on Spengler, Whitehead, Frazer, and the Cambridge anthropologists (*NFC*, 61–62). Whatever minor interest Frye had in reading theology, it gradually waned over the years as he discovered that visionary texts, like Blake's, provided a more adequate account of the stages and the end of the quest—thus the attraction that the Avatamsaka Sutra held for him.[78]

The Avatamsaka Sutra is a massive, dense, extravagant, and repetitive text that forms the basis of the Chinese Hua-yen school of Buddhism, founded by Tu-shun, the first patriarch of Hua-yen, and codified at the end of the seventh century in the *Hua-yen* (flower ornament) of Fa-tsang (643–712). In India the Avatamsaka (Sanskrit for "flower ornament") was a central text of the Yogacharins. In Japan the Avatamsaka sect was known as Kegon, and a large portion of the scholarship on Hua-yen is Japanese.

There is no evidence that Frye read the Avatamsaka Sutra outside the selections in the third series of D. T. Suzuki's *Essays in Zen Buddhism*. In fact, in one of his notebooks Frye says, "I can't make any sense out of these infernal Sutras: they seem designed for people who really can't read"

(*LN,* 2:616).[79] But what Frye did fasten on from the sutra was the idea of the identity of everything and the interpenetration of all elements in the world. Suzuki calls this the "fundamental insight" of the sutra.[80] "It is," he adds, "philosophically speaking, a thought somewhat similar to Hegel's conception of concrete universals. Each individual reality, besides being itself, reflects in it something of the universal, and at the same time it is itself because of other individuals. A system of perfect relationship exists among individual existences and also between individuals and universals, between particular objects and general ideas. This perfect network of mutual relations has received at the hand of the Mahayana philosopher the technical name of interpenetration."[81]

This is the idea that captivated Frye. The sutra represents the idea in experiential and intuitive rather than philosophical terms. Suzuki's commentary on the sutra, which is based chiefly on book 39 ("The Entry into the Realm of Reality"), is often presented philosophically (he calls interpenetration a "doctrine"), even though he recognizes that philosophical language is inadequate: "In the world of the *Gandavyuha* [book 39] known as the Dharmadhatu [realm of dharma, reality], individual realities are folded into one great Reality, and this great Reality is found participated in by each individual one. Not only this, but each individual existence contains in itself all other individual existences as such. Thus there is universal interpenetration, so called in the Dharmadhatu. . . . This is not philosophical penetration of existence reached by cold logical reasoning, nor is it a symbolical representation of the imagination. It is a world of real spiritual experience."[82] Suzuki traces the several ways that Chinese thinkers speculated on the philosophical meaning of the Gandavyuha from the sixth through the ninth centuries. This speculation tended to identify the philosophy of book 39, with the fourfold doctrine of the Dharmadhatu:

> (1) the Dharmadhatu as a world of individual objects, in which case the term *dhatu* is taken to mean "something separated"; (2) the Dharmadhatu as a manifestation of one spirit (*ekacitta*) or one elementary substance (*ekadhatu*); the Dharmadhatu as a world where all its particular existences (*vastu*) are identifiable with one underlying spirit; and (4) the Dharmadhatu as a world where each one of its particular objects is identifiable with every other particular object, whatever lines of separation there may be between them all removed.[83]

In the margin of his copy of Suzuki's book Frye wrote four words, each corresponding to one of the four rungs on this ladder from the many to the one: "particulars," "unity," "universal," and "interpenetration." Such passages in Suzuki were doubtless what Frye remembered when he was preparing his Emmanuel College lectures, some forty years after he had encountered Suzuki's *Essays in Zen Buddhism*. Like Suzuki, Frye often speaks of interpenetration as an experience.[84] But in the Avatamsaka Sutra interpenetration is also represented imagistically. The sutra may be called a *flower* ornament scripture, but by far its most frequent image is that of the jewel, the text sparkling with literally thousands of jewel images. In Hua-yen Buddhism the crowning jewel, so to speak, is found in the metaphor of the celestial jeweled net that hangs above the palace of Indra, the emperor of the gods. As Tu-shun describes it, this net "is made of all jewels: because the jewels are clear, they reflect one another's images, appearing in one another's reflections upon reflections, ad infinitum, all appearing at once in one jewel, and in each one it is so—ultimately there is no going or coming."[85] Nowhere in his writings does Frye refer to the net of Indra, but he would have encountered it in his reading of Suzuki and Capra. In any event, this representation of the structure of reality as an infinitely reflecting net of jewels is a subtle yet powerful metaphor for interpenetration—the poet's way of energizing such abstractions as the concrete universal. In book 39 of the Avatamsaka, the tower with innumerable towers inside it becomes another image for interpenetration. For Thomas Cleary, the indefatigable translator of Eastern texts, book 39 represents "the most grandiose, the most comprehensive, and the most beautifully arrayed of the Buddhist scriptures." Cleary concludes that the repeated-tower image symbolizes "a central Hua-yen theme represented time and again throughout the scripture—all things, being interdependent, therefore imply in their individual being the simultaneous being of all other beings."[86] Put this way, the relationship between the one and the many may be closer to what Frye means by decentralization, but Cleary's interpretation of interdependence does have affinities with the hologram model.

As an experience, interpenetration implies process and is thus a temporal term, related to *mythos* rather than to *dianoia:* "[T]he conception of interpenetration has to apply to movements of time" (*RT,* 92). But Frye often speaks of interpenetration as a concept, and therefore as a thematic or spatial idea, as in this notebook entry: "Any thematic stasis of the Christian *commedia* is likely to sound a trifle Buddhist, as the Eliot quartets do. So does the *Paradiso,* for that matter. The fictional emphasis is on escape from prison; the thematic on smashing the walls of a mental prison, the iron bar in Zen. Romance, which presents this as contained, leads fictionally to Jerusalem & Eden; thematically to the Avatamsaka conceptions of universal identity and interpenetration" (*TBN,* 29).[87] On still other occasions Frye, aware of the limitations of spatial and temporal categories, seeks to push language beyond Spenglerian time and Whiteheadean space. "The third chapter," he says in one of his *Words with Power* note-books, "goes beyond space into the conception of interpenetration, the fourth one beyond time into the conception of 'mystical dance,' or time as interiorly possessed contrapuntal movement" (*LN*, 2:558). The inter-penetrating vision, which is the climax of the anabatic quest, comes when space is annihilated (*LN*, 1:30–31).[88]

Philosophical systems can themselves interpenetrate: "I suspect," Frye says, ". . . that the key to philosophy is the exact opposite of what philosophers do now. It's the study of the great historical systems, each of them a palace and a museum, that's genuine philosophy. At a certain point they interpenetrate into a house of many mansions, a new Jerusalem of verbal possibilities, but that's a tremendous state of enlightenment" (*LN*, 1:123). Religions interpenetrate as well.

In 1935 Frye wrote, with particularly acute prescience, to Helen Kemp: "I propose spending the rest of my life, apart from living with you, on various problems connected with religion and art. Now religion and art are the two most important phenomena in the world; or rather the most important phenomenon, for they are basically the same thing. They constitute, in fact, the only reality of existence" (*NFHK*, 1:425–26). As it turned out, Frye, who was twenty-two at the time, did devote his whole career to seeking the unified vision of religion and art. To discover verbal formulas for expressing that vision was, again, at the center of his mission. When in "The Aleph" Borges's narrator arrives at the "ineffable core" of his story, he reflects that "all language is a set of symbols whose use among speakers assumes a shared past. How, then, can I translate into words the limitless Aleph, which my floundering mind can scarcely encompass? Mystics, faced with the same problem, fall back on symbols."[89] The au-thors of the Avatamsaka Sutra also fall back on symbols—mirrors, many-faceted jewels, the pores of Buddha, the net of Indra. Frye, less given both to symbolism and to falling back, reaches forward to interpenetration as one of his central verbal formulas. Of all the contexts for his use of the word, the most frequent one in the notebooks is clearly a religious or spir-itual one. "The Holy Spirit, who, being everywhere at once, is the pure principle of interpenetration" (*LN*, 2:562). Frye also associates interpen-etration with anagogy, kerygma, apocalypse, spiritual intercourse, the vision of plenitude, the everlasting gospel, the union of Word and Spirit, the new Jerusalem, and atonement. These are all religious concepts. This paradox involved for Frye a continuous restating of the claim that X is Y, that X identifies itself with Y, that X interpenetrates Y, that X incarnates itself in Y. Incarnation, or Blake's human form divine, is perhaps the ultimate radical metaphor for Frye. "That God may be all in one," he says, "that's the text for interpenetration" (*RT,* 339). Or, in a notebook from the late 1960s, the Incarnation (along with identity, mutual awareness, and natural inclusion) is synonymous with interpenetration: "The conception of interpenetration is that of natural inclusion. We are in God; God is in us. Therefore there are two worlds, as at the end of *Paradiso,* one the other turned inside out. My consciousness of things put those things inside me, but whatever is conscious has me inside them. I fell over this years ago in dealing with art & nature: in art nature is turned inside out. But I didn't see it as interpenetration, or an aspect of it. Perhaps this mutuality of awareness *is* identity" (*TBN,* 253).[90] In *Words with Power* Frye observes that the sacred marriage in the New Testament (Christ as bridegroom, redeemed people as bride), as well as the intensely erotic way this relation is represented in mystical literature, is an expansion of the one-flesh union of Adam and Eve "into an interpenetration of spirit" (224).

We noted earlier that the Incarnation is a liberating force for Frye. Its *telos* is freedom, as we see in this exchange with Bill Moyers:

> MOYERS: *I noticed that the inscription on Victoria College is . . .* "You shall know the truth, and the truth shall make you free." *What kind of truth?*
> FRYE: In its original context in the Gospel of John, Jesus says that He is the truth, meaning that the truth is a personality and not a set of propositions, and that the truth about him was the union of divine and human natures. The feeling that the human destiny is inseparably involved with something divine is for Jesus what makes one free.
> MOYERS: *Is that true for Northrop Frye?*
> FRYE: Yes.
> MOYERS: *No separation of the secular and the sacred—even in learning?*
> FRYE: Oh, there are separations, yes. But the separations are in many contexts much less important than the things they have in common. Everything in religion has a secular aspect. Everything in secular life has a religious aspect.
> MOYERS: *What do you mean by the divine?*
> FRYE: . . . I think that in human terms it means that there is no limit toward the expansion of the mind or of the freedom and liberty of mankind. Now, of course there are aspects of freedom and liberty, such as wanting to do what you like—which really means being pushed around by your social conditioning.
> MOYERS: *—your appetites, as well.*
> FRYE: Yes. But the feeling that the genuine things you want, like free-

dom, are inexhaustible and that you never come to the end of them—
that's the beginning of the experience of the divine, for me.[91]

Two notebook entries that center on the Incarnation are instructive.
The first is from 1946, when Frye was reading the Lankavatara Sutra, and
the second from 1989, when he was preparing his lectures on the "double
vision."

> I can take no religion seriously, for reasons I don't need to go into here,
> that doesn't radiate from a God-Man, & so Christ & Buddha seem to
> me the only possible starting points for a religious experience I don't
> feel I can see over the top of. Hinduism has the complete theory of this
> in Krishna, and perhaps Judaism in the Messiah, but I'm not satisfied
> that even Hinduism is really possessed by the God-Man they under-
> stand the nature of so clearly. Now in Christianity & Buddhism I reject
> everything involved with the legal analogy, the established church, &
> so cling to Protestantism in the former & Zen in the latter. I'm just be-
> ginning to wonder if Protestantism & Zen—not as churches but as ap-
> proaches to God-Man—aren't the same thing, possessed by the same
> Saviour. (*RT,* 46)[92]

> I want to proceed from the gospel to the Everlasting Gospel, and yet
> without going in the theosophic direction of reconciliation or smile-
> of-a-fool harmony. The synoptics make Jesus distinguish himself from
> the Father, as not yet more than a prophet: it's in the "spiritual" gospel
> of John that he proclaims his own divinity. (That's approximately true,
> though one has to fuss and fuddle in writing it out.) Yet John is more
> specifically and pointedly "Christian" than the synoptics: the direction
> is from one spokesman of the perennial philosophy and a unique incar-
> nation starting a unique event. Buddhism and the like interpenetrate
> with the Everlasting Gospel: they are not to be reconciled with it. (*LN,*
> 2:618–19)

Juxtaposing these two passages, separated by more than four decades,
may help us see the interpenetration, as it were, of East and West in Frye's
thought. In his published work one gets little sense that Eastern art and
religion are formative. Notebook 3, most of which was written between
1946 and 1948, contains several extended reflections on the Lankavatara
Sutra. When we read in Eastern religious texts, Frye says "that all things
exist only insofar as they are seen of Mind itself [*Cittamatra*], that suggests
pantheism to a Western mind. Such pantheism corresponds to the hazy
impression the Westerner has of all 'Eastern' philosophy: that it is an at-

tempt to forget that one is an ego & try to hypnotize oneself into feeling that one is a part of the great All. But it is clear, first, that the Lankavatara is based on a conception of a divine man; second, that it does not teach a doctrine but inculcates a mental attitude" (*RT,* 46). Here is another version of the divine man in Buddhism, as Frye formulates it in his 1950 diary:

> [T]he study of physics does not imply that the physical universe exists, but that it is totally intelligible. Similarly with the verbal universe. Theology goes on to make an existential affirmation about each (the unmoved mover *is* God, the one word *is* Christ) which makes them descriptive & the subject of affirmation an object. . . . I can't indefinitely go on saying that literature refuses to affirm or deny the identification of the verbal universe with Christ. Sooner or later . . . I have to come to grips with the total form of human creative power. Now that, as I see it (and as Blake saw it) contains divinity within its intelligibility: it doesn't add divinity to it existentially. I know Thomism comes within a hair's breadth of saying what I say, but it can't quite say it or it couldn't remain within the Church. What I say is the straight Lankavatara line: the doctrine of Mind-only arising out of Paratantra [interdependence]. (*D,* 257)

The divine man is perhaps the epitome of interpenetration for Frye. What Frye doubtless has in mind is the Mahayana idea of *trikaya,* which includes the Buddha as both a transcendental reality and an earthly form.[93] In Christianity, the interpenetration of the human and the divine is the descending movement of the Incarnation and the ascending one of the Resurrection. "In the Incarnation the Word comes down and the Spirit, having finished his job, goes up. Here the Spirit is the Father of the Word. In Acts 1–2 the Word goes up and the Spirit comes down. Here the Spirit is the successor or Son of the Word" (*LN,* 1:213). The "Logos as incarnation," Frye says in Notebook 12, "gives place . . . to the interpenetrating epiphany" (*TBN,* 145). In another of his late notebooks Frye recalls that a "student asked me about the difference between analogy and metaphor. I said that such a statement as 'God is love' could mean that love, a mere finite word, was being used as an analogy to something infinite, or that the two were being metaphorically identified. It then occurred to me that the metaphorical meaning was only possible in an incarnational context. Useful people, students" (*LN,* 2:478).[94] In *Words with Power* this gets translated, in the context of a discussion of *soma pneumatikon* (spiritual body), into "fluidity of personality," meaning that "the spiritual body of the risen Christ is everywhere and in everyone." And the complete form of this fluidity is interpenetration (126).

"All religions are one," Frye writes, quoting Blake, "not alike: a metaphorical unity of different things, not a bundle of similarities. In that sense there is no 'perennial philosophy': that's a collection, at best, of denatured techniques of concentration. As doctrine, it's platitude: moral maxims that have no application. What there is, luckily, is a perennial struggle" (*LN,* 1:110).[95] Frye engaged in that struggle—which had its beginnings with Blake and his doctrine of contraries, his passion to erase dualities, his desire to get beyond the cloven fiction of the subject-object split, and his desire "to see a world in a grain of sand"—over the course of some sixty years. Francis Huxley concludes *The Way of the Sacred* by noting the parallels among the hologram model of coherent light, the experience of "total synecdoche" represented in the Gandavyuha (the last section of the Avatamsaka Sutra), the experience of Jacob Boehme's theory that the external world is a signature or figure of an internal spiritual world, and Lady Julian of Norwich's vision of God as existing in all things. In one of Frye's two copies of Huxley's book (both are extensively marked and annotated) he underlined the words "hologram" and "interpenetration" in Huxley's description of the "total synecdoche" of the Gandavyuha, and beside the account of Lady Julian's vision of the one and the many he wrote "grain of sand."[96]

In his exposition of the two concepts at the center of Kabbalistic thought, Charles Poncé writes that the "Primordial or Smooth Point," an attribute of *Kether,* "is not a point in the normal sense of the word, a dot on a piece of paper; it is a monad of pure energy." In his copy of Poncé's book Frye put parentheses around "monad of pure energy" and then wrote in the margin, "the everything everywhere." And in Poncé's commentary on the point of creation as understood by the sixteenth-century alchemist John Dee ("this universal monad is contained within man as well as in space"), Frye notes in the margin that Dee "has a good sense of interpenetration." Frye made a number of marginal annotations throughout this book. He also typed his response in a set of detailed notes, quoting the passage about the "universal monad" and remarking, "that's well said and worth saying." He writes in the same typescript that "Luria's doctrine of retraction followed by expansion seems an effort to incorporate the notion of interpenetration into the creation scheme."[97]

Such annotations and markings confirm that for Frye the principle of interpenetration exists in such divergent traditions as medieval mysticism, Mahayana Buddhism, and the Kabbalah, further explorations of which we will turn to in later chapters.[98] But he worked out his own complex definition of the principle. In one of his notebooks for *The Great Code* he writes that for more than thirty years he had thought about "interpenetration as one of the last mysteries to be explored and revealed in the book" (*RT,* 267). And for *Words with Power* he has a similar plan for the conclusion: he wants the final chapter to include "Thou art That and the flight of the dove to the dome, the dialogue of Monos & Una," Poe's dialogue, *The Colloquy of Monos and Una* (1841), this chapter to serve as one of his many efforts to overcome the separation between conscious existence and spiritual reality. But "that's still at least metaphorically individualized," Frye continues, "and I have to work out the assumption (in the theological sense) of the interpenetrating world. Perhaps the last word could be Tom o' Bedlam's 'Methinks it is no journey.' Tom o' Bedlam is a shaman, & I start off Part Two with the shaman's ladder. It passes through the prophet, with his 'the Word came to' and 'I will pour out my spirit upon'" (*LN,* 1:290). Fortunately, Frye expanded this elliptical passage in an earlier notebook entry and in *Words with Power.* In the former we learn that the hypostasis of hope, rather than simply the way it is signified fictionally in even the most intensely subjective poets, is contained in the prophetic utterance, and in prophecy "Word and Spirit are no longer proclaimer and listener, but the same thing, Jesus metamorphosed with Moses and Elijah" (*LN,* 1:286). This means that there is no longer a distinction between signifier and signified: in such a totally verbal world, words *are* spiritual realities. The Tom o' Bedlam line, glossed in *Words with Power,* is for Frye an example of how the journey takes us beyond the "wide world's end" where the subjective and the objective interpenetrate (*WP,* 96). Subject and object collapse when they are identified, as Blake said. We turn now to Frye's elaboration of this central concept of identity.

2 Identity

The metaphor is a microcosm of language, the myth is a microcosm of narrative. A lot here to think about. In fact, I've never thought much about anything else.
—*Late Notebooks,* 1:58

It would perhaps be a reasonable characterization of religion to say that a man's religion is revealed by that with which he is trying to identify himself.
—*The Stubborn Structure,* 37

Frye's extensive speculations on metaphor have received practically no attention: in the extensive literature on this trope, his name seldom appears.[1] But among the numerous theories of metaphor—from Aristotle's transference view through the well-known theories about metaphor as substitution, comparison, transaction (I. A. Richards), and interaction (Max Black)—Frye's theory is unique, based as it is on the principle of identity.[2]

Frye says very little about metaphor in *Fearful Symmetry,* preferring to speak about the principle behind Blake's poetic thought as symbolism. The word "metaphor" appears in that book only three times, but one of those instances does contain the kernel of what Frye would later develop: "Whenever we take our eye off the image we slip into abstractions, into regarding qualities, moral or intellectual, as more real than living things. So Blake opposes to 'Similitude' the idea of 'Identity,' the latter being the metaphor which unites the theme and the illustration of it" (*FS,* 117). In *The Book of Urizen* Blake writes, in a passage quoted in *Fearful Symmetry* in another context, "Demonstration Similitude & Harmony are Objects of Reasoning / Invention Identity & Melody are Objects of Intuition."[3] Here again the opposing terms are "Similitude" and "Identity." Similitude, for Blake as for Frye, is related to abstraction and to debased rather than genuine allegory. It is a form of the comparison view of metaphor frequently found in contemporary handbooks, where the principle underlying metaphor is said to be analogy rather than identity.[4] The analogical position is critical Arianism: the two items in the trope are of similar but not the same substance.[5] But in Frye's radical view of metaphor, when one thing is linked with another by the copula or even by juxtaposition, no similarity, analogy, or comparison is involved. The model is a grammatical one (X is Y), and there is always paradox involved, because we all know that in such expressions as "Grecian urn is unravished bride" X is in fact not Y. Like zen koans, metaphor paralyzes the discursive reason (*RT,* 468).

Language

Frye's views on metaphor form a part of his expansive theory of language, in which identity is both a grammatical and a religious principle as well as a principle for defining the sense of self (personal identity). In *Anatomy of Criticism* the connections between religion and metaphor are often muted or at best only implicit, but in his last three books Frye worked hard to establish the connections between them. The source of this connection is language. "The characteristics of language," he says, "are clearly the essential clue to the nature of everything built out of language" (*MM,* 108). The key to Frye's view of both poetic and religious language is his conception of literal meaning. Traditionally, he notes, literal meaning has been regarded from the point of view of natural language as simply the descriptive meaning: what is literally true is what is descriptively accurate. But such a view of language does not work in the area of either literature or religion. "Literalism of this kind in the area of the spiritual," says Frye, "instantly becomes what Paul calls the letter that kills" (*DV,* 14). The view of language that does work is first-phase or poetic language, where metaphor is the powerful key, and metaphor, as just noted, operates on the principle of identity.

Identity as both a principle of literary structure and a religious category is embodied in the anatomy of language that Frye elaborated in his two books on the Bible. The first chapter of *The Great Code* "is concerned with language—not the language of the Bible itself, but the language that people use in talking about the Bible and questions concerned with it, such as the existence of God" (xxi). The chapter, in typical Frye fashion, is elaborately schematic. It begins with Vico's notion of the three ages of humanity and then moves through more than a dozen different categories to classify the tripartite phases that language has, more or less historically, passed through: the poetic, the heroic, and the vulgar; the hieroglyphic, the hieratic, and the demotic; the mythical, the allegorical, and the descriptive; the metaphorical, the metonymic, and the similic, and so on. Frye glances at the historical locus of each of these phases, the way each formulates subject–object relations, the meaning of such words as "God" and "Logos" in each, and the typical form that prose takes in each phase. All of this anatomizing, devoid of Frye's examples and illustrations, is summarized in chart 1 in the appendix.

The problem Frye faces in applying his schematic account of language is that the Bible does not fit well into one or more of the phases. His way out is to devise another framework to account for the Bible's metaphorical origins and its "concerned" or existential quality. Thus he posits a fourth form of expression that is a special kind of rhetoric: kerygma. The three phases of language more or less disappear in Frye's subsequent writing, and except for the metaphoric phase Frye does little with the three phases in the other chapters of *The Great Code*. But kerygma, as we shall see, does not disappear.

Frye was apparently dissatisfied with this account of language in *The Great Code*. In *Words with Power*, in any case, he takes a somewhat different approach, developing a thesis about four modes of verbal communication: the descriptive, the dialectical, the ideological, and the imaginative. Each mode is connected to its successor by what Frye calls "the excluded initiative," "initiative" meaning the motive necessary to get the verbal process going and "excluded" referring to what remains in the background in one mode as an unexamined assumption but which comes to the foreground in the succeeding mode. Frye replaces the tripartite analysis of *The Great Code* with a quadripartite one, represented in chart 2 in the appendix.

In Frye's new formulation, the function of the descriptive or information-centered mode of writing is to transmit the nonverbal. The descriptive mode minimizes tropes; its criterion is truth; its typical narrative forms are histories, textbooks, and reference works. Its excluded initiative is syntax, the word-ordering process. That is, our attention as readers is directed away from the word-ordering process because in the descriptive mode language is assumed to be a transparent vehicle of communication: nature is the content reflected by language. Frye also refers to the descriptive mode as "perceptual" because descriptive language reflects what we see in nature. When the descriptive initiative is no longer excluded, it becomes the shaping force of the next mode, the dialectical or conceptual, which functions to coordinate verbal elements. This is the mode of metaphysical systems, the mode in which data are arranged and arguments constructed and in which nature is the content not reflected but contained by language. The excluded initiative in this mode—what begins the process of objective conceptual prose but which is not the focus—is subjective energy or desire. Again, when subjective energy does become the focus, the writer and what is written become identified, and we enter the ideological or rhetorical mode. Dialectic is incorporated into rhetoric in order to rationalize authority. The excluded initiative in this mode is what Frye calls "the non-human personal," a somewhat curious locution for the numinous or the divine: the personal nonhuman world is the world of the gods. Finally, once this initiative is no longer excluded, we enter the mythological mode, the mode where the fundamental element is no longer descriptive truth or conceptual argument or persuasion in the interest of ideology, but the conceivable. This is the poetic and metaphorical mode of the imagination. Myth, in short, is the excluded initiative of ideology.

In this four-part sequence of linguistic modes, where the emergence of the previously excluded initiative represents the Hegelian *Aufhebung,* we can see the close connection in Frye's thinking between the religious initiative and the fundamental principles of literature: metaphor and myth. This is one of the ways Frye puts it:

> Myths take us back to a time when the distinction between subject and object was much less continuous and rigid than it is now, and gods are the central characters of myth because they are usually personalities identified with aspects of nature. They are therefore built-in metaphors. . . . There is an infinite number of individual myths, but only a finite number—in fact a very small number—of *species* of myths. These latter express the human bewilderment of why we are here and where we are going, and include the myths of creation, of fall, of exodus and migration, of the destruction of the human race in the past (deluge myths) or the future (apocalyptic myths), of redemption in some phase of life during or after this one, however "after" is interpreted. Such myths outline, as broadly as words can do, humanity's vision of its nature and destiny, its place in the universe, its sense both of inclusion in and exclusion from an infinitely bigger order. So while nothing ontological is asserted by literature as such, the imaginative or poetic mode of ordering words has to be the basis of any sense of the reality of non-human personality, whether angels, demons, gods, or God. (*WP,* 22–23)

The schematic theories of language outlined in *The Great Code* and *Words with Power* move in opposite directions: from the poetic to the descriptive in the former; from the descriptive to the poetic in the latter. In addition, the progression in the former is more or less historical; in the latter, this movement is reversed. At this point in the mental diagram of Frye's second schema there is no excluded initiative for the poetic mode. But there is an initiative that has generally been excluded from Frye's previous works, and this is the experience of metaphor by the reader, especially what Frye calls existential or ecstatic metaphor. He refers to this "something else" as beyond the literary, and this something else turns out to be the excluded initiative of the poetic, though it takes him another seventy-five pages to say so. In *Words with Power* the excluded initiative or the real kerygma is, similarly, "a mode of language on the *other side* of the poetic" (*WP*, 101). The reference here is to the reader's experience of the Bible, but the power of the experience applies to poetic works as well. In fact, Frye says that we have to "go through the territory of literature" to get there, and this is the point at which *Words with Power* makes a radical departure from his previous work. "Spirit," he says in a different formulation, "is the initiative excluded from literature" (*LN*, 1:272).

The excluded initiative of the poetic is what permits the reader to move from the panoramic apocalypse, a detached vision, to the participating apocalypse, an engaged one—which is a kind of *paravritti* or reversal for Frye himself. He does not emphasize this in *Words with Power*, but he does remark in one of his notebooks for this book that "the recovery and incorporating of the excluded initiative of experiencing literature marked the first step from the *Anatomy* that I've taken" (*LN*, 1:297). Kerygma moves beyond the poetic, embracing the reader's existential experience. It is a key principle in Frye's expanded theory of language.

Kerygma

In *The Great Code* Frye adopts the word "kerygma" to indicate that while the Bible has obvious poetic features, it is more than literary because it contains a rhetoric of proclamation. Kerygma, the form of proclamation made familiar by Bultmann, thus designates the existentially concerned aspect of the Bible, as opposed to its purely metaphoric features.[6] Bultmann sought to "demythologize" the New Testament narrative as an initial stage in interpretation: the assumptions of the old mythologies, such as demonic possession and the three-storied universe, had to be purged before the genuine kerygma could be "saved," to use his word.[7] Frye, of course, has exactly the opposite view of myth: "[M]yth is the linguistic vehicle of *kerygma*" (*GC*, 30).

But having made his point about kerygma, Frye drops the word altogether from the rest of *The Great Code,* except for a passing reference toward the very end of the book (231). In *Words with Power* the word kerygma is completely absent from Frye's analysis in the "sequence and mode" (or "language") chapter; we have to wait until chapter 4, where we learn that the excluded initiative—what lies hidden in the background of the poetic—is what leads to kerygma, even though Frye does not initially put it in these terms. He begins by saying, "Our survey of verbal modes put rhetoric between the conceptual and the poetic, a placing that should help us to understand why from the beginning there have been two aspects of rhetoric, a moral and a tropological aspect, one persuasive and the other ornamental. Similarly, we have put the poetic between the rhetorical and the kerygmatic, implying that it partakes of the characteristics of both" (*WP*, 111).[8] The *Aufhebung* process now begins its lifting operation, as Frye expands the meaning of kerygma far beyond what it meant in *The Great Code*. It now becomes synonymous with the prophetic utterance, the metaliterary perception that extends one's vision, the Longinian ecstatic response to any text, sacred or secular, that "revolutionizes our consciousness."[9] Kerygma takes metaphorical identification "a step further and says: 'You are what you identify with'" (116), a point to which we will return. We enter the kerygmatic realm when the separation of "active speech and reception of speech" merges into a unity (118).

This leads to an absorbing account of the "spiritual" as it is embedded in the descriptive, conceptual, and rhetorical "factors of the poetic," and the "spiritual" as extending the body into another dimension so that it reaches "the highest intensity of consciousness" (119–21, 128). Then, some twenty pages after Frye began his exploration of kerygma, he arrives finally at the excluded initiative of the poetic. He does not say what we might expect, that the excluded initiative is kerygma. What he says, in a statement that appears to be something of an anticlimax after all the elevated probing of Spirit, is that the excluded initiative of the poetic "is the principle of the reality of what is created in the production and response to literature" (128). This teasing understatement has been anticipated by the declaration about the unity of "active speech and reception of speech" just quoted. Or as Frye puts it in Notebook 53 in less pedestrian terms, kerygma is "the answering voice from God to the human construct" (*LN*, 2:615).

But what is this "principle of reality" that is "neither objective nor subjective"—the excluded initiative of the poetic? The short answer is religious faith. The long answer is Frye's commentary on Hebrews 11:1 ("the substance of things hoped-for, the evidence of things not seen"), which he translates into "the reality of hope and of illusion," concluding with an exposition of spiritual presence that goes beyond the conventional formulations of dialectic and doctrine. The "reality of what is created in the production and response to literature" turns out to be the presence of spiritual vision, the interpenetration of the human and the divine. Ironically, the proclamation is said to be beyond words, at least in one of Frye's formulations: "What's the initiative excluded from the higher kerygma? Something that goes outside the verbal, which is why it can't have much of a role in my book. It starts after we've finished the Bible and accepted its invitation to drink [Rev. 22:17]. But Zen & others say that it's a renewal of vision, the same world but seen in enlightenment. . . . the conception of interpenetration can't be avoided" (*LN,* 1:271). In the kerygmatic world one is released from the burden of speech and writing: "The gospels are written mythical narratives, and for casual readers they remain that. But if anything in them strikes a reader with full kerygmatic force, there is, using the word advisedly, a *resurrection* of the original speaking presence in the reader. The reader is the logocentric focus, and what he reads is emancipated both from writing and from speech. The duality of speaker and listener has vanished into a single area of verbal recognition" (*WP,* 114).[10] We do not speak in the kerygmatic world, but God does, which is why the voice of revelation is rhetoric in reverse (*LN,* 2:660). When Frye uses kerygma in the sense of the prophetic or metaliterary utterance, human speech or writing does enter the picture, and while there is no metaliterary style, there is a metaliterary idiom which takes the kerygmatic as its model (*LN,* 1:369). Frye even projects his own kerygmatic anthology. He says, without commentary, that it would include Blake's *The Marriage of Heaven and Hell,* Buber's *I and Thou,* and selections from Dostoevsky, Kafka, Rimbaud, and Hölderlin (*LN,* 1:366).[11]

In *The Double Vision* Frye says about kerygma only that the New Testament's myths to live by and its metaphors to live in are a transforming kerygmatic power "coming from the other side of mythical and metaphorical language" (18). The word kerygma does not appear in either *The "Third Book" Notebooks* (1964–72) or the notebooks on romance (1944–89), and it appears only twice in the notebooks for *The Great Code*. But in the *Late Notebooks* (1982–90) there are more than 160 instances of the word kerygma, an indication of the energy Frye devoted to searching for the other side of the poetic during the last decade of his life. In fact, kerygma as *on the other side* of the poetic or as *beyond* the imaginative gets emphasized in the notebooks,[12] and never satisfied with the point at which he has arrived, Frye even wonders at one point, "What's on the other side of kerygma?" He soon answers the question: "the world of words as seen by the Word" (*LN,* 1:343). Otherwise in the *Late Notebooks*—and it is an extensive otherwise—kerygma is said to announce a world beyond speech (*LN,* 2:715) and to be the purloined-letter archetype ("the verbal message everybody wants to kidnap but can't get hold of") (*LN,* 1:219). It is the transformation of Kierkegaard's "aesthetic" category (*LN,* 1:251);[13] it combines the counterhistorical myth and the counterlogical metaphor (*LN,* 2:695); it is spiritual rhetoric (*LN,* 1:306, 403) and revelation (*LN,* 1:342); and it serves as a new context for the Logos in John's gospel (*LN,* 2:647). In the kerygmatic universe the gods and spirits of myth have been transformed into God and Spirit (*LN,* 1:270). The "kerygmatic breakthrough always contains some sense of 'time has stopped.' The sequential movement has become a focus, or fireplace. In intensified consciousness the minute particular shines by its own light (or burns in its own life-fire)" (*LN,* 1:290).

As already intimated, the notebooks contain a distinction between lower and higher kerygma, a distinction Frye did not retain for *Words with Power.* Lower kerygma is the social proclamation that derives from dialectic, "the stage of law, full of prohibitions & penalties, & increasingly given to censorship in the arts," as in Plato's restriction of art in the *Republic* (*LN,* 1:265). The lower kerygma of the notebooks is actually the rhetorical mode of language in *Words with Power,* and higher kerygma is what Frye calls simply kerygma in that book. Higher kerygma in the *Late Notebooks* is defined as the interpenetration of Word and Spirit and as close to Martin Buber's "Thou" (*LN,* 1:209), and it entails the sense of complete "otherness" (*LN,* 1:271). It therefore goes beyond its conventional New Testament associations. Even the antithesis between esoteric and exoteric does not hold in the kerygmatic world (*LN,* 1:334).

Kerygma, because it lies beyond the poetic, is all content and so without form, as we see in this notebook riddle: "In descriptive writing the *verbal* content (not what we usually think of as content in that connection) is syntactic prose. When this content turns into form, a content of metaphor reveals itself within. When *that* becomes form, myth (order, narrative, time, quid agas) becomes the content. When myth becomes form, kerygma becomes the content" (*LN,* 1:269). In this enigmatic aphorism we have another *Aufhebung,* one that moves through four stages of content and form:

$$
\begin{array}{l}
\text{form of myth} \rightarrow \text{content of kerygma} \\
\quad \uparrow \\
\text{form of metaphor} \rightarrow \text{content of myth} \\
\quad \uparrow \\
\text{form of prose} \rightarrow \text{content of metaphor} \\
\quad \uparrow \\
\text{verbal content of prose}
\end{array}
$$

Kerygma is too discontinuous to assume a form itself, except in the provisional form it takes in sacred texts (*LN,* 1:269).

This brief survey of the numerous meanings that cluster around the word kerygma illustrates Frye's dogged determination to clarify the mystery of spiritual rhetoric. He keeps struggling to find the proper verbal formula. It illustrates as well Frye's fundamental desire during the 1980s to move beyond the poetic world into a world of spiritual vision. This does not mean that Frye abandons his interest in the first-phase language of metaphor in *The Great Code* or the fourth, imaginative mode of language in *Words with Power*. Far from it. According to the principle of *Aufhebung,* the poetic is never canceled but lifted up and preserved at a higher level.

Imaginative Literalism

Frye consistently argues for what he calls imaginative literalism. His view of literal meaning appears embryonically in *Fearful Symmetry,* is developed in the *Anatomy,* and becomes an insistent theme in his subsequent books.[14] By identifying poetic, metaphorical, and spiritual meaning with literal meaning, Frye is, of course, violating common usage. His line of reasoning begins with the assumption that "the centripetal aspect of verbal structure is its primary aspect" (*GC,* 60). Because what words primarily do with precision and accuracy in poetry is to hang together as a verbal structure rather than refer to something outside themselves, the literal meaning and the metaphorical meaning are the same. Here is the way Frye puts it in writing about biblical metaphor:

> The Bible means literally just what it says, but it can mean it only without primary reference to a correspondence of what it says to something outside what it says. When Jesus says (John 19:9), "I am the door," the statement means literally just what it says, but there are no doors outside the verse in John to be pointed to. . . . Metaphorical meaning as I use the term, like myth, has for me a primary and a derived sense, the primary one being so broad that it is really a tautology. All verbal structures have a centripetal and a centrifugal aspect, and we can call their centripetal aspect their literary aspect. The primary and literal meaning of the Bible, then, is its centripetal or poetic meaning. It is only when we are reading as we do when we read poetry that we can take the word "literal" seriously, accepting every word given us without question. The primary meaning, which arises simply from the interconnection of the words, is the metaphorical meaning. (*GC,* 60–61)

The principle of identity in metaphor takes us back to Frye's theology of immanence. Again, this derives from Blake, who "by postulating a world of imagination higher than that of sense," Frye says, "indicates a way of closing the gap [between the divine and the human] which is completed by identifying God with human imagination. . . . Man in his creative acts and perceptions is God, and God is man" (*FS*, 30). The counterlogical connections that define metaphor lie, therefore, at the heart of religious language, but the paradoxes of identity are paradoxes only at the level of descriptive and conceptual prose where there is a separation between subject and object. If we think of the world, à la John Locke, as being separated into the perceivers and the perceived, then we are, so to speak, locked into a world of subjects and objects. But the world of metaphor—what Frye calls "metaphorical literalism" in *The Double Vision*—collapses this distinction. In one of his *Words with Power* notebooks Frye writes: "Metaphor is the attempt to open up a channel or current of energy between subject and object. It begins in ecstatic metaphor (Stone Age painting and 'primitive' music), and literature develops in proportion as the sense of a split between subject and object becomes habitual. The link with religion is there because metaphor creates a 'Thou' world between the 'I' and the 'it,' and the god is the stabilized metaphor" (*LN*, 2:537). In his account of metaphor in the New Testament (John 14:8–17), Frye observes that when Philip asks Jesus to be shown the Father, he gets the answer "there is nothing there; everything you need is here. In the synoptics Jesus makes the same point in telling his disciples that the kingdom of heaven, the core of his teaching, is among them or within them. Nothing Jesus says seems to have been more difficult for his followers to grasp than his principle of the hereness of here" (*WP*, 94–95). So once again we have the great code of immanence: an identification of the human and divine that is brought to life by metaphor. The phrase about the location of the kingdom of God in Luke, *entos hymon* (17:21), is translated as "within you" in the Authorized Version, as "in the midst of you" in the Revised Standard Version, and as "among you" in the New English Bible and the New Revised Standard Version. But whether the kingdom of God is emphasized as individual and psychological (within) or social and communal (among), the immanent and the transcendent interpenetrate in either case.[15]

Throughout his work Frye returns to metaphor time and again, trying to work out the implications of identity. In *Anatomy of Criticism,* he differentiates between "identity as" and "identity with," the two forms deriving from Blake's view, referred to at the beginning of this chapter, of the two ways the imagination perceives identity. When a thing is identified *as* itself, the emphasis falls on the "living form" or "image" of its experienced reality. Frye says that Blake's own images and mythological forms "are minute particulars identified with their total forms."[16] Identity *as* means to see the class as individual, or the individual with the whole as a part of it.[17] When things are seen as identical *with* each other, they are of one unified essence; the individual is part of a greater whole. "A work of literary art," Frye says, "owes its unity to this process of identification *with,* and its variety, clarity, and intensity to identification *as*" (*AC,* 123). The identity of experience (identity *as*) is combined with the identity of knowledge (identity *with*) in what Frye calls the royal metaphor (*RT,* 295; *GC,* 87).

The most extensive exposition of these two forms of identity is found in the tables of apocalyptic and demonic imagery in *The Great Code* (166–67), where the various categories of imagery on each level of the chain of being are identified *with* Christ, while each individual image (bridegroom, lamb, temple, and so on) is identified *as* itself.[18] A quarter century after *Anatomy of Criticism,* Frye continues to work out the implications of his view of metaphorical identity, as we see suggested in the title of a collection of his essays from the 1980s, *Myth and Metaphor.* And Frye fills his notebooks with practically endless speculations on metaphor, the most expansive taxonomy of which he sketches in a set of notes from the 1980s:

> A metaphor ("Joseph is a fruitful bough," etc.) is a statement of identity, A is B, which at the same time conveys a much stronger sense of denial: anybody can see that A is not B. What follows from this includes:
>
> 1. The ironic. Metaphors of this kind are tentative: they say "even if this isn't true, and it's utterly obvious it isn't, still it's worth making statements of this kind." It's irony in the face of glum reality. Casual couplings, not life-time marriages.
>
> 2. The apophatic. Such a metaphor can be easily turned inside out, made an assertion by means of denial. Chairman introducing guest of honor at a banquet: "I will not remind you of his innumerable public services," etc., and goes on for half an hour listing them. What the metaphor says is rather different apophasis from this: it says "maybe not this, but—well, something beyond." That is, it's a temporary assertion of an identity that in a very long run actually exists. Counter-logical, not illogical.
>
> 3. The tentative, as above. The metaphor can be easily abandoned, because it isn't taken very seriously in the first place. Even metaphors like "Christ is God and Man," which are the basis of Christianity because the real nitty-gritty of any religion can only be expressed in metaphors, are like a rope bridge across a gorge. You may commit your life to a belief that it will get you across, but there will be moments when you wish you hadn't.

4. The participative. Every metaphor suggests an identity between an aspect of personality (Joseph) and an aspect of natural existence (fruitful bough). It opens up a current of energy between subjective and objective worlds, and points the way towards the first serious kind of metaphor, the god, who, whether sea-god or sun-god or whatever, identifies a personality with an aspect of nature.

5. The questing. Every metaphor, however casual, is ready to embark on a journey toward the myth, as above. As I said in AC [*Anatomy of Criticism*] about the drowned Mary in Kingsley's poem, it's not a question of "pathetic fallacy" but of being an embodiment of myth [*AC*, 36]. Reversing this principle, metaphors are the exfoliation of myths. Fictions, literary stories, are the dialectic of mythology.

6. The juxtaposing. This is the Ezra Pound principle that you don't need the "is," and that a metaphor is two images copulating, so to speak, trying to become one flesh, the "is" being often an unnecessary pedantry. Eros is the muse of poetry.

7. The centripetal. There is no metonymic "this is put for that" about the metaphor: there isn't any separate order of signifieds. Hence the arbitrary relation of word to its meaning hardly comes into the discussion at all; hence too the differences among words are not primary. If it's conceivable that Joseph is a fruitful bough, it's equally conceivable that Issachar is, or that Joseph is a strong ass. Hence, as above, the relation of words in metaphor is erotic.

8. The metaphor doesn't point to a signified but to a solid & permanent union of spirit and nature. The *royal* metaphor points to an identity of the one & the many.

9. It's metonymy that's apophatic: part of the Biblical reversal of myth–metaphor from hypothetical to existential.

10. Leibnitzian optimism: words chosen are the best of all possible words. (*LN*, 2:487–88)

In these freewheeling speculations we have the seeds of the three levels of metaphorical experience that Frye eventually settled on in *Words with Power*: the imaginative, the erotic, and the existential or ecstatic. As we move up the ladder of metaphorical experience, the difference between identity and difference continues to lessen until the highest level, an ecstatic state in which, Frye says, "there is a sense of presence, a sense of uniting ourselves with something else" (85). This is, mutatis mutandis, quite like the anagogic level of meaning in Frye's theory of symbols in *Anatomy of Criticism*. It is the level of vision, a word we encounter everywhere in Frye's work and to which we devote the next chapter. It is the level of kerygma or revelation or apocalypse. It is the level of spirit, a word that plays a substantial role in the fourth chapter of *Words with Power*.[19] This kind of language—spirit, ecstasy, revelation, anagogy, vision—suggests that we have moved a great distance from a theology of immanence. But in Frye's Hegelian dialectic, as we will see in our chapter on vision, transcendence never cancels immanence. As he says in one notebook, vision as an expanded present is the spiritual world that exists here and now (*LN*, 2:657).

Personal Identity

"Identity means a good many things," Frye observes in *The Secular Scripture* (54), an understatement confirmed by a glance at any philosophical dictionary. Identity, as Arthur O. Lovejoy said of Romanticism, is a word we must use in the plural, and for Frye in this case plural means scores. The word is omnipresent ("identity" and its congeners, "identify" and "identification," along with their inflected forms, appear 357 times in *Words with Power* and the notebooks for that volume), and its meaning is bewilderingly fluid.[20] But while identity is a structural principle of metaphor, it is also a structural principle of narrative or myth, a meaning embedded in the title of Frye's first collection of essays, *Fables of Identity*. His most fully developed exploration of narrative identity is in *The Secular Scripture*, where the context is restricted primarily to romance, even though it is a principle in any genre: "This story of the loss and regaining of identity is," Frye says in *The Educated Imagination*, "the framework of all literature" (55). Still, the losing and finding of identity is especially foregrounded in romance, which for Frye is "the structural core of all fiction" (*SeS*, 15). What is lost and regained is in its simplest form the state of existence in Eden before the Fall, and so it is what exists on the other side of the world of absurdity and alienation. Identity, Frye writes, "is existence before 'once upon a time,' and subsequent to 'and they lived happily ever after'" (*SeS*, 54). It expands, however, beyond this to a state of self-recognition, "which is what all recognition scenes really point to" (*SeS*, 152). These statements apply to identity as a structural principle of romance—to literature rather than to life. But Frye often makes the transition from identity as a principle of myth and metaphor to personal identity or what defines the character of a person.

This shift to personal identity is especially apparent in Frye's later work, but the seed is present even in *Fearful Symmetry*, where Frye speaks of identity as "the construction of a character" and as expressing "individual and social integration" (248, 249). The context here is Albion's emergence into eternity in Blake's Orc cycle, but the movement from literature to life, what Frye calls "the journey toward one's own identity" (*SeS*, 166), is a movement he returns to again and again, especially in his late work. "The business of life," he writes, "is to make a path for the incarnation" (*RT*, 354), the ultimate form of the divine-human identity. The essential point is that, outside of our genes, our identity is what we identify with. Frye's own identity, as he remarked to several interviewers, was a function of his identification with his university, the United Church of Canada, and the Cooperative Commonwealth Confederation. Such identification has to do with social continuity. As Frye says in *Words with Power*, "[A]ll the deeper forms of human dignity and self-respect are bound up with an identification of the individual with a church, a nation, a social revolution, the advancement of learning, or whatever seems to connect the past with the future, or realize Burke's contract of the dead, the living and the unborn" (255).

Identity is also constructed by our identification with other people, represented, say, in the marriage ceremony as two becoming one or in the Eros tradition, about which Frye writes so compellingly.[21] If metaphor is defined by identity, personal identity is often in Frye's writing defined by metaphor. In *The Educated Imagination*, for example, we have the metaphor of ingestion: our identity is defined by what the imagination "swallows" and takes into itself. "We study literature in order to possess its powers" (*RT*, 376), and we are defined by what we "possess." Or again, "What you identify with possesses you, and operates as an informing principle in your mind" (18.116). The two metaphors are combined in the remarkable example of Ezekiel's eating the roll of a book (2:9–3:3): Ezekiel is possessed by the Word and so he takes it into himself, the literal and the metaphorical in this case being the same thing. The penultimate chapter of one of Frye's many outlines for *The Great Code* (this one was to have sixty-four chapters) was entitled "The Swallowed Roll: Reader as Hero" (*RT*, 265), suggesting that the reader's identification with what has been ingested is a heroic act.[22] This is what Frye means by the participating apocalypse, which will be considered in the next chapter. A similar example of this metaphor of identity is embodied, to use that word metaphorically, in Montaigne's remark, mentioned in the previous chapter and referred to on several occasions in Frye's notebooks, that he was consubstantial with his book.[23] Another example of such possession is Frye's oft-quoted phrase from Milton, the Word of God in the heart, which he describes as "the key to identity" (*RT*, 91).[24] These bodily metaphors signify the idea that our identity is what we internalize from outside the self and are therefore possessed by.

The ultimate Christian metaphor for such ingestion, deriving from the primary concern of food, is the Eucharist. Such possession can be demonic as well as apocalyptic, and it can be erotic, deriving from the primary concern of sex: "Love means entering into and identifying with other people and things" (*LN*, 1:210). When we have reached this stage, we have entered a spiritual order of being beyond the identities of myth and metaphor. We have entered, that is, the existential universe.[25] "[A] man's religion is what he wants to identify himself with," Frye writes (*LN*, 2:595).[26] Another version of the same idea comes from an early notebook: "Surely the discovery of the self and the unifying of vision are and always must be the same thing" (*RT*, 11). The more abstract but still metaphorical word Frye often uses to describe this process of internal possession is "decentering," which is a reversal of the metaphor of the individual as contained in and fulfilled by membership in a group. From the decentered perspective the individual is the microcosm of the whole. Decentralization, then, is a form of interpenetration.

The existential universe is the universe of "myths to live by," a phrase—borrowed from the title of a book by Joseph Campbell—that Frye used on occasion.[27] "Myths to live by" are existential and so related directly to life, rather than to the detached vision of the hypothetical. Frye has a straightforward statement of this "second shift"—from the hypothetical to the existential—in one of his *Great Code* notebooks: "The shift from mythos to dianoia, therefore, is the shift from somatic to mental response, and from the individual known by sense to the universal really known. There's a second shift from the mental to the pneumatic, the existential response required by religion (*and* ultimately by all scripture, including literature) which recaptures some of the somatic spontaneity & challenge to *action* (hence the role of commandment in religion)" (*RT*, 89). Myths to live by spring from existential response. Even the highest forms of literature do not provide myths to live by, or if they do, Frye says, they betray their literary purpose (*NFR*, 163). They are models for action, belonging to the myth of concern (what a society is most devoted to learning and preserving), although retaining the defining feature of the myth of freedom (the tolerance that permits an openness to other myths to live by).

A "myth to live by" lies beyond the metaphorical-literal level that Frye describes in *The Double Vision*, "transformed from the kind of story we can construct ourselves to a spiritual story of what has created and continues to re-create us" (*DV*, 76–77), and the realized form of a myth to live by is kerygma, the driving force behind the reality of the spiritual life and removed from the rationalizations of ideology (*LN,* 1:306). Myths to live by "convey a vision of spiritual life that continues to transform and expand our own" (*DV,* 17). This expansion is primarily an expansion of consciousness. We have already noted that Frye associates kerygma with the revolutionizing of consciousness, and in *Words with Power* this expansion is repeatedly said to be an intensification of consciousness or awareness. "Awareness" was the key term Frye used for a ten-year period beginning in the early 1960s, as he struggled to define a third level of consciousness beyond subject–object perception. "For a long time," Frye writes in 1990 (several months before his death), "I've been preoccupied by the theme of the reality of the spiritual world, including its substantial reality" (*LN,* 2:720). His extensive notebook reflections on "the three awarenesses" were a part of this preoccupation, which is anticipated by a remark in *Anatomy of Criticism* about the reader's response to culture being "a revolutionary act of consciousness" that becomes a revolution in "spiritual productive power" (344).

The Three Awarenesses

In Notebook 19, which dates from the mid-1960s, Frye writes, "One of my present master keys seems to be a recapturing of something that suddenly crystallized one Sunday morning & was written down in one of the brown notebooks. It puzzled me at the time, because it seemed inconsistent with or peripheral to my main line of thought. It's turned up again as the three forms of awareness" (*TBN,* 39). The "brown notebook" is Notebook 32 (early 1950s), in which Frye speculates on the relations among body, mind, and soul in the context of mysticism, and these speculations parallel what he later calls the "three awarenesses." They parallel even more closely an outline of the three stages of religion that he developed several years later (1969–70) in Notebook 11f. Notebook 19 (1964–67) contains the earliest extant account of the three awarenesses, which is a series of schematic reflections on the stages of mythical consciousness. Frye then develops his ideas about the three awarenesses in the late 1960s and early 1970s, first in Notebook 21 (1969–71) and more extensively in Notebook 24 (1970–72). At about the same time, in Notebook 15 he sketches a related schema about the four levels of vision.[28]

The speculations about the three awarenesses are connected with two projects. The first was the Birks Lectures at McGill University, but when the three-awarenesses thesis kept expanding, becoming too large for a series of lectures, Frye saw his ideas developing into a book (*RT,* 148). "It's a damn big book," he announces, "& it's mostly the book on its side, what I thought of as *following* the Third" (*RT,* 148).[29] A year or so later Frye planned to develop the themes of the Birks Lectures ("shorter version") into a book devoted to the three awarenesses ("longer version"), although now the length of the book is somewhat reduced, projected to be about the size of *The Critical Path* (*RT,* 154). The Birks Lectures apparently turned out to be a typological reading of the Bible,[30] and the book on religion, of course, never came to fruition. But a large portion of Notebook 21 is devoted to Frye's typically freewheeling ideas about the content of his book on religion, and at the center of his speculations are scores of entries, which he expanded over a period of some eight years, having to do with the development of human consciousness from its natural to its imaginative or mythical (sometimes mystical) state. These entries are typical of the dizzily complex, schematic, and often repetitive free play that characterizes much of Frye's notebook writing. Frye had the uncanny ability to keep track of the proliferation of his categories. But for us it is difficult to follow the pattern and to keep his numerous sets of terms clearly in mind without the help of a training aid. Charts 3–7 in the appendix re-create material from four different notebooks (ca. 1965– ca. 1972), containing summary outlines of the three awarenesses, beginning with their early incarnations of body, mind, and soul.

The Spengler-like progressions represented in these charts spring from Frye's conviction that the end of art must be identified "with some kind of total unification, in which the soul & its object or creature of contemplation are alike universal, & identical therefore with each other" (32.62). The charts reveal that very little is said about literature. Even though a half-dozen poets are said to be commentators on one or another of the three awarenesses, Frye's speculations are not literary criticism in any conventional sense. They form a schematic historical progression, or what Michael Dolzani refers to as a "scheme of the evolution of religious consciousness,"[31] and so they provide the framework for an essay in comparative religion or mythology. But Frye's goal is not simply to reveal the revolutionary, or even the evolutionary, movement of human consciousness, still less to catalogue the different forms that such consciousness assumes.[32] We are reminded again of Coleridge's remark that we can distinguish where we cannot divide.[33] Frye, the consummate anatomist, distinguishes with a vengeance, but his end is not division. It is unity and identity.

The third column in charts 3–7 reveals that with the third awareness we have moved from historical progression into the pure vision of the imagination. The great commentator of the third awareness has not yet been born (*TBN,* 304); Frye leaves blank the historical locus of the third awareness in his speculations in Notebook 24 (chart 7), but it would be what he calls the "eternal now." It should not go unnoticed that he sees himself as the representative of the third stage of the third awareness (*TBN*, 315). The cycle moves, then, from history to vision. While many of the categories Frye uses to exemplify the substance of the third awareness have religious connotations (e.g., "mystical experience," "total unification," "the revelation of the Word," "interpenetration," "apocalypse," "the numinous"), the third awareness is still essentially an imaginative one. Thus, in Hegelian fashion, Frye writes:

> [T]here clearly has to be a *fourth* awareness. This arises from the point on the first page of this book, that no human language can constitute a revelation. Something must arise from contemplating the infinite variety of literature, of the sort indicated in the epilogue to *The Tempest*. Of course this makes the literary critic a prophet, or at least gives him a prophetic function, but I can't help that. Hear the voice of the Bard. Whatever the Bard has heard himself, he's making too much noise to hear himself, or, more accurately, what most bards have heard is a damn garbled version of the Holy Word. (*RT*, 153)[34]

In a series of entries in Notebook 21 Frye pursues the mysterious form of the fourth awareness. It is a "recapturing of the whole progression" (*RT*, 154) of the first three awarenesses and thus an *Aufhebung*, and it begins at the point where the imagination has been released (*RT*, 154). The "form of the fourth" is a biblical phrase: in the book of Daniel the startling presence in Nebuchadnezzar's fiery furnace, "the form of the fourth," is said to have "the appearance of a god."[35] Frye does not put it in quite these terms in Notebook 21, but the fourth awareness does turn out to be revelation, which is the excluded initiative of the imaginative. Notebook 21 dates from 1969 to 1971, more than fifteen years before Frye developed the idea of the excluded initiative, but there are clear parallels between the four modes of language in *Words with Power* with their excluded initiatives and the four awarenesses. In any event, what the fourth awareness does is reverse the current of the first three awarenesses. Frye finds the idea of reversing the current to be "a very suggestive notion: it's in fact the notion inherent in conversion, paravritti, Milton's peripeties, & the like." Such reversal is "the making of all things new" (*RT*, 155). "Revelation as the reversal of the current of awareness. I don't know all of what this implies, but its importance is pretty crucial. Inspiration as creation reversed; insight. . . . Only it isn't individual only but a social vision as well. Reversal is the *opposite* of projection: that's a *very* important principle. Resurrection is the reversal of rebirth" (*RT*, 156). Archaic societies regard the gods as projections of certain aspects of the human imagination. The intuition, for example, of some mysterious power external to humanity is projected as the will of the gods. Or divine creation is projected from the human ability to create. Such projections eventually become submerged in second-phase thinking (ideologies), and our task now, according to Frye, is to recover the original projections, which identify some power in nature with the gods. "A god who isn't just a concept has to be an incarnate god. There are no gods except incarnate ones" (10.42). In *Words with Power* he speaks of the need to "rehabilitate" and "restore," synonyms for "recover," the primitive form of awareness (xxiii, 90). We need to recover, in short, the original mythical and metaphorical consciousness.

In Frye's *Late Notebooks* the recovery of projection and the recovery of myth are synonymous.[36] For our present purposes the important point is that the recovery of projection occurs with the third awareness, so that if reversal is the opposite of projection, the movement of the fourth awareness is from east to west, as it were. "So what is revelation?" Frye asks. And his answer: "What comes through human language the other way" (*RT,* 154). And what comes through from the other way is, in conventional terms, the voice of God, or in Frye's terms, a divine current of energy that consolidates the arts of myth and metaphor so that the human and the divine interpenetrate (*RT,* 156). What bridges the gap between the third and fourth awarenesses, Frye writes in Notebook 15, is "divinely initiated dialogue, God's willingness & ability to speak (God as Spirit particularly)" (*RT,* 314). This spirit is identified in another notebook as the "spirit of interpenetration" (*RT,* 319).

Expanded Consciousness

As indicated above, awareness as a category tends to disappear from Frye's vocabulary in the 1980s.[37] The fourth *awareness* of the notebooks is transformed into speculations about higher levels of *consciousness.* For Frye one of the central archetypal scenes of the intensity of consciousness that arises from the desire to identify is found in the Paleolithic cave drawings, references to which appear on more than thirty occasions in his work. The cave drawings, another example of the meander-and-descent pattern, represent "the titanic will to identify" (*MM,* 112).

> When one considers the skill and precision of these works, and the almost impossible difficulties of positioning and lighting surrounding their creation, we begin to grasp something of the intensity behind

them to unite human consciousness with its own perceptions, an intensity we can hardly imagine now. Magical motives, such as maintaining a supply of game animals by picturing them on the cave walls, seem
utterly inadequate: for one thing, many of the figures are evidently
human beings in animal skins. In any case such caves are the wombs of
creation, where conscious distinctions have no relevance and only pure
identity is left. (*WP,* 250)

The cave drawings at Lascaux, Altamira, and elsewhere are an example of
what Lévy-Bruhl called *participation mystique,* the imaginative identification with things, including other people, outside the self, or an absorption
of one's consciousness with the natural world into an undifferentiated state
of archaic identity.[38] In such a process of metaphorical identification the
subject and object merge into one, but the sense of identity is existential
rather than verbal (*LN,* 2:503).

But what does the intensity or expansion of consciousness entail for
Frye? This is a difficult question to answer with certainty, for Frye reflects
on the implications of the phrase only obliquely. But this much we do
know:

1. It is a function of kerygma. Ordinary rhetoric

seldom comes near the primary concern of "How do I live a more
abundant life?" This latter on the other hand is the central theme of all
genuine kerygmatic, whether we find it in the Sermon on the Mount,
the Deer Park Sermon of Buddha, the Koran, or in a secular book that
revolutionizes our consciousness. In poetry anything can be juxtaposed, or implicitly identified with, anything else. Kerygma takes this
a step further and says: "You are what you identify with." We are close
to the kerygmatic whenever we meet the statement, as we do surpris-
ingly often in contemporary writing, that it seems to be language that
uses man rather than man that uses language. (*WP,* 116)

2. It does not necessarily signify religion or a religious experience,
but it can be "the precondition for any ecumenical or everlasting-gospel
religion" (*LN,* 1:17).

3. Whatever the techniques used to expand consciousness (e.g.,
yoga, Zen, psychosynthesis, meditation, drugs), or whatever forms it
takes (e.g., dreams, fantasies, the "peak experiences" described by Abraham Maslow, ecstatic music), the language of such consciousness always
turns out to be metaphorical. Thus literature is the guide to higher consciousness, just as Virgil was Dante's guide to the expanded vision represented by Beatrice (*LN,* 2:717; *WP,* 28–29). Still, Frye believes that

language is the primary means of "intensifying consciousness, lifting us into a new dimension of being altogether" (*LN*, 2:717).

4. *Vision* is the word that best fits the heightened awareness that comes with the imagination's opening of the doors of perception. What the subject sees may be "only an elusive and vanishing glimpse. Glimpse of what? To try to answer this question is to remove it to a different category of experience. If we knew what it was, it would be an object perceived in time and space. And it is not an object, but something uniting the objective with ourselves" (*WP*, 83).

5. The principle behind the epiphanic experience that permits things to be seen with a special luminousness is that "things are not fully seen until they become hallucinatory. Not actual hallucinations, because those would merely substitute subjective for objective visions, but objective things transfigured by identification with the perceiver. An object impregnated, so to speak, by a perceiver is transformed into a presence" (*WP*, 88).

6. Intense consciousness does not sever one from the body or the physical roots of experience.

> The word spiritual in English may have a rather hollow and booming sound to some: it is often detached from the spiritual body and made to mean an empty shadow of the material, as with churches who offer us spiritual food that we cannot eat and spiritual riches that we cannot spend. Here spirit is being confused with soul, which traditionally fights with and contradicts the body, instead of extending bodily experience into another dimension. The Song of Songs . . . is a spiritual song of love: it expresses erotic feeling on all levels of consciousness, but does not run away from its physical basis or cut off its physical roots. We have to think of such phrases as "a spirited performance" to realize that spirit can refer to ordinary consciousness at its most intense: the *gaya scienza*, or mental life as play. . . . Similar overtones are in the words *esprit* and *Geist*. (*WP*, 128)

Or again, St. John of the Cross makes "a modulation from existential sex metaphor (M_2) to existential expanding of consciousness metaphor (M_1)" (*LN*, 1:120). As in *Aufhebung*, things lifted to another level do not cancel their connection to the previous level: "M_2" is still present at the higher level. Chapter 6 ("The Garden") of *Words with Power* "is concerned partly, if not mainly, with getting over the either–or antithesis between the spiritual and the physical, Agape love and Eros love" (*LN*, 2:451). Again, "spiritual love expands from the erotic and does not run away from it" (*WP*, 224).

7. Intensified consciousness is represented by images of both ascent and descent: "[I]mages of ascent are connected with the intensifying of consciousness, and images of descent with the reinforcing of it by other forms of awareness, such as fantasy or dream. The most common images of ascent are ladders, mountains, towers, and trees; of descent, caves or dives into water" (*WP,* 151). These images, which arrange themselves along the *axis mundi,* are revealed with exceptional insight in some of Frye's most powerfully perceptive writing—the last four chapters of *Words with Power.* In these concentrated chapters Frye illustrates how four central archetypes connect the ordinary world to the world of higher consciousness: the mountain and the cave emphasizing wisdom and the word, and the garden and the furnace emphasizing love and the spirit.

8. Expanded consciousness is both individual and social.

9. The raising of consciousness is revelation (*LN,* 1:61).

Love

But what does it mean to say that the kerygmatic higher consciousness reveals how we can lead a more abundant life? Our survey of the various concepts surrounding the concept of identity (metaphor, kerygma, possession, the fourth awareness, higher consciousness) should lead us, Frye says, to "myths to live by." But what are these existential myths that come from "the other side" of the imaginative? What are the "coherent lifestyles" that Frye hopes "will emerge from the infinite possibilities of myth" (*WP,* 143)? Although Frye often appears hesitant to give a direct answer to these questions, preferring to assume the role of Moses on Mt. Pisgah, the answer does surface in the conclusions of his last three books, where the gospel of love becomes the focus of discussion.

Frye's speculations on love begin early. In Notebook 3 (1946–48) he probes the meaning of love in different contexts: his own erotic and fantasy life, his attitude toward the church, his reflections on yoga and on time. Here are two representative reflections:

> Joachim of Floris [Fiore] has a hint of an order of things in which the monastery takes over the church & the world. That is the expanded secular monastery I want: I want the grace of Castiglione as well as the grace of Luther, a graceful as well as a gracious God, and I want all men & women to enter the Abbey of Theleme where instead of poverty, chastity and obedience they will find richness, love and *fay ce que vouldras;* for what the Bodhisattva wills to do is good. (*RT,* 17)

Each dimension of time breeds fear: the past, despair & hopelessness & the sense of an irrevocable too late: the present, panic & sense of a clock steadily ticking; the future, an unknown mystery gradually assuming the lineaments of the consequences of our own acts. Hope is the virtue of the past, the eternal sense that maybe next time we'll do better. The projection of this into the future is faith, the substance of things hoped for. Love belongs to the present, & is the only force able to cast out fear. If a thing loves it is infinite, Blake said, & the act of love is itself a vision of a timeless world. (*RT,* 59)[39]

His speculations on love reappear some thirty-five years later in the conclusion of *The Great Code,* where he probes the meaning of the Word of God in the context of biblical language. This language, Frye says, is enduring, inclusive, welcoming, and beyond argument, and it can move us toward freedom and beyond the anxiety structures created by the human and divine antithesis (231–32). *The Great Code,* however, provides little concrete guidance about the function of love in the myths we are to live by. But during the eight years following *The Great Code* Frye devoted a good deal of energy to working out the implication of the language of love. In Notebook 46 (mid- to late 1980s) he writes, "Love is the only virtue there is, but like everything else connected with creativity and imagination, there is something decentralized about it. We love those closest to us, Jesus' 'neighbors,' people we're specifically connected with in charity. For those at a distance we feel rather tolerance or good will, the feeling announced at the Incarnation" (*LN,* 2:696). This "only virtue" idea gets developed in *Words with Power,* where love, Paul's *agape* or *caritas,* is said to be "the only genuine form of human society, the spiritual kingdom of Jesus" (89), and the idea gets repeated elsewhere.[40] At the conclusion of "The Dialectic of Belief and Vision," a seminal essay to be examined in the next chapter, love as the "only virtue" makes its appearance at the stage of imaginative identity, where human initiative ceases and the divine initiative begins. Frye says he is not qualified to write about the divine initiative, but in his last two books and in their notebooks, he writes a great deal about love. As mentioned in chapter 1, he even considered using a line from the *Pervigilium Veneris* as a motto for *Words with Power:* "And those who have loved now love the more" (*LN,* 1:145).

Summarizing the "moral" of the garden or Eros archetype of *Words with Power,* Frye writes in Notebook 27, "[L]ove is interpenetration, but it has to extend beyond the sexual interpenetrating of intercourse. Every act of hostility is penetration with a threat, with a desire to dominate or acquire for oneself. Love means entering into and identifying with other people and things without threats or domination, in fact without retaining an ego-self. That's what the woman-garden expansion means. The rejuvenating of the mother into the bride means (a) the internalizing of the maternal (b) the equalizing of a figure of authority" (*LN*, 1:209–10). Here we have an expansion of Frye's own vision. In his early work he too easily identified the feminine half of the species with Blake's Female Will, and the natural world, with its repetitive cycles and Druidic analogies, was too much aligned with natural religion for Frye to work it into his structure of mythology as of primary significance. But the feminine principle gets renovated in *Words with Power*, where we find Frye writing about the importance of the symbolically female Jerusalem and about how "man is redeemed by or through woman" (*WP*, 192). Moreover, he is drawn to the Jungian suggestion that the Trinity be expanded to a Quaternary "by adding a representative of humanity, specifically female humanity, as a fourth term" (*WP*, 193), and he says that the sexual bias in the conventions of love poetry can be reversed, so that the female becomes symbolically, like Blake's Emanation, the natural environment (*WP*, 200–201).[41] In one of a series of notebook entries, written in 1986 when Frye was seeking to allay his grief over the death of his wife Helen, he writes, "[T]he last 'm'amour' fragment of Pound reveals (though Pound may not have known it) the profundity of Blake's 'emanation' conception: the objectivity one identifies with, with the woman one loves as its incarnate centre" (*LN*, 1:142).[42]

Frye worries about arriving at the seminal idea for *Words with Power* that will answer the question, so what? for the unsympathetic reader (*LN*, 1:210). From all that he says about love, especially in the concluding pages of the book, it seems clear that the seminal idea turns out to be love— what he had earlier called "the supreme clue to otherness" (*RT*, 333):

> For the New Testament, the Word clarifies, the Spirit unifies, and the two together create what for it is the only genuine form of human society, the spiritual kingdom of Jesus, founded on the *caritas* or love. (*WP*, 89)

> The word love means perhaps too many things in English and for many has an over-sentimental sound, but it seems impossible to dissociate the conceptions of spiritual personality and love. The capacity to merge with another person's being without violating it seems to be at the center of love, just as the will to dominate one conscious soul-will externally by another is the center of all tyranny and hatred. (*WP*, 126)

At the end of the *Paradiso* Dante has reached the top of the *axis mundi,* and is in the presence of God, where the question "what happens next?" has no answer and no meaning. The goal of the creative ascent is the transcending of time and space as we know them, and the attaining of a present and a presence in another dimension altogether. The present is the expanded moment of awareness that is as long as recorded human history; the presence is the love that moves the sun and the other stars. (*WP,* 303)

These themes get repeated in *The Double Vision,* where Frye quotes approvingly Auden's line "We must love one another or die" (34). But Frye is much more explicit in *The Double Vision* than in *Words with Power* in extending the power of love from the human world, both individual and social, to the natural world: "[T]he feeling that nature should be cherished and fostered rather than simply exploited is one of the few welcome developments of the last generation or so" (*DV,* 34). Looking at nature as an object of love rather than simply as an intellectually coherent order is, Frye says, a "central theme" of *The Double Vision* (84).

If love emerged as the central myth to live by in Frye's late work, it also became one of the two organizing principles for the last four chapters of *Words with Power* (the other is wisdom). Throughout his *Late Notebooks* Frye struggles doggedly to find an organizing pattern. One early formulation comes from the phases of revelation in chapter 5 of *The Great Code.* Another is a series of dialogues between word and spirit, which we will consider in chapter 7. It is enough to note here that climbing the ladder of higher love, which is central to the dialectic of word and spirit, takes us back to the principle of identity.[43] In the chapter "Metaphor and Identity" in *Words with Power* Frye distinguishes, as we have noted, three kinds of metaphorical experience: the imaginative, the erotic, and the ecstatic. About these he writes,

> The imaginative is an experience of the arts, including literature, in which we watch the dance of metaphors in a poem, joining them or retreating from them at pleasure. In the erotic we enter into an act of union followed by a separation, but not a separation into a simple subject–object relationship. According to Plato, using an image that will dominate the rest of this book, the lover climbs a ladder of refining experience: at the top of the ladder there is still a contrast between identity and difference, but this time he knows what it is: on the top level of experience, identity is love and difference is beauty. In the ecstatic state there is a sense of presence, a sense uniting ourselves with some-

thing else, even when it soon turns into a sense of absence. Here too are gods, says Heraclitus, lighting a fire; Heidegger, 2500 years later, picks up the water jug on his lecture table and says essentially the same thing. (85)

The identification that occurs in the experience of ecstatic metaphor is, again, the moment of revelation, and this kind of revelation, as opposed to its doctrinal embodiments, is often found among mystics, medieval visionaries, and Neoplatonists. We will examine Frye's interest in these traditions in chapter 5.

Purgatory

One final form of identity comes from what Frye calls the purgatorial progression or, following Keats, life as a "vale of soul-making."[44] "My whole conscious life," he writes, referring to the shape of his career, "has been purgatorial" (*LN,* 1:89). Like the vision of love, which is a myth to live by in this world, purgatory is for Frye an event, not a place where the spirit resides outside of time or a doctrine about the course of the soul in an afterlife.[45] Frye sometimes speaks of purgatory as an order, existing between the levels of lower (physical) and higher (spiritual) nature, but purgatory for him is fundamentally a pilgrimage that serves as a crucible for the purified mind and the emancipated vision. Its centrality in Frye's own imaginative journey is signaled by the concluding chapter of *Words with Power,* where, in the Promethean vision, purgatory as *Weltgeschichte* leads to love as *Heilsgeschichte.* As against those who see Frye simply as an idealizing and escapist visionary, the coda of *Words with Power* (the final sections of the final chapter of the final book published in Frye's lifetime) should stand as a response. Purgatory is decidedly immanent, even though the purgatorial quest may lead to transcendence. It is the informing vision of "life in this world" (*TBN,* 15). "Hell is human life as 'mere nature,' as Blake says: purgatory is the effort of the spirit to emerge from this" (*LN,* 1:253).

The central purgatorial images are fire (with its technological form, the furnace) and the ladder or spiraling stairway. The refining fire relates to how we are to live morally in this life, and the purgatorial way leads upward toward freedom, perfection, and original innocence at the top of the spiraling mountain or ladder. Dante is understandably the chief purgatorial source for Frye. Although he never wrote an extended study of Dante, the *Commedia* is omnipresent in his published and unpublished work, and he devoted an entire notebook to a commentary on the *Purgatorio* and the first ten cantos of the *Paradiso*.[46] The Dantean purgatorial progression leads from *quid agas* (the moral level in the polysemous medieval scheme) to *quo tendas* (the spiritual or anagogical level). Thus, while the purgatorial progression is a journey through life, it is a journey of ascent. "The destiny of man as purgatorial, an ascent from the lower to the higher level of creatureliness" (*LN,* 2:571).

In the chapter on the furnace archetype in *Words with Power* Frye writes that there are four components of the Promethean vision: the purgatorial, the technological, the educational, and the Utopian (294). The four components actually turn out to be subsets of a larger purgatorial crucible, whose various images Frye surveys from the Bible and Homer through Eliot and Yeats (294–306). Again, he distances himself from the view that purgatory represents the removal of sin in some after-death state. The purgatorial experience has to do with self-education in this life, with present restoration, with the transforming of the physical body into a spiritual one, with the development of creative skill through habit and practice.[47] Otherwise, Frye says that in the purgatorial progression "existence [is] taken over and shaped by a moral force" (*FT,* 115). The context of the regaining of moral identity is the return to the original human state in Eden, the earthly paradise, represented by, among other things, Spenser's faerie world.[48] The Edenic theme derives from Dante, who reaches the Garden of Eden at the top of the purgatorial mountain, at which point, in Frye's reading, he begins his return backward to his original state.[49] The upward purgatorial quest of the spirit is motivated by grace:"[G]race must descend before merit can ascend";[50] "the presence of God is what makes purgatorial sense of life" (*LN,* 1:358). But the means of the purgatorial ascent are law, morality, education, religion, and the sacraments.[51] These institutions are part of the progression of habit and practice just mentioned. Finally, the biblical analogue to purgatory is the deliverance theme in Exodus: the sojourn in the Egyptian "furnace of iron," the wandering in the wilderness, and the entry into the Promised Land (*WP,* 299).

The purgatorial progression actually contains all four of the "variations on a theme" that Frye treats in the last half of *Words with Power:* the mountain, the ladder, the cave, and the furnace. We arise from the oracular cave and are purged in the crucible of the furnace as we ascend the spiraling mountain and then move backward to the original garden. This is the earthly paradise, where the purgatorial virtues would include eros and *philia,* though not *agape.*

This chapter began with an account of metaphor in Frye's theory of language. It concludes with a typically concise *Aufhebung* that moves, by a series of identities, from word through spirit and love to God, representing epigrammatically four of the key stations along the path of Frye's own quest: "[T]he language of metaphor is the language of the spirit and the language of the spirit is the language of love and the language of love is the language of God" (*LN,* 2:613).[52] This is *agape* or higher love, paradisal virtue that exists at the level of vision. We turn now to consider vision, another central term in Frye's critical dictionary.

3 Vision

The conscious subject is not really perceiving until it recognizes itself
as part of what it perceives. The whole world is humanized when
such a perception takes place.

—*The Double Vision,* 23

Well, the dialectic of belief and vision is the path I have to go down
now.

—*Late Notebooks,* 1:73

Mythos and *dianoia,* and all the associations these two terms have for Frye,
are central to the way he thinks, since he conceives of literature as either
moving in time or forming a pattern in space. The other two key Aristotelian terms for Frye are *melos* and *opsis.* Frye was a pianist, and he wrote
a good deal about music,[1] but of the second pair of terms, *opsis* is far more
important when we look at the broad contours of his work.[2] "Doodle"
is more important than "babble"; the eye more important than the ear.
Thus, imagery becomes a central category in Frye's poetics.

> If there is such a thing as a key to my critical method, it is that I look at
> the image as revealing or illustrating the essential shape of the author's
> thought. I never think of it as purely decorative, & this means, of
> course, that I find any author who does deficient in his sense of re-
> ality. . . . if I were a creative writer, say a novelist, I should adopt the
> same principle to a technique of studying character. Character is re-
> vealed in the images we choose; in the concreteness of our thinking,
> never in the generalities we pack around them like excelsior. (34.1)

The emphasis on what the eye "sees" means that Frye is not primarily a "singing" critic but a visionary one. Although visionaries can hear,
and many have reported experiences in which words or the Word issued
audibly from elsewhere, the word *visionary,* as the Latin root indicates, has
primarily to do with seeing. But the word, as we are using it here, expands
in many directions, characterizing, on the one hand, the extraordinarily
visual way in which Frye thinks (he can hardly put pen to paper without
a schematic diagram in his head) and, on the other hand, the content of
what the expanded consciousness "sees" in its most heightened moments,

as in the "panoramic apocalypse." Frye's says that for Blake vision "meant the capacity to live with one's eyes and ears in what he calls a spiritual world" (*NFC,* 54). But in the book of Job, which represents the epitome of the Bible for Frye, Job's ears do him little good: it is only when he "sees" the new creation (42:5) that he comprehends the message from the whirlwind.

Insight

In the introduction we noted several experiences that afforded Frye particularly keen insights. From the hints he provides it appears relatively clear that two of these epiphanies are part of the dialectic that occurs along the *axis mundi.* The first, which he refers to nearly a dozen times as his Seattle illumination, is an epiphany he had when he was teaching summer school at the University of Washington in 1951.[3] The references to this epiphany are somewhat cryptic: they center on what Frye calls the passage from oracle to wit. The oracle was one of Frye's four or five "kernels," his word for the seeds or distilled essences of more expansive forms. He often refers to the seeds as kernels of scripture or of concerned prose. The other microcosmic kernels are commandment, parable, aphorism, and (occasionally) epiphany. Frye sometimes conceives of the kernels as what he calls comminuted forms, fragments that develop into law (from commandment), prophecy (from oracle), wisdom (from aphorism), history or story (from parable), and theophany (from epiphany). There are variations in Frye's account of the kernels (aphorism is sometimes called proverb, for example, and occasionally periscope and dialogue are called kernels),[4] but those differences are not important for understanding the oracle-wit illumination.

Oracle is almost always for Frye a lower-world kernel. It is linked with thanatos, secrecy, solitude, intoxication, mysterious ciphers, caves, the dialectic of choice and chance, and the descent to the underworld. The locus of the oracle is the point of demonic epiphany, the lower, watery world of chaos and the ironic vision. The central oracular literary moments for Frye include Poe's Arthur Gordon Pym's diving for the cipher at the South Pole, the descent to the bottom of the sea in Keats's *Endymion,* Odysseus in the cave of Polyphemus, the Igitur episode in Mallarmé's *Coup de dés,* the visit to the cave of Trophonius, and, most important, the oracle of the bottle in Rabelais, who was one of Frye's most admired literary heroes.[5] As for wit, in the context of the Seattle illumination it is related to laughter, the transformation of recollection into repetition, the breakthrough from irony to myth, the *telos* of interpenetration that Frye found in the Avatamsaka Sutra, new birth, knowledge of both the future and the self, the recognition of the hero, the fulfillment of prophecy, revelation, and detachment from obsession.[6] The oracular and the witty came together for Frye in the finale of Verdi's *Falstaff*.[7]

Frye calls the Seattle illumination a "breakthrough," and the experience, whatever it was, appears to have been decisive for him. He was thirty-nine at the time, literally midway through his journey of life. One can say with some confidence that the Seattle epiphany was a revelation to Frye that he need not surrender to what he spoke of as the century's three A's: alienation, anxiety, absurdity; that he realized there was a way out of the abyss; that he embraced the view of life as purgatorial; that, in short, he accepted the invitation of the Spirit and the Bride in Revelation 22:17. "The door of death," Frye writes, "has oracle on one side & wit on the other: when one goes through it one recovers the power of laughter" (*TBN*, 162). And laughter, for Frye, is the "sudden release from the unpleasant" (33.34). Oracles are, of course, ordinarily somber, and wit, in one of its senses, is lighthearted. Pausanius tells us that the ritual of consulting the oracle in the cave of Trophonius was so solemn that the suppliants who emerged were unable to laugh for some time, but they did recover their power to laugh.[8] There is a "porous osmotic wall between the oracular and the funny," Frye writes in Notebook 27 (*LN*, 1:15). Similarly, in *Gargantua and Pantagruel*, when Panurge and Friar John consult the oracle of the Holy Bottle, there is, if not literal laughter, an intoxicating delight that comes from the oracle's invitation to drink; and we are told that the questers then "passed through a country full of all delights."[9] This is why "Rabelais is essential to Dante" (*LN*, 1:15). But laughter here is more than a physical act. It is a metaphor for the sudden spiritual transformation that is captured in the *paravritti* of Mahayana Buddhism. *Paravritti* literally means "turning up" or "change," and according to D. T. Suzuki it corresponds to conversion in religious experience.[10] In the Lankavatara Sutra we are told that in his transcendental state of consciousness the Buddha laughed "the loudest laugh," and in his marginal annotation of this passage Frye notes that "the laugh expresses a sudden release of Paravritti."[11]

In *Anatomy of Criticism* Frye describes the oracular mind, whose original archetype is the cave of Trophonius, as lying beneath the conscious one (353). This is the world of the *perseroso* mood—the return to the womb or the imaginative withdrawal that we get in sixth-phase romance. To escape from what Frye calls the "oracular cave" (*TBN*, 198) is to enter the world of the "awakened critical intelligence" or wit (*AC*, 185–86). It is, as described in Notebook 21, "the passage from dream to waking" (*RT,* 227). To leave the dream cave is to turn one's back on what in the *Anatomy* Frye refers to as the reductio ad absurdum, "which is not designed to hold one in perpetual captivity, but to bring one to the point at which one can escape" (233). This means that the movement of oracle to wit is the movement from the world of magical nothingness to full awareness or recognition.[12] In *Beyond the Body: The Human Double and the Astral Planes,* Benjamin Walker concludes that what ultimately happens to the soul is that it loses its body on earth and loses its sense of individuality in the celestial abodes. Reacting to this conclusion, Frye wrote in the margin of Walker's book, "you don't *lose* anything: you lose the lower sphere, or nothingness."[13] What you gain, by contrast, is self-knowledge and creative energy. In one of his more revealing commentaries on oracle, this one on the oracle at Delphi, Frye writes,

> The motto of Delphi was "Know thyself," which suggests that the self intended was a conscience far below the ego with its anxieties of self-interest, far below all social and cultural conditioning, in short the spiritual self. For that self to "know itself" would constitute the unity of Word and Spirit in which all consciousness begins and ends. Such a spirit could produce its own oracles, and they would be not only genuinely prophetic but genuinely witty. *Finnegans Wake* is the only book I know which is devoted entirely to this hidden intercommunion of Word and Spirit, with no emergence into the outside world at any point, but of course the creative energy involved has produced all literature. (*WP,* 251)

We will have more to say in the final chapter about the unity involved in the dialogue of Word and Spirit.

Wit is both an efficient and a final cause of satire. One of the differences between irony and satire is that the former represents humanity in a state of bondage, whereas the effort to escape from bondage marks the latter. In one of his notebooks for *Anatomy of Criticism* Frye writes, "[S]atire goes up the ladder of laughter, through the low norm of the experiential & the high norm of the innocent, to participating in the laughter of the gods at the fallen state of man (which is sadistic if God & man are not mutually involved). That gives me a Lankavatara quote" (35.70), the Lankavatara quotation being the "loudest laugh" passage, mentioned above, that Frye annotated in his copy of the Lankavatara Sutra. This is apparently what Frye means when he writes that by moving in a Lankavatara direction he hopes "to bust the supremacy of the existential" (36.10), with all its ritual bondage and poker-faced angst. By the time he came to write *The Secular Scripture,* some twenty-five years after the

Seattle experience, Frye put the *axis mundi* movement in these terms in his chapter "Themes of Ascent":

> As the hero or heroine enters the labyrinthine lower world, the prevailing moods are those of terror or uncritical awe. At a certain point, perhaps when the strain, as the storyteller doubtless hopes, is becoming unbearable, there may be a revolt of the mind, a recovered detachment, the typical expression of which is laughter. The ambiguity of the oracle becomes the ambiguity of wit, something addressed to a verbal understanding that shakes the mind free. This point is also marked by generic changes from the tragic and ironic to the comic and satiric. Thus in Rabelais the huge giants, the search for an oracle, and other lower-world themes that in different contexts would be frightening or awe-inspiring, are presented as farce. *Finnegans Wake* in our day also submerges us in a dream world of mysterious oracles, but when we start to read the atmosphere changes, and we find ourselves surrounded by jokes and puns. Centuries earlier, the story was told of how Demeter wandered over the world in fruitless search of her lost daughter Proserpine, and sat lonely and miserable in a shepherd's hut until the obscene jests and raillery of the servant girl Iambe and the old nurse Baubo finally persuaded her to smile. The Eleusinian mysteries which Demeter established were solemn and awful rites of initiation connected with the renewal of the fertility cycle; but Iambe and Baubo helped to ensure that there would also be comic parodies of them, like Aristophanes' *Frogs*. According to Plutarch, those who descended to the gloomy cave of the oracle of Trophonius might, after three days, recover the power of laughter. (129–30)

"The moment of illumination," Frye writes in one of his marginalia to the Rig-Veda, is "humorous & not pompous."[14] A further gloss on the Seattle experience is Frye's juxtaposition, in one of his sets of typed notes for *The Secular Scripture*, of the recovery of laughter in the cave of Trophonius, located at the south point of his mandala, with "Blake's boy born in joy." This is a reference to the boy in *The Mental Traveller* who "was begotten in dire woe"[15]—another example of the gleeful release arising from the gloomy, oracular depths. Or, as Frye says in Notebook 21, "Laughter means hostility in the ironic direction & assimilation to the paradisal one" (*RT,* 231).

Finally, the oracle-wit distinction is parallel to a number of Frye's other bipolar distinctions. By collapsing the distinctions we experience in ordinary waking reality, the oracular is metaphorical. The process is like that of condensation in Freud's account of dream work—accidental slips, allegories, and the like: a single word or image comes to represent two or more ideas, memories, or feelings. In contrast, the witty, having to do with recognition, is metonymic; one thing is put for another, as in Freudian displacement, and so is accommodated to waking experience once we have ascended from the oracular cave. Condensation occurs in a prerecognition state. Displacement belongs to the daylight world where one recognizes the point of the joke—the "oh-I-see" moment of release and illumination. Similarly, to use another of Frye's distinctions, oracle represents a centripetal movement into the identities of metaphor, as in the interrelationship of words in *Finnegans Wake;* and wit, a centrifugal movement out into the world of realistic awareness, as in the continuous narrative of *War and Peace,* where myth has been adapted to the canons of plausibility.[16]

Precisely what happened in Seattle and why it happened will no doubt remain mysteries. Since oracle belongs to the complex of things Frye associates with metaphor, and wit with those things associated with myth, perhaps the Seattle experience had to do with the realization that these two principles would become the backbone of the *Anatomy.* In any case, there is no difficulty in accepting Frye's judgment that the intuition was a breakthrough; it certainly helps to explain his treatment of the themes of romance in the secular scripture and the last four chapters of his second book on the sacred scripture. Nor is there difficulty in understanding what he means when he says, "I've spent nearly eighty years trying to articulate intuitions that occupied about five minutes of my entire life" (*LN,* 2:636).

The Seattle illumination may not have involved only laughing in the face of irony—the telling moment that Frye saw in Trophonius and Rabelais and in the pure detachment of the Buddha's laugh. It may also have been related to the vision of dice throwing in Mallarmé's *Igitur,* which Frye summarized some years later this way: "[I]n Mallarmé the dice represent a world where, in Yeats's phrase, choice and chance are one. Throwing dice is a commitment to chance that does not abolish chance, but is in itself a free act, and so begins a negating of negation that brings something, perhaps ultimately everything, into being again" (*WP,* 292). The dice throwing seems also to be linked (one of Frye's favorite words) with the metaphorical-game tradition, which explores the metaphorical foundation of discursive prose and which Frye sees as characterizing some of his own work. "The word game," he writes, "is linked to the fact that its centre of gravity is that mysterious area I've talked so much about, where the oracular and witty seem different aspects of the same thing" (*RT,* 301). In *The Secular Scripture* Frye writes that in comedy the device that breaks the spell of death or paralysis is the recognition scene, and the word *recognition,* as Aristotle and *Oedipus the King* remind us, has to do with figurative seeing, whether comic or tragic. And here again the recognition scene "transforms a story into a kind of game" (*SeS,* 130).

The point of all this for Frye is that the abyss must be entered and the nightmare vision confronted before a triumphant reversal can occur.[17] It may not be for Frye, as it was for Heraclitus, that the way up and the way down are one and the same, but he sometimes comes close to suggesting that:"The principle of the higher or unfallen world is harmony or concord; the principle of the lower world is metamorphosis, the passing out of one state of being into another. But perhaps a sufficiently penetrating wisdom could see in metamorphosis itself a kind of harmony, a principle of change moving in correspondence with the worlds above."[18] To pass through the door of wit permits one to embark on the purgatorial journey, that journey of spirit making that figures so importantly in the notebooks and finally gets articulated in chapters 4–8 of *Words with Power* and in *The Double Vision.* In any event, moving in both directions on the *axis mundi* is part of the double movement of the spiritual vision that defines and is defined by Frye's religious quest.

The content of the St. Clair illumination or enlightenment (both words are Frye's)—the second event mentioned at the beginning of this section, referred to in sixteen notebook entries—is somewhat more difficult to understand. Frye says that this experience, which happened on St. Clair Avenue in Toronto, was about "the passing from poetry through drama to prose" (*LN,* 2:621), a passage that took the form of a gyre or vortex.[19] The transition he is speaking about is connected with the movement between two of the units in his eight-book project (the ogdoad)— from Tragicomedy, which was to focus on ritual and drama, to Anticlimax, which was to center on prose or continuous thematic forms, such as satires, confessions, romances, and other quests for identity. By prose in this context, Frye means the possession of a consolidated vision. In this respect, the movement or transition that he speaks of as suddenly bursting in upon him is not unlike the *paravritti* of the Seattle experience. In fact, in one notebook Frye speculates that the two were "essentially the same illumination, perhaps: the movement from the esoteric to kerygma" (*LN,* 2:621). The two differ, however, in that the Seattle illumination was not specifically connected in Frye's mind with any of the various parts of his ogdoad project.

The Seattle and St. Clair epiphanies also appear to be different in kind from the experiences Frye had with Spengler in Edmonton and twice with Blake in Toronto, all three of which were visions of coherence, of things fitting together into a mythological framework.[20] In an interview, Frye describes all of these experiences as "visions" (*NFC*, 48), but in Notebook 19 he clarifies the difference between the mystical, visionary experience and moments of inspiration:

> I have never had the sort of experience the mystics talk about, never felt a revelation of reality through or beyond nature, never felt like Adam in Paradise, never felt, in direct experience, that the world is wholly other than it seems. I don't question the honesty, or even the factuality, of those who have recorded such experiences, but I have had to content myself with the blessing to those who have not seen & yet have believed—if one can attach the word "belief" to accepting statements as obviously true as the fact that I have seen New York. The nearest I have come to such experiences are glimpses of my own creative powers— Spengler in Edmonton and two nights with Blake—and these are moments or intervals of inspiration rather than vision. (*TBN*, 60)

In these latter epiphanies, then, things began to form themselves into patterns and make sense, and Frye was able to realize that he had something to say about Spengler and Blake as a critic, or, as he told one interviewer, they were sudden "visions ultimately of what I might be able to do" (*NFC*, 48). In a letter Frye also distinguishes between "visionary experiences" and occasions when he was suddenly aware of the shape of what he was doing.[21] He clearly wants to avoid the impression that he was confronted with some mystical visitation. The Seattle and St. Clair experiences were not mystical visitations either, but they were brief moments of intense awareness when the shape of at least two parts of the writing project he had outlined (the ogdoad) began to take form. The words "gyre," which Frye borrows from Yeats, and the less familiar "vortex" come from his account of the St. Clair illumination in Notebooks 12 and 24 (*TBN*, 333 and 179). What does he mean by vortex? And how does it relate to vision?

Vortex

Vortex comes from the Latin *vertex* for "whirlpool," "top of the head," or "summit," and *vertex* itself derives from *vetere*, "to turn." Thus a vortex can be a maelstrom, or the point farthest from the base of a figure, or the place where lines or curves intersect, or the zenith. The idea of turning is explicit in maelstrom and implicit in the others. We should keep all these meanings in mind in considering Frye's use of the term, which is in some ways conventional and in others idiosyncratic. (He even invents the ungainly verb "vorticized.") Blake uses "vortex" in both *The Four Zoas* and *Milton,* and the central passage for Frye comes from the latter:

> The nature of infinity is this: That everything has its
> Own vortex; and when once a traveler thro Eternity.
> Has passed that Vortex, he perceives it roll backward behind
> His path, into a globe itself infolding; like a sun
> Or like a moon, or like a universe of starry majesty.[22]

Here is Frye's gloss on the passage:

> Blake says that everything in eternity has what he calls a "vortex" (perhaps rather a vortex-ring), a spiral or cone of existence. When we focus both eyes on one object, say a book, we create an angle of vision opening into our minds with the apex pointing away from us. The book therefore has a vortex of existence opening into its mental reality within our minds. When Milton descends from eternity to time, he finds that he has to pass through the apex of his cone of eternal vision, which is like trying to see a book from the book's point of view; the Lockian conception of the real book as outside the mind on which the vision of the fallen world is based. This turns him inside out, and from his new perspective the cone rolls back and away from him in the form of a globe. That is why we are surrounded with a universe of remote globes, and are unable to see that the earth is "one infinite plane." But in eternity the perceiving mind or body is omnipresent, and hence these globes in eternity are inside that body. (*FS*, 350)[23]

Vortex for Frye is an active or moving geometric shape, an image that helps him to visualize different events, particularly transformative ones, in the structure of literary and religious narrative and meaning. In his published writing the word appears only occasionally: in *The Secular Scripture* he uses it to describe the passage of the action through a recognition scene in Terence's *Andria* (91), and in *Words with Power* to characterize the pattern of creative descent in Melville (284–85). But in his notebooks Frye repeatedly calls on the vortex to assist him in visualizing, particularly, passages from one state to another, as in Blake's account of Milton's descent. Vortexes can move in two directions: they can whirl upward or spin downward. They can attach themselves to each other at the point of the cone, or they can expand outward into an apocalyptic or demonic universe.

Since Frye conceives the various movements visually, perhaps a diagram will help us here. In diagram 1 we can see a ladder image in the background, Blake's four levels on the left, and Dante's three on the right.

But the ladder or chain-of-being image is insufficiently dynamic to capture the radical changes that can occur in human consciousness—thus the
vortex, which for Frye is often an image of revolutionary change. Vortical movements can occur on any level, though they mostly take place in
the purgatorial area between Ulro and Eden. Here is one of Frye's lists of
vortices on the different levels:

> the Charybdis or Maelstrom sucking from Generation down into non-
> entity; or, coming back the other way from the sea, the cornucopia or
> female phallic symbol pouring fruits from the place of seed. The for-
> mer is in Dante's hell. Then there's the Orc one . . . which stretches to
> the upper limit of nature & reason & when frozen becomes Leviathan
> or the symbol of hierarchy (the rhythm of the pyramid (step) & zig-
> gurat recurs in the tiers). Third, there's the Paravritti, the Beulah-Eden
> vortex through the ray of fire which opens out into the mystic rose, an-
> other female phallic symbol, in Dante one of an inviolate virgin because
> of the Babel nature of Purgatory. This elusive vortex is satirized as the
> δῖνος in Aristophanes' *Clouds.* (7.33)[24]

Revolutionary changes can be individual moments of transformation,
recognition, or enlightenment, or they can be social. In Notebook 8 Frye
speaks of the "vortical explosion" in the revolutionary consciousness that
comes into the modern world with Marx, Kierkegaard, and Nietzsche
(8.191). Dante's two vortices—the swirling descent into the inferno and
the circular climb up the purgatorial mountain—are, of course, central
examples for Frye. Similarly with Yeats, as the diagram is reminiscent of
the double gyres of *A Vision.*

But Frye writes about the vortex mostly in relation to a sudden
awareness that moves one from a lower state of being to a higher one.
Opsis is the underlying category. One bursts through to a new awareness
where things can now be *seen* differently. "When the action passes from
one level to the other through the recognition scene, we have a feeling of
going through some sort of gyre or vortex" (*SeS,* 91), and recognition
scenes are often accompanied by reversals, as in the case of *Oedipus the
King,* where the central metaphors are light and darkness, blindness and
sight.[25] But nothing is ever purely visual in Frye: there is always a dialectic of space *and* time, and the vortex can apply to both categories, as we
see in this notebook entry, which is an abstract parallel to what Milton experienced in Blake's poem:

> The cycle of the Word is a series of epiphanies—creation, law,
> prophecy and apocalypse—and the cycle of the Spirit is a series of re-
> sponses—exodus, wisdom, gospel and participating apocalypse. The

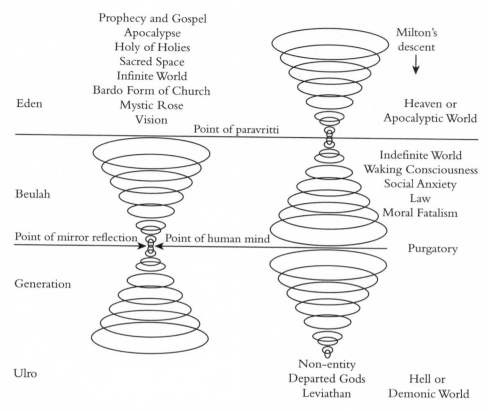

Diagram 1. Vortex: Anabatic and Katabatic Spirals

true response is the historical one turned inside out. Not just upside-down: that's the other half of the Word cycle. But the Bible uses the up-down metaphors in the crucial first two chapters of Acts [the descent of the Spirit, the ascent of the Word]. What gets turned inside-out, as I said in GC [*The Great Code*] and have been stumbling over all my life, are the categories of time and space. At present we tend to think of eternity and infinity as time and space indefinitely extended, which they are anyway, and they have to go into a real reverse, another vortex. (*LN*, 2:462)

Frye's vortices do not interpenetrate like Yeats's, but as the diagram indicates, they can come together at their apexes to form an hourglass figure. This point of contact takes place in the human mind, and after the vortical explosion has occurred, we can look back from where we've come, as if in a mirror. Blake's *Jerusalem,* Frye says, "attempts to show that the vision of reality is the other one inside out. The poem shows us two worlds, one infinite, the other indefinite, one our own home and the other the same home receding from us in a mirror" (*FS,* 384). Frye writes about the vortex in forty-six notebook entries, some of which are cryptic enough to qualify as speaking in tongues.[26] But the effect of the whole, the demonic descents notwithstanding, is another of Frye's verbal formulas, this one a dynamic image, for trying to grasp what happens when one bursts through to a moment of "illumination," which is the word he uses to describe his St. Clair revelation (*TBN,* 179). As an image in the notebooks, the vortex is as endlessly fascinating as a poetic conceit, but what if it is only that? This is a question that Frye poses for himself, though in a somewhat different form: what is the relationship between belief and vision?

The Hegelian Dialectic of Belief and Vision

In one of his notebooks from the mid-1980s Frye writes, "What I'm hoping to get away with is a paper on 'The Dialectic of Belief and Vision,'" and seven entries later he remarks that "the dialectic of belief and vision is the path I have to go down now" (*LN,* 1:71, 73). Not long after projecting this journey, he *did* go down that path, writing an address called "The Dialectic of Belief and Vision" which he gave at the School of Continuing Studies, University of Toronto, in December 1985.[27] A bit later in the same notebook Frye remarks, in a passage already noted, that he would like to help "make religion interesting and attractive to many people of good will who will have nothing to do with it now" (*LN,* 1:74). He seems to have his projected paper in mind as a way of achieving this goal. The paper was written when Frye was in the middle of his eight-year struggle to produce *Words with Power,* and so it relates to a number of the issues addressed in that book. But it provides a capsule version of Frye's thinking at this point about the relation between literature and religion. "What place," he asks, "does the creative imagination, and the kind of response that we make to a work of literature, have in the study of religion in general, or of the text of the Bible in particular?" (*MM,* 93).

The history of criticism is replete with commentaries and debates about critical language. We still have little assurance that we know with certainty what Plato meant by *mimesis,* Aristotle by *katharsis,* Longinus by *ekstasis,* Sidney by "figuring forth," Dryden by "nature," Keats by "Negative Capability," and so on, but making our best effort to understand the material cause of criticism is still an essential first step. The same of course is true with poets. We do not get very far in reading Blake without struggling to understand the special meanings that words like "memory" or "emanation" or "intellectual powers" have in his poems, and anyone who has tried to catalogue the various meanings that cluster around such a word as "myth" in Frye's work has faced a similar challenge. In confronting an essay like "The Dialectic of Belief and Vision" we need to be aware, therefore, that a word like "dialectic" means more than argument, which is what it means in its one appearance in *Fearful Symmetry*.

Frye begins by calling his title "somewhat forbidding," and this gambit seems intended to call our attention to the word "dialectic" itself, which has as many connotations clinging to it as *dianoia* does in *Anatomy of Criticism* and elsewhere. Of course Frye may mean, or mean as well, that if we take dialectic to signify simple opposition we confound normal expectations: faith and belief are not ordinarily seen as opposing pairs; we tend rather to oppose belief and doubt, vision and blindness. In any case, we need to be attentive to the word dialectic (Greek, *dialektos*), which originally meant debate or dialogue, the latter word deriving from the same root. Thus Platonic dialectic was the discipline of drawing rigorous distinctions. In the medieval trivium, dialectic as a form of rational debate was the companion of grammar and rhetoric in the educational system. Frye is clearly using the word in this sense. But "dialectic" throughout his writing is more complicated than this. It is certainly one of his more frequently used words, occurring several hundred times in *The Great Code* and *Words with Power*, in the notebooks for these two volumes, and in *The "Third Book" Notebooks*.[28] In these texts dialectic is sometimes a conceptual mode of writing, sometimes a simple opposition (apocalyptic vs. demonic, liberal vs. conservative, repression vs. confrontation, faith vs. doubt, and any number of additional either/or pairs), sometimes a synonym for ideology. At other times Frye uses the word to signify a process, as when he speaks about the movement from law to wisdom or prophecy to gospel. Here we have the Marxist view of dialectic hiding in the background. At still other times, the word means being able to hold two points of view at the same time. Frye says, for example, "Prophecy indicates the path of human folly into inevitable disaster, and the restoration of Israel by God in a metaphorical future which is really an expanded present. Commentary on prophecy is a dialectic between the social setting & the incremental tradition, & that's what criticism of literature should follow as a model" (*LN*, 1:68). Here Frye is not recommending that advocates of the two positions debate with each other or that literary criticism make a choice between the two. Rather, the literary critic must be attentive both to the original setting of the prophetic word and to what it means in an "expanded present."

Frye also uses dialectic in the sense of *Aufhebung*, which, as we have noted in the two preceding chapters, means for Hegel the process of canceling, preserving, and lifting up. Take, for example, his account of the opposing views of Calvin and Blake: "Calvin couldn't make any sense out of the book of Revelation because he was obsessed by belief. He couldn't imagine a vision as a completion of a belief. Blake, on the other hand, could hardly make any sense out of the stages leading up to vision, partly because he was a painter. . . . The contrast between belief and vision, the emphasis that makes Calvin and Blake so diametrically opposed, has to be reconciled according to the Hans Denck principle," the Hans Denck principle being that "whoever leaves an antithesis without resolving it lacks the ground of truth."[29] Although Frye does not refer to *Aufhebung* in "The Dialectic on Belief and Vision," the *aufgehoben* process lies behind his resolving of the belief and vision antithesis. A close look at the progression of Frye's own engagement with the dialectic will reveal how the resolution emerges.

Frye begins by presenting us with a "crude form" of the relation of faith and belief: belief is a state of mind, and faith an expression of belief in action. This may not strike us as particularly extraordinary, even though it seems to run counter to the more or less common understanding of faith—that faith is an expression of belief. But Frye rejects outright the notion that faith is a matter of what goes on in our heads.[30] What began, then, as the dialectic of belief and vision has now become a dialectic of faith and belief. Does Frye mean to equate *vision* and *faith*? If so, why the switching of terms?[31]

The answer to these questions is postponed momentarily because Frye, in a typical move, has to develop a *framework* for posing the question. The framework is the process of reading, based on the familiar time-space categories: reading is both a linear, temporal, narrative movement, related to the ear and to musical metaphors, and a spatial, patterned, conceptual act of attention, related to the eye and to architectural metaphors. This is a version of the familiar *mythos* and *dianoia* opposition: things move in time (we "listen" to the sequence), and things organize themselves in space (we "see" the pattern).

The second aspect of the act of reading permits Frye to introduce the concept of structure, and at this point in the essay he digresses to consider two "confused metaphors" about structure. The first, advanced by Marshall McLuhan, is that while the book is a linear process, the electronic media present us with a simultaneous vision. The second is Jacques Derrida's elevation of the speaker's presence in writing (*écriture*) as the crucial issue. Frye dismisses each "metaphor," not so much by argument as by counterassertion. Against McLuhan, Frye notes that the book has to be understood (experienced as *dianoia* or comprehended spatially) as well as read (experienced as *mythos* or in a linear way), and electronic media have a narrative or sequential shape as well as a simultaneous pattern. Against Derrida, Frye says simply that because prose depends on rhythm, it has a written structure, and that the issue of the speaker's presence is just a conventional pretense. The important thing for Frye is that there is *structure* in written discourse: we respond to the structure of prose, not to the writer's presence.

Having elevated the importance of structure for understanding literary works, Frye cautions against believing that complete understanding is ever possible: interpretations have a history and a future, so it is impossible to arrive even theoretically at a definitive meaning of a literary text. Here he introduces his own theological metaphor for the reading process, saying that literature suggests "the paradox of the incarnation, the enclosing of the infinite in a finite form" (*MM*, 96). Then, after a paragraph illustrating the close connection in religious ritual between hearing and seeing—drawing illustrations from the Mass, the Eleusinian mysteries, and Zen Buddhism—Frye returns to the issue of belief as it relates to the reading process. His purpose now is to differentiate between the willing suspension of disbelief in the reading of literature ("a continuous process of acceptance" and the "postponing of response") and the continuous reactions of belief and disbelief in the reading of the descriptive prose of a newspaper (*MM*, 96–97). Belief and disbelief have been conventionally associated with what is called "literal meaning" with respect to history and doctrine. But literal meaning, in Frye's familiar formulation, is really a matter of internal coherence, the relationship of the words of a poem to each other, not to external correspondence. Extroverted forms of biblical literalism in the conventional sense lead to hysteria; introverted forms to crises of faith.

Here we have one of the cruxes of the essay. In Notebook 27 Frye writes that his paper on the dialectic of belief and vision is "the resolution of the 'is' and the 'as though' I've circled around since at least the AC [*Anatomy of Criticism*]. I suppose one first attacks the conventionalizing of subject and object involved in 'I' (who's I?) believe 'that' (what's that?)" (*LN*, 1:71). This note is developed in the essay itself into the following formulation: "The assertion 'I believe that' is not simply meaningless but actively dangerous when we still don't know who 'I' is or what 'that' is" (*MM*, 98). It is dangerous because it is based on the assumption of a unified mind. But the divided mind behind the hysteria of literalism cannot distinguish "what one believes from what one thinks or believes one believes" (*MM*, 98).

Faith, then, is not a matter of professed belief, for which Frye's shorthand is *quid credas*. Faith, rather, is revealed in the consistency of one's actions throughout life, and actions (*quid agas*) are powered by vision. Frye presents a number of formulations of this principle—that actions speak louder than words—especially in his later writing. One is in *The Double Vision*, another in his interview with David Cayley, still another in his sermon "Symbols." But the germ of the dialectic goes all the way back to *Fearful Symmetry*.[32]

At this point Frye introduces the Hegelian distinction between the *for itself* and the *in itself*: "Faith is the continuous struggle of a time-bound man to pursue the *for itself* which is the burden brought into the world by consciousness. Vision is focused on an aspect of a model world which is the *in itself,* a model that is ineffective if separated from the *for itself*" (*MM*, 98). The *for itself* represents the world of external reality, where things are temporally contingent and historically determinate. The *in itself* represents timeless, unchanging, universality—the imaginative world on which vision focuses. Frye's understanding of genuine faith, as opposed to professed belief, derives primarily from the passage in Hebrews that he so often puzzled over: "faith is the substance of things hoped for, the evidence of things not seen" (Heb. 11:1). In Frye's exegesis this means that faith is "the activity of realizing a visionary model in the mind produced by hope" (*MM*, 100), with the visionary model now completely distanced from any notion of professed belief or religious creed. "*My* approach to faith," Frye writes in one of his notebooks, "turns it into *gaya scienza*, a joyful wisdom: most of the conventional approaches turn it into a burden of guilt feelings. Critics who distrust me because I don't seem too worried about inconsistencies . . . can't tune into this notion of faith as a dancing ballet of intuitions, affirmations, counter-affirmations, 'doubts' or retreats from dogma, & a pervading sense of 'anything may be "true" or "false," but whatever it is, the whole pattern has a design and a movement'" (*LN*, 1:234). There is no long-faced solemnity, then, in Frye's understanding of faith; he sees it as a lively process and not a sober product, such as a creed, and it is "under entropy except to the degree that it's transmuted into hope" (*RT,* 312).[33] Thus, he concludes, expanding his dialectic, belief without vision issues in anxieties over moral and other secondary concerns, and vision without belief focuses on the *in itself* at the expense of the *for itself.*

How, then, can one get beyond, on the one hand, the bad faith of vision without belief and, on the other, the narrow ideology of belief without vision? The answer comes through a process very similar to

Hegel's *Aufhebung*. In his *Phenomenology of Spirit* Hegel, in vexingly dense language, describes the problem of the alienated self as a problem of two opposing forces—the division between self-consciousness, actuality, human law, the external world of culture and civilization, and the *for itself*, on the one hand; and consciousness, possibility, faith, harmony, consciousness of the Notion (*Begriff*), the spiritual world, and the *in itself*, on the other. The gulf between these two worlds is collapsed by an insight into what Hegel calls Enlightenment, and Enlightenment lifts the self to a level of "absolute freedom" and "absolute Being." The *in itself* and the *for itself* are united at the level of Spirit.[34]

Frye's version of *Aufhebung* comes in his movement from seeing and hearing and from time and history to the Apocalypse. From the point of view of the Hegelian model, seeing is negated but we pass through the negation to another level of vision, for the Apocalypse "is primarily a vision of a body of imagery, where the images of every category of being, divine, angelic, paradisal, human, animal, vegetable, and inorganic, are all identified with the body of Christ" (*MM*, 101). Both Frye and Hegel are climbing a spiraling ladder to a higher level of being, except, as Frye goes on to illustrate in "The Dialectic of Belief and Vision," he is moving upward by way of the language of myth and metaphor. "If Hegel had written his Phenomenology in *mythos*-language instead of in *logos*-language," Frye remarks in one notebook, "a lot of my work would be done for me" (*LN*, 1:192).[35]

It is perhaps worth noting that in Frye's notebooks Hegel often becomes a preoccupation. Hegel's use of *Begriff* or concept in his journey up the ladder of being and his view of dialectic as *Aufhebung* get mentioned in passing in *The Great Code* and *Words with Power*, but Hegel and Hegelianism are referred to in the notebooks more than 220 times, and Frye declares in Notebook 53, "The rush of ideas I get from Hegel's Phenomenology is so tremendous I can hardly keep up with it" (*LN*, 2:631). Elsewhere Frye gives an eloquent testimony to Hegel as "the great philosopher of *anabasis*" (*TBN*, 89) and to *Phenomenology of Spirit* as the "tremendous philosophical masterpiece" that through its upward thrust finally abolishes the gap between subject and object:

> The programme of spiritual awareness laid down in that tremendous philosophical masterpiece, Hegel's *Phenomenology of Spirit*, turns on two principles that are relevant here. First is Hegel's introductory principle, "The true substance is subject." That is, the gap between a conscious perceiving subject and a largely unconscious objective world confronts

us at the beginning of experience. All progress in knowledge, in fact in consciousness itself, consists in bridging the gap and abolishing both the separated subject and the separated object. . . .

Spirit, says Hegel, enters the picture as soon as "We" and "I" begin to merge, when the individual speaks as a discriminating and independent unit within his society. In his "substance is subject" principle Hegel continues a philosophical tradition going back to the Latin church fathers, brooding on the relation of person and substance in the Trinity and translating *hypostasis* not as *substantia* but as *persona*. The problem is to define what is at once spiritual and substantial, the spirit which is also a body. The mirror, where a subject sees an object which is both itself and not itself, is a central metaphor of knowledge, and such words as "speculation" and "reflection" point to its importance. Hegel is in search of a self-awareness that culminates, for him, in "absolute knowledge," where we finally break out of the mirror, the prison of Narcissus. (*DV,* 36)[36]

Frye makes one final move that looks very much like another Hegelian *Aufhebung.* It hinges on the distinction between the identity of subject and object in metaphor and what he calls "ultimate identity" in life. Ultimate identity is a matter of existential power and religious experience. To take the language Frye uses to describe this experience in other contexts, it is a movement from the panoramic to the participating apocalypse.[37] The panoramic or spectacular apocalypse is an objective vision, related to the Mosaic law in the Old Testament and, in the book of Revelation, to the Last Judgment and the vision of St. John on Patmos. "Every eye shall see him," John announces at the beginning of the book of Revelation (1:7), referring to the Second Coming of Christ. This means that the Word is something to be seen, an object of vision in the panoramic apocalypse, rather than simply something to be heard. The participating or existential apocalypse, on the other hand, represents the reintegrated vision in which "time and space disappear into synchronicity and interpenetration respectively" (*RT,* 304).

This is, again, a metaphorical structure in which subject and object are identified, just as in Eden before the Fall there was an identity of the human and the natural. The function of literature is, in part—to use the refrain that is sounded throughout Frye's work—"to keep the metaphorical habit of thinking in identities alive" (*MM,* 106).[38] This stage of imaginative vision is fundamentally religious: "No one can read far . . . in mystical literature without feeling the urgency of the question of whether there is an identity of the kind that the verbal metaphor suggests but does not assert. In fact some sense of ultimate identity of the kind implicit in the Hindu formula 'thou art that,' seems to lie behind nearly all the profoundest religious feelings and experiences, whatever the actual religion, even when the ideological censor forbids its expression as a doctrine" (*MM*, 106). It is at this stage of imaginative identity that love or *agape* emerges from the *for itself* of faith and the *in itself* of hope.

Frye does not refer to the dialectic he has followed in this essay as *Aufhebung*. But he keeps pushing his way up the ladder, passing beyond each series of opposites, until he arrives at the point of revelation, just as Hegel kept climbing to get beyond subject and substance to arrive at Spirit or Absolute Knowledge.[39] Even though Hegel tried to arrive at an apocalyptic vision, he did not quite get there, Frye suggests, because his millennialism prevented him from seeing that the apocalypse was not a future vision but a "vision of the expanded present, the world of physical concerns taking on a spiritual dimension" (*LN*, 2:653–54). "We soon realize," Frye says, concluding the dialectical journey in this essay, "that at a certain point we enter into a vaster operation where human personality and will are still present, but where the self-begotten activity no longer seems to be the only, or even the essentially, active power. The initiative is now usually seen to come from, not some unreachable 'in itself' world, but from an infinitely active personality that both enters us and eludes us" (*MM*, 107). This is the vision of the divine–human encounter called revelation, revelation signifying, as the root of the word indicates, that it is now possible to see anew, to see a totally transformed reality, because the veil has been removed. In the context of the Bible, Frye writes, "Revelation is not visualized, but it is a 'seeing' of what the Bible means. From there it passes into the reader and becomes the participating apocalypse, which is also a type of a new creation, the ultimate antitype of everything" (*RT*, 364).

On several occasions in his notebooks Frye notes a correspondence between the medieval four levels of interpretation and Hegel's *Phenomenology of Spirit*,[40] and in one of his unpublished lectures he makes the connection explicit: "Hegel's *Phenomenology of the Spirit*, the cornerstone of modern philosophy, was in fact the same [medieval] doctrine of different levels of meaning all over again. In fact, even the metaphor of levels is preserved in Hegel's key term *Aufhebung*."[41] The medieval view of polysemous meaning is, of course, omnipresent in Frye. In a condensed but revealing outline in Notebook 27 he writes:

History is the (literal) Exodus response.
Philosophy is (allegorical) Wisdom response.

> The total body of imagination (Blake's Golgonooza) is the (everlasting)
> Gospel or tropological response.
> The response to Apocalypse is the interpenetrating vision. (*LN,* 1:41)

Here we have another formulation of the goal reached at the end of the ladder of polysemous meaning, which is vision as apocalypse, yet rather than negating the first three levels, apocalypse interpenetrates with them. The second and third levels, corresponding to the *quid credas* and *quid agas,* terms already glanced at that Frye appropriated from a fourth-century jingle, are thus resolved by an *Aufhebung* to the fourth or anagogic level, the *quo tendas* vision of reality or the spiritual world toward which we are directed.[42] In *The Well-Tempered Critic* Frye equates the highest level of the use of words with *quo tendas,* "a vision of the nature and destiny of man and the human situation," and he adds that we may or may not associate this level of language with religion (*WTC,* 49). But Frye himself associates it with religion elsewhere, including the final two paragraphs of *The Well-Tempered Critic* (*WTC,* 155–56),[43] and in one notebook he even identifies religion with "constructing verbal patterns" (7.97). The literary form most indebted to anagogy, we know from *Anatomy of Criticism,* is apocalyptic revelation (120), and this is what Frye's journey in "The Dialectic of Belief and Vision" leads to—the *quo tendas* level of vision. In *Aufhebung* the process of lifting to another level means that there is a continual process of ascent, whether it is the Hegelian ladder or the ladder of polysemous meaning. In the coda to Frye's essay "On the Bible," he actually identifies the dialectic with ascending the ladder, this time Jacob's: "[P]ursuing the dialectic of belief and vision until they merge is the first step on the ladder that Jacob saw in his vision: the first entrance into the *mysterium tremendum,* a mystery that is really a revelation, which is mysterious only because its revelation has no end" (*NFR,* 165). If belief and vision merge on the first step, they interpenetrate on the last one.

In his workshop notes for "The Dialectic of Belief and Vision," Frye writes, "The apocalyptic revelation at the end of the Bible presents all this simultaneously to the eye, as it were. . . . This is the stage of vision, the elevation of the host, the exhibition of the reaped ear of corn, where you stop believing things and simply 'see' what it all means."[44] Revelation follows elevation, one might say, and revelation is literally an unveiling. What is "seen" as a result is a function of imaginative energy. As Frye says in the opening paragraph of "The Dialectic of Belief and Vision," he is continuing his study of the role of the imagination in the study of religion.

The Imagination

Frye's poetics is clearly a Romantic poetics, forged from the prophetic works of Blake. Frye sees Romanticism as the most important cultural revolution in the Western tradition because it, more than (say) the Renaissance or the Enlightenment, turned upside down the Judeo-Christian and Greek cosmology, with its doctrine of creation and all the conventional structures of imagery in the great chain of being. In the pre-Romantic cosmos Frye's visionary poetics can be traced back to Longinian *ekstasis,* the state of being put out of one's place and transported into another realm altogether.[45] In the Romantic and post-Romantic cosmos his poetics is closely linked to Shelley's revolutionary views ("poetry redeems from decay the visitations of the divinity in man")[46] and to Martin Heidegger, from whom he borrows the idea of ecstatic metaphor. But it is from the nineteenth-century expressive tradition as we find it in Blake, Coleridge, Shelley, and Keats that Frye derives his theory of the imagination.[47]

No account of the importance of vision in Frye's work would be complete without reflecting on this central term in his poetics. The locus classicus for the subject is in chapter 13 of the *Biographia Literaria:* "The primary IMAGINATION," says Coleridge, "I hold to be the living Power and prime Agent of all human Perception, and as a repetition in the finite mind of the eternal act of creation in the infinite I AM." Here the two obvious powers Coleridge attributes to the imagination are perception and creation. Attached to the latter is the radically immanent idea that human creation repeats *the* Creation; human creation is, therefore, a divine activity, repeating what God does. In the only extended essay Frye ever wrote on Coleridge, he maintains, as against his colleague Kathleen Coburn, that the real coordinating principle in Coleridge is not the psychological one of the imagination but the religious and philosophical one of the Logos.[48] Frye may be wrong in claiming that in Coleridge the imagination is to be understood solely in psychological terms (others have made the case that Coleridge's "imagination" is a critical, poetic, and philosophical principle),[49] but he is in complete agreement with Coleridge that the imagination is the human power that permits us to see and to make. It is a perceptive and therefore a visionary faculty; it is a creative and therefore a constructive faculty.[50] In the notebook most fully devoted to exploring kerygma, Frye suggests that Coleridge's statement about the "eternal act of creation" is a metaliterary, kerygmatic text (*LN,* 1:369).

Frye did not have to turn to Coleridge, however, to understand the dual nature of the imagination. Coleridge simply provides an aphoristic account of what Frye had already learned from Blake, and he spends the first two chapters of *Fearful Symmetry* illustrating the importance of seeing and making in Blake's conception of the mind. From chapter 1: "If man perceived is a form or image, man perceiving is a former or imaginer, so that 'imagination' is the regular term used by Blake to denote man as an acting and perceiving being. . . . To be perceived, therefore, means to be imagined, to be related to an individual's pattern of experience, to become a part of his character" (*FS,* 19). All people possess imagination (what Coleridge calls the "primary imagination"), and for Blake the difference between those who see the sun only in terms of the simile, likening its fiery disk to a guinea, and those who see it metaphorically as a hallelujah chorus of the heavenly host is a difference in imaginative power: "more imagination has gone into perceiving it" (*FS,* 21). This is the visionary phase of the imagination. Again, from chapter 1 of *Fearful Symmetry:* Blake's "'All Religions are One' means that the material world provides a universal language of images and that each man's imagination speaks that language with his own accent. Religions are grammars of this language. Seeing is believing, and belief is vision: the *substance* of things hoped for, the *evidence* of things not seen" (*FS,* 28).[51]

Chapter 2 of *Fearful Symmetry* begins with an explanation of the way that Blake sought to overcome the gap in Berkeley's theory of perception, which was still based, like Locke's, on the separation of subject and object and on the wide distance between human and divine perception. In his annotations to Berkeley's *Siris* Blake wrote, "Man is All Imagination. God is Man & exists in us & we in him," and in his Laocoön engraving Blake said, "The Eternal Body of Man is The IMAGINATION. / God himself / that is . . . / The Divine Body / It manifests itself in his Works of Art (In Eternity All is Vision)."[52] Frye's commentary on these two aphorisms is as striking in its scope as Blake's is in its paradoxes: "Man in his creative acts and perceptions is God, and God is Man. God is the eternal Self, and the worship of God is self-development. This disentangles the idea . . . of the two worlds of perception. This world is one of perceiver and perceived, of subject and objects; the world of imagination is one of creators and creatures. In his creative activity the artist expresses the creative activity of God; and as all men are contained in Man or God, so all creators are contained in the Creator" (*FS,* 30). Here we have the doctrine of poetic Incarnation writ large, but in the context of our present inquiry into vision, the important point is to note the link between perception and creation. For Blake, as for Coleridge, these are the two distinguishing features of the imagination. The difference is that Coleridge does not directly identify divine and human creation: human creation *re-*

peats the "eternal act of creation." But for Blake "Man in his creative acts and perceptions is God," and the creative power of the artist is what Blake meant by "vision" (*FS*, 25). As Frye says in *The Educated Imagination*, the imagination gives birth to vision and fosters it (151). Even in *Anatomy of Criticism*, where the emphasis on the formal structures of literature tends to overshadow its spiritual power, Frye can write, "The work of imagination presents us with a vision, not of the personal greatness of the poet, but of something impersonal and far greater: the vision of a decisive act of spiritual freedom, the vision of the recreation of man" (94). The perceptive and creative qualities of the imagination turn out to be not just closely linked but inseparable. As Frye wrote in the margin of Samuel Alexander's *Space, Time, and Deity,* "to perceive is to identify and hence to create."[53] Such aphorisms are themselves a function of the structure or *dianoia* of seeing: "The aphorism is a verbal *perception:* that is, it's a verbal analogy of a *Gestalt* perception. We often speak of it as a perception. And the quality I so admire in Burton and struggle for myself is verbal *outline,* a verbal analogy of powerful sketching that contains a great mass of facts" (*TBN*, 25).

Like Coleridge, Frye holds that the imagination is a unifying power. In the *Biographia Literaria* Coleridge speaks of the imagination as blending, fusing, balancing, and reconciling a host of opposing qualities. The imagination is a "synthetic" power that works toward a "spirit of unity,"[54] which is similar to Shelley's claim at the beginning of his *Defence of Poetry.* In "The Symbol as a Medium of Exchange" Frye also maintains that "imagination" is a unifying power. It enables the conscious faculties to unite with the unconscious ones, the language of feeling with the language of reason (*MM*, 36). Frye sees this unifying power most fully realized in the French *symbolistes*—in the completely symbolic peak experiences in Huysmans's *À rebours*, in Villiers de L'Isle-Adam's *Axël,* and especially in Mallarmé, who, after Blake, is perhaps Frye's greatest poetic hero. Mallarmé

> speaks in his letters of a symbolic death and resurrection that he has attained through his search for a pure poetry, and speaks also of the poet who creates in the teeth of *the* creation, so to speak, as though he were the vehicle of a holy spirit. "Man's duty," he says, "is to observe with the eyes of the divinity; for if his connection with that divinity is to be made clear, it can be expressed only by the pages of the open book in front of him." He also describes himself, in a letter to Cazalis, as "one of the ways the Spiritual Universe has found to see Itself, unfold Itself through what used to be me. . . . Mallarmé's symbolic world . . . is not a Platonic world above the physical one [as in the Romantics], nor a world of buried

treasure below it [as in the post–Freudians], nor a private world inside it [as in the other *symbolistes*]. It is the world where human creation comes to be, where meaning is, where chance is not abolished but where a world that within itself is not chance has taken shape." (*MM,* 39)

Mallarmé's world, in short, like the world of Rilke's *Duino Elegies* and *Sonnets to Orpheus,* is a completely metaphoric and symbolic world, a world where divinity can be expressed only by the poetic word. The word expressed and then heard means that the receptive ear is still integral to the visionary experience. As Frye notes, God "comes to us as a linguistic event" (*NFC,* 189), which is perhaps what he means by saying that words have "an incarnational context" for him (*RT,* 321). But the ear is a means to the ultimate end, what Sidney calls the "ending end" or *architectonike,*[55] which is spiritual vision. One of the meanings of "spiritual" (*pneumatikon*), at least in the New Testament, is "metaphorical" (*GC,* 56; *WP,* 119), metaphor being, along with myth, the primary agency of the visionary imagination. With the *symbolistes* and Rilke we have moved *beyond* the poetic, *beyond* what Frye calls the "hypothetical."

Beyond

Frye notes that most prepositions imply spatial relationships. When words like "up" and "down," "inside" and "outside," "ahead of" and "behind," "over" and "under" are used metaphorically, they express, or at least imply, concepts and diagrammatic structures of thought (*AC,* 335).[56] Frye's most extended application of this observation is in *A Study of English Romanticism,* where he illustrates that the difference between the pre-Romantic and Romantic mythological structures is a difference, among other things, in the spatial diagrams embodied in prepositions:

> For the quest of the soul, the attaining of man's ultimate identity, the traditional metaphors were upward ones, following the movement of the ascension of Christ, though they were there even before the Psalmist lifted up his eyes to the hills. In Romanticism the main direction of the quest of identity tends increasingly to be downward and inward, toward a hidden basis or ground of identity between man and nature. . . . Romanticism brought in a new mythological construction. We can still think of it as a four-tiered structure, but it is much less concretely related to the physical world as we ordinarily perceive it. What corresponds to heaven and hell is still there, the worlds of identity and of alienation, but the imagery associated with them, being based on the opposition of "within" and "without" rather than of "up" and "down,"

is almost reversed. The identity "within," being not purely subjective but a communion, whether with nature or God, is often expressed in imagery of depth or descent. (*SER*, 33, 46–47)

The power that prepositions have to reveal a structure of thought can be telling, as in the difference between "within" and "among" as translations for *entos* in Luke 17:21, mentioned in the previous chapter.

Turning Frye's principle back on his own writing uncovers prepositional metaphors everywhere, such as this typically Romantic one: "The function of art is to awaken faith by making us aware of the imaginative world concealed within us" (*RT*, 246). But the most revealing preposition in Frye's religious quest is "beyond," a preposition that takes on special significance only late in his career. During the last decade of his life he uses the word repeatedly as both a spatial and a temporal metaphor. Having arrived at a particular point in his speculative journey, over and over he reaches for something that lies *beyond*. Notebook 27 (1985) begins with a series of speculations about getting to a plane of both myth and metaphor beyond the poetic, and Frye even confesses that there is no reason at all to write *Words with Power* unless he can get to that plane (*LN*, 1:67). The Bible implies that there is a structure beyond the hypothetical (*LN*, 1:8, 14). Many things are said to be beyond words: icons, certain experiences, the identity of *participation mystique* (*LN*, 1:15, 16).

"Faith," Frye writes, "is the recurring sense of revelation, i.e., an existential reality beyond the hypothetical. This revelation is the vision of a 'new' creation—new to us, that is. Such a faith, if attained, redeems and justifies all literature" (*LN*, 1:14). Or again, "On one side of the metaphor is ecstatic identification, the mob frenzies of the Bacchanals, the self-hypnotism of the shaman, the hysteria of the sorcerer. Then comes the ironic distancing of the hypothetical poetic metaphor. On this level art is possessed: it doesn't take possession. But beyond this is the counter–ironic aspect of metaphor, the sense of revelation recaptured by a (spiritual) community which is what the word 'gospel' is all about" (*LN*, 1:16).[57] The kerygmatic announces a world that is beyond speech and beyond the duality of experience and understanding (*LN*, 2:715). In a half-dozen passages in *The Great Code* Frye uses "beyond" in the sense of something (God, eternity, verbal revelation, dialectic, levels of vision) that is out of reach or far from being comprehensible in our ordinary temporal and spatial existence.[58] Similarly, in *Words with Power* he writes in another half-dozen places of going beyond the imagination, beyond time, beyond myth, beyond ordinary common sense, beyond the creative process.[59] "All mythology," writes Susanne Langer, "requires the notion of a 'Beyond.'"[60]

In *The Double Vision* Frye uses the word only once in this sense: "[W]e may speak of 'inspiration,' a word that can hardly mean anything except the coming or breaking through of the spirit from a world beyond time" (55).

The notebooks, however, are filled with expressions of Frye's desire to reach a world that lies *beyond,* as in this sampler, with italics added:

[L]iterature is the obvious guide to whatever passes *beyond* language, just as Dante's obvious guide to states of being *beyond* life in 13th c. Italy was Virgil. (*LN,* 2:717)

The kerygmatic, whether the Vico-Joyce thunderclap or the Blakean "Awake, ye dead, and come to Judgment!," is presented as verbal, but it's really announcing a world *beyond* speech. (*LN,* 2:715)

Where religion & science can still get together is on [David Bohm's] conception of the objective world as an "unfolding" of an "enfolded" or unborn order, which is *beyond* time and space as we experience them. (*LN,* 1:105)

The perspective of prophecy as seeing the direct challenge of what lies *beyond* (one's own) death. (*LN,* 2:474)

Theseus' lunatic & lover are behind the poet, suggesting an existential identity *beyond* the literary kind. (*LN,* 1:107)

The quest as question is of course future-directed, & its ultimate answer, which goes *beyond* any origin or first-cause answer (as in Job), is resurrection in the present. (*TBN,* 223)

There's a good *beyond* good-and-evil, a life *beyond* life-and-death, and a heaven or presence *beyond* heaven-and-hell. (*RT,* 213)

[T]he risen Christ as one with the Spirit in man, leading us into a world *beyond* the natural world of time and place. (*LN,* 2:667)

The third chapter [in *Words with Power*] goes *beyond* space into the conception of interpenetration, the fourth one *beyond* time into the conception of "mystical dance," or time as interiorly possessed contrapuntal movement. (*LN,* 2:558)

Altogether there are some seventy-six notebook entries, all but fourteen of them in the *Late Notebooks,* that contain the word "beyond" as a signal of what in *The Critical Path* Frye calls the "third order of experience," an order beyond the dialectic of freedom and concern (170). Like Tennyson's Ulysses, who wants "To follow knowledge like a sinking star, / Beyond the utmost bound of human thought," Frye keeps struggling to reach beyond the limits of imaginative desire. In *The Educated Imagination* he writes, "Religions present us with visions of eternal and infinite heavens or paradises which have the form of the cities and gardens of human civilization, like the Jerusalem and Eden of the Bible, completely separated from the state of frustration and misery that bulks so large in ordinary life. We're not concerned with these visions as religion" (29–30). But he is clearly concerned with such visions as religion in his notebooks and, as we continue to see, in much else that he wrote.

For Frye there seems always one more rung on the ladder to be climbed. The process of going *beyond* is another example of the Hegelian *Aufhebung.* For Hegel, as we have seen, Spirit can know itself as Spirit only when it comes to embrace both the *in itself* and the *for itself.* Such knowledge is Absolute Knowledge, the point at which Hegel arrives after five hundred pages of torturously opaque prose, having moved from self-consciousness through reason and spirit until he reaches the end of his quest.[61] For Frye, the goal of the ascent up the *axis mundi* is Absolute Vision. "Perhaps," writes Frye, "we can eventually get past [Blake's tiger] to some vision of creation which will include his glowing and sinister splendour. But such a vision of creation would have to be at the end of a long journey to somewhere on the far side of the tiger" (*NFR,* 70). Still, this "far side" is neither a space nor a place. Although Frye keeps saying that the ultimate vision is beyond language and beyond speech, he nevertheless doggedly persists in tying to name and to give content to that which lies *beyond.* The name ordinarily turns out to be one of his familiar single-word designations: kerygma, revelation, enlightenment, apocalypse, interpenetration. The content is all of the meanings associated with these terms, such as those linked with "interpenetration" or *anagnorisis.* Such language is the language of *Heilsgeschichte,* which offers a perspective "beyond imagination" (*NFR,* 21).

The persistent effort to move *beyond* is, as just indicated, typical of Frye's late work. We can see the *Aufhebung* at work, for example, in the first half of *Words with Power,* the four chapters of which have dialectical pairs in their title: sequence and mode, concern and myth, identity and metaphor, and spirit and symbol. At the end of each of these chapters Frye advocates going *beyond* the dialectic that he has established. At the end of chapter 1 he speaks of the need for "wider verbal contexts," of finding "an open gate to something else" beyond the limitation of language (27, 29). This something else turns out to be the "intensifying of consciousness," the *Aufhebung* that takes the theory of language with its four modes and the sequence of their excluded initiatives to another level.

Similarly, at the end of chapter 2, what emerges from the dialectic of concern and myth is the entry of the "personal" into myth and into "history's dream of revelation," and the *Aufhebung* carries Frye to the "principle of going beyond myth" (62). Chapter 3 concludes with a gloss on Tom o' Bedlam's song, where Frye urges "a further stage of response": after the *mythos-dianoia* dialectic "something like a journeying movement is resumed, a movement [*Aufhebung*] that may take us far beyond the world's end, and yet is still no journey" (96). Finally, the end of chapter 4 resolves the antithesis between the human subject and divine object, between the creation of Genesis and the new creation of Revelation by the *Aufhebung* of the Incarnation, "which presents God and man indissolubly locked in a common enterprise" (135). In each of these cases we are lifted to a level beyond the terms of the dialectic, the terms themselves being preserved while their opposition is canceled. And in each of these cases the end, in the sense of both the termination and the goal, is an expanded vision.

Recognition

If "beyond" is the most telling preposition in Frye's poetics, "re-," in all three of its senses (again, back, and against) is its most telling prefix. Thus we have a series of words, all connected to some extent with the word "religion" (to bind again),[62] appearing repeatedly throughout Frye's work: "recover" (to receive again), as in the phrase "recovery of projection" or "recovery of myth";[63] "recreate" (to form anew in the imagination); "renewal"; "reversal" (turning back); "resurrection" (rising again); "rebuild" and "reconstruct"; "repetition" (going back, seeking again), in Kierkegaard's sense; "renewal"; "revolution" (rolling back); "return"; "regenerate" (to beget again); "reconstitute" (to set up anew); "rebirth"; "response" (promising or replying again); "redeem" (to take or buy again); "regain" (to earn again); "resemble" (to be like again); "reconciliation" (restoring, conciliating again); "revive" (to live again); and "revelation" (against covering or veiling). All these words are embedded in Frye's disposition to privilege the conventional, the radical in its sense of foundational roots, the original in its sense of returning us to beginnings, and the traditional as opposed to the individually talented. The condition of being in a lost paradise requires the return of Eden. This key disposition in Frye is not nostalgia for the Golden Age but a concern for what is primary. The "re-" word most directly connected with vision is "recognition."

We have spoken already of recognition scenes, especially in connection with the movement from oracle to wit. "To recognize" means literally "to know again," but like many other words having to do with knowledge, it figuratively means "to see." Recognition (*anagnorisis*), a central category in Aristotle's theory of dramatic tragedy, is a fundamental component of Frye's visionary world. In his definitive study of recognition as a poetic category, Terence Cave sees recognition as lying at the very center of Frye's literary theory.[64]

In the Third Essay of *Anatomy of Criticism* Frye represents his four central literary forms—comedy, irony, tragedy, and romance—as parts of a single, universal story or monomyth, which he calls the quest-romance. The central theme of this story is the killing of the dragon, and the ritual analogy to such a story is connected to the myth of the dying god. This myth has four aspects, which are connected with the four central *mythoi*:

agon (conflict)	the archetypal theme of romance
pathos (suffering or death)	the archetypal theme of tragedy
sparagmos ("tearing to pieces")	the archetypal theme of irony
anagnorisis (discovery or recognition)	the archetypal theme of comedy

We find this myth in a variety of forms in Western literature, but the myth always has the same general shape, having to do with the disappearance and return of a divine being. The various forms of literature are episodes, and all the episodes add up to the monomyth. In the Gospel narrative, for example, the tragedy of Christ's Crucifixion is part of a larger comic structure which is resolved in the Resurrection, the final rebirth and recognition scene: "[T]he gospel is the world's great recognition scene" (*RT,* 324). And for Frye one cannot "develop a serious belief in either a salvation or an enlightenment religion without accepting the validity of the comic structure" (*TBN,* 29).

In *Anatomy of Criticism* and much of his other published work Frye often uses *anagnorisis* in the conventional or Aristotelian sense of an element in the plot whereby characters come to discover or recognize something about themselves they did not previously know, the discovery involving a movement from ignorance to knowledge.[65] For Aristotle, the recognition, if properly handled, will evoke the emotions of pity and fear in the audience, but the recognition itself is something that happens to heroes and heroines. But more often than not, Frye greatly expands the structural or centripetal usage in Aristotle, as he does with his other adaptations of terms from the *Poetics*. Here, for example, is Frye's definition from the *Harper Handbook to Literature*:

> *Oedipus Rex* begins with the king determined to discover why his land is suffering from a drought: the reader or audience assumes that his discovery of the reason will end the play. He eventually discovers that *he*

is the reason; he has killed his father and lives in incest with his mother. Two things are involved here: one is "reversal" (*peripeteia*), or sudden change in fortune; the other is "discovery" (*anagnorisis*) [*Poetics*, 10, 11]. The word *anagnorisis* could also be translated as "recognition," depending on how much of a surprise it is. In some plots, such as those of detective stories, the *anagnorisis* is a discovery, because it is a surprise to the reader; in others, such as those of most tragedies, it is a recognition by members of the audience of something they have come to realize long before, though it may still be a surprise to the chief character.[66]

In this definition we move from Oedipus's discovery and our assumption that it will complete the parabolic shape of the story to our own discovery as readers or members of an audience—with the additional distinction, which Frye also makes elsewhere, between the two usual translations of *anagnorisis* as "discovery," referring to a new awareness by the audience, and "recognition," referring to knowledge the audience has had all along.[67] Here, recognition has become an entirely functional and centrifugal concept, far removed from its structural sense in Aristotle. Frye, so to speak, recognizes this himself: "Functional analysis belongs to anagnorisis alone" (38.9). At one point he makes the connection between *anagnorisis* and the reader by speculating that *anagnosis,* the word ordinarily used in the New Testament for the reading of the scriptures, "is derived from *anagnorisis,* which I believe also can mean reading" (54–6.16).[68] Another intriguing suggestion Frye makes, not found in Aristotle, is that the recognition in tragedy is individual and subjective and in comedy social and objective (7.261). This is still an internal distinction, referring to what happens in the plot, though it does not necessarily involve a movement from ignorance to knowledge.

But when we turn to Frye's unpublished works, where the word *anagnorisis* appears repeatedly, we find the meaning of recognition expanding in a number of directions.[69] In one diary reflection about the experience of hearing the Bach B Minor Mass, Frye uses *anagnorisis* to describe what in *Anatomy of Criticism* he calls the anagogic experience:

> The B minor Mass was a glorious performance. . . . Though a very Protestant mass, with the weight thrown on the Kyrie & the Credo, it's pure revelation, & that's why it's so brilliant & buoyant. It's such a contrast to the Beethoven mass, where the predominant feeling is mystery, & the big climax is the Messianic Benedictus, which is dependent on a violin solo. Bach takes mystery in his stride: the key word of the mass, for him, is "gloria," & he gives you pure mandala vision. He's also given the real meaning of sacrament, which is commedia, recognition, anag-

norisis, epiphany. It's the exact opposite of sacrifice: in sacrifice, which is tragedy, something is killed: in sacrament something is brought to life. That something is the real presence of a single mind which contains both the Mass & the participating audience. No external God can be adored with music He did not compose. (*D*, 324–25)[70]

Here the visionary or perceptive experience is an epiphany of the ear, but the recognition is still a matter of figuratively seeing. "Emblematic focus," he says, seems to be the radical of recognition."[71] But recognition of the "real presence" is as paradoxical as the counterlogic of the Incarnation: "This doctrine of epiphany is important to me because the visibility or appearance of God, who is practically by definition invisible, seems to me a more momentous paradox than the alternative form of stating the same paradox: God becomes man in the Incarnation. Perhaps epiphany is to pneuma what incarnation is to logos: the everlasting gospel again" (*RT,* 322).

At times Frye speaks of *anagnorisis* as the reader's perception of the total shape of the tragic plot—a parabola formed by the rising action (the *desis* or complication) through the peripeteia to the falling action (the *lysis* or solution) (13.95).[72] "Recognition of *total shape* (anagnorisis)," he writes, "is crucial" (37.43), the linear experience of *mythos* now having become spatialized as *dianoia.* "Seeing" as a metaphor for what Frye calls the "final act of understanding the whole" is an observation about structure, but for the ideal presence of this final act he says that he actually prefers the term *anagnorisis* to "structure" (*MM,* 6). Recognition is like interpenetration, he writes, because both involve the surrender of the ego.[73] *Anagnorisis* is what gives coherence to a work of literature, but in life it is "the moment of truth" (*LN,* 1:356). Given Frye's boundlessly analogical habit of mind, it is an easy step for him to associate the structural coherence of the parabola with a cycle, for the *anagnorisis* takes us back to the beginning, as in the movement in the epic, which begins in the middle and moves back to the beginning, "which are, more or less, the same point" (35.135, 137).

Frye's next expansion—not quite so easy a step perhaps—is to see the recognition pattern in terms of renaissance, rebirth, and repetition: "[B]oth repetition & efflorescence seem to combine in *anagnorisis,* the recognition of the end as like the beginning" (42.135). Or again, Kierkegaard's "repetition is really Aristotle's *anagnorisis,*" he writes in one notebook (36.97).[74] In another notebook, *anagnorisis* is said to be "the recovery of *memory*"—Plato's *anamnesis* (35.42). Frye was fascinated by the implications of Kierkegaard's repetition, and in *The Great Code* he links the idea to Plato's *anamnesis:* "Kierkegaard's very brief but extraordinarily suggestive book *Repetition* is the only study I know of the psychological contrast between a past-directed causality and a future-directed typology. The mere attempt to repeat a past experience will lead only to disillusionment, but there is another kind of repetition which is the Christian antithesis (or complement) of Platonic recollection, and which finds its focus in the Biblical promise, 'Behold, I make all things new' (Revelation 21:5)" (*GC*, 82).

Here Frye is moving toward the idea of *anagnorisis* as religious vision, and in a number of places he makes the identification explicit. In *The Return of Eden,* for example, he remarks, "Epiphany is the theological equivalent of what in literature is called 'anagnorisis' or 'recognition'" (*RE*, 143).[75] Similarly, the teleological movement of romance away from fantasy, which has no end beyond itself, is a movement of recognition that turns into revelation or epiphany:

> If I look at my circle of dramatic genres, I see four zones in it, epiphany, spectacle, mimesis & irony, the middle two being archetype & allegory. These are the Eden, Beulah, Generation & Ulro forms of art. Art begins in Beulah with the romance, & as it ages goes into realism & Generation. There are two ways of hypothesizing: fantasy, or the use of a let's pretend world, and selection, & these two give us the middle terms. But fantasy as an end in itself lacks a teleological point: this is anagnorisis or revelation (epiphany), the thing revealed being the infinite form of the innocent world, the form of work. The emergence of this from romance raises romance to scripture, & as the real presence of this world is the central teaching of all religions worth anything, we learn about it mostly from religious literature. The arrival at epiphany is the end of the quest, the consummation, a new birth, a marriage & a fertile fuck all identical with the burning of experience. (7.199)

Here *anagnorisis* marks the point of the movement from word to spirit, "raising" literature to the "real presence" found in scripture.

In Notebook 11b Frye writes, "Recognition means both discovery of the new & *recognition* of the old. The latter is the total comprehension of the work or spectacular apocalypse; the former is the absorption into the personality. But this identifies recognition with imagery, not with narrative. Perhaps there's a stage of identification that bridges the gap between reversal (of *movement*) and recognition. I'm looking for a Mosaic or Pisgah view, the first or preliminary apocalypse" (11b.37). The Pisgah view is what Frye would later call the panoramic apocalypse, and this stage of *anagnorisis* is, as he remarks, "still incomplete without the rebuilding of Jerusalem" (11h.23). He completes the pattern by postulating a second stage or level of *anagnorisis*, which is the participating or existential apocalypse. This second level is found in four different places in Frye's notes for his ogdoad project in the mid- to late 1960s, when he was energetically formulating scheme after scheme for his projected "third book." The six and seventh books of this unfulfilled project were to be what he called "two gigantic anagnorisis summaries" (*TBN*, 133). They are labeled "Anagnorisis I" and "Anagnorisis II" in an outline for the ogdoad that Frye jotted down on the inside front flyleaf of Notebook 45, and in a similar form of the outline that appears in Notebook 19, written about the same time (*TBN*, 85), "Anagnorisis I" is associated with the encyclopedic vision of plenitude and education as a quest myth, and "Anagnorisis II" with wisdom and religion. Twenty-three entries later Frye worries about his use of the word, saying "the anagnorisis *has* to be literary, not with an eye swivelling out to education & religion" (*TBN*, 89), although he immediately recurs to the two phases of *anagnorisis* with still another prospectus for the ogdoad in which the six and seventh parts are projected as follows:

> The Anagnorisis, Phase One . . . The commedia of Eros in Plato & Dante; Shelley & Hegel; the symposium & the triumph of dialectic. . . . The Anagnorisis, Phase Two . . . The Bible & the final commedia: the double gyre with the dead; rephrasing of [the *agon*] in terms of total identity. (*TBN*, 89)

In one of his eight-part compass diagrams Frye locates apocalypse at the northern point of the circle, where it is coincident with the birth of God, and he comments that *anagnorisis* or recovery is connected with this stage of the hero's quest. This is also the stage of the rebuilding of Jerusalem, and "rebuilding the Temple is putting the body of Christ together again, making one body out of a society. But it must be a spiritual body" (*LN*, 2:716).

Frye eventually favored "apocalypse" over *anagnorisis* for characterizing the penultimate and ultimate stages of the quest, but the differences in language are not important; for in the vocabulary of Frye's religious speculations *anagnorisis* is interchangeable with apocalypse (as in 7.279 and 8.248), revelation and epiphany (as in 7.199 and *RT*, 34), rebirth (as in 6.39), the reversal into the vision of Logos (as in *LN*, 1:139), the place where death is destroyed (as in *TBN*, 82), and spiritual self-discovery (as in 7.261). What we have discovered about "discovery" is another example of a movement from literature to religion. Frye's appropriation of Aristotle's poetic term moves up through a series of elaborations to the level of interpenetration, where poetic vision becomes spiritual vision, although given the *Aufhebung*, the former stages are never canceled.

This is the vision embodied in *Oedipus the King*, already mentioned in connection with the vortex of recognition. At the level of literary *anagnorisis* Oedipus discovers who murdered King Laius, and he comes to recognize that he is guilty of parricide and incest. But if we leave the story at that, we have only a detective story, and if Sophocles' play were only a murder mystery, then it would have long since disappeared into the dustbin of history. Something else in the play is compelling, and this something else is the vision Oedipus has at the moment of recognition and reversal—the moment he blinds himself and screams out against Apollo. This vision does not cancel our experience of the literary level; it lifts the detective story to another level, forcing Oedipus now into the role of a cosmic detective. What Oedipus *discovers* at this level is difficult to articulate, just as it is difficult for Frye to articulate the content of what he calls moments of intensified consciousness. But surely it has to do with his awareness of both the limitations of his own human power and with his hope, even when he feels most polluted and helpless, that genuine self-knowledge and social enlightenment might come to him if he patiently endures the suffering he must undergo. Although Frye doesn't use the word *paravritti* in connection with any of his speculations about *anagnorisis*, he would doubtless consider Oedipus's recognition to be a *paravritti*—the complete conversion of Oedipus's mind and soul at the moment of his deepest desolation. Finally, recognition is connected with the vision of love we examined in the previous chapter: "If the ultimate reality in the world is love, there can be no love without recognition. . . . Every individual turns out to be a functioning community. And if everything is community, and love is reality, love must include recognition, which is also discovery, anagnorisis. Recognition is the 'moment of truth' in a real and not a slang sense" (*LN*, 1:356).

The survey we have been making of the different meanings that cluster around *anagnorisis*, especially as the word is used in the notebooks, can perhaps help us better understand Frye's remark, confirming the centrality of recognition in his own approach to literature, "Much of my critical thinking has turned on the double meaning of Aristotle's term *anagnorisis*" (*WP*, xxiii); better understand his comment in Notebook 24 about one of the reading assignments he had been given, "As always, my approach was through *anagnorisis*" (24.209); better understand his very early observation that while Milton and Bunyan were the great Protestant poets of the *agon*, Blake was the great Protestant poet of the *anagnorisis* (5.22);[76] and better understand, finally, the concluding sentences of his last and posthumously published book: "In the double vision of a spiritual and a physical world simultaneously present, every moment we have lived through we have also died out of into another. Our life in the resurrection, then, is already here, and waiting to be recognized" (*DV*, 85).[77]

Seeing the World: The Double Vision

Vision is, of course, a metaphor in the contexts we have been considering, imaginative and otherwise. Vision for Frye leads, or should ultimately lead, to what he refers to often in his later work as expanded consciousness. This is the moment of intense perception or, in Blake's terms, the power to see the world with a twofold vision:

> For double the vision my Eyes do see
> And a double vision is always with me:
> With my inward Eye 'tis an old Man grey;
> With my outward eye a Thistle across my way.[78]

When such inward or metaphorical perception takes place, "the whole world is humanized" (*DV*, 23). Seeing only the thistle is an example of a conscious, single-vision subject looking at a natural object. But

> metaphor, as a bridge between consciousness and nature, is in fact a microcosm of language itself. It is precisely the function of language to overcome what Blake calls the "cloven fiction" of a subject contemplating an object. . . . Language from this point of view becomes a single gigantic metaphor, the uniting of consciousness with what it is conscious of. This union is Ovid's metamorphosis in reverse as it merges with articulated meaning. In a more specifically religious area this third order would become Martin Buber's "Thou," which comes between a consciousness that is merely an "I" and a nature that is merely an "it" (*MM*, 115).

This union of consciousness and its object produces, in still another *Aufhebung*, the religious awareness of Buber's "Thou," and it comes to those possessed of a double vision, the phrase Frye used for the title of his last major writing project, *The Double Vision*. The book began as a series of lectures in 1990 at Emmanuel College, where he had completed his theology studies fifty-four years earlier. His plan was to make the assignment "one of my three-lecture books providing a pocket-sized summary of my GC [*Great Code*] and WP [*Words with Power*] theses, more particularly the latter, in the way that the Masseys [*The Educated Imagination*] were a pocket-sized Anatomy" (*LN*, 2:613). The three lectures were on the double vision of language, nature, and time. But when Frye came to publish the book he felt it necessary, "after considerable hesitation," to complete the argument by adding a fourth chapter on the "double vision of God" (xvii). The reason for the hesitation is uncertain. In the mid-1980s he remarks that if he were writing a book on religion he would call the Bible an "archetypal model of a perennial philosophy or everlasting gospel" (*LN*, 1:28). As a literary critic, Frye may not have wanted his last major writing project to culminate so explicitly with a religious accent. But he did write the book on religion (*The Double Vision* is subtitled *Language and Meaning in Religion*), and so his career culminates with that part of the ogdoad he had been brooding over for many years. The fact that Frye's last major writing project concludes with the double vision of God is, from the point of view of my thesis, not simply an appropriate but an inevitable final act of his quest.

Seeing with double vision hinges on what appears to be an oxymoronic phrase, "metaphorical literalism." But Frye's criticism, like the Zen koan, is driven by such paradoxical expressions. As we know from his theory of symbols in *Anatomy of Criticism* (and have glanced at in chap. 2), Frye reverses the ordinary meaning of "literal"—language used to convey descriptively accurate truths or to represent historical information without any ambiguity.[79] This would be the view implied by the expression "literal-minded" and asserted by the Biblical "literalist." The reversal of "literal" to mean "metaphorical" is perhaps anticipated in *Fearful Symmetry,* where Frye calls Blake a "literalist of the imagination," but Frye almost always uses "literal" in his study of Blake in the conventional sense, as a kind of meaning opposed to the symbolic or allegorical.[80] In his understanding of Dante's polysemous theory of meaning, "The ultimate significance of a work of art is simply a dimension added to its literal meaning" (*FS,* 121). But ten years later this has all changed: "The literal meaning of Dante's own *Commedia* is not historical, not at any rate a *simple* description of what 'really happened' to Dante," and Frye now conceives of literal meaning as a poem's centripetal meaning, the "inner structure of [its] interlocking motifs" (*AC,* 77). After still another decade Frye began to modify this view of literal meaning even further: his new understanding is one that equates the literal and the metaphorical. The first indication of his revised view comes in the late 1960s in Notebook 11f:

> The great cry on the cross ["My God, my God, why hast thou forsaken me"] seems less human when identified as a quotation from Ps. 22; the realistic detail of Judas' 30 pieces of silver less realistic when referred back to Zech. [11:12–13] & so on. But nobody takes the Bible literally

in this sense. "The Kingdom of Heaven is within you" [Luke 17:21]. We may disagree on what that means, but we all agree on what it does not mean: it does not mean, "literally," that the k. of h. is inside us in the sense in which the food we have just eaten is inside us. Consequently all discussion of the meaning of the sentence has to start with the interpretation of a metaphor. It is the same even with doctrine: Christ is God & Man; his body & blood are the bread & the wine, are doctrines expressible only in metaphor. It is the attempt to translate them into "literal" or reasonable language by such concepts as hypostasis that is not simple. (*RT*, 72–73)

Several years later Frye writes, "I'm getting through to something, I think: the secrets of Being can only be expressed in that Homeric phase of language in which the metaphorical is the literal. We can recapture this only poetically; but our poetic apprehension has to transcend everything we think of as literary into a new kind of super-'literalism'" (*RT*, 292).[81]

What Frye is "getting through to" is the direct identification of the literal and the metaphorical, the position he explicitly defends in *The Great Code*.[82] In *The Double Vision* he refers to this identity, first, as "imaginative literalism" (17, 18) and then as "metaphorical literalism" (69–74), the latter phrase deriving not from Dante but from the commentary on the *Commedia* by Dante's son Pietro.[83] Metaphorical literalism, the hinge referred to above, looks back to the literal-descriptive that is based on truth as correspondence. It looks forward to a literal-descriptive based on truth as coherence, which is the imaginative approach to the Bible or any other literary work. This is the single-vision and essentially passive approach. But the double vision takes us "beyond [that word again] the suspended judgment of the imaginative" (*DV*, 71). Thus, in the final manifestation of *Aufhebung* in Frye's writing, we learn that the genuine form of literal meaning, one that passes through the metaphorical level and thus enables us to see doubly, is spiritual meaning.

4 The East

That is not to say . . . that we can't learn infinitely and indefinitely from Oriental religions.

—*Northrop Frye in Conversation*, 195

I seize on every resemblance there is, invent a great many there aren't, and disregard all differences, determined to find an analogy in the teeth of the facts—not that there are any facts, of course.

—*"Third Book" Notebooks*, 211

Frye was always forthright in acknowledging the significance of the "mythological framework" he inherited. He was inescapably conditioned, he says, by the "cultural envelope" of the classical and Christian traditions of Western culture, the Methodist heritage of his upbringing, and his white, male, middle-class identity. The antifoundationalists, along with others more interested in difference than identity, refer fashionably to this commonplace as a social construction. The implication has often been that Frye was unable to step outside his Western conditioning to take a broader and more inclusive view of things, so that what we end up with is an insular, ethnocentric, and outmoded structure of thought— thus Jonathan Culler's attack on Frye for being a dogmatic religious ideologue and Terry Eagleton's for his being a middle-class liberal and Christian humanist.[1] While there can be no doubt that Frye was rooted in the tradition of Western liberal humanism in its classical and Christian forms, his notebooks reveal that he was more influenced by Eastern thought than is commonly imagined and thus able not simply to engage worlds outside his own cultural envelope but to assimilate their religious principles into his own worldview.

Frye's readers will be aware of the occasional references to the religion and culture of the East—from his comments on Zen Buddhism in *Fearful Symmetry* at the beginning of his career to those on Eastern techniques of meditation in his posthumous *Double Vision*—but no one would take such occasional comments as significant features of Frye's grand vision. In the *Anatomy* one runs across references to the Brihadaranyaka Upanishad, Chinese romances, the No drama, the *Mahabharata* and the *Ramayana,* Chinese and Japanese lyric poetry, and Lady Mura-saki's *Tale of Genji,* and Frye makes an occasional comment on the East-West connection in his other books.[2] In *A Study of English Romanticism,* for example, he calls attention to the similarity between Shelley's use of "interpenetration" in *A Defence of Poetry* and the apocalyptic visions of the Eastern poets (160).

But in most cases Frye is using these texts for purposes of illustration only, and if they were removed nothing much would be lost. Sometimes Eastern literature has a more functional role to play in Frye's argument, as in his use of *The Dream of the Red Chamber* and Kalidasa's *Sakuntala* in *The Secular Scripture* (103–9, 147–48). But in the published work Eastern literature is not at all fundamental to Frye's criticism. Similarly, with Eastern religion and philosophy: There are scores of references to Hinduism, Buddhism, and Taoism scattered throughout Frye's work, from *Fearful Symmetry* to the two Bible books. But his interest here is primarily in the occasional analogue; Eastern religion and philosophy lie on the periphery of his major concerns.

In the notebooks, however, the attraction that the East holds for Frye is considerably less marginal. Notebook 3, for example, contains extensive entries on the path of Patanjali's eightfold yoga, which Frye turns to in order "to codify a program of spiritual life" for himself (*RT,* 32). He also writes about other forms of yoga: Bhakti yoga, the path to the devout love of god, and Jnana yoga, the path of abstract knowledge. On the verso of the flyleaf of Notebook 3 is the neatly written entry "Paravritti of July 26/46," *paravritti,* Sanskrit for "the highest wave of thought," meaning, as we have seen, the complete conversion of the mind. Frye defines it in different ways: "epistemological apocalypse," "Wiederkehr [return]: the descent through & return through the vortex," the "reversal of the current . . . the notion inherent in conversion," a "revolutionary leap of sudden deliverance," "the regaining of liberty," and a "turning around."[3] *Paravritti* is another way Frye tries to capture the sense of apocalyptic reversal and recognition. He also has entries on bardo, the "in-between" state in Tibetan Buddhism that connects the death of individuals with the rebirth that follows. And the notebook includes several extended reflections on the Lankavatara Sutra, a key text, as we have seen, for Frye's understanding of interpenetration.

Frye was aware of the dangers of what he called the "cleaned-up versions" of Eastern religion, the kind that issue from extracting yoga or Zen from its own culture, and he kept in mind Coleridge's principle that we can distinguish where we cannot divide, meaning that he could differentiate, for example, between the Logos vision of Christianity and the Thanatos vision of Buddhism, Hinduism, Taoism (the "Oriental big three," as he calls them), and Confucianism. The Eastern religions have no clear sense of the resurrected spiritual body, of a personal god, and of the existential transformation that is found in Christianity outside its institutional forms. The focus of Buddhism, Hinduism, and Taoism is instead on what Frye calls the "evaporation" of the soul (*RT,* 180). Again, while there is a parallel between Jesus and the humble hero of the Tao-te Ching, "the supreme sacrifice of dying for the people does not appear to be anything that would appeal to a Taoist" (*DV,* 73–74). Frye makes no effort to reconcile these differences. Still, he claimed that we can "learn infinitely and indefinitely from Oriental religions" (*NFC,* 195). What, then, did he learn from three very different traditions of Mahayana Buddhism (the sutras, Zen, and the *Tibetan Book of the Dead*), from Hinduism (Patanjali's yoga and Kundalini), and from Taoism and Confucianism?

Mahayana Buddhism: The Sutras

Frye was familiar with several of the Mahayana sutras. He annotated his own copies of the Diamond Sutra and Lotus Sutras, and he was at least familiar with the Prajna–paramita Sutra. But the first two are never mentioned in the notebooks, and the last is referred to in Notebook 3 only in passing as the sutra on the void. The Lankavatara and the Avatamsaka Sutras, however, appear with some regularity in the notebooks and diaries. The Lankavatara Sutra ("Sutra on the Descent to Sri Lanka") is a Mahayana Buddhist text that stresses inner enlightenment, the erasing of all dualities, the concept of emptiness, and the truth of *cittamatra* or "mind only." The Avatamsaka Sutra is an extravagant and often ponderous text that stresses the identity of all things or the interpenetration of all elements in the world.[4] The Avatamsaka is the only Mahayana text Frye ever mentions in his published work. But there are forty-eight entries in the diaries and notebooks where Frye records his observations on one or the other of the two sutras. For all their complexity,[5] the Lankavatara and the Avatamsaka Sutras became for Frye, as he says in one notebook, "vade mecums of practical meditation" (*LN,* 2:714). Both sutras advance a form of absolute idealism, which has a Western analogue in Hegel's *Phenomenology of Spirit,* but the Avatamsaka presents it in a mode that is often concrete and metaphoric, whereas the Lankavatara favors an abstract, almost Hegelian mode over the symbolic.[6]

Sometimes Frye seems to regard what he finds in the sacred texts of the East as analogies of Western ideas, as when he observes that the Protestant conception of conversion, different from the straight line of Dante's *Commedia* or the parabola of rise and descent in tragedy, is like the vortex of transformation he finds in the Lankavatara: they are not identical, but they "point in the same direction" (*RT,* 21). Similarly, Frye sees in the miraculous power that often accompanies Eastern enlightenment an analogue of the miracles in the New Testament (*DV,* 55–56) and of Christian salvation without all the legalism that was never purged from the doctrine (*GC,* 105). At other times Eastern and Western conceptions seem to be practically identical for Frye. In the Buddhist conception of maya (the illusion of the phenomenal world which the unenlightened mind takes as the only reality) Frye finds both an affirmation and a denial of the law of noncontradiction, and he remarks that the "Christian conception of evil as the product of original sin & a fallen world is really exactly the same: the same combination of something that exists & yet cannot exist" (*RT,* 43–44). When identity rather than similarity underlies the East-West conjunction, the result is an insight that helps to define Frye's own position; in such cases Eastern ideas are constitutive.

Frye is wary of framing the connections in philosophical terms. He is attracted to the Lankavatara idea of *cittamatra* (mind only), but he finds that it "suggests pantheism to a Western mind" and that its parallel doctrine of *vijnaptimatra,* is "very like Platonic idealism" (*RT,* 46).[7] Still, Frye recurs to the Yogacara doctrine of "mind only" throughout the notebooks, not simply because it corresponds well to his holistic view of apocalypse but also because it helps to define it. *Citta* means generally the storehouse of thoughts and actions, and specifically, when used in conjunction with *matra,* it is synonymous with *alayavijnana,* "storehouse consciousness," or the fundamental consciousness of everything that exists. Frye's knowledge of *cittamatra* is indebted to Suzuki's technically intricate commentary, which comes down to this: *cittamatra* is both a psychological theory of the way the mind operates and an ontological and religious theory, the grasping of which enables one to get beyond dualistic ways of thinking.[8] In the Buddhist *citta,* Frye writes in an essay on Jung, "the self becomes fully enlightened by realizing its identity with a total self, an indivisible unity of God, man, and the physical world" (*NFCL,* 120).

But Frye is more interested in the ontological and religious theory, the initial postulate of which is a spiritual unity that transcends logic and the opposites found in all forms of dialectic. In reflecting on a novel he wants to write, he identifies *cittamatra* with the goal of the apocalyptic quest: "Ever since I read Dante, I have been fascinated by the possibilities of the ascent or anabasis form (less by the Inferno, because so many others, like Orwell and Sartre & Koestler, have done that better than I can do). I think vaguely of seven or eight metamorphoses on various levels of the spiritual world that a dead man's soul goes through, including a Utopia, a vision of Bardo, an apocalypse, and finally a withdrawal into the Lanka-vatara 'mind itself'" (*D,* 561). One of the goals of the apocalyptic quest is unified consciousness, and the emphasis on unity in *cittamatra* appeals more strongly to Frye than does the psychological half of the phrase, as we see in this extraordinary passage on the holism of total form, where the word "one" functions like a power-laden symbol of a secret mantra:

Anagogy begins with the postulate of the verbal *universe* & its corol-lary, the *one* word. Aristotle's physics leads to the conception of *one* mover at the circumference of the world. . . . To make sense of the shape of any subject, you have to assume an omniscient mind. No *one* mind comprehends the whole of physics, but the subject wouldn't hang together unless it were theoretically possible for *one* mind to compre-hend it, all at once. And if there is such a thing as "the whole of" physics, the subject must have an objective *unification* at its circumfer-ence. This *universal* mind is not God, in any religious sense, for it doesn't necessarily exist: it is necessary only as a hypothesis completing a human mental structure. . . . But the fact that the guarantor of all our knowledge is a *universal* mind, of which we can say only a) that we have no reason to suppose that it differs from other human minds except in the amount of knowledge it has, and b) that we have no reason to sup-pose that it "exists," certainly makes a lot of sense of the Lankavatara Yogacara doctrine [of *cittamatra*]. Anyway, the point is that allegorized bodies of knowledge assume an objective single or total form. The mu-sical *universe* leads to the *one* chord, the music of the spheres. The his-torical *universe*, or the *universe* of events, leads to the *one* event, or nature, that which is born, the *one* thing that is & has happened. The mathematical *universe* leads to the *one* number, or as we should say the *one* equation, which is what Pythagoreanism was all about. The philo-sophical *universe* leads to the Form of Forms, the *One* Idea. Similarly, literature, the verbal *universe*, leads to the *One* Word. I don't know yet how many of these *universes* there are, or how few they can be reduced to. Thus biology leads to *one* organism. Blake's Polypus, & Samuel But-ler's known God, the *anima mundi* who in Browne is the Holy Spirit, at the circumference of the biological *universe*. But that seems to disap-pear in the physical *universe*, where the *one* form is nature, the *one* organism plus the *one* environment. Also, where does the difference between the descriptive & the hypothetical disciplines come in? I've found only the word & the number. Nonsense: there's a musical *uni*-verse, & there should be a pictorial & a sculptural *one* & an architectural *one,* though the last three seem to disappear into the *One* Man who is *one* building. Certainly it's important that all social & political questions disappear in the *One* Man. . . . Chemistry, the analysis of the mixture of elements, lead[s] to *one* element at the circumference of the *uni*verse, in other words quintessence. This, if we identify quintessence with the elixir, which shouldn't be too hard, was the point about alchemy. Many of these *one*-form structures are superstitions, i.e., premature, but the development of modern sciences is in the direction of their original vision. (38.13; emphasis added).

This is Frye's reading of *cittamatra.* In the Lankavatara, *cittamatra* is the discarding of all discrimination in spiritual discipline, which for Suzuki is the ultimate goal of the Lankavatara.[9] In the passage just quoted Frye extends the principle to everything in the verbal universe.

In the Lankavatara the Buddha denies any number of dualities with repetitive insistence (for example, to select from a large catalogue of oppositions: birth and no-birth, being and nonbeing, oneness and otherness, bothness and not-bothness, existence and nonexistence, perceived and perceiving, evolution and cessation, individuality and generality, different and not-different). "The gate of highest reality," declares the Buddha in the Lankavatara, "has nothing to do with the two forms of thought-construction [subject and object]."[10] The Lankavatara in its dogged determination to preach the truth of *cittamatra* (mind only) insists on unity at the expense of everything else. One of the ways Frye sees this formulated in the sutra is in the difference between "not" and "non-":

> The fascination the Lankavatara has for me has something to do with my feeling that art is the zero of knowledge, the no-fact that turns out to be the essential fact, the unnumbered Fool of the greater trumps, my eighth book & Blake's eighth eye. There seem to be two antithetical forces here: there is the Hegelian dialectic of A and not-A, which leads to revolutionary dialectic action by turning ideas into half-ideas, truths into half-truths, in order to sharpen their cutting edge; and there is the cultural dialectic of spiritual authority, the dialectic of A and non-A, of "this is" and "let this be," the ultimate in conservation & the ultimate in liberality. Perhaps non-A will turn out to be the Kantian noumenon after all, except that the noumenon also "is." (*RT,* 66–67)[11]

. . . the statement A is never also not-A is true, as it asserts the eternity of form; but the statement A is never also non-A is bullshit. I learned that from the Lankavatara Sutra, produced by the same Indian genius that said: it is absurd & inept to imagine that no-number could also be a number. O.K. Let's see what happens when it does. The result was the discovery of zero, and all mathematics turns on similar postulates: a line, a thing of length without breadth, neither exists nor does not exist. That's the doctrine of Maya, the attempt to get off the Beulah mattress of a substantial or objective world. (*RT,* 43–44)

The distinction between the philosophical not-A and the spiritual non-A brings us back to the principle of identity, and the Lankavatara is written in a kind of primary-phase language based on identity. The Lankavatara, Frye says, "does not teach a doctrine but inculcates a mental attitude" (*RT,* 46). Thus it stresses not just hearing or understanding the word but "actually possessing it" (*RT,* 46), possession being one of the common metaphors in Frye (as we saw in chap. 2) for the mystery of metaphor itself, the complete identity achieved when A internalizes B and becomes one with it. For Frye the ultimate Christian metaphor is the Incarnation, and we have already noted that for him the Lankavatara Sutra "is based on a conception of a divine man" (*RT,* 46). Here is the mental attitude involved:

> When we read the history of Western philosophy we pass Aristotle & Plotinus & then find ourselves suddenly reading about "Christian" philosophers. Where did these Christians come from? Well, from Jesus. And what was his philosophical position? Well, he didn't exactly have one. Philosophy disappears into a vortex at that point. So with the Buddha here, who stigmatizes every attempt to make him define his "position" as "materialism," who answers all Mahamati's 108 questions by ignoring them all completely & then trying to make him grasp the mental attitude that will make answering them unnecessary. Buddha is not Mephistopheles, promising esoteric knowledge in exchange for your soul, & you can't talk to him in those terms. The Buddha is very subtle in analyzing the unconscious motive of panic in the desire to understand. Knowledge grasped at out of fear & bewilderment of ignorance remains grasped knowledge, that is, imperfect & inadequate knowledge. (*RT,* 47)[12]

Frye writes in the 1940s that he wishes he could get a good translation of "the Avatamsaka, or enough of it, & one of another Sutra, perhaps the one on the void [the Prajna-paramita Sutra], [so that he] might do a series of three essays called 'certain wise men'" (*RT,* 65). He was unable to get a translation until the mid-1980s, but he continues to refer, in four different notebooks spanning almost a decade, to his "Avatamsaka hunch."[13] This hunch, as we have seen, is an intuition about the universal decentralized vision and identity of interpenetration.

The one reference to the Avatamsaka in Frye's published work appears in the context of his explaining what he means by "the expanding of vision through language" and what Blake means by seeing a world in a grain of sand. This, Frye writes,

> would lead us to something like the notion of interpenetration in Buddhism, a type of visionary experience studied more systematically in Oriental than in Western traditions. The great Buddhist philosopher D.T. Suzuki gives an account of it in his study of the Avatamsaka or Gandavyuha Sutra, the Buddhist scripture that is most fully devoted to it. Suzuki speaks of it as "an infinite mutual fusion or penetration of all things, each with its individuality yet with something universal in it." As he goes on to speak of the "transparent and luminous" quality of this kind of vision, of its annihilating of space and time as we know them, of the disappearance of shadows (see Song of Songs 2:17) in a world where everything shines by its own light, I find myself reminded more and more strongly of the Book of Revelation and of similar forms of vision in the prophets and the gospels. (GC, 167–68)[14]

As for the essays on "certain wise men," Frye goes on to say that the "Preface would explain that I know nothing first-hand about oriental culture, & that experts who do don't need to read me. I'm just trying an experiment in the translation of ideas. That today we find both a lot of false antitheses about Eastern vs. Western thought & a general vague hunch that these antitheses *are* false" (*RT,* 65). Perhaps the phrase "an experiment in the translation of ideas" best describes what Frye is doing in Notebook 3. He is trying to translate rather than reconcile. A year after he wrote this notebook, Frye reviewed F. S. C. Northrop's *The Meeting of East and West* in the *Canadian Forum.* Northrop's goal was somehow to unify what he called the Eastern "immediate apprehension of experience," which he called "aesthetic," with the Western "theoretical construction made from experience." Frye thought that such a synthesizing project was doomed to fail, and he concluded the review by saying, "I imagine that whatever an Oriental philosopher tries to tell us about his Tao, his Citta, his Nirvana, his Brahman, he is also telling us, in Eastern language, that an intellectual and cultural synthesis that gets everything in and reconciles everyone with everyone else is an attempt to build a Tower of Babel, and will lead to confusion of utterance" (*NFCL,* 110).

But there is the gift of tongues as well as their confusion (if we do not try to reconcile all differences), as we see in this commentary on the Lankavatara Sutra, written when Frye was in his early thirties.

> The Lankavatara says there are three levels of understanding: imaginary or materialistic, interpenetrative, & detached. Learning a language by

laboriously boning it up is knowledge on the first stage; getting a swift intuitive knack or flair for languages belongs to Paratantra [interdependence]: the gift of tongues is on the third level.

One thing I didn't have too clearly in mind when I wrote the Blake book is that the total imgve. [imaginative] power we feel in a language or a religion is, like the Bible, sifted by tradition so that it is a cultural product, & a cultural product suggests imgve. totality as no one man can ever do. The individual's powers are limited & predictable, or if they aren't he soon passes out of range. But a big library really has the gift of tongues & vast potencies of telepathic communication. You can't "substitute art for religion" without making art include religion, & so recovering it from the individual or ego-centric sphere. That's really what I'm trying to do.

The 18th c. English philosophers, reflecting a mercantile civilization, thought of ideas as possessed things; Plato, reflecting a community, thought of them as an order to be entered. We have to disentangle ourselves from such subjects & objects. (*RT,* 52)

The detached vision, the gift of tongues, imaginative totality, escaping the ego-centric sphere, moving beyond subject-object distinctions, interpenetration, the three levels of understanding—these are themes Frye circled around for the next forty-five years, and in order to find the right verbal formulas he continually translated in his notebooks and diaries between East and West. Sometimes the translation is an analogue, a parallel, or what he calls a "counterpart" in *The Great Code* (xx). At other times the East-West dialogue clarifies or even helps to constitute Frye's thinking, as we see in this diary entry: "To think of light as created is to think of it as potentially lovable, its real source the Word that produces it. Thus the Christian idea of Creation turns out to be the same thing as the Eastern doctrine of Maya: the created world is not reality but manifestation, a fact that doesn't make it 'unreal,' of course. The same ambiguity is in Job's Leviathan, which means both creation and chaos. It looks as though I can hardly avoid a climax in the triumph of hypothesis over thesis, when the conceivable becomes our closest approach to the existent. That is getting increasingly clear as the goal of my speculations about Christianity, as it has always been my understanding of such things as the Lankavatara Sutra" (*D,* 497–98).

There is no question, in other words, that the hypothetical or conceivable does not mean the "unreal" in the Lankavatara, and it is this awareness that is urging Frye in 1952 to adopt a similar attitude toward Christianity, replacing Christian doctrine ("thesis") with an imaginative hypothesis. Frye says in one notebook that the Lankavatara is a religious scripture that provides techniques for the "breaking up and escaping from doctrines" (*LN*, 2:526; cf. 421). The Lankavatara also undermines the law of noncontradiction. It "continually insists on the distinction between hearing or understanding something & actually possessing it. It distinguishes words from meaning to such an extent that even 'all things are unborn,' after having been accepted as true earlier, is then denied as a statement. The thing it means is true, but its form is that of a thesis, with an implied negation or antithesis, & the Buddha will accept no statement of which an opposite can be predicated" (*RT*, 46–47).

Frye is clearly attracted to the holism he found in the Hua-yen metaphysics. Thomas Cleary sees the value of the Avatamsaka primarily in instrumental terms, saying that the Hua-yen philosophy

> may be considered not so much the establishment of a system of thought for its own sake or as an object of belief or ground of contention but rather as a set of practical exercises in perspective—new ways of looking at things from different points of view, of discovering harmony and complementarity underlying apparent disparity and contradiction. The value of this exercise is in the development of a round, holistic perspective which, while discovering unity, does not ignore diversity but overcomes mental barriers that create fragmentation and bias.[15]

Unity in diversity is the insistent theme throughout Frye's career, whether he is writing about the symbols, myths, archetypes, and genres of literature or about the modes of religious experience.

Mahayana Buddhism: Zen

The second major connection Frye makes with Mahayana Buddhism is through Zen, and here the emphasis is not on such metaphysical abstractions as *cittamatra* or such visionary principles as interpenetration but on the experience of enlightenment and the paradoxes embodied in the koans. An exoteric school of Mahayana Buddhism, Zen was a religion that sprang up in the sixth and seventh centuries in China, combining meditative practices (*dhyana*) and Taoism with an attentiveness to the Lankavatara Sutra.[16] But the word Zen is also used to signify an esoteric, mystical experience, not attached to religion. The scores of references to Zen throughout Frye's work, the large majority of which are in the notebooks, suggest that he was drawn to both the exoteric and esoteric forms. There seems to be no evidence that he practiced Zen meditation, but we know that he read fairly widely in Zen literature and its commentaries: of

the nine books in his library devoted exclusively to Zen, including three
by D. T. Suzuki, all are annotated.

Frye championed the view that both literature and religion provided
a critique of both pure reason and the cause-effect explanations found in
the single-vision paradigm. Zen, for Frye, was part of that critique. The
Zen paradox, he says in *The Great Code,* "enlightens the mind by paralyz-
ing discursive reason" (*GC,* 55).[17] In Notebook 33, where he speculates
on the various stages of prose, he writes that when we pass beyond the
stage of the aphorism and commandment, we enter the stage of the teacher
who doesn't write. At this point, he declares, "we find the koan of Zen
Buddhism, the paradox designed to arrest & break the flow of conceptual
causality, which also in Christianity would be identification with pure
Being, i.e., the creating Word whose commandments are dialectic axioms
for projected existence" (33.51). The emphasis in Zen on meditation and
silence and on the alazon-eiron dialogue between the master and the pupil,
and Zen's drive to recover spontaneity also appealed to Frye.[18] And he
turns to Zen not infrequently for illustrations and examples. In one notebook he refers to the story of the Buddha's holding up a golden flower at
the end of a sermon (*LN,* 2:590, 596). The story then gets used in *Words
with Power* as an example of the principle of metaphorical seeing (70), and
Frye used the story in four of his essays as well.[19]

But more than these, Zen is a way of achieving full spiritual vision.
Zen, Frye writes in one notebook, is one of the Eastern ways of entering
the world that the Resurrection stands for in Christianity. "It's a world
in which the dead from the past are redeemed and the future has lost its
remoteness, apocalyptic but not millennial. God is all in all there, not a
sovereign whom everyone wants to dethrone. . . . we should not think of
resurrection as a survival after death, but as an awakening from death,
which includes ordinary life" (*LN,* 2:657). Zen provides a way of reaching this world. Finally, in one of the elaborate schemes for the "three
awarenesses" summarized in Chart 6 (see appendix), Frye notes that the
highest development of the spiritual awareness might well be identified
with Zen (*RT,* 151).

Mahayana Buddhism: Bardo

In Mahayana Buddhism, bardo, a concept that dates back to the second
century, is the in-between state, the period that connects the death of
individuals with their following rebirth. The word literally means "between" (*bar*) "two" (*do*). The *Bardo Thödol,* or "Liberation through Hear-

ing in the In-Between State," distinguishes six bardos, the first three having to do with the suspended states of birth, dream, and meditation and the last three with the forty-nine-day process of death and rebirth. In *The Tibetan Book of the Dead,* which is the principal source for Frye's speculations on bardo,[20] a priest reads the book into the ear of the dead person.[21] The focus is on the second three in-between states or periods: the bardo of the moment of death, when a dazzling white light manifests itself; the bardo of supreme reality, in which five colorful lights appear in the form of mandalas; and the bardo of becoming, characterized by less-brilliant light. The first of these, Chikhai bardo, is the period of ego loss; the second, Chonyid bardo, is the period of hallucinations; and the third, Sidpa bardo, is the period of reentry.[22]

In recounting one of his Monday sessions with Peter Fisher in 1949, Frye writes, "[W]e went on to discuss the life-Bardo cycle. Normally we are dragged backwards through life & pushed forwards through Bardo, & attempt to find some anastasis at the crucial points, or else go through a vortex or Paravritti which leads us, not to escape, but to implement charity by going forwards through life, as Jesus did, & withdraw in retreat from Bardo" (*D,* 118). Here we have the fundamental dialectic so often encountered in Frye: the raising up (*anastasis*) or removal to another level (*Aufhebung*), represented by bardo, or the vortical descent, which is a turning away from what bardo represents. The anastasis is the moment of illumination—the timeless moment or the moment Satan can't find, to use the line from Blake that Frye repeatedly quotes.[23] This—the Chikhai bardo—is the resurrection (*anastasis*), or the ultimate recognition scene (*TBN,* 35), the apocalypse or the fulfillment of life:

> Nobody can move toward it [the *anastasis*]: inspiration, providence, instinct, intuition, all the metaphors of involuntary accuracy, including grace itself, are groundswells carrying us along in a counter-movement, forward to the moment. We go by relaxing ourselves, & trying to put ourselves in the organized receptivity, the "negative capability," of being ready to listen to or look at whatever comes along. If it never comes, that's not our business. If death brings it, as the Tibetans say, that's the point about death. But to have something shown you & then refuse to admit that you saw anything of the kind: that's the sin against the Holy Spirit of inspiration which is not forgiven (i.e. makes it impossible for you to arrive at release or anastasis) either in this world or the next (Bardo). You can't expect something, or you'll find an oracle in every spiritual breeze that passes over you; you can't expect nothing, or you'll have in yourself no principle of escape. (*D,* 140–41)

For Frye the context of bardo is often death. If the visions the soul encounters immediately after death are repressions from which it can be released, then, as Frye says in *The Great Code,* deliverance from the power of such repressions can occur immediately (137). In "The Journey as Metaphor" he remarks on the *Tibetan Book of the Dead* in the context of reincarnation:

> Here [in *The Tibetan Book of the Dead*] the recently dead soul is informed, by the reading of the book to him, that he will see a series, first of benevolent, then of wrathful deities, and that as all of these are hallucinations projected from his own mind, he should not commit himself to any belief in their substantial existence. In practically all cases the discarnate soul is assumed to wander in an intermediate world between death and birth known as "Bardo," until he is finally attracted to the female womb and enters it. Here again there is a continuing cycle within which all journeys take place. (*MM,* 220–21)

Frye's copy of *The Tibetan Book of the Dead* contains 240 annotations, including marked passages, and bardo is a subject he returns to repeatedly in his diaries and notebooks, even though he mentions it on only four occasions in his published work.[24] What exactly does bardo mean for Frye? Sometimes he uses the word simply to describe a moment of daily illumination—the "moment of opportunity to take the right direction," as he puts it in a marginal annotation.[25] One suddenly gets a sense "of the right thing to do, the courteous & beautiful act [Chikhai bardo], instantly smothered under a swarm of spawning Selfhood illusions of timidity, laziness, selfishness & the rest [Chonyid bardo], whereupon the moment of what we rightly call inspiration passes, and we return to the ordinary level of existence [Sidpa bardo]" (*RT,* 8). Or it might be the feeling of enthusiasm when we are unexpectedly confronted with something new (*RT,* 26). But more often Frye thinks of bardo as one of the metamorphoses the soul goes through in its journey to the spiritual world just mentioned. In one of his diaries he describes this journey in four stages: "Utopia, a vision of Bardo, an apocalypse, and finally a withdrawal into the Lankavatara 'mind itself'" (*D,* 561). Thus, bardo is one of the stages in the *mythos* of the spiritual quest. In one of Frye's more ambitious schemes—his plan for a book of one hundred sections—bardo represents the end of a cyclical process (sections 90–99) that moves toward the point of epiphany (*RT,* 131). Similarly, in his account of the quest romance in Notebook 14, bardo represents the recognition scene and final reconciliation (14.40, 51). It is linked with the Harrowing of Hell in Christian drama and with similar crises of spirit in other dramatic forms (8.47). But Frye also conceives of bardo as *dianoia*. In spatial terms, it is the land of Blake's Beulah, the green and golden world of faeries (7.90).[26] Or at least, Frye says, bardo may be able to makes sense of the world that survives in "in ghosts, fairies, gnomes, elves, the powers in Paracelsus, devils & demons, the world of magic & spiritualism, of divination & *astrology,* of automatic writing, poltergeists & controls," the "mezzanine" world of Yeats and Blavatsky (37.11), the mezzanine being, again, Blake's world of Beulah between the death of Generation (physical experience) and the rebirth of Eden (spiritual experience). It is also the world of Prospero's island, especially in the court party's demons of wrath (8.47). All these associations are of course metaphorical or, as one of his annotations has it, pictorial.[27]

Frye got glimpses of the Bardo world in Yeats, Gogol, Joyce, and William Morris.[28] These and other writers trigger the desire, which lasts for some years, of writing a bardo novel himself. He first entertains the notion in the 1940s, when he proposes writing a novel from the point of view of a dead narrator looking at the world—a supernatural novel, but one based on intellectual paradox and without morbidity (30m.20).[29] He writes that all of his fictional ideas

> tend to revolve around Rilke's idea of the poet's perceiving simultaneously the visible & the invisible world. In practice that means a new type of ghost or supernatural story, possibly approached by way of some science-fiction development. The idea is a vision of another life or another world so powerfully plausible as to make conventionally religious & anti-religious people shake in their shoes. I've begun notes on this many times, but threw away my best notebook, written in Seattle, in a London (Ont.) hotel. By "shake in their shoes" I don't mean threats, but the ecstatic frisson or giggle aroused by plausibility. (20.1)

By 1949 Frye has begun to find some models for such a work: Robert Nathan's *Portrait of Jennie,* a romantic fantasy about a young girl who, defying time, mysteriously vanishes and reappears, and Henry James's *A Sense of the Past,* an unfinished ghost story in which characters disappear from one century and resurface in another. When Frye discovers Charles Williams's *All Hallows' Eve,* a supernatural tale that explores a world parallel to our own, with characters, some dead and some alive, who interact with our own, he temporarily loses his ambition to write the bardo novel—Williams has already done it. But in 1962 the idea gets resurrected: "How the hell would one write a good Bardo novel?" Frye asks (2.13), and he then outlines in some detail the narrative of a character who prepares for death, does die, and wakes up in bardo not knowing that he has died but living in some vision of a liberated world. Just as *All*

Hallows' Eve had earlier dissuaded Frye from pursuing his fiction-writing project, so now the appearance of Katherine Anne Porter's *Ship of Fools* (1962) makes him realize, again, that he has been preempted. Thus he concludes, "My Bardo novel is not something to write, but a *koan* to think about and exercise the mind" (2.18).[30] And exercise his mind he does: once he has abandoned the novel project, he engages in a series of speculations about bardo.

Two aspects of bardo proved to be enigmas for Frye: its relation to purgatory, which he worries about in a dozen or so notebook and diary entries,[31] and what he refers to as chess-in-Bardo, a "will-o-wisp I've been chasing for thirty years" (*TBN*, 340). The in-between state of purgatory is the obvious Christian link: "Purgatory was invented by the R.C.Ch. [Roman Catholic Church] to bring Bardo into Xy [Christianity]" (*D*, 131). Frye appears to see purgatory finally not as a translation but as an analogy. It turns out to be too Catholic, and Catholicism always raises a red flag for Frye. He says, in any event, that purgatory is "an illegitimate adaptation of Bardo" (*D*, 142) and that bardo as a "hyperphysical form of the Church" leaps over purgatory by virtue of the vortex creed of Protestantism (31.52).[32]

As for the cryptic phrase "chess-in-Bardo," Frye associates chess throughout the notebooks and diaries with the theme of ascent and the world of romance—what he calls the Eros archetype.[33] Solving the "chess-in-Bardo problem," he writes, "will give some indication of what it means to live in a totally mythical universe" (*TBN*, 56). Frye circles around the "problem" throughout his notebooks, associating chess-in-bardo with the *agon* or contest, with the recognition scenes in *Alice in Wonderland*, *The Tempest*, and *Finnegans Wake*,[34] and with a vision opposite from that of the dice throw in Mallarmé (the Adonis archetype). By the time he came to write *The Secular Scripture* (1976) Frye had caught up with the ignis fatuus he had been tracking since the 1940s. In that book he provides a clue to the meaning of chess-in-bardo in a brief commentary on *Alice in Wonderland:*

> Alice passing through the looking-glass into a reversed world of dream language is also going through a descent. . . . Before long however we realize that the journey is turning upwards, in a direction symbolized by the eighth square of a chessboard, where Alice becomes a Psyche figure, a virginal queen flanked by two older queens, one red and one white, who bully her and set her impossible tasks in the form of nonsensical questions. Cards and dice . . . have a natural connection with themes of descent into a world of fatality; chess and other board games,

despite *The Waste Land,* appear more frequently in romance and in Eros contexts, as *The Tempest* again reminds us. As Alice begins to move upward out of her submarine mirror world she notes that all the poems she had heard have to do with fish, and as she wakes she reviews the metamorphoses that the figures around her had turned into. (155–56)

Chess-in-bardo, then, involves a dialectic of two opposing forces: *agon* and *anagnorisis,* choice and chance, descent and ascent. Neither of the opposite forces can abolish the other, for each has "its own centre" (*TBN,* 288), as in the magic of Prospero and its renunciation. Frye says that *The Tempest* leans in the direction of chess-in-bardo (*TBN,* 340). But at the same time, chess-in-bardo appears to be related to reversal, as in the ascent of Alice. "Chess in Bardo? Is it a modulation of dice in Bardo?" Frye asks. "A chess move is a decisive choice that may not abolish chance, but sets up a train of consequences that forces it to retreat into the shadows" (*LN,* 1:318). Chance may never completely disappear in chess, but each move works toward an eventual reversal. The entry in Notebook 50 following the one just quoted appears to be related: "Perhaps sacrifice is the carrying out of death *in reverse,* identification through death to union with God—well, obviously it's that. This identity with death turns into an identity across death" (*LN,* 1:318). This is another way of describing the movement from death to rebirth in *The Tibetan Book of the Dead.*

Frye writes that completing *Anatomy of Criticism* left him free to engage in unrestrained speculations about bardo (*TBN,* 190; 2.245; 20.10), which is a movement from structure to spirit and vision. What then is bardo? It is a link, to use one of Frye's favorite words, to a number of features in what he calls his "metaphysical cosmology" (19.92). It is a link with the reconciliation that emerges from the *agon* (*TBN,* 150; 2.81; 14.40), with "the opportunity for the inspired act" (*D,* 131), with the timeless moment (14.31), with a "plunge into another order of being" (2.19), and then with a movement toward the point of epiphany (31.85; *TBN,* 150), with "the archetypal dream-state achieved after death" (33.20), with the resurrection from Blake's Beulah world, and with the "vision of all forms as identified."[35] Frye almost always refers to bardo in a telic sense. It is not the end of the quest, as the dozen linkages with Beulah indicate, but it is a stage toward that end. Frye ordinarily speaks of it as the stage before Eden or apocalypse (*D,* 561; *RT,* 90). But if it is a stage in the universal story, it was also a stage in Frye's own life. Here is the way he puts it, using the editorial "we," in one of his early notebook entries on the bardo insight born of negative capability:

The Tibetans say that when you die you get a flash of reality (Chih-Kai [Chikhai] Bardo) that for everyone except a yogi saint is bewildering & unrecognizable, whereupon you pass into a plane of hallucination (Chonyid Bardo) & then seek a womb of rebirth (Sidpa Bardo). I don't know about after death, but it's an excellent account of all other crises of the spirit, & so may be true of that one. So often it happens in meeting someone who needs help & can be helped (or encouraged) there comes a sudden flash of the right thing to do, the courteous & beautiful act, instantly smothered under a swarm of spawning Selfhood illusions of timidity, laziness, selfishness & the rest, whereupon the moment of what we rightly call inspiration passes, and we return to the ordinary level of existence. It's only rarely that we even recall having such a moment, & perhaps the capacity for having them could be destroyed. One of the major efforts of all discipline is to unbury the consciousness of the moment that Satan can't find, as Blake calls it. Hence the importance of achieving spontaneity, Butler's unconsidered control. In social relationships we always admire the person who acts, to quote Blake again, from impulse & not from rules, and we assume, however unconsciously, that such impulses can be trained to achieve adequate & accurate expression. That is perhaps why Jesus stresses the unconsidered life—I'm not thinking of the lily passage so much as the instructions to the apostles not to rehearse their speeches. It is true, however, that the way of achieving such development is to concentrate on the present moment, which implies that all idealization or brooding over the past, and all idealization or worry over the future, are diseases of the soul—hence the lily passage. (*RT,* 8)

Yoga

One of the forms of yoga that figure importantly in Frye's notebooks, especially Notebook 3, is that of Patanjali, the founder of the Hindu yoga philosophy in the second century B.C.[36] Patanjali was interested, not in metaphysics, but in spiritual freedom through physical practices. In the 1940s Frye set out to follow Patanjali's eightfold path, devoting a number of pages of Notebook 3 "to codify[ing] a program of spiritual life" for himself (*RT,* 32). He does not get beyond the fourth stage—*pranayama,* the control of breathing—but he outlines in some detail what he proposes to do in the first three stages—*yama* (withdrawal from negative habits), *niyama* (concentration and proper timing), and *asana* (meditative exercises and postures) (*RT,* 32–37). Frye yearns for moments of withdrawal and concentrated attention, times when he can turn off what he later calls the incessant babble of the drunken monkey in his mind (*LN,* 1:161, 173,

236). He looks to Patanjali for almost purely personal reasons, feeling that the Yoga-Sutras provide sound advice on how to cleanse the temple of his own psyche, to overcome the timidity and irritability of his cerebrotonic self, to repair the weakness of his body, to defeat inertia, to establish a proper, relaxed rhythm in his life. Although he makes his way through only half of the eight stages ("genuine withdrawal, the pratyahara or fifth stage, is away out of my reach as yet" [RT, 34]),[37] Patanjali nevertheless provides him the occasion to engage in serious self-reflection and critique, and his interest in the posture and breathing exercises of zazen began early and appears to have continued for some years.[38] Here the East-to-West translation has to do with his own physical, moral, and mental habits. Frye does find analogues between certain Western ethical principles and Patanjali's *sattva,* the ideal of harmoniousness, uprightness, and composure—the noblest of the three *gunas* or fundamental qualities:

> Patanjali says Sattva, Castiglione (or Hoby), grace and recklessness, Aristotle the mean. All three mean what Samuel Butler means when he speaks of complete knowledge as unconscious knowledge. The first stage of awareness is a "morbid" self-consciousness of which schizophrenia is the opposite, as lunacy is the opposite of creating forms & conditions of existence & atheism the opposite of secular mysticism. Then comes, with practice and a continuous relentless analysis, a gradual overcoming of the rigidity begotten by this self-consciousness. (*RT,* 5–6)

But there is a speculative side to Frye's interest in yoga that goes beyond Patanjali's *raja* or royal yoga, and his less-personal speculations provide another example of the East-to-West re-creation. "I seem to be trying," Frye writes, "to interpret as much of the Gospels as possible in Yoga terms" (*RT,* 14–15). Here is one such interpretation:

> The Christian Gospel and Indian Buddhist systems associated with the word yoga seem to me to make sense of this process [of liberation from a fallen world], & perhaps the same sense. The advantage of using the latter is that Hindu Buddhist conceptions have for us fewer misleading associations of ideas left over from childhood, and the thunder of their false doctrines is less oppressive in our ears than the thunder of ours. . . . When Jesus speaks of "righteousness" the word is an English word . . . which in turn translates an Aramaic word I don't know translating a concept with a Hebrew background. I have to recreate it into something more like "rightness," but think how clear such a word as Tathagata is! (*RT,* 4–5)[39]

Frye is speaking here of Bhakti yoga, the path to the devout love of god.[40]
He associates Bhakti with both militant monasticism in Christianity and
with Western mysticism, and finds Bhakti to be wanting because it is too
partial and fragmentary, too much removed from the world (*RT,* 14–17).
It is "the expanded secular monastery I want," Frye announces, adding
that "there isn't much for me in high Bhakti, & Jnana if not Mantra . . . is
my road" (*RT,* 17, 19). He says little about Jnana yoga, but unlike Bhakti,
which relies on intuition and which for Frye remains on the Beulah level
of existence, Jnana is the yoga of the intellect, in a Platonic or Shelleyan
sense. *Jnana* in Sanskrit means "to know," and it has to do with both general knowledge and spiritual wisdom or illumination. Mantra is the form
of yoga that aims to achieve union with God through the repetition of
God's name. With the stress Frye puts on the repetitive rhythm of practice and habit, one can understand how he would be drawn to the principle, at least, underlying Mantra yoga. "Yoga," he says, "attaches great
importance to 'muttering' ritual forms (dharani) and to the working
word, the mantra or verbum mirificum," and the Western analogue he
finds is in the discipline of listening to music without any sense of "panic
& laziness" (*RT,* 6).

The problem Frye has with the yogas of whatever school is, finally,
that they have no place for art and no real theory of creation. He thus proposes to develop one, which he calls, reversing Patanjali's terms, Sutra-
Yoga. Such a yoga, Frye says, "would be identical with what I have been
calling anagogy" (*RT,* 21), a unifying principle that spiritualizes the law
(*RT,* 27). He explains the growing interest in poets such as Rilke and
Rimbaud as stemming from their having made "a yoga out of art"; they
"have employed art as a discipline of the spirit that takes one all the way.
Rimbaud is the great denier & Rilke the great affirmer of this aspect of
art" (*RT,* 23).

Toward the end of Notebook 3 Frye returns to the sense of calm
watchfulness he finds in Patanjali, combining it, in a rare third-person reference to his own approach to the life of the spirit, with the change in
consciousness that is always for Frye the end of the universal quest:

> The wind bloweth where it listeth, and thus the unconscious will is not
> on the same time clock as the conscious one, the S of U [Spectre of
> Urthona] which is always getting into a dither every time the clock
> strikes. We must not *do* things, but let them happen. This is the Chi-
> nese *wu wei,* Keats' negative capability, which imitates Milton's God in
> withdrawing from the causation sequence and simply watching with
> prescience. In Frye's thought this faithful watching is the literal appre-

hension of art, the willing suspension of disbelief which is the prelude to all understanding (at least all *detached* understanding). What the consciousness *can* do, perhaps, is take out the obstacles hindering the union of life & consciousness, the Indian yoga, the Chinese Tao (which means "head-going"). (*RT,* 61)[41]

The union of life and consciousness is a state of identity. Patanjali writes, "In the case of one the transformations of whose mind have been annihilated, the complete identity with one another of the cogniser, the cognition and the cognized, as well as the entire absorption in one another is brought about, as in the case of a transparent jewel." In his copy of the *Yoga-Sutras of Patanjali,* Frye underlined the word "identity" here and wrote opposite the reference to the transparent jewel, "world in a grain of sand."[42]

Frye's notebooks contain more than a dozen entries on Kundalini yoga, the Hindu form of yoga sometimes identified with Tantra.[43] *Kundalini* in Sanskrit means "snake" or "she who is coiled." The essential goal of Kundalini is to awaken, through purification rites, breathing exercises, and the practice of certain yoga positions, the spiritual energy or "serpent power" that is said to lie inactive at the base of the spine. When this power is awakened, it passes through six centers (chakras) along the spine, finally achieving the wisdom and bliss in the seventh center at the top of the head. Frye may have become aware of Kundalini from the passing references in Jung's *Psychology and Alchemy*[44] and from Jung's commentary on *The Secret of the Golden Flower,*[45] but the principal source of his reflections is Gopi Krishna's *Kundalini,* which he read in the late 1980s. In his 1990 notebook he writes, "I'm reading a book that impressed me, Gopi Krishna's *Kundalini.* The introduction writer says we in the West need a new vocabulary for spiritual reality, a thing I strongly felt in writing Chapter Four [of *Words with Power*]. . . . Even the commentary [by James Hillman] is rewarding" (*LN,* 1:353). Krishna believes that what the Indic texts refer to as Kundalini is actually a biological and psychological mechanism responsible for creativity and genius (it also has destructive and demonic manifestations) and that through certain spiritual practices we can activate this energy and reach states of expanded consciousness. Frye refers to this locked up energy as "the seed of the spiritual body" (*LN,* 1:357). He distrusts Krishna's evolutionary hypothesis, but he finds the process involved instructive, as we see in this notebook entry, written forty years before he read Gopi Krishna: "If nature is the fallen human body turned inside out, & if the true form of both is a human spiritual body, which we have to approach through ourselves & not through nature, then wisdom must be partly a growing of the fallen body into the spiritual form of itself. This is the principle of Yoga with its awakening of Kundalini" (7.56). For Frye, Kundalini, dependent as it is on the central image of the spine, is part of the symbolism of the apocalyptic ladder. In several notebook entries Frye calls attention to the serpent archetype;[46] this, and its kindred form the ouroboros, have symbolic import for him as well.[47] Beyond the archetypal significance, however, is Frye's speculation at one point that he might be a better visionary if he were suddenly awakened by the serpent power (*LN,* 1:173). This was doubtless only a wish-fulfillment fantasy, as whatever awakening Frye was able to achieve came through words (and the Word). Even though he says that "maybe religion today has to pass through the Oriental meditation techniques" (*LN,* 2:526), he was unable to invest in disciplinary meditation himself. Still, the awakening of Kundalini held for him a certain fascination as a form of higher consciousness, the articulation of which became the focus of so much of his late work. Kundalini became another Eastern verbal formula—part of the new spiritual vocabulary that Frederic Spiegelberg, in his introduction to Krishna's *Kundalini,* called for.[48]

Taoism: The *Tao-te Ching* and the *Chuang-tzu*

Frye's knowledge of Taoism and Confucianism came largely from the *Tao te-Ching,* which he read in Lin Yutang's translation,[49] from the *Chuang-tzu,* and from his two editions of the *I Ching.*[50] There were numerous secondary sources, including the books on Taoism in his own library,[51] Aldous Huxley's *The Perennial Philosophy,* various studies by Mircea Eliade in comparative religion,[52] and Francis Huxley's *The Way of the Sacred.*

The "Tao" for Frye is, among other things, one of the terms for trying to capture what is meant by "the totality of imaginative vision" (*LN,* 1:261). Among those other things is the metaphor of "the way":

> In the Bible "way" normally translates the Hebrew *derek* and the Greek *hodos,* and throughout the Bible there is a strong emphasis on the contrast between a straight way that takes us to our destination and a divergent way that misleads or confuses. This metaphorical contrast haunts the whole of Christian literature: we start reading Dante's *Commedia,* and the third line speaks of a lost or erased way: "Che la diritta *via* era smarrita." Other religions have the same metaphor: Buddhism speaks of what is usually called in English an eightfold path. In Chinese Taoism the Tao is usually also rendered "way," by Arthur Waley and others, though I understand that the character representing the word is

formed of radicals meaning something like "head-going." The sacred book of Taoism, the *Tao te Ching,* begins by saying that the Tao that can be talked about is not the real Tao: in other words we are being warned to beware of the traps in metaphorical language, or, in a common Oriental phrase, of confusing the moon with the finger pointing to it. But as we read on we find that the Tao can, after all, be to some extent characterized: the way is specifically the "way of the valley," the direction taken by humility, self-effacement, and the kind of relaxation, or nonaction, that makes all action effective. (*WP,* 91–92)[53]

This nonaction, as we have already seen, is *wu wei,* the Taoist idea of unmotivated action (literally, "nondoing" in Chinese). Only out of this nonaction, as Frye says in *The Double Vision,* can any genuine action really come (*DV,* 73). The way of the valley, then, is preparatory to still another way: perhaps this is "the way of heaven," a phrase that only occurs, with two exceptions, in the last ten chapters of the *Tao-te Ching.* While Lao-tzu says that "the way conceals itself in being nameless,"[54] this did not prevent him from trying to name it and from investing *tao* with the import of some metaphysical first principle and universal law ("the One"). *Tao* can mean "teaching" as well, especially in Confucian texts. Lao-tzu says, "My words are very easy to understand and very easy to put into practice, yet no one in the world can understand them or put them into practice."[55] In his marginal annotation to this passage, Frye writes, "a very brief statement of the essential paradox of the great religions."[56] The teaching most often mentioned by Frye is the Taoist idea of the balance or harmony between heaven and earth, between yin and yang.[57] Frye learned this not from the *Tao-te Ching,* which contains a number of stanzas about heaven and earth but none in the context of balance, but from the *Chuang-tzu,* which also gives central importance to *wu wei,* and doubtless also from Richard Wilhelm's commentary on *The Secret of the Golden Flower.*[58] But the *tao* itself, as what gives rise to the universe, precedes heaven and earth. "Turning back is how the way moves," says Lao-tzu. "The myriad creatures in the world are born from / Something, and Something from Nothing."[59] For all the significance Frye attaches to the creation myth, this notion of primordial nothingness had its own appeal for him, and on a blank page at the end of book 4 in his edition of Lao-tzu he penned these tongue-in-cheek but telling lines, entitling them "Laotse's Commentary on Genesis:"

> In the beginning God created heaven and earth.
> That was where the trouble started.
> Before, there was chaos,

Which is what the wise man still seeks.
He divided light from darkness, dry land from sea,
But we got sea and darkness anyway.
Silly blundering old bugger,
Why couldn't he have left well enough alone."[60]

Heaven and earth are the concrete manifestations of yin and yang, two opposing yet intertwined principles. In Notebook 27 Frye writes, "Note that the new heaven and the new earth is the real Tao, yang & yin in perfect balance" (*LN*, 1:10). The one passage about yin and yang in the *Tao-te Ching* points to sexual union as one of the creative processes of nature: "The myriad creatures carry on their backs the yin and embrace in their arms the yang, and are the blending of the generative forces of the two."[61] And the only passage Frye himself ever quotes from the *Tao-te Ching*— one he ran across in Norman O. Brown's *Life against Death*—has sexual suggestions as well:

He who knows the male, yet cleaves to what is female
Becomes like a ravine, receiving all things under heaven
(Thence) the eternal virtue never leaks away.
This is returning to the state of infancy. (*LN*, 1:257)

But Frye recognizes that the sexual symbolism of yin and yang is a tricky business and, as he says, such references can become "distortions of a quite comprehensible metaphorical design" (*LN*, 1:177). When he recurs in his notebooks and elsewhere to the Taoist polar principles, the context is wider: yin and yang represent concentrating and diffusing rhythms, an identification Frye picked up from Nathan Stiskin's *The Looking-Glass God* (*LN*, 1:46). Or they represent the earth and fire imagery in Berkeley's *Siris* (*LN*, 1:127). Yin and yang are elements of the mythical universe in space: the centrifugal hunt and the centripetal hearth, the world mountain and world tree (male extension) and the serpent and *temenos* (female enclosure) (*LN*, 2:609). Frye wishes that in English we had "some such conception as the Chinese yang and yin, where images of male and female represent aspects of experience that often include the sexual but expand from it in various metaphorical directions" (*WP*, 196). He makes a similar remark in *Creation and Recreation* (*NFR*, 58). In Taoism, therefore, Frye encounters a principle with no real counterpart in the West, although, as we have just seen, he does point to a number of instances where translation, or what he refers to in one notebook as "cross-pollenization" (*RT*, 332), can occur.

Alchemy, about which more later, is of course replete with yin-yang dualities. While the dualities are opposites, they are nevertheless connected, as we see in the hyphenated word and in the well-known symbol of the two tadpolelike forms, one black and the other white, swirling together inside the encompassing circle with each half containing the seed of the other: ☯. The first known reference to yin-yang appears in chapter 5 of *The Book of Changes* or the *I Ching:* "One yin, one yang, that is the Tao." We turn now to consider the influence that this Confucian book of oracles and wisdom had on Frye.

Confucianism: The *I Ching*

The *I Ching* is an ancient Chinese book of wisdom and divination, often taken as the most important of the Five Classics of Confucianism.[62] The geometric icons that make up the original form of the book symbolize forces of change at work in the cosmos and offer instruction on how to respond to the natural and social worlds. As an oracular device, the *I Ching* relies on a series of broken (yin) and unbroken (yang) horizontal lines. The original formula of an unbroken line represented the answer "yes" to a question, and a broken line "no." This eventually developed into a more complex system formed by eight trigrams—some combination of three broken and/or unbroken lines. These trigrams were then combined in pairs to produce sixty-four hexagrams. The exegetical texts in practically all editions of the *I Ching* catalogue the hexagrams and indicate the objects of their symbolism, their attributes, images, and family relationships. The Ch'ien trigram, for example, is composed of three unbroken lines, symbolizing the creative impulse, strength, heaven, and the father. To consult the *I Ching,* one uses yarrow stalks or coins to arrive at a hexagram. The process involves dividing and counting off the yarrow stalks or flipping the coins so as to establish a numerical value for each line, beginning with the bottom line and working toward the top. Before beginning this process, one frames a question to be answered. Among Frye's papers is a typed set of instructions about how to use the yarrow stalks to discover one's hexagram.[63] Frye recognizes that his interest in the *I Ching* might appear to be curious, if not bizarre: "As a child I had a board with 33 hollows for marbles, the central one empty. The puzzle was by jumping over marbles & removing them from the board to leave one in the middle. There were four side areas to be cleared. This game has the solution to my projected book on an I Ching or model of augury. I record this because anyone reading these notes would assume that they were the work of a psychotic, so I may as well furnish the definitive proof of the fact" (*TBN,* 192).

The image Frye projected as a teacher, writer, and academic citizen quietly attending to his university duties, lecturing all over the world, continuously writing, fulfilling his social obligations, and living a life that he once described as "completely without incident," seems altogether incompatible with that of the Eastern guru, sitting cross-legged on the floor with his copy of the *I Ching* and his yarrow stalks. But on two occasions in Notebook 27 Frye reveals that he once consulted the *I Ching* (*LN*, 1:4, 257–58). Having no yarrow stalks available, he used toothpicks. As for the question, Frye reports that he "didn't want an answer to a specific problem but general advice about what to do and be." And the message he got, "without qualification or 'moving lines,'" was the K'un hexagram. The chief feature of this hexagram (six pairs of unbroken lines) is receptivity, and it symbolizes one who is devoted and yielding. Its image is the earth, and its family relation centers on the mother. About his divination experiment Frye says only, and with complete disinterestedness, that he supposed he was "to be a 'feminine' or receptive writer" (*LN*, 1:4).[64] He reports in another notebook that the Spirit, as opposed to the Father and the Son, is "residually female, the K'un respondent I've always felt was my particular area in the I Ching setup" (*LN*, 1:376). The resemblance between Frye's own personality and the symbolism of the K'un hexagram is rather uncanny, and one wonders what his having consulted the *I Ching* subsequently would have revealed. But if he engaged in such ritual divinations on other occasions, he is silent about them.

Frye does, however, report in another notebook that he is able to make a connection between his one *I Ching* experiment and the lines from the *Tao-te Ching* quoted above:"He who knows the male, yet cleaves to what is female / Becomes like a ravine, receiving all things under heaven." The link comes by way of "Jung's notion of the soul as the embryonic female (*anima*) a man carries around within him" (*LN*, 1: 257–58). The point here is that Frye is using the *I Ching* for self-analysis, or perhaps self-understanding: his *anima* nature emerges from what he discovers from his yarrow stalks, and this is driven home to him in the passage from the *Tao-te Ching*. Admittedly, Frye's sketchy account does not reveal any deep probing and does not issue in any profound disclosure. But it is, in any event, consistent with what we know about his Jungian analysis of his dreams and of his relations with women, as he records them in his diaries from the late 1940s. He notes the strong current of *anima* within himself but suffers anxiety because women cannot recognize it but instead want to turn him into an *animus* figure.[65] Although Frye says that he is in Jungian terms the thinking type, he also observes that he is frequently possessed by undifferentiated feelings that sweep over him (*D,*

250), and beside the text of the K'un hexagram in his copy of the *I Ching* he writes, "hexagram of the feeling type." His experiment with the yarrow stalks appears to have confirmed what he already realized.[66]

The major context for Frye's use of the *I Ching* is not finally psychological but schematic. He says that the eight trigrams of the *I Ching* are connected with the Great Doodle (*TBN,* 209), the all-containing diagram described above, in the introduction. He then lists the trigrams, gives their broken and solid symbols, overlays one form of the Logos diagram with the eight trigrams of the *I Ching,* placing the four pairs at the appropriate point of the north-south and east-west points of his Great Doodle. He also makes connections between the trigrams and his pre-Romantic and Romantic spatial projections and those of Jacob Boehme; suggests links between the *I Ching* on the one hand and alchemy, astrology, and Blake's Four Zoas on the other;[67] and notes *I Ching* patterns in the imagery in *Sir Gawain* and Rossetti.[68] Michael Dolzani has shown how Frye derived the basic pattern for his *I Ching* reflections from the diagrams in the Wilhelm and Baynes edition, combining his categories with those of the primal and inner-world arrangements.[69] These are two arrangements of the trigrams in an ogdoadic circle were proposed by Fu-hsi in the fourth millennium B.C. in order to "show fully the attributes of the spirit-like and intelligent (operations working secretly) and to classify the qualities of the myriads of things." These things, we are told vaguely, were located either in the natural world or within human beings.[70] Of the other arrangements of the eight trigrams, the best known is by King Wen (12th century B.C.). His arrangement was based on family relationships, the K'un trigram representing the mother, Ch'ien representing the father, and the other six representing their children, three sons and three daughters.

One can understand Frye's attraction to the ogdoadic pattern, with its compass points and seasonal cycle. What he has actually done with the *I Ching* is superimposed his HEAP cycle with its Nomos and Nous axis onto the primal-arrangement ogdoad, adding his own version of King Wen's trigrams to it, and superimposed on Fu-hsi's ogdoad, with its seasonal cardinal points, his own version of the natural cycle. But more than this, as we learn from the diagrams Frye drew, he reversed the direction of the cycle for both the primal and the inner-world ogdoads.[71] Frye's *I Ching* speculations, as difficult to follow as they are, embody a certain ingenuity, and he himself recognizes their fanciful recklessness: "Thus, noting that Blake's Zoa-Emanation scheme & the I Ching trigrams are both an ogdoad [the Fu-hsi scheme] and a Noah's Ark family of eight [the King Wen pattern], I seize on every resemblance there is, invent a great many there aren't, and disregard all differences, determined to find an analogy in the teeth of the facts—not that there aren't any facts of course" (*TBN*, 211). He even muses that the eight characters in one of the novels he plans to write could represent the eight trigrams.[72]

Beyond the game of finding or inventing resemblances, what is the point of it all? Frye provides a direct answer in Notebook 24. Speaking about his search for an "alphabet of forms," he writes, "The feeling that this 'sequence' [of epiphanies] ought to suggest the cycle of totality produces the conception of the Logos as an alphabet of forms. The I Ching, the Tarot pack, & the like, are the Alpha-Omega aspect of the Word. These schemes are used for divination, as is natural, because they're conceived as above time, but they are expressions of the schematic ('all imagination') shape of mythical apprehension of reality. Yeats' circle of the moon and Poe's Eureka cloud of unknowing" (*TBN*, 110–11). The phrase "all imagination" is Frye's shorthand for Blake's interpenetrative understanding of the incarnation: "Man is All Imagination God is Man & exists in us & we in him."[73] The syllogism in this epigram, or at least the train of thought, is this: Reality has a mythical (poetic and imaginative) shape. This shape, which is ultimately about the divine-human connection (as in Blake, Yeats, and Poe), is schematic. Schema, therefore, are incarnations of the myth-making power of the poetic imagination. The unstated premise in all this is that nothing else finally matters. Seen in this context, Frye's experiment with the yarrow stalks and his cryptic analogizing is fundamentally another of his many efforts to probe the imaginative world in search of its great code, its "third awareness," its interpenetrating vision. While there is a hint in Frye's two references to his "divination" experience that he believed his toothpicks more or less magically, like a Ouija board, told the truth, it was not any "belief" in the *I Ching* that mattered for Frye. It was rather a matter of vision, a matter of the conceivable—or the hypothetical, as he liked to call it.

But before concluding our account of Frye's journey to the East, it is perhaps worth observing that "the Way" can be traversed in two directions. Easterners, even with little or no knowledge of Frye's interest in the Mahayana sutras, Patanjali, bardo, and Lao-tzu, have been drawn to Frye's work in ways that seems disproportionate to what one might expect. There are now thirty-six translations of his books into Japanese, Korean, and Chinese,[74] three conferences on his work have taken place in Korea and China, and three collections of essays on Frye's China connection have appeared in both Chinese and English.[75] So just as Frye for more than fifty years sought to assimilate the East into his grand encyclopedic vision, a growing number of readers in the East have been engaging Frye's world.

II Esoterica

5 The Traditions

The progress from 'literal' to spiritual meaning . . . is . . . often
identified with an exoteric-esoteric movement.
—*Late Notebooks,* 1:131

I'm beginning to feel that I really am the man who's found the lost
chord, somebody who really can, on the basis of literature, put the
Tarots & alchemy & kabalism & the rest of it together into a coherent
speech & language.
—*Notebooks and Lectures on the Bible,* 109

Although religious doctrines and institutions have little appeal for Frye,
the highly personal and often idiosyncratic religious speculations we have
been considering are nevertheless firmly rooted in Western and Eastern
exoteric traditions. But he read fairly widely in the various esoteric traditions, and his notebooks, especially, record the depth and breadth of his
interest. The word *esotericism* was not coined until the nineteenth century,
when Alphonse-Louis Constant (Eliphas Lévi) used it to designate certain
occult practices—alchemical, kabbalistic, and magical.[1] Esotericism remains another essentially contested concept, even though the Western
esoteric tradition is generally considered to include alchemy, astrology,
Gnosticism, gnosis, magic, mysticism, Rosicrucianism, and secret societies. Yet in the scholarly study of esotericism, a relatively recent development, the esoteric tradition includes much more than these eight
bodies of arcane and mysterious thought. The expanded accounts of esotericism are illustrated by two of the more studious expositors of the subject, Wouter J. Hanegraaff and Antoine Faivre. Hanegraaff distinguishes
five different meanings of the word esoteric:

1. Esoteric as a synonym for the occult: here we would have a wide
variety of writings on the paranormal, exotic Wisdom traditions, New
Age spiritualities, and the like.

2. Esoteric as secret teachings: the discipline of the arcane with its
distinction between initiates and noninitiates.

3. The *philosophia perennis* in religious studies: here esoteric is a

metaphysical concept referring to the "transcendent unity" of exoteric religions.

4. Esoteric as gnosis, in the sense of various religious phenomena that emphasize experiential rather than rational and dogmatic modes of knowing and that favor mythical or symbolic over discursive discourse.

5. Esoteric as a complex of interrelated traditions that arise from Renaissance "hermeticism": alchemy, Paracelsianism and Rosicrucianism; Christian and post-Christian Kabbalah; theosophical and Illuminist currents; and various occultist and related developments during the nineteenth and twentieth centuries.[2]

Antoine Faivre maintains that we can distinguish Western esoteric thought by four "intrinsic characteristics":

1. The belief that there are correspondences between all aspects of the visible and invisible worlds which are meant to be decoded. Correspondences can be (a) within nature itself (e.g., the seven metals and seven planets of astrology), or (b) between nature, history, and sacred texts (e.g., Jewish and Christian Kabbalah).

2. Nature is felt to be essentially alive in the cosmos (e.g., Paracelsianism, *Naturphilosophie*).

3. The imagination is the faculty for revelation and mediation.

4. Transmutation, metamorphosis, "second birth."[3]

There are naturally debates in the study of esotericism, which has become an established field of inquiry,[4] about the nature of the field, the definition of its subject, and its methods of inquiry. These lie beyond the scope of our study. But the meanings given to *esoteric* by these two well-recognized scholars in the field do provide a framework for considering Frye's interests, and they indicate the broad scope of those traditions taken to be esoteric. These traditions provide the foundation for Hanegraaff's encyclopedic study of spirituality in the alternative cultural trends of the last two or three decades, *New Age Religion and Western Culture: Esotericism in the Mirror of Secular Thought.*[5]

Frye is drawn to most of the features of esotericism that Faivre and Hanegraaff take to be central, but before considering his speculations on the esoteric tradition, we can gain a sense of the breadth of his reading by looking at the list presented below, in the next section. Although only a small percentage of the writers and texts in the list are mentioned in Frye's published works, taken together they appear hundreds and hundreds of times in the notebooks. The categories in section 1 of the list, "Esoteric Traditions," derive largely from Antoine Faivre's "Ancient and Medieval

Sources of Modern Esoteric Movements."[6] The other twelve categories, some broadly inclusive and others quite narrow, catalogue what we know of Frye's sources from the annotated books in his library and from references in his notebooks. The classification here is indebted to Hanegraaff's *New Age Religion.*[7] The list includes Eastern traditions, but it excludes studies of comparative mythology and books on ancient myth, folklore, ritual, the Grail legend, and romance—works that often treat or border on such topics as magic, mystery cults, and other esoteric subjects. It excludes as well science fiction, speculative and fantastic fiction, magical realism, and fantasy, though it does include a few works of fiction (e.g., novels based on the Tarot by Piers Anthony and Italo Calvino, Bulwer-Lytton's *Zanoni,* Charles Williams's *The Great Trumps,* George MacDonald's *Phantastes,* and the novels of Carlos Castaneda). The problem in compiling such a list is the same as that faced by library cataloguers: some books might just as easily have been placed in another category, and some belong in more than one category. Moreover, arguments could be made for excluding altogether some books from Frye's library that I have included and including others I have passed over. Whatever the failures of classification, the intent of the list is primarily to reveal the range of Frye's familiarity with esoterica.

The Sources of Frye's Knowledge of Esoteric Traditions

In the following list an asterisk indicates that the copy of the book in Frye's library has marginal markings or comments or both. These are sometimes extensive, sometimes minimal. A double asterisk means that the book or author is not in Frye's library but that there is evidence from the notebooks that he read the book or read about it in some related secondary source. A triple asterisk means that Frye owned the book but did not annotate it.

1. Esoteric Traditions	Frye's Sources
Hellenistic Judaism	
Philo of Alexandria (ca. 20–15 B.C. to 45–50 A.D.)	★*Works*
Alexandrian Hermeticism	
Hermes Trismegistus	G. R. S. Mead, ★*Thrice-Greatest Hermes: Studies in Hellenistic Theosophy and Gnosis*

Corpus Hermeticum — Frances Yates, ★*Giordano Bruno and the Hermetic Tradition*
Norman O. Brown, ★*Hermes the Thief*

Neoplatonism
Philostratus (171?–247) — ★*Life of Apollonius of Tyana*
Porphyry (234–ca. 305)
Iamblichus (ca. 250–ca. 330) — ★*On the Mysteries of the Egyptians, Chaldeans, and Assyrians*
Macrobius (fl. ca. 430) — ★*Commentary on the Dream of Scipio,*
★*The Saturnalia*

Christian Esotericism
Clement of Rome (1st cent.)
Clement of Alexandria (d. ca. 215) — ★★★*The Exhortation to the Greeks; The Rich Man's Salvation; and The Fragment of an Address Entitled "To the Newly Baptized"*
Frances Yates, ★*Giordano Bruno and the Hermetic Tradition*

Pseudo-Dionysius (1st cent. A.D.) — ★*The Divine Names,* ★*The Mystical Theology*
Frances Yates, ★*Giordano Bruno and the Hermetic Tradition*

Boethius (ca. 480–ca. 525) — ★*The Consolation of Philosophy*
Martianus Capella (fl. 5th cent.) — ★★*The Marriage of Philology and Mercury*
★*Martianus Capella and the Seven Liberal Arts*
John Scotus Erigena (ca. 810–ca. 880) — ★★*On the Division of Nature*
Bernardus Silvestris (fl. 12th cent.) — ★*The Cosmographia of Bernardus Silvestris*
Joachim of Fiore (ca. 1145–1202)
Albertus Magnus (1206–80) — ★*The Book of Secrets of Albertus Magnus*
Ramon Lull (ca. 1232–1316) — ★*Blanquerna.* See also Frye's paper on Lull in *SE*.
Meister Eckhart (1260–1328) — ★ *Meister Eckhart: A Modern Translation,* ★*Meister Eckhart: The Essential Sermons, Commentaries, Treatises, and Defense*
Jan van Ruysbroek (1293–1381) — ★*Spiritual Espousals*
Julian of Norwich (ca. 1341–ca. 1413) — ★*Revelations of Divine Love*
Nicholas of Cusa (1401–64) — ★*The Vision of God*
Pico della Mirandola (1463–94) — ★*Oration on the Dignity of Man*

Cornelius Agrippa (1486–1583/84)	★ *Three Books of Occult Philosophy or Magic: Book One: Natural Magic*
Theophrastus Paracelsus (1493–1541)	★ *The Prophecies of Paracelsus: Occult Symbols, and Magic Figures with Esoteric Explanations*
St. John of the Cross (1542–91)	★ *Ascent of Mt. Carmel,* ★ *Dark Night of the Soul,* ★ *Living Flame of Love,* ★ *Spiritual Canticle*
Giordano Bruno (1548–1600)	★ *The Expulsion of the Triumphant Beast* Dorothy Singer, ★ *Giordano Bruno* Frances Yates, ★ *Giordano Bruno and the Hermetic Tradition*
Jacob Boehme (1575–1624)	★ *The Signature of Things;* ★ *The Aurora,* ★ *Six Theosophic Points,* ★ *The Three Principles of the Divine Essence*
William Law (1686–1761)	★ *Characters and Characteristics of William Law* ★ *Selected Mystical Writings of William Law* ★★★ *A Serious Call to a Devout and Holy Life* Aldous Huxley, ★ *The Perennial Philosophy*
H. P. Blavatsky (1831–91)	★ *The Secret Doctrine,* ★ *An Abridgement of The Secret Doctrine*
Alchemy	Elias Ashmole, ★★★ *Theatrum chemicum Britannicum* Titus Burckhardt, ★ *Alchemy: Science of the Cosmos, Science of the Soul* Chao Pi Ch'en, ★ *Taoist Yoga: Alchemy and Immortality* Mircea Eliade, ★ *The Forge and the Crucible* Marie-Louise von Franz, ★ *Alchemy: An Introduction to the Symbolism and the Psychology* C. G. Jung, ★ *Psychology and Alchemy,* ★ *Mysterium Coniunctionis* Stéphane Mallarmé, ★ *Poems and Letters* Artur Rimbaud, ★ *Poems* Herbert Silberer, ★ *Problems of Mysticism and Its Symbolism* Thomas Vaughan, ★ *The Works of Thomas Vaughan*
Astrology	Franz Cumont, ★ *Astrology and Religion among the Greeks and Romans* Warren Kenton, ★ *Astrology: The Celestial Mirror* Nostradamus, ★★★ *The Complete Prophecies*

Rosicrucianism	Frances Yates, ★*The Rosicrucian Enlightenment*
	Israel Regardie, ★*The Golden Dawn*
	Edward Bulwer-Lytton, ★*Zanoni: A Rosicrucian Tale*
Tarot	Piers Anthony, ★*God of Tarot: Book I of the Tarot Sequence;* ★*Vision of Tarot: Book II of the Tarot Sequence,* and ★*Faith of Tarot: Book III of the Tarot Sequence*
	Papus (Gérard Encausse), ★*The Tarot of the Bohemians*
	Italo Calvino, ★*The Castle of Crossed Destinies*
	A. E. Waite, ★*A Pictorial Key to the Tarot*
	Charles Williams, ★*The Greater Trumps*

2. Astral Projection, Out of Body Experiences, and After Death States

Stanislav and Christina Grof	★*Beyond Death: The Gates of Consciousness*
Arthur E. Powell	★*The Astral Body and Other Astral Phenomena*
Benjamin Walker	★*Beyond the Body: The Human Double and the Astral Planes*
Herbert B. Greenhouse	★*The Astral Journey*
Raymond Moody	★*Life after Life: The Investigation of a Phenomenon—Survival of Bodily Death*
Kenneth Ring	★*Heading toward Omega: In Search of the Meaning of the Near-Death Experience*
Marcia Moore	★*Hypersentience: Exploring Your Past Lifetimes as a Guide to Your Character . . .*
Lyall Watson	★*The Romeo Error*
Glenn Williston and Judith Johnstone	★★★*Discovering Your Past Lives: Spiritual Growth through a Knowledge of Past Lifetimes*

3. Channeling and Other Paranormal Phenomena

Jane Roberts	★*The "Unknown" Reality: A Seth Book*
James A. Pike	★★*The Other Side*
Jess Stearn	★*Edgar Cayce—The Sleeping Prophet*
David Haisell	★*The Missing Seven Hours*
Immanuel Velikovsky	★*Worlds in Collision*
Charles Fort	★*The Books of Charles Fort*
Brian Inglis	★*Natural and Supernatural: A History of the Paranormal*
Lawrence L. Le Shan	★*Clairvoyant Reality: Towards a General Theory of the Paranormal*

Nostradamus	★★★*The Complete Prophecies*
John Taylor	★*Superminds: An Investigation into the Paranormal*
Joel L. Whitton and Joe Fisher	★*Life between Life: Scientific Explorations into the Void Separating One Incarnation from the Next*
Guy Lyon Playfair and Scott Hill	★*The Cycles of Heaven: Cosmic Forces and What They Are Doing to You*

4. Cosmic Consciousness, Peak Experiences, Fourth-Force Psychology

C. Muses and A. M. Young, ed.	★*Consciousness and Reality: The Human Pivot Point*
Charles T. Tart, ed.	★*Altered States of Consciousness*
John White, ed.	★ *Frontiers of Consciousness*
Annie Besant and C. W. Leadbeater	★*Thought-Forms*
Ken Wilber	★*The Spectrum of Consciousness*
Stephen Larsen	★*The Shaman's Doorway: Opening the Mythic Imagination to Contemporary Consciousness*
Robert E. Ornstein	★*The Psychology of Consciousness*
Martin Ebon, ed.	★*The Signet Handbook of Parapsychology*
Maria Beesing, et al.	★*The Enneagram: A Journey of Self-Discovery*
Alex Comfort	★*I and That: Notes on the Biology of Religion*

5. Eastern Traditions

R. Wilhelm and C. F. Baynes, trans.	★*I Ching*
James Legge, trans.	★*I Ching*
D.T. Suzuki, trans.	★*The Lankavatara Sutra*
Thomas Cleary, trans.	★*The Avatamsaka Sutra*
Kazi Dawa-Samdup, trans.	★*The Tibetan Book of the Dead*
W. Y. Evans–Wentz, ed.	★*The Tibetan Book of the Dead, or, the After-Death Experiences on the Bardo Plane*
W. Y. Evans–Wentz, ed.	★*The Tibetan Book of the Great Liberation, or, the Method of Realizing Nirvana through Knowing the Mind*
Shankara	★*Shankara's Crest-Jewel of Discrimination*
Chuang-tzu	★*Chuang-tzu: Genius of the Absurd*
Confucius	★*The Analects*
John Blofeld	★*The Tantric Mysticism of Tibet*
W. Y. Evans–Wentz, ed.	★*Tibetan Yoga and Secret Doctrines, or, Seven Books of Wisdom of the Great Path*
Chao Pi Ch'en	★*Taoist Yoga: Alchemy and Immortality*

Chung-yuan Chang, ed.	*Tao: A New Way of Thinking
Gopi Krishna	*Kundalini: The Evolutionary Energy in Man
Lao-tsu	*Tao te Ching; *The Wisdom of Laotse
R. A. Nicholson, ed.	*Rumi: Poet and Mystic
Patanjali	*The Yoga-Sutras
James N. Powell	*The Tao Symbols
Philip Rawson	*Tantra: The Indian Cult of Ecstasy
P. Rawson, L. Legeza	*Tao, the Chinese Philosophy of Time and Change
Holmes Welch	*Taoism: The Parting of the Way
Eugen Herrigel	*Zen in the Art of Archery
D. T. Suzuki	*Essays in Zen Buddhism (3rd series)
D. T. Suzuki	*Zen and Japanese Culture
D. T. Suzuki	*Zen Buddhism: Selected Writings
Shunryu Suzuki	*Zen Mind, Beginner's Mind
Ernest Wood	*Yoga
Walt Anderson	*Open Secrets: A Western Guide to Tibetan Buddhism
Mircea Eliade	*Yoga: Immortality and Freedom
Yu-lan Fung	*The Spirit of Chinese Philosophy
A. K. Ramanujan, ed.	*Speaking of Siva
Edwin A. Burtt , ed.	***The Teachings of the Compassionate Buddha
B. Kato and W. E. Soothill, trans.	*The Threefold Lotus Sutra: Innumerable Meanings, The Lotus Flower of the Wonderful Law, and Meditation on the Bodhisattva Universal Virtue
Herbert V. Guenther	*The Tantric View of Life
W. Y. Evans-Wentz, ed.	*Tibet's Great Yogi Milarepa
Paul Reps, ed.	*Zen Flesh, Zen Bones: A Collection of Zen and Pre-Zen Writings
Tomio Hirai	*Zen and Meditation Therapy
Christmas Humphreys	***Buddhism
Bhagwan Shree Rajneesh	*The Book of the Secrets—I: Discourses on "Vigyana Bhairava Tantra"
Nahum Stiskin	*The Looking-Glass God: Shinto, Yin-Yang, and a Cosmology for Today
Mark Tatz and Jody Kent	*Rebirth: The Tibetan Game of Liberation
Arthur Waley	*The Way and Its Power
Paramhansa Yogananda	*Autobiography of a Yogi, *The Science of Religion

6. Faeries and Elementals

Maureen Duffy	*The Erotic World of Faery
George MacDonald	*Phantastes
W. B. Yeats	*Irish Folk Stories and Fairy Tales

Jacob Grimm	*The Complete Grimm's Fairy Tales
Edmund Spenser	*The Faerie Queene
Shakespeare	*A Midsummer Night's Dream and The Tempest
Milton	*Comus
John Crowley	*Little, Big

7. Gnosticism

Bentley Layton, ed.	*The Gnostic Scriptures
James M. Robinson, ed.	*The Nag Hammadi Library
Jacob Needleman	* The Sword of Gnosis: Metaphysics, Cosmology, Tradition, Symbolism
Hans Jonas	*The Gnostic Religion
G. R. S. Mead	*Thrice-Greatest Hermes: Studies in Hellenistic Theosophy and Gnosis
G. R. S. Mead, ed.	*Pistis Sophia: A Gnostic Miscellany
Pheme Perkins	*The Gnostic Dialogue

8. The Kabbalah

Gershom Scholem	*Major Trends in Jewish Mysticism, *On the Kabbalah and Its Symbolism
S. L. MacGregor Mathers, trans.	*The Kabbalah Unveiled
Z'ev Ben Shimon Halevi	*Kabbalah: Tradition of Hidden Knowledge
Migene Gonzalez-Wippler	*A Kabbalah for the Modern World: How God Created the Universe
Charles Poncé	*Kabbalah: An Introduction and Illumination for the World Today
Leo Schaya	*The Universal Meaning of the Kabbalah
Carlo Suarès	*The Cipher of Genesis: The Original Code of the Qabala as Applied to the Scriptures; *The Qabala Trilogy: The Cipher of Genesis, The Song of Songs, The Sepher Yetsira; *The Sepher Yetsira, Including the Original Astrology according to the Qabala and Its Zodiac
Gershom Scholem, ed.	*Zohar: The Book of Splendor

9. Kook Books

| Robert Anton Wilson | *Cosmic Trigger: The Final Secret of the Illuminati |
| Itzhak Bentov | *Stalking the Wild Pendulum |

Dmitry Merezhkovsky   *Atlantis/Europe*
Michael Baigent, et al.   **Holy Blood and Holy Grail*

10. Magic and Shamanism

E. M. Butler   *Ritual Magic*
Francis King   *Magic: The Western Tradition*
Louis Pauwels and   *The Morning of the Magicians*
  Jacques Bergier
John Matthews   *At the Table of the Grail: Magic and the Use of the
                             Imagination*
Alphonse Louis Constant   *The History of Magic*
Joseph Ennemoser   *The History of Magic*
Francis Hitching   *Earth Magic*
John Baptista Porta   *Natural Magick*
Kurt Seligmann   *Magic, Supernaturalism and Religion*
John Wilcock   *A Guide to Occult Britain: The Quest for Magic in
                             Pagan Britain*
Mircea Eliade   *Shamanism: Archaic Techniques of Ecstasy*
I. M. Lewis   *Ecstatic Religion: An Anthropological Study of
                             Spirit Possession and Shamanism*
Joseph L. Henderson and   *The Wisdom of the Serpent*
  Maud Oakes
Lyall Watson   *Gifts of Unknown Things: A True Story of Nature,
                             Healing, and Initiation from Indonesia's "Dancing
                             Island," *Lightning Bird*

11. Mysticism, Mystery, and the Occult

Anonymous   *The Cloud of Unknowing* (two annotated copies)
Immanuel Swedenborg   *The Divine Love and Wisdom, *Heaven and Hell,
                             The True Christian Religion
George Trobridge   *Swedenborg: Life and Teaching*
Thomas Taylor   *The Eleusinian and Bacchic Mysteries*
Evelyn Underhill   *Mysticism, *The Golden Sequence*
Valmiki   *The Ramayana of Valmiki*
William R. Inge   *Christian Mysticism*
Anne Fremantle, ed.   *The Protestant Mystics*
R. C. Zaehner   *Mysticism: Sacred and Profane*
A. J. Arberry   *Sufism: An Account of the Mystics of Islam*
Jill Purce   *The Mystic Spiral: Journey of the Soul*

Herbert Silberer	*Problems of Mysticism and Its Symbolism*
Joachim Neugroschel, ed.	*Yenne Velt: The Great Works of Jewish Fantasy and Occult*
Agrippa von Nettesheim	*Three Books of Occult Philosophy or Magic*
August Strindberg	*From an Occult Diary*
Paul Waldo-Schwartz	***Art and the Occult*
Frances Yates	* *The Occult Philosophy in the Elizabethan Age,* *The Art of Memory*
Franz Cumont	*The Mysteries of Mithra*
Rudolf Otto	*Mysticism East and West*
Sidney Spencer	***Mysticism in World Religion*
Alan Upward	*The Divine Mystery*
Arthur Versluis	*The Egyptian Mysteries*
Edgar Wind	*Pagan Mysteries in the Renaissance*
Leo Frobenius	*The Childhood of Man*
Piers Anthony	*Macroscope*
Margaret Alice Murray	*The God of the Witches*
Ronald Curran, ed.	*Witches, Wraiths and Warlocks*
Maulana Jalal al-Din al-Rumi	*Rumi: Poet and Mystic*
Gustav Meyrink	*The Golem*
A. E. Waite	*The Holy Grail, *The Quest of the Golden Stairs, *The Unknown Philosopher: The Life of Louis Claude de Saint-Martin and the Substance of His Transcendental Doctrine*
Lyall Watson	*Supernature: A Natural History of the Supernatural*
Harold Bailey	*The Lost Language of Symbolism*
Roger Cook	*The Tree of Life: Symbol of the Centre*
Aleister Crowley	*Moonchild*
Sheila Ostrander and Lynn Schroeder	***Psychic Discoveries behind the Iron Curtain*
Reginald Scott	*The Discoverie of Witchcraft*
Nicholas and June Regush	*Mind-Search*
John Sharkey	*Celtic Mysteries*

12. New Age Science and Religion

Ken Wilber, ed.	*The Holographic Paradigm*
Geoffrey Chew	***Lectures on Modelling the Bootstrap*
Fritjof Capra	*The Turning Point, The Tao of Physics*
Stanislav Grof	*Realms of the Human Unconscious*
Marilyn Ferguson	*The Aquarian Conspiracy*

Adam Smith	*Powers of Mind*
G. I. Gurdjieff	*All and Everything*
Kenneth Walker	*A Study of Gurdjieff's Teaching*
P. D. Ouspensky	*In Search of the Miraculous*, *A New Model of the Universe*, *The Psychology of Man's Possible Evolution*, ***Tertium Organum: The Third Canon of Thought, a Key to the Enigmas of the World*
Rudy Rucker	*Infinity and the Mind*
Carlos Castaneda	*The Fire from Within*, *Journey to Ixtlan: The Lessons of Don Juan*, *The Teachings of Don Juan: A Yaqui Way of Knowledge*, *A Separate Reality: Further Conversations with Don Juan*, *Tales of Power*
W. B. Yeats	*A Vision*
Abraham H. Maslow	*Toward a Psychology of Being*
Aldous Huxley	*Doors of Perception*
Colin Wilson	*The Philosopher's Stone*
Joseph Chilton Pearce	*The Crack in the Cosmic Egg*, *Exploring the Crack in the Cosmic Egg*
John D. Barrow	*The World within the World*
J. W. Dunne	*An Experiment with Time*
Stan Gooch	*Guardians of the Ancient Wisdom*
David Hay	*Exploring Inner Space: Scientists and Religious Experience*
Richard Moss	***The I That Is We*
Claudio Naranjo	*The One Quest*
Russell Targ and Harold E. Puthoff	*Mind-reach: Scientists Look at Psychic Ability*
Carl Sagan	*The Cosmic Connection: An Extraterrestrial Perspective*
Elisabet Sahtouris	*Gaia: The Human Journey from Chaos to Cosmos*
John C. Lilly	*The Center of the Cyclone: An Autobiography of Inner Space*

13. Synchronicity

C. G. Jung	**Synchronicity*
Lyall Watson	*Lifetide*
Robert Anton Wilson	*Cosmic Trigger: The Final Secret of the Illuminati*
Arthur Koestler	*The Roots of Coincidence*

Elementals and Madame Blavatsky

This catalogue of 271 books (252 annotated) illustrates that Frye's reading in the esoteric tradition was considerable. As already suggested, it would be impossible to infer from Frye's published work that he was broadly familiar with esoterica as defined by Hanegraaff and Faivre. But the notebooks reveal that Frye was no stranger to the unusual, mystical, extraordinary, paranormal, and off-beat. In a set of notes written sometime after 1985 he says, "I had a strong impulse the other day to write an article called 'Fairies and Elementals.' It branches out in so many directions that it becomes bewildering, and worse, it takes me back to the days when I wanted to read every kooky book in the world as a background for Blake" (55–3.1). He is doubtless referring to Swedenborg, Blavatsky, and Boehme, among others. Faeries and elementals were for Frye one strand of the "elemental" occult tradition, the other two chief strands being bardo and "the total magnet or anima mundi which accounts for mesmerism, telepathy, clairvoyance, second sight & magical healing cures" (*RT*, 54). Frye calls this the soul-world or *akasa* (Sanskrit for "space" or "ether"), a term that he adapted from Madame Blavatsky.[8] His interest in elemental spirits—spirits neither angelic nor demonic, or as he says in Notebook 3, "non-human forms of more or less conscious existence" (*RT*, 54)—appears to have been motivated by what he found in the early Milton, especially *Comus,* where the elementals are the Attendant Spirit, Sabrina, and Comus himself.[9] In *Anatomy of Criticism,* faeries and elementals are said to belong to the existential projection of romance (64), meaning that these writers of romance accept the world of fantasy as "true" and so populated their stories with fairies, ghosts, demons, and the like. They also belong to what Frye called in his first essay on Yeats "the hyperphysical world."[10] Twenty years later he describes this in a notebook as

> the world of unseen beings, angels, spirits, devils, demons, djinns, daemons, ghosts, elemental spirits, etc. It's the world of the "inspiration" of poet or prophet, of premonitions of death, telepathy, extra-sensory perception, miracle, telekinesis, & of a good deal of "luck." In the Bible it's connected with Lilith & other demons of the desert, with the casting out of devils in the gospels, with visions of angels, with thaumaturgic feats like those of Elijah & Elisha, & so on. Fundamentally, it's the world of buzzing though not booming confusion that the transistor radio is a symbol of. The world of communication as total environment which inspires terror. Shakespeare's *Tempest* as heard by the imprisoned crew. Chaucer's Houses of Fame & Rumor (because *no* information that gets on that circuit is really reliable). The world of drugs, multiple

personality, and hallucination. Before we come out on the other side of it, we recognize that ordinary life is a part of it, a Bardo perspective out of which apocalypse, or stage 2, finally comes. It's the polytheistic world of contending & largely unseen forces; it's the world of terror that McLuhan associates with the oral stage of culture: twitching ears, & a poor sense of direction. (*RT,* 90)

But the remark about wanting to write an article on faeries and elementals, a remark that gets repeated a half-dozen times in Frye's notebooks,[11] was triggered by his having read Maureen Duffy's *The Erotic World of the Faerie,* which is pretty close to a "kooky book."[12] And in the 1985 notes Frye's mind begins to branch in every direction indeed: backward to Shakespeare's Puck and Ariel and further back to Lyly's *Endymion* and Peele's *Old Wives' Tale;* forward to Lewis Carroll's *Sylvie and Bruno* and George Macdonald and Tolkien's essay on fairy stories; then to John Crowley's *Little, Big,* and from there to Giordano Bruno, science fiction, Celtic mythology, James's occult fiction, and finally to the Theosophists. To move from Shakespeare to Madame Blavatsky is to move from the center to the circumference.

Frye had read Blavatsky's *The Secret Doctrine* for *Fearful Symmetry,* and he had turned to her again when he was trying to crack the code of Yeats's *A Vision* in the first major paper he wrote after *Fearful Symmetry.*[13] Why the attraction to the Theosophist Blavatsky? "Whenever I read Blavatsky and other deifiers of the void," Frye says, "I realize that Xy [Christianity] & the other great religions are, so to speak, phenomenological: they deal with the infinite only in terms of what the infinite has revealed" (*RT,* 207). Blavatsky's Theosophy was, for Frye, "the connecting link between myth and science," a kind of thinking that was not quite poetic and certainly not rational but, as Frye says, "a synthetic and mythical reasoning [which is] known as occultism" (31.5). "I don't want to dismiss the 'mezzanine' world of Yeats and Blavatsky as purely unreal: some such theory as Bardo might make sense of it, as I've always thought" (37.11). What Frye is referring to is Blavatsky's cosmic view that our world is attached to another one, an idea that Frye links to William Morris's revolutionary romances. He describes this as Blavatsky's dumbbell- or hourglass-shaped cosmos, the stem of the two figures symbolically connecting the worlds of Generation and Beulah—an image Frye picked up from reading Yeats's *Trembling of the Veil.*[14] Morris's romances are similar to Blavatsky's cosmos in that they represent a state "before birth and after death meeting somewhere around the universe, east of the sun and west of the moon, where the archetypes of the psyche fight their Valhallas, and where the revolutionary drive in all romance isn't perverted or kidnapped by some social institution" (54-13.24).

Frye worries a good deal about such social institutions, including the social institution of second-phase rational thought. If literature can be a critique of pure reason, so can the occult. In his 1947 essay on Yeats, Frye says of Madame Blavatsky, "*The Secret Doctrine,* whatever else it is, is a very remarkable essay on the morphology of symbols, and the charlatanism of its author is less a reflection of her than on the age that compelled her to express herself in such devious ways" (*FI,* 221). As his extensive annotations of *The Secret Doctrine* reveal, Frye read Blavatsky with a great deal of attention.[15] Frye sees Blavatsky as continuing the tradition of the Neoplatonic "mystagogues" from Paracelsus, the Cambridge Platonists, and Thomas Taylor to Schelling and Goethe. This tradition, with its references to elementals and magnetism, Frye writes,

> has a quasi-experimental side to it, the basis of which is, to put it bluntly, rumor. The people who have discovered the alkahlest, or oil of gold, or can keep lamps burning for centuries, or can reconstruct a plant from its ashes, or a man's appearance from his signet ring, are always, like the person of unimpeachable veracity who will vouch for the truth of a rumor, just around the corner. To say it is all rubbish is to say that only untruths & impossibilities get rumored, which is nonsense. My plan is not to compare this rumor with fact, but to analyze it as though it were myth, classifying & comparing the mythical themes in it. (32.53)

In other words, if we shift our perspectives, Blavatsky is not a charlatan or purveyor of rubbish at all. This is why Frye writes in the margin of the abridgement of *The Secret Doctrine* the phrase "Grammar Symbolism,"[16] meaning that Blavatsky provides us with a symbolic syntax, just as Jung, Eliade, Campbell, Graves, and other mythographers do. One also finds such a grammar in the romantic hermeticism of such novels as Bulwer-Lytton's *Zanoni,* one of Frye's favorite occult works of fiction.[17] For the grammarian of symbolism, as Frye see it, the issues of truth and belief do not apply, even though Blavatsky herself is interested in constructing doctrine from her hermetic sources.[18] Such a shift of perspective away from the truth of correspondence and toward an imaginative truth of coherence is one of the driving forces of Frye's agenda. Here's the way he puts it in a relatively early notebook:

> Now let's go back to the occult threshold. . . . Mysticism can come to terms with the dogmatic systems: the soul accepts what the mind hands it just as the mind accepts sense data from the body. . . . All mental

systems are symbolic forms, & are held in suspension by the spirit with a detachment beyond all skepticism. The mystic is thus naturally attracted by a 'why not?' sense of the relativity of reality, & likes to return to the free speculation of the primitive, who thinks a dream is experienced by his soul when leaving the body. Sophisticated reasoning conventionalizes & orders reality, & uses the word 'coincidence' to dismiss any form of unusable design. So he wonders what would happen if he shifted the perspective; . . . occultism has a continuously satanic role to play, as Blavatsky shows. (32.66)

By "satanic role" Frye means the deviousness with which Theosophy forces a shift in perspective away from the conventions of Cartesian thinking. He does not see mysticism itself, to which we now turn, as devious, but it does offer another shift in perspective back to the primitivism of free speculation.

Mysticism

"I have very few religious books," Frye declares, "& those I have stress the mystics" (*LN*, 1:35). This declaration is hardly an accurate representation of the more than 5,100 titles in Frye's library, hundreds of which could be described as religious, and of these only a small portion are mystical texts or commentaries on mysticism.[19] Frye may of course be using the word "mystics" here to refer to esoteric books in general. But whatever the intended reference, the remark does reveal at least a perception he had about the general thrust of his reading of religious texts, and a study of his religious views is obliged to explore his interest in mystical literature. As we indicated in chapter 3, Frye reported that he himself had never had the sort of experience reported by the mystics (*TBN*, 60). But if he never had a mystical experience himself, he writes a good deal about the experiences of others, or rather about the accounts of those experiences, the experiences themselves being mute and inaccessible by direct observation. His books, essays, and unpublished manuscripts contain numerous references to mystics and mysticism—more than 250 altogether.

The only thing close to a sustained account on the topic is in Frye's essay, written when he was an Emmanuel College student, on the thirteenth-century philosopher, theologian, and mystic Ramon Lull. Lull, as Frye sees him, is a Neoplatonic mystic because of his view of religion "as communication between the individual soul and the divine spirit" (*SE*, 227). The essay focuses on Lull's *Book of the Lover and the Beloved,* and the quality of its "airy and abstract" mysticism is for Frye, as it is for other commentators, "difficult to define." The Lover and the Beloved are always soaring upward, and the book contains, Frye says, no sense of "the intense agony, the profound humiliation, the symbolism of the descent into hell and a rise through purgatory that we find in the mystics who have gone through what is called the dark night of the soul" (*SE,* 231). Moreover, in Lull there is no erotic symbolism of the kind found in, say, Sufi mysticism, the Song of Songs, St. John of the Cross, and St. Teresa. Lull is strictly contemplative, and the end of contemplation for him is "that mystic *extasis* in which joy and sorrow are surpassed in a fervour of devotion too concentrated to permit of any emotional criticism" (*SE,* 232).[20] We see, then, that Frye's understanding of mysticism in this student paper includes three strands—the contemplative, the erotic, and the *via negativa.*

Frye also introduces mysticism into an earlier Emmanuel College paper (he was twenty-one at the time) in which he sets down an embryonic form of the truth, beauty, goodness triad that he developed twenty years later at the beginning of the Fourth Essay in *Anatomy of Criticism.* In this earlier essay, "The Relation of Religion to the Arts," the members of the triad are truth, beauty, and justice, and the corresponding human faculties, reason, feeling, and will. Religion, for Frye in this paper, derives from a synthesis of the will and reason. This is what produces the good life or "the imperative which brings together all souls around one concept, thus establishing the relationship of God to man" (*SE,* 308). He does not say what this concept is, but it can be expressed only symbolically, and he argues that the religious synthesis becomes one-sided if either the will dominates the reason or the reason dominates the will. The former produces mysticism and the latter theology. Mysticism is not congenial to art, Frye maintains, because the individual is withdrawn "into a timeless absolute" where communication becomes difficult and is achieved only by compromise. "A mystic poet, for example, must sacrifice to the poet the mystic's self-absorption to be able to become articulate, while he must surrender to the mystic the poet's love for a deceptive nature and his rapturous acceptance of the sense world" (*SE,* 309). Mysticism, then, in this student essay, has little to recommend it from the point of view of art. If art leans too far in either direction, the mystical or the theological, it undermines its purpose. Frye would continue to explore the relations between mysticism and art, especially in Notebook 3, which he began writing nearly a decade after completing his Emmanuel College studies and which he calls his "mystical notebook" (*TBN,* 162).

The most important published commentary on mysticism early in Frye's career is in the note at the end of *Fearful Symmetry.* This brief statement, which addresses the question whether Blake was a mystic, isolates three meanings of mysticism: contemplative quietism, spiritual illumination resulting in unspeculative piety, and the visionary transformation of the human mind (*FS*, 422). These three definitions illustrate that mysticism is another essentially contested concept. In an appendix to his Bampton Lectures, Dean Inge lists twenty-six definitions.[21] Frye adds still another in an expanded exposition of his third category, saying that if Blake is to be considered a mystic, then mysticism has to be defined as an "effort of vision . . . conceived neither as a human attempt to reach God nor a divine attempt to reach man, but as the realization in total experience of the identity of God and Man in which both the human creature and the superhuman creator disappear" (*FS*, 431). The key idea here is the total experience of identity.

In his authoritative study of Western mysticism Bernard McGinn argues that the dichotomy between mystical experience or the mystical way of life, on the one hand, and mystical theology (the reflection on or understanding of the experience), on the other, is a false dichotomy. Mystical "experience," with its suggestions of altered or rapturous states, does not in fact capture what mystics themselves have emphasized. Such experience, which is itself inaccessible, is available to us only through mystical interpretation. Mysticism, in other words, is always mediated textually and theologically. McGinn's own historical approach is to consider Western mysticism in three different contexts: "mysticism as a part or element of religion; mysticism as a process or way of life; and mysticism as the attempt to express a direct consciousness of the presence of God."[22] Frye does not examine mysticism in such a systematic way, although most of his speculations and commentaries would fall into one or the other of McGinn's contexts. He does sometimes speak of the mystical experience in his notebooks, but he realizes the vagueness of the term, and he is aware that all we possess are mystical texts. Criticism, he would say, is to literary experience as religious interpretation is to mystical experience. If, as McGinn maintains, a new level of awareness or heightened consciousness more accurately describes the mystical encounter, then Frye's view that the kerygmatic breakthrough to the "spiritual" level is the highest intensity of consciousness could be described as "mystical." This breakthrough for Frye, as we have seen in chapter 2 and as Frye spells out again in the *Fearful Symmetry* note, is the identity of the human and the divine presences through an act of vision. If the word "mystic" is to be applied to Blake, then it must be seen as a synonym for "visionary."[23] But Frye uses the word "mystical," as we shall see below, in ways that qualify this somewhat loose equation.

Still, the *Fearful Symmetry* note anticipates a good deal of what Frye says about mysticism elsewhere. Mysticism, which is a word Blake never used, is relevant to the study of Blake only if the mystics are seen as struggling

> to describe the divine One who is all things, yet no thing, and yet not nothing; to explain how this One is identical with the self yet as different from the self as it can be; to make it clear how the creaturely aspect of man does not exist at all and yet is a usually victorious enemy of the soul. . . . The true God for such visionaries is not the orthodox Creator, the Jehovah or Isvara or Nobodaddy who must always be involved with either an eternal substance or an eternal nothingness, depending on the taste of the theologian, but an unattached creative Word who is free from both. Unity with this God could be attained only by an effort of vision which not only rejects the duality of subject and object but attacks the far more difficult antithesis of being and non-being as well. (*FS*, 431)

Nowhere does Frye comment on the four marks of the mystical experience outlined in William James's *The Varieties of Religious Experience:* ineffability, noetic quality, transiency, and passivity.[24] But he was attracted to two ideas in James's *Varieties,* which he calls "an almost definitive book on its subject" (*LN,* 1:366). The first is the notion of expanded consciousness, close to the visions of parallel worlds in science fiction that arise from dreams and drug-induced states—what Julian Jaynes calls "hallucinations."[25] The second is the hint throughout James that the mystical experience is neither subjective nor objective but an identity of subject and object in the Blakean sense (*RT,* 228, 231, 242). The paradoxes in the note on Blake's mysticism in *Fearful Symmetry* take us to the core of Frye's visionary poetics. Frye is speaking here about the implications of mysticism for Blake's view of art, and Frye's own almost mystical language points in the direction of the freedom that comes from the spiritual discipline of yoga, the paradoxes of Zen Buddhism, and the speculations of the German mystics from Eckhart to Boehme.[26] In fact, in his *Fearful Symmetry* note Frye remarks that all three of these traditions are analogous to the visionary metamorphosis in Blake. We have examined Frye's connection with the first two. To explore further his speculations on mysticism, we turn now to the third.

The Deification of the Void

Frye encountered in the medieval mystical tradition, especially in Meister Eckhart and Jacob Boehme and in the fourteenth-century mystical treatise *The Cloud of Unknowing*, what he calls the "deification of the void," the apophatic disposition to discover God through the *via negativa*. In Eckhart this was the God behind or beyond God, in Boehme the abyss or nothingness of the *Urgrund* (Unground), and in *The Cloud of Unknowing* the idea of a "hid divinity." Boehme, especially, is a Hermes or psychopomp figure for Frye and so represents a descent into the dark night of the soul that the *Urgrund* symbolizes. "I used to call this Unground mysticism the deification of the void," Frye writes in a marginal annotation to Boehme's *Six Theosophic Points*, "which apparently is just what it is."[27] Versions of the void appear in Carlyle and Blavatsky as well.[28]

Frye did not react approvingly to the "deification of the void" early in his career, calling it a form of false occultism (32.32). What he found objectionable was the absence of a personal Creator. While Boehme does have the idea of a Father-God, this Nobodaddy God can be rescued, for Frye, only after it is humanized by the idea of the Son, which overcomes all the wrath associated with the God of the deified void.[29] Frye finds Boehme unsatisfactory because *katabasis* involves more than deifying the void, and finds him difficult because of the prolixity of his style: "I've also been trying to read Boehme because of his fire imagery and the way he talks about Urgrund and nothingness, but I've never got much out of Boehme" (*LN,* 2:480). Still, he continues "to struggle with Boehme and his abyss–fire–wrath world" (*LN,* 2:550), a struggle that had begun in the writing of *Fearful Symmetry,* where he calls Boehme's often impenetrable works, arising from the Anabaptist and alchemical traditions, "visionary poems" (153).

Frye appears to have gradually altered his opinion. In one of his notebooks from the 1980s he writes, "Boehme is making more sense as I move closer to light and signature symbolism," adding that "it's not that I 'believe' him but that this is the kind of link between the Bible and the creative imagination that I'm looking for" (*LN,* 1:35). This is a reference to the *Signatura Rerum,* where Boehme advances the theory, not unlike that of Paracelsus, that the inner qualities and properties of all things are displayed in their outer forms, just as the character of a person shows itself in his or her facial expression.[30] He advised everyone to study Nature with this in mind, assuring them that "the greatest understanding lies in the signatures, wherein man (viz. the image of greatest virtue) may not only learn to know himself, but also the essence of all essences."[31] Then, in *Words with Power* we discover that, for Frye, Boehme takes his place alongside the Neoplatonists, Dionysius the Areopagite, Eckhart, and Ruysbroeck as one who approaches revelation by way of ecstatic metaphor (86). When Frye comes to his katabatic chapter on the furnace, which was the end of his own quest, he calls on Boehme to help illuminate the imagery of the radical creative descent and its Heideggerean distinction between nothing and Nothing:

> Of those in the Christian theological tradition, perhaps Boehme is the most thoroughgoing, in showing that the conception of God is essentially connected with nothingness, that the presence of God appears in an *Urgrund* from which all conditions and attributes of being have been withdrawn. Boehme's vision of the creation anticipates Hegel in speaking of a negating of negation, a transforming of God from nothingness to an infinite something, which left the nothingness behind as a kind of vacuum suction, drawing everything within its reach into non-being. The abandoned nothingness is the principle of evil, the Lucifer or light-bearer which turns into the adversary of light, or Satan, after the light or Word has freed itself. This may sound difficult, but Boehme is difficult. The essential point is the association of nothingness and divine creation, an association that fascinated Yeats, who refers to Boehme in his play *The Unicorn from the Stars,* in which the climactic phrase is "Where there is nothing, there is God." (*WP,* 289)

The tradition of the hidden divinity or *deus absconditus* is no less difficult, since its advocates claim that to seek God, who remains always hidden by a cloud of unknowing, one must abandon all ideas and images beneath a "cloud of forgetting." In Frye's outline of the three stages of religion, glanced at in chapter 2 and summarized in chart 4 (appendix), the hidden divinity belongs to the second stage. Here the conceptions of God range from a personal creator at one end of the spectrum to a hidden God at the other, and the context is the ascent of the spirit. The spirit progresses first through the moral or sacramental stage of religion (as represented by Dante's *Purgatorio* and Spenser's faerie world). This is followed by the mystical ascent to the God beyond God. But the "hid divinity" complex is wordless, because language, which is naturally finite, cannot in the end capture the essence of the infinite. That is what the anonymous author of *The Cloud of Unknowing* was trying to get at: God may know us, but whatever apprehension we have of God is finally beyond language. Thus the "hid divinity" tradition has no place in the scheme of language Frye outlined in *The Great Code.* It does not belong to the analogical or metonymic phase of language (this is put for that), and it is not metaphoric, for the "hid divinity" tradition eschews images altogether. As Frye says in *The Great Code,* for Eckhart and *The Cloud of Unknowing,* "no word, such as 'Being,' is strictly applicable to God, because words are finite and God is not: the real God is 'hidden,' beyond all thought, and *a fortiori* beyond words. This tendency in thought seems to point in the direction of a nonverbal mysticism, like that of some Oriental religions, notably Tao and Zen" (*GC,* 12).[32]

Another version of the God beyond God is Eckhart's *Gottheit*—God as emptiness, silence, absence. The *Gottheit,* Frye writes, "is nothing because he's transferred everything to God. Sounds like what the God-is-dead people say about kenosis. It's the void that's the antitype of 'vanity' (apocalyptic fullness, rather), the absolute spirit that's the apocalyptic contrast to hebel or mere breath. It's the silence that's the echo of speech" (*LN,* 1:35). A contemporary form of the *Gottheit* would be the vision of vacancy in Eliot's *Four Quartets* (*RT,* 103). Frye is clearly indebted to Rudolf Otto's *Mysticism East and West* for his understanding of Eckhart, but his source for Eckhart's *via negativa* is Aldous Huxley's *Perennial Philosophy,* and the passage in Eckhart he is referring to is this: "The Godhead gave all things up to God. The Godhead is poor, naked and empty as though it were not; it has not, wills not, wants not, works not, gets not. It is God who has the treasure and the bride in him, the Godhead is as void as though it were not."[33] Frye says that the *Gottheit,* which is a matter of experience rather than knowledge (*RT,* 130), is implicit in Christianity, "which has never denied that God *in himself* is bigger than his revelation" (*RT,* 207). The most frequent reference to Eckhart in Frye's notebooks— less a mystical point than a theological one—is to the mythical and metaphorical understanding of the Virgin Birth that Frye ran across in one of Eckhart's sermons: every Christian is a virgin mother responsible for giving birth to the Word.[34] It is worth noting that Frye is attracted to Eckhart as well because of the accusation against him for heresy, such accusations always being for Frye, the dissenting nonconformist, a signal that the accused had defended something important.[35]

The Perennial Philosophy

One of Frye's primary sources for mystical texts was Huxley's *The Perennial Philosophy,* where he finds his "oft-thought good ideas well-expressed as well as my bad ones" (*RT,* 24). The *philosophia perennis,* a phrase popularized by Leibnitz, is for Huxley the timeless and universal ground of all Being—what he calls "the divine Reality." Metaphysically, the divine Reality underlies everything in the world, including human minds. Psychologically, it is the same thing as the soul. Ethically, the ultimate end of the human enterprise is to be found in the immanent and transcendent ground of Being. Huxley proposes that this ground of Being in all religions is one and the same and that it constitutes the essential core of each religion.[36] His book, which Frye read shortly after it was published in 1945, is an anthology of selections from the tradition of the *philosophia perennis,* alternating with Huxley's commentary.[37]

Frye is initially skeptical of Huxley's project, because he finds him to be like the proponents of Bhakti yoga, "ducking out the back door." Bhakti yoga, the shortest and easiest of the four paths to union with God in Hinduism (the path of the devout love of God), is analogous for Frye to orthodox Christian mysticism. It is a form of an escape from the world: by slipping out of the world by the back door, it provides no opportunity for "exercising the larger regenerative power of the prophet & the artist" (*RT,* 16). Huxley is "not in there slugging. And that rather unhealthy (as I think) mildness in him makes him miss the point of the great scherzo people—Blake most obviously, the Zen Buddhists, perhaps Rabelais" (*RT,* 24). "Scherzo," or what Frye sometimes calls the *schalk* features of the imagination, is the lighthearted, roguish, and comic disposition that serves as an antidote to high seriousness and moral propriety and is rooted in ordinary reality. And this is not to be found in Huxley. Moreover, Huxley has no sense of the paradox in the spiritual energy of, say, Zen (*RT,* 24), and his "weak irritation seem[s] to miss the point of the real people— Eckhart, for instance—and bring down to the reader the whole monastic conception of the spiritual exercise as what to do to keep from jerking off when you're alone" (*RT,* 26). Eckhart, that is, knows what a genuine spiritual exercise is. But Frye finds that as he continues to read *The Perennial Philosophy,* Huxley improves, and more than thirty years later he even announces that he must "keep in touch" with the book.[38]

One of Frye's plans for *The Critical Path* was a three-chapter book, of which the third chapter, on biblical typology, would lead up to the question of what religion says "when considered, not as *religio* or social observance, or as symbolism, which doesn't *say* anything, but as doctrine, in the sense of an imaginative vision which is also existential and committed" (*RT,* 110). This would be an essay on "what comparative religion compares" and so would amount to a version of the perennial philosophy. Frye adds that although he does not *believe* in a perennial philosophy, "there *is* something there" (*RT,* 110). This something would be "a total religion, a *telos* of religious impulses" (*RT,* 113). These speculations occur in the late 1960s and early 1970s, the time when Frye was working out his view on the three awarenesses that we examined in chapter 2. The perennial philosophy was part of the second awareness:

> The second stage is the mind's withdrawal from creation into the
> death-consciousness of contemplation and observation. God here be-

comes a first cause and (as in St. Thomas) a clearing-house of absolute terms—essence, being omni- this and that. Here everything is focussed on the judgement that accompanies death, which in turn is the inevitable consequence of an *act* of creation, a making of the world. As it proceeds, its one God becomes less personal, & the stage ends in "Thou art That" mysticism, the so-called perennial philosophy. (*RT*, 100)

This is the second stage of religion in one of Frye's body-mind-soul formulations (see chart 4), the first stage being natural religion (the Druid analogy) and the third stage a biblical and revolutionary monotheism focusing on the Word. In Notebook 11f, where Frye gives a capsule version of the three stages of religion, he calls the second stage the perennial philosophy, and mysticism is the final form of the second stage of awareness.[39]

The most extended sketch we have of the three stages is in Notebook 12, where Frye outlines three parts of the Great Doodle (described in the introduction), his circular diagram with its vertical Logos-Thanatos axis, its horizontal Nomos-Nous axis, and its four quadrants divided into thirty-three sections. He develops a Great Doodle for his Druid analogy and gives a few hints of what the biblical one might look like (*TBN*, 240–42). Between these he gives his own "version of the 'perennial philosophy,'" the four components of which are represented in diagram 2. The movement of the cycle here is counterclockwise, beginning with the Adonis quadrant. Frye refers to the Eros complex as "the mystical, idealistic ladder-climbing quadrant" (*TBN*, 175). Mysticism, then, as he conceives it in his anticipated book on religion, is a concluding or Eros phase of the second awareness. The Eros archetype, like the other three "gods" in Frye's Hermes-Eros-Adonis-Prometheus (HEAP) cycle, keeps dissolving and reformulating itself in Frye's notebooks, but it represents higher love (*agape*) as an *axis mundi* image, gospel and the participating apocalypse as a phase of revelation, spirit as the object of epiphany, and redemption as a biblical analogue. Mysticism, then, so long as it is not self-hypnosis, is part of the Eros vision, or what Frye calls in Notebook 21 "the imgve. apoc. [imaginative apocalyptic] vision of the transfigured world the poets help us to get, the vision symbolized in the Bible by miracle, especially the miracle of healing. A community's art is its spiritual vision." Frye adds that the northeast quadrant is the locus of mysticism as well (*RT*, 206).

In Frye's *Late Notebooks*, the distinction between the perennial philosophy and the perennial religion tends to collapse. At one point Frye appears to equate the two, saying that "the Bible is an archetypal model of a perennial philosophy or everlasting gospel" (*LN*, 1:28). The Everlasting Gospel meant for Frye what it meant for Blake: the religion of Jesus,

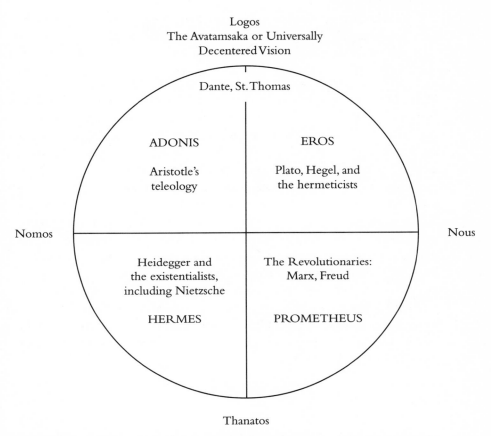

Diagram 2. The Perennial Philosophy (from Notebook 12, *TBN*, 174, 241)

which is the embodiment of Blake's "all religions are one" thesis. As Frye explains in *Fearful Symmetry,* "Blake does not mean by one religion the acceptance of a uniform set of doctrines by all men: he means the attainment of civilized liberty and the common vision of the divinity and unity of Man which is life in Jesus" (*FS*, 340). The epitome of the perennial philosophy in the New Testament is not found in the Synoptics but in the Gospel of John. As Frye is working out his third lecture for what became *The Double Vision,* he writes in Notebook 53,

> I want to proceed from the gospel to the Everlasting Gospel, and yet without going in the theosophic direction of reconciliation or smile-of-a-fool harmony. The synoptics make Jesus distinguish himself from the Father, as not yet more than a prophet: it's in the "spiritual" gospel of John that he proclaims his own divinity. . . . Yet John is more specifically and pointedly "Christian" than the synoptics: the direction is

from one spokesman of the perennial philosophy and a unique incarnation starting a unique event. Buddhism and the like interpenetrate with the Everlasting Gospel: they are not to be reconciled with it. (*LN*, 618–19)

Here the perennial philosophy has moved from the position it had for Frye in the 1960s and 1970s, as a separate stage in the progression from natural to biblical religion. It is now equated with the biblical vision of the Everlasting Gospel, and it interpenetrates with Buddhism. The focus here is not on similarity but on unity. As Frye writes in Notebook 44, there is no perennial philosophy if all we see are similarities between, say, the wisdom of the Bible and the wisdom in Egypt or Sumeria. Such similarities lead to a perennial philosophy that is nothing more than "denatured techniques of concentration" (*LN*, 1:110). But in the sense of "all religions are one" the perennial philosophy is the metaphorical unity that Frye refers to as "Thou Art That" mysticism; and insofar as there are layers of the self above the consciousness of the ego, then "the self becomes fully enlightened by realizing its identity with a total self, an indivisible unity of God, man, and the physical world. This conception is the basis of Aldous Huxley's 'perennial philosophy,' the mystic's axiom 'Thou art That'" (*NFCL*, 120).

Thou Art That

Frye appears to have first encountered the Hindu precept of "Thou Art That" (*tat tvam asi*) in Huxley, whose first chapter, entitled "That Art Thou," reproduces from the Chandogya Upanishad the story of Svetaketu's receiving these three celebrated words from his father.[40] According to Huxley's translation, *tat tvam asi* means that "the True" is the Self. And for a person to know the "That" which is the "Thou," he or she may look inward to the God that is within, outward to discover the unity of others with God, or, optimally for Huxley, "both from within and from without."[41] When Frye equates the perennial philosophy with the "Thou Art That" in the second stage of religion, he sees the Hindu formula as pointing to a mystical similarity:

> The key to stage two is monotheism: you can't have recreation or apocalypse without that. The key to stage three is divine humanity, which gets past mysticism of the "Thou art That" type. (*RT*, 90)

> "Thou art That." Who says so? Whoever it is, he begins with "Thou," & so implies a communication of particulars as well as identity. I'm a

theist because I think the human is divisible, part of it being "all too human" & only a part divine. Man is a twofold being, Blake says. But I don't want an unseen likeness-link, whether it's God or being or what the hell. It's partly a question of context: it can't ultimately be true that the divine is *part* of anything, whether human or not. We're all panthe-ists in the resurrection, when God is all in all. (*RT,* 93)

But in contexts other than the stages-of-religion scheme, Frye's reading of "Thou Art That" turns away from the mystical "likeness-link" toward metaphorical identification. The more orthodox, though no less para-doxical, interpretation of the Hindu formula takes "That" to refer to *brahman* (the absolute or eternal) and "Thou" to *atman* (absolute con-sciousness or soul). The joining by the copula *asi* of the two parts of the statement means that we have a metaphor, the intention of which is to ex-press an intuition of oneness—the identity of the individual soul and the supreme soul.[42] In the dozen or so places where Frye writes about "Thou Art That," the context is usually metaphorical. In "The Dialectic of Be-lief and Vision" he says—in a passage quoted in chapter 3—that the sense of ultimate identity that lies behind the most profound religious intuitions is suggested by the metaphorical "Thou Art That" formula. It is under-standable, then, as we have seen in chapter 1, that Frye would associate "Thou Art That" with interpenetration.

In Notebook 50 Frye writes that "Thou Art That" will be a part of chapter 8 of *Words with Power.* He adds that he still has "to work out the assumption (in the theological sense) of the interpenetrating world," one example of which is in *The Colloquy of Monos and Una,* a dialogue by Poe that seeks to overcome the separation between conscious existence (*at-man*) and spiritual reality (*brahman*) (*LN,* 1:290). "Thou Art That" is not a hypothetical metaphor of the panoramic apocalypse but an ecstatic one of the participating apocalypse, the locus of identification (*LN,* 2:600).[43] Hypothetical metaphor, however paradoxical, still operates in the ordi-nary world, but existential metaphor creates a "mystical identity above time and space" (*LN,* 1:107). In one of his sermons, Frye says,

The basis of knowledge is the individual: I know, you know, he or she knows. The basis of wisdom is the community; it is what others may get from us, either because of what we say or, much more frequently, in spite of what we say. The next step is that of the poet Rimbaud, who remarks that one should not say "je pense," but rather "on me pense." The point is not that "I think;" the point is rather that somebody or something is thinking with me. Rimbaud is expressing the kind of experience that the great mystics struggle for, the moment the Upanishads express in the formula "Thou art that," the moment when "I know" goes into reverse and becomes something more like "I am known." This is a tentative sense of a total scheme of things, which can be grasped only by an infinite mind, yet a scheme of things where we belong and find our own place and our own identity. Such phrases as these are not assumptions or hypotheses, much less definitions: they are attempts to put into words feelings which, while they express a sense of complete certainty and conviction, are always in themselves expendable.

This is of course what Paul is talking about when he says that we now know in part, but that there is a state of being where we know even as we are (now) known [1 Cor. 13:12]. For Paul, it follows that the process we call death is the highest adventure of the questing spirit, where we go from knowledge to what would be more accurately called revelation; where we come to the end of all things for ourselves and therefore come around to the beginning again, the beginning of life within the power that can make all things new. (NFR, 310)[44]

Similarly, Frye concludes one of his undated prayers by expressing the hope that "we may attain a glimpse of thy city where there is no distinction of creator and creature, where there are no men but only man, and where thou art that man, one with God in eternity, yet one with us in the mirage of time" (NFR, 382). It seems clear, then, that the religious implications of the perennial philosophy and "Thou Art That" are not all that different from the versions of the kerygmatic breakthrough that Frye associates with identity, revelation, vision, and re-creation.

Mystical Mediators

In addition to Huxley's book, Frye read two of the most popular studies of mysticism, R. C. Zaehner's *Mysticism Sacred and Profane* (1957) and Evelyn Underhill's *Mysticism: A Study in the Nature and Development of Man's Spiritual Consciousness.*[45] Zaehner, a Roman Catholic convert, distinguishes between the mysticisms of nature and of God, the latter taking either monistic or theistic forms, and he asserts that theistic mysticism is the highest form. But Frye cannot agree with this division, and he thinks that Zaehner's Roman Catholicism skews his judgments (RT, 212).[46] Frye read Underhill at the same time he was reading Rudolf Otto's *Mysticism East and West* and Patanjali's *Yoga-Sutras,* along with other yoga texts. Otto's book posits two mystical paths—the inward way of introspection and the way of unifying vision—and both paths, Otto argues, can be found in the two representative figures he studies, Eckhart and Sankara.

But Frye, always seeking identity rather than difference, thinks that Otto's dichotomy, like Zaehner's, is a false one: "Surely the discovery of the self and the unifying of vision are and always must be the same thing" (*RT,* 11).

As for Underhill, Frye's notes on her are more extensive, but he does not find her view of mysticism, especially as it is developed in the first part of her book, as having much to recommend it. She sees mysticism as the "haphazard appearance of genius" (an experience removed from discipline and practice), she is not open to secular forms, and she tends to see only one mystical path.[47] But as Frye continues to read Otto and Underhill, he comes to understand that mysticism bifurcates:

> On the one hand, it relates to a specific tradition & approach, a high Bhakti yoga or practice of communion with Being in love. As such, it seems to me (this is subject to change without notice) perfectly valid as far as it goes, but inclined by its temperament & symbols to stay on the Beulah level of the married creature: fragmentary & disjointed in utterance, . . . humorless, because its search for unity makes it determined to overlook the incongruous, tending to apotheosize the female will, . . . tending to make its last court of appeal subjective, & of the type of mysterious orthodoxy which insists on how possible it is to have one's Nobodaddy & eat him too. On the other hand, if Plotinus & Eckhart & Sankara are mystics, one begins to see in what sense Plato, St. Thomas Aquinas & Dante, who all get extensively quoted in any serious study of mysticism, are also mystics. Here the term mystic tends to mean that large & more powerful comprehensiveness of mind (*and* speech *and* soul *and* all the other words) which makes a poet a Dante & not a Shelley, a composer a Bach & not a Wagner, a philosopher a Plato & not a Descartes, a contemplative a St. Theresa & not a Guyon. Now one can illegitimately confuse these meanings, as I think the Underhill woman unconsciously does, so as to suggest that *a* way is actually *the* way. Or one can unite the partial to the total, & see the complete mystic way as one of a group of means of developing the soul. I feel that this perception, this ability to see the whole process in perspective, is the true Raja Yoga, which differs from all others in being the power of perceiving other approaches as Yogas. (*RT,* 15–16)

All of these speculations are early, and they form a part of the direction that Frye is trying to set for his own life in the 1940s. The path he decides to take is not that of high Bhatki yogins, who "have a ferocity of spirit that enables them to break & twist themselves, to pluck out eyes that offend them, to eliminate the centrifugal in matters of faith," and who withdraw into their monastic cells while the heretics are burning outside the gates. "I do not deny Loyola's kind of courage," Frye writes, "but I am more impressed by the heretics' kind, & hope it will prove more acceptable to God" (*RT,* 18, 19). Frye rejects, then, what he calls the Bhakti mystics because they are humorless, with no sense of imaginative "scherzo," and because they have a very limited conception of art. Thus, as we have seen in chapter 4, Frye opts for the path of Patanjali, the way of discipline, combined with Jnana yoga, the way of the artist.

Frye perceives other dangers in mysticism. Mystics who ignore the phenomenological relation between the world and the Word, instead looking for the *deus absconditus* or noumenal God only within themselves, can become narcissistic, their platitudes surrounded by "an aura of secret knowledge" (*RT,* 210–11). Frye is interested in anagogic forms of mysticism, not psychological ones (*RT,* 23). And there are perils in mystical knowledge that is said to be beyond words: "[t]he mystic keeps running out of language" (*LN,* 1:62). Mystics are not alone in describing God as beyond words: one finds the same tendency in Gnosticism and in some theologians. But mystics often claim that God is "above anything you can possibly put into words. O.K. But how could so stratospheric a conception be a character in a human story, which is what he consistently is in the Bible?" (*LN,* 1:276). Frye draws back, then, from those forms of mysticism that take what he calls the flight-of-the-dove approach (*LN,* 1:347).[48] Without the mystic's vision being rooted in physical reality, there can be no place for the Incarnation. Mystics who insist that their vision corresponds to *the* way are also to be mistrusted (*LN,* 1:209). Nor does Frye think that mysticism without a sense of community—individualized mysticism, as in Plotinus—has much to recommend it (*LN,* 1:347). But he does affirm mysticism as a comprehensiveness of soul and as a stage in the religious quest that leads ultimately to dialogue. Still, something more than an intense ecstasy is required:

> [O]n my way from 2nd to 3rd awareness I have to by-pass mysticism in the sense of a deliberate effort to transcend ordinary consciousness. This is because of the *conservatism* of mysticism: what it doesn't try to transcend is the quality of awareness, only its intensity. Hence a curiously *facile* element in its (mainly allegorizing) treatment of myth: Browne's "easy & Platonick" description. The profundity of St. John of the Cross on the Song of Songs is very great, but it would make an O.T. scholar shudder. Imagination unites sanity & the ecstatic, as in Shaw's St. Joan. (*RT,* 152)

Frye approves of the formulation of Sir Thomas Browne, who wrote, "Since I was of understanding to know we knew nothing, my reason hath

beene more pliable to the will of faith; I am now content to understand a
mystery without a rigid definition in an easie and Platonick description."[49] Frye's critique here is a form of reason dominating the will that
he outlined in his student paper "The Relation of Religion to the Arts."
The distinction in the passage just quoted is between the limitations of
generalized and abstract definitions (allegory), on the one hand, and the
"quality of awareness" that comes with a metaphorical approach to myth,
on the other. Philosophical description is always restricted for Browne, as
it is for Frye. The *Aufhebung* involved in all of this is a movement to an
imaginative level beyond the oppositions of the sane and the ecstatic,
philosophical description and intensity of awareness, or, as in the student
paper and in Browne, the reason and the will. At this point, Frye's understanding of mysticism is somewhat more circumscribed than its Blakean
sense noted at the beginning of this chapter—an expanded consciousness
that is synonymous with the visionary and kerygmatic breakthrough.

Mystical mediators can be gurus, such as G. I. Gurdjieff, where the
emphasis is on oral teaching, as in the tradition of yoga. Gurdjieff, the
Russian spiritual teacher, began his work in 1912 and several years later
was joined by the philosopher P. D. Ouspensky, whose *In Search of the
Miraculous,* a record of eight years of conversations with Gurdjieff, is the
most complete account we have of his teachings. Frye read Gurdjieff's
All and Everything—or at least part of this gargantuan work[50]—but his
knowledge of Gurdjieff came primarily from Ouspensky's book and from
Kenneth Walker's *A Study of Gurdjieff's Teaching.* Frye makes two substantial references to Gurdjieff in his published work, both accompanied by a
measure of skepticism and suspicion.[51] The first reference, which comes
in the context of the allegory of self-transformation in the "great work"
of the alchemists, is in Frye's autobiographical essay "Expanding Eyes."
"Such a work of transformation," Frye writes,

> is the work specifically of saints, mystics and yogis. However the al-
> chemists managed, it seems to require teachers, oral instruction, and
> joining a school, and it is so unimaginably difficult that very few get far
> along the way, though they undoubtedly make a big difference to the
> world when they do. The transmission of such teaching, however, is
> often accompanied, especially in the East, by a total unconcern for so-
> ciety as a whole, or else, especially in the West, by an over-concern with
> the preserving of the unity of the transmitting body. In any case some
> powerful force of social entropy seems to affect it wherever it appears.

One of the most impressive figures in this tradition in our own century, Gurdjieff, distinguishes two elements in man: the essence and the

persona, what a man really is and what he has taken on through his social relationships. Gurdjieff clearly thought of the kind of training that
he could give as essentially a developing and educating of the essence.
Perhaps there is also a way to development through the persona,
through transforming oneself into a focus of a community. This includes all the activity that we ordinarily call creative, and is shown at its
clearest in the production of the arts. What is particularly interesting
about alchemy is the way in which it uses the same kind of symbolism
that we find in literature to describe the "great work" of the mystic. If
spiritual seeker and poet share a common language, perhaps we cannot
fully understand either without some reference to the other. (*SM*,
119–20)[52]

The methods that Gurdjieff used to lead his pupils along the path of a
"fourth way"—a path different from those of the fakir, the monk, and the
yogi—sought to achieve an esoteric awareness that would overcome the
fragmentary character of ordinary experience.[53] Gurdjieff's focus was on
the higher consciousness of the self, rather than on spirituality as an institutional or social form.

But for Frye, Gurdjieff's speculations about the contemplative life
lack any sense that art can also reflect states of higher consciousness.
"There's no evidence that Shakespeare or Bach habitually attained higher
consciousness, but what they wrote certainly manifests that world." And,
Frye wonders, cannot one attain a genuine Logos vision by reading
Shakespeare and listening to Bach (*TBN*, 195)? Passive contemplation
may lead to Gurdjieff's "essence," but this will always for Frye be at the expense of the active participation of the "persona" and the creative focus of
a community.

The second published reference is in *The Great Code*:

The twentieth-century guru Gurdjieff is said to have taught his followers that practically everything we consider art is "subjective" art,
where the artist is taken over by the conventions and conditions of his
art, and whose appeal to his audience is both restricted and haphazard.
Beyond this is an "objective" art which sounds like a propagandist's
wish-fulfilment dream, where the artist knows exactly what effect he
wants to produce and can produce it at will, influencing his public as he
wishes. The examples given of objective art are the Sphinx, a statue in
India that only Gurdjieff had seen, the objective music that brought
down the walls of Jericho, and, in the verbal area, the gospels. I get a
strong impression, which may be quite unfair, that Gurdjieff did not

really know what he was talking about, but had derived the notion from someone who did. Yet the questions his distinction raises of the role of the "objective" in the arts, of the degrees of authority and persuasive power in the works of any given cultural heritage, of the meeting point of the sacred book and the work of literature, are worth exploring, however tentatively. (GC, 216)[54]

In his notebooks Frye is somewhat less guarded, thinking that Gurdjieff must be a better teacher than a writer (RT, 144) and that his theory of universal symbols, called enneagrams, might well be a "put-on" (TBN, 195). Frye's notebook reflections on Gurdjieff are not extensive, but he clearly thinks there is something genuine in the teachings that Gurdjieff had accumulated from his youthful travels to various monasteries and other spiritual sites in Central Asia and the Middle East. At the same time, he is aware that a great deal gets lost when the teachings of the spiritual master are written down by students such as Ouspensky, Gurdjieff's principal interpreter, and Walker—and by Gurdjieff himself in All and Everything.

Beelzebub's Tales to His Grandson, part 1 of All and Everything, is a huge (1238-page) allegory, narrated by the Orc-like Beelzebub, about the causes of human alienation. Throughout, according to Jacob Needleman, "Beelzebub continually brings his perceptions back to the same cosmic laws that govern both the working of nature and the psychic life of humans and, in so doing, bodies forth the picture of a living and conscious universe. In this universe, humanity, falling further away from an understanding of its source and the place it can occupy, has forgotten its function and lost all sense of its direction."[55] Needleman confesses that the meaning of Beelzebub will yield itself only after repeated readings, largely because of its complex style and recurring neologisms. This is perhaps why Frye's comments about Beelzebub's Tales to His Grandson refer not to the book's conceptual argument about cosmic laws and the psychic life but to its literary form. Beelzebub's Tales is at once a "satiric oracular descent," keeping company with Melville's Mardi, Lucian's Kataplous, Apuleius's Golden Ass, and Rabelais' Gargantua and Pantagruel (TBN, 201); a form of sentimental romance, keeping company with E. R. Eddison's The Worm Ouroboros and the Mormon Bible (TBN, 316); and an encyclopedic epic, keeping company with Joyce's Finnegans Wake, Derrida's Glas, and Francesco Colonna's Hypnerotomachia (RT, 305). This move from the conceptual level to the imaginative one is typical of Frye's engagement with esoteric traditions, including the occult arts.

The Kabbalah: From Yates to Yeats

Kabbalism for Frye was one of the four occult arts, the other three being magic, alchemy, and astrology (31.14, 33.15). From the last three emerged the sciences of physics, chemistry, and astronomy, a version of Spengler's idea that each science emerges from the "world-feeling" of a particular culture.[56] From the body of mystical teachings that form the Kabbalah, with its emphasis on the alphabet of forms, emerged philology.[57] There are more than three dozen notebook entries devoted to one or more aspects of Kabbalism, and more than twenty references in Frye's published work. In terms of the dialectic of belief and vision the Kabbalah was a source of things seen rather than heard: Talmudism, like Calvinism, listens to the scholastic unfolding of doctrine; Kabbalism, like the Anabaptist-Quaker tradition, looks for the mystical, apocalyptic pattern (*LN*, 1:80).

Frye's library contains ten books on the Kabbalah, all annotated, but from among these he seems to have relied principally on Gershom Scholem, Charles Poncé, and S. L. MacGregor Mathers's translation of *The Kabbalah Unveiled*.[58] His copy of Scholem's *On the Kabbalah and Its Symbolism* is heavily annotated throughout, and about two-thirds of Scholem's *Major Trends in Jewish Mysticism*, which is quoted in *The Great Code* (60), has numerous marginal markings and annotations. The extensive marginalia in Frye's copy of Poncé's *Kabbalah: An Introduction and Illumination for the World Today* indicate that he read it with a great deal of attention (Frye even corrects Poncé's Hebrew). Although he sometimes gets annoyed by what he encounters in the Kabbalah,[59] its "naked mythology" (10.114) nevertheless held a certain visionary power for him.

In addition, Frye was schooled in the Kabbalah by Dame Frances Yates's studies of Renaissance hermeticism, particularly her treatments of Pico della Mirandola and his follower Johannes Reuchlin and of the culminating survey of Renaissance magic and the occult by Cornelius Agrippa.[60] Pico, convinced that the Kabbalah contained a divine revelation that could unlock the secrets of Greek (Pythagoras, Plato, the Orphics) and Christian thought, commissioned the translation of a large number of Kabbalistic texts. Among the nine hundred theses Pico offered for debate was the proposition that "no science can better convince us of the divinity of Jesus Christ than magic and the Kabbalah."[61] Frye read and annotated Pico's *Oration on the Dignity of Man* and the first of Cornelius Agrippa's *Three Books of Occult Philosophy or Magic*. He also read and annotated the works of two nineteenth-century French occultists—Gérard Encausse's (pseud. Papus) *The Tarot of the Bohemians*, and Eliphas Lévi's

(Alphonse Louis Constant) *The History of Magic*—although their interests in *l'occultisme* was much broader than simply the Kabbalah. But as Frye's notebooks reveal, Yates was his primary source for Renaissance Kabbalism and other speculations about hermeticism. What appeal, then, did the Kabbalah have for Frye?

The Kabbalah, which means "to receive," contains first of all what Frye calls positive analogies. "Analogy" is a word that functions in many ways in Frye's thought, but here it means the resemblances one finds between biblical and Christian myth, on the one hand, and classical versions of the myth, on the other.[62] Thus, the flood in Ovid is a positive analogy of the flood in Genesis. Although the resemblances can be negative analogies (demonic parodies) of the biblical material, the use of classical myths in Christian stories and poems is generally a positive analogy. Positive analogies can be found in doctrines as well. The classical muses are "a positive analogy of Eckhart's theological doctrine of the birth of the Word in the Soul" (*LN*, 1:153). *Eros* is a positive analogy of *agape*. In the second half of *Words with Power* Frye treats scores of such analogies. The Kabbalistic tree of life, commonly depicted as a treelike diagram of the ten Sefiroth in the *Sepher Yetzirah*,[63] is a positive analogy to the biblical tree in Eden, the book of Revelation, and elsewhere—or to any other *axis mundi* image in the Bible, such as Jacob's ladder. The numerical schemes of the Kabbalah are a positive analogy of such things as the 666 symbolism in Revelation. Even the Kabbalistic respect for the letter can be seen as a positive analogy of God as Alpha and Omega. The idea in the Kabbalah that God created the world by withdrawing from it is a positive analogy of what the creation account in Genesis 1 at least suggests, and the image of the original *adam* as androgynous, the male body assuming an already existing female one, is a positive analogy of the creation account in Genesis 2.[64]

There are no archetypal giants, like Adam Kadmon of the Kabbalah, in the biblical Creation accounts,[65] but the idea of creation suggested by a line in the *Sepher Yetzirah*, which Frye considered using as an epigraph for the last four chapters of *Words with Power* (*LN*, 1:180), contains another version of his own idea that the doctrine of Creation is best understood not as an event but as the awakening of human consciousness. The *Sepher Yetzirah* (The Book of Creation or Formations), one of the foundations of Kabbalism, is a brief, anonymous work of mystical cosmology that aims to account for the mystery of creation, which is seen as issuing from "thirty-two wondrous paths of wisdom" (1.1) according to an alphabetic and numeric arrangement: the twenty-two letters of the Hebrew alphabet and the ten primordial numbers. In *Words with Power* Frye writes,

What is really dramatic and powerful about a creation myth is not any account of how the order of nature came into being, but the account of how the sense of nature as an order dawns on a conscious mind. Again, creation carries little conviction when presented as an event occurring at the beginning of time, as time for the imagination really has no beginning. Creation is rather an intensely vivid image of the objective world as a spread-out picture of intelligibility awaiting discovery and interpretation. Traditional religion claims that creation is a product of the Word of God, the creation itself being a second Word of God, an infinite source of what is intelligible to man and can be responded to by him:

Set the Word at its origin and put the Maker in his place.

So counsels the *Sepher Yetzirah* (Book of Formations), a pioneering work of Jewish kabbalism that takes the letters of the Hebrew alphabet, along with the numbers they also stood for, to be the formative principles of the cosmos. (*WP,* 155–56)[66]

The context here is Frye's relating the stairway image to the creation myth, and his point is that the Creation is not something that happened in time but is presented in space as a "spread-out" image. In this image the word is at the top and the creator at the bottom of the spatial projection. The word, that is, always trumps the event. In one of his notebooks for *Words with Power,* Frye quotes the same line from the *Sepher Yetzirah,* but this time in an autobiographical context, saying that throughout fifty years of changing fashions in literary criticism he has taken its counsel "to refer to the ordering of one's own mind, and in that context have tried to follow it" (*LN,* 1:176). In other words, whatever the place of the Maker ("place" is rendered as "base," "foundation," and "throne" in other translations),[67] the creative principles of the world begin, as in the first verse in the Gospel of John, not with a Faustian act, but with the Word.[68] Creation, as Frye puts it in a notebook entry, "is a world to things to be read" (*LN,* 2:520). Because the Word is the real creator, it is human as well as divine. Frye therefore locates in the language-centered mysticism of the *Sepher Yetzirah* a riddling injunction that conforms to, and perhaps even helps define, his view of Creation as a linguistic event, rather than a cosmological or historical one. Whereas the Kabbalistic tree may stretch from Adam Kadmon to the descent into the belly of the leviathan, it is still a map of Creation "presented in the present" (*LN,* 2:655) for human consciousness to interpret. Here we are not too far from the idea, stretching from Pythagoras to modern science, that the ultimate formulas behind the created universe are mathematical.

The Kabbalah, focusing as it does on Creation and the Word, is part of an imaginative myth itself and thus congenial to Frye's way of thinking. This takes us back to the shift from scientific to poetic thinking, which Frye saw as occurring in the other occult "sciences" as well. That is, when alchemy develops into chemistry, alchemy loses its scientific worth but retains its poetic value. Similarly, Kabbalism as an alphabet of forms is replaced by philology and etymology. It will seem foolish to those who are not initiates of the Kabbalah to base an entire hermeneutics on the correspondences between the Hebrew alphabet and the created world, or on gematria, the conversion of letters to a numerical equivalent, a process that is said to reveal correspondences between words that have the same numerical value. But for Frye the apparent arbitrariness of such schemes for post-Enlightenment thinking does not gainsay the validity of the mental outlook they assume. The science of philology, particularly historical etymology, simply takes the form of what Frye calls poetic etymology, the sphere of value being shifted from the scientific to the poetic. This move is not without a measure of wit, but as Frye says, "[C]riticism (which is energetic response to literature) must itself be imaginative, not afraid of humor or paradox, which latter are as essential to poetic truth as accuracy of observation is to botany. Criticism can never be a branch of philosophy or science" (34.97). Here is one of several examples of Frye's poetic etymology:

> From the historical point of view most verbal coincidences are accidents: Kunst nach Gunst; Der Mensch ist, was er isst?; God is good; the Italian version of "a translator is a betrayer," and so on. From my point of view I am not so sure. The whole crisis in Christian doctrine over whether Christ was an allegory or a reality, of like or of the same substance, was fought over literally one jot of difference: homoousian vs. homoiousian that seems to me the historical crisis of the whole argument. Again, cabbalism based on YHWH may have been foolish, but is not the sound identical with Iove which does not seem to be etymologically related? And what about Christ & Krishna? In English there is one *l* of a difference between the Creator & the Creature, the Word & the World. Dante's whole allegory, political & moral, rests on a palindrome: Amor-Roma, just as Parmenides' philosophy of being rests on the ambiguity of "is" as copula & verb of existence. (30n.2)[69]

Although Frye never followed up on his plans to devote a section of one of his books to the study of such eccentric verbal associations and accidental puns,[70] he never abandoned his interest in folk etymologies, wordplay, and the like, even though he recognized that the effort to synthesize meanings from words that simply sound alike was fanciful if not absurd from the perspective of comparative linguistics (30n.1). More than thirty years after the passage just quoted, Frye writes, "In poetry, accidental resemblances among words create sound patterns of rhyme, alliteration, assonance, and metre, and these have a function in poetry that they rarely have outside it. The function of these sound–patterns is to minimize the sense of arbitrariness in the relation of word and meaning, to suggest a quasi-magical connection between the verbal arrangement and the things it evokes. Puns and different or ambiguous associations bound up in a single word seem to be structural principles rather than obstacles to meaning" (*MM*, 109). All of this is close to the metaphorical-game tradition we noted in chapter 3.[71] Of course the Kabbalah is not the only source of Frye's interest in poetic etymology (Joyce is another obvious one), but viewing the Kabbalah as a work of first- rather than third-phase language leads him to conclude that "the cabalistic view of reality is one of enormous importance" (31.14) as an imaginative construct.

One final feature of this imaginative construct returns us to the seen-rather-than-heard distinction—the "spread-out picture of intelligibility." Everyone who writes about the Kabbalah must necessarily represent its material schematically: thus all the charts and diagrams, pentagrams and six-pointed stars, mandalas, schematic trees, the human body overlaid with all manner of correspondences, tables of letters and numbers, magic seals, ringed solar cycles, and the like that one encounters in any Kabbalistic exposition. Frye always insisted that his own diagrams, whether actually drawn or not, were the inevitable consequence of the schematic nature of poetic thinking: criticism is schematic because myth and metaphor are. He comments on the diagrammatic character of the Kabbalah only in passing, and there is nothing to remark about this except to note the obvious—that the Kabbalah, whatever else it might be, is for him an imaginative creation. In *Anatomy of Criticism* he says that the paradigms of Kabbalism and the other occult arts, which are similar to his tables of archetypal imagery, are for the literary critic, "simply reference tables" (359). But they turn out to be much more than reference tables, as we will see in our continuing examination of Frye's interest in the occult arts.

In one of his early notebooks (1946), when Frye is attempting to come to terms with Yeats's *A Vision* in preparation for writing one of his first major essays, "Yeats and the Language of Symbolism," he confesses his ignorance of the evidence that would lead him to judge Yeats in any "scientific" sense. But he goes on to say that after Freud and Jung it is not inconceivable that a genuine study of anagogy might reveal a Yeatsian dictionary of types. At this point, Frye says, he could deliver his "Galenic sermon," meaning apparently that in his Yeats paper he should note that while the sympathies and antipathies of Galenic medicine have no natural existence, such forces do exist in the mind and thus have a verbal reality. This, combined with the "mathematical diagrams" in our prepositions ("up," "down," "beside," "between"), leads Frye to wonder whether "cabalistic diagrams" might "produce mystical visions." He then concludes with one of his own metaphorical games as an illustration of such "diagrammatic" thinking, an illustration that contains a good measure of delight, if not instruction, and that brings to an end this survey of Frye on the Kabbalah:

> We live in an intuitive world of abstract, geometrical, arbitrary symbols: traffic signs, dates, a geometrical alphabet (note how words today break down into letters & Robot words, O.K., F.B.I., UNRRD, & a world dominated by U.K., U.S.A., & U.S.S.R.: a man in the Army speaks almost nothing else) flags (swastika & rayed sun, a flag with 13 red & white bars & 48 stars are potent symbols), arbitrarily conventionalized shapes (the v-shaped "heart" of cards & St. Valentine's day; the star-shaped star), & so on. The lazy mind always wants to make as much of this "just coincidence" (= mentally unorganized design) as possible; the imaginative mind wants to make more, though it often makes too much. But the latter has all the facts. Right now it is 5:24 p.m., Eastern Daylight time, Saturday, May 11, 1946. To the lazy mind that seems a simple & literal statement; but it is actually a complex whirlwind of astrological [week & hour], cosmological [month], mythological [May], historical [1946] & scientific [Daylight] symbols, with some anthropology [Saturday, the week] & geography [Eastern] thrown in. The really [more nearly] literal statement would be more like: "now I am designating a moment of time" (this is still all pure symbolism, but it seems more literal) which has a vaguely poetic sound to most ears. Somewhere in here I should bitch the whole Carnap positivism in a sentence or two, or a paragraph or two at most, & develop, perhaps out of *Sartor Resartus,* my intuition that variable symbolization is the fundamentally human act. (31.15)[72]

Alchemy

Frye's interest in alchemy goes back at least to his Emmanuel College days, but he does little more in his student essays than link alchemy with other forms of occultism. But one passage in his essay on Ramon Lull does anticipate much of what he writes later about alchemy as symbolizing the transformation of the soul from the material state (the *prima mate-*

ria) to the state of original identity (the *lapis*). In making the point that Lull is not an alchemist, Frye writes that alchemy "is the one branch of occult thinking which excludes [numerology]. It rests on the Aristotelian entelechy. . . . the mineral world is the most completely material, and, therefore, the least actualized; all earths are to metals as matter to form; the other metals bear the same relation to gold, and the transmutation of all metals into gold is symbolically connected with the regeneration of mankind. Thus, its premises are quite consistent with Thomism; too consistent to win the approval of Aristotle's great opponent [Lull]" (*SE*, 230).[73]

Frye's knowledge of alchemy in his early years apparently derived mainly from Spengler, whom he read when he was nineteen, and from his readings in comparative mythology.[74] By the time he came to write *Fearful Symmetry* he had read Paracelsus in order to discover how Blake was influenced by alchemical philosophy and the "inner light" of the Anabaptists as these traditions came together in the apocalyptic philosophy of Boehme. The connection turns out to be primarily a correspondence between Blake's view of the imagination and that found in Boehme, whose works are really "visionary poems" (*FS*, 153):

> To the alchemic visionary, gold, the material of the New Jerusalem, was the quintessence of the mineral world, that is, the dead or opaque part of the creation, the "Hermaphroditic Satanic world of rocky destiny" [*Jerusalem,* pl. 58, line 1]. A process of transforming metals to gold would be a redemption of this world: it would symbolize, or even cause, by some form of sympathetic magic which the writer does not pretend to understand, the resurrection and apocalypse of man. The ultimate object of alchemy, from this point of view, was exactly what Blake said the object of his art was, "to Restore what the Ancients call'd the Golden Age." (*FS*, 152–53)

To locate alchemical symbols in Blake (iron, fire, furnace, smith, stone, and so on) is a natural step for Frye, although he was assisted in this effort by M. O. Percival's *William Blake's Circle of Destiny* (1938), which points to a number of alchemical analogues in Blake.[75] An analogue is not a source, and Blake may have known little about alchemy directly. But this does not concern Frye, as the alchemic symbolism is in the Bible anyway and so is evidence for the universality of archetypes.

In *Anatomy of Criticism*, alchemy is seen as a repository of archetypes (rose, stone, elixir, flower, jewel, fire). Drawing on Herbert Silberer's *Problems of Mysticism and Its Symbolism* and C. G. Jung's *Psychology and Alchemy,* Frye writes that in apocalyptic symbolism the fiery bodies of heaven, sun, moon, and stars, are all inside the universal divine and human body. The symbolism of alchemy is apocalyptic symbolism of the same type: the center of nature, the gold and jewels hidden in the earth, is eventually to be united to its circumference in the sun, moon, and stars of the heavens; the center of the spiritual world, the soul of man, is united to its circumference in God. Hence there is a close association between the purifying of the human soul and the transmuting of earth to gold, not only literal gold but the fiery quintessential gold of which the heavenly bodies are made. The golden tree with its mechanical bird in *Sailing to Byzantium* identifies vegetable and mineral worlds in a form reminiscent of alchemy. (146)

Silberer's book, later published as *Hidden Symbolism of Alchemy and the Occult Arts,* is an analysis of a Rosicrucian alchemical text called "The Parable." Silberer, a psychoanalyst and member of the Vienna school, gives a Freudian analysis of the text, which turns out to be an alchemistic hieroglyph. "The Parable," once deciphered, reveals a version of the Oedipus complex; and the attendant red-white, male-female symbolism, plus the various ideas of substance as procreative, are familiar alchemical symbols and themes. In one of his notebooks Frye catalogues several dozen of these that he has drawn from Silberer's book (34.98). But Silberer has a theory of polysemous meaning, so in addition to his psychoanalytic reading of "The Parable" and several other stories, he also offers philosophical or scientific interpretations and religious or anagogic ones. The psychoanalytic reading probes "the depths of the impulsive life" of the psyche; the anagogic reading explores the heights of hermetic mysticism.[76] One of Frye's early outlines for a book he planned to write on symbolism and the Bible shows that the book was to include a chapter on "occult traditions." The eighth chapter was to include a study of Kabbalism and then a study of the "meaning of philosophical alchemy, following the general approach of Silberer; its connection with a) secret societies with a symbolism concealed from censorship like the so-called Rosicrucians b) apocalyptic enthusiasts like Fludd & the precursors of the 'fifth-monarchy' people. Nothing particularly occult, rather fashionable, about occultism in Tudor times. Distinction between occult philosophy & the folklore of witches & familiars that became attached to it. Paracelsus" (34.86).[77] The Bible book eventually assumed a different shape, but the note indicates the philosophical direction Frye wanted to take.

Jung, writing a generation after Silberer, also uncovers a host of resemblances between alchemical concepts and dream symbolism, but his encyclopedic study is directed toward his own psychotherapeutic practice. Thus, Jung finds parallels in alchemy between the process of individuation on the subjective side and the collective unconscious on the objective. On the subjective side he treats the alchemical Great Work (that is, the transmutation of metals), as Frye puts it, "as an allegory of self-transformation, a process of bringing an immortal body (the stone) to birth within the ordinary one (the *materia prima*). Such a work of transformation is the work specifically of saints, mystics and yogis" (*SM,* 119). On the objective side, he argues that the process of symbol formation in alchemy provides evidence for the existence of the collective unconscious. Frye sometimes expresses anxieties about being considered a Jungian, but he was much more deeply immersed in Jungian thought than is commonly imagined. His most extensive commentary on alchemy is his review of *Psychology and Alchemy,*[78] where he gives an overview of the Christian form of alchemy, which was based on biblical commentary. Thus, the alchemical experiments repeat the Creation, and the principle of complementary opposition introduces a host of additional analogies related to the Fall, the church, Christ, the immortal soul, and the doctrine of transubstantiation. "The essential point to remember," writes Frye, "is that when alchemy loses its chemical connections, it becomes purely a species of typology or allegorical commentary on the Bible."[79] This means that regardless of what one thinks of the parallels between alchemy and psychoanalytic principles, Jung's book, like Silberer's, is "a grammar of literary symbolism."[80]

Frye later read Mircea Eliade and Frances Yates on alchemy. Eliade's *The Forge and the Crucible* turned out to be for Frye another sourcebook for the language of myth and metaphor, particularly the Los symbolism of the alchemical furnace and the symbolism of the dying-god vegetative world applied to the mineral world (*LN,* 1:301; *TBN,* 321–22). As for Yates, her interests, like Eliade's, were obviously much broader than the alchemical arts. She does, however, treat alchemy in each of the four books of hers that Frye read, especially in *The Rosicrucian Enlightenment,* where she argues that alchemy in combination with Kabbalism is to be found in the work of such typical Rosicrucian thinkers as John Dee.

Earlier we noted Frye's debt to Yates, one of a group he calls the "wise women."[81] "Frances Yates is wonderful," he declares, "the combination of sober documentation and the wildest guesswork is very exhilarating" (*LN,* 1:51–52). What was not guesswork was Yates's demonstration that many Christians, far from being hostile to the esoteric arts during the Renaissance, actively supported the coexistence of Christian doctrine and hermetic philosophy and that furthermore, as against the widely held view that science had vanquished the esoteric arts, the two could coexist in the minds of many people. Frye thinks that Yates's book on Bruno gets sidetracked by her obsession with the errors in dating hermetic literature, but he values her assumptions about the nature of the imagination.[82] Her book *The Art of Memory* shows how the Renaissance memory theaters were based on the spatializing of knowledge, and these memory theaters, Frye says, hold "all the ghosts of imagination" (*TBN*, 79).[83] This synthetic view of the imagination and its products achieved its full flowering in *Anatomy of Criticism,* and although Frye completed the *Anatomy* before he had read Yates, both critics understand the imagination as an encyclopedic repository of the things the imagination constructs. This means that even the most bizarre texts, literary and otherwise, are potentially valuable. "There is, in fact, nothing in past literature that cannot become a source of imaginative illumination. One would say that few subjects could be duller or less rewarding than the handbooks studied by Miss Frances Yates in *The Art of Memory,* yet her study has all the mental exhilaration of the discovery of a fine new poet" (*StS,* 69–70).

Frye says the same thing about many other discursive thinkers. Whatever one thinks of Spengler as a historian or Frazer as an anthropologist or Jung as a psychoanalyst—and Frye recognizes they are vulnerable from the perspective of current social-scientific methods—such writers are nevertheless astonishingly rich resources for understanding primary concerns, their imaginative representation, and the architecture of the spiritual world. Thus, when Yates speaks of creative melancholy in her book on Renaissance occultism—the descent below hell that is a necessary prelude to creative ascent—she becomes in effect a literary critic, triggering a series of associations for Frye, some alchemical: "Dürer's Saturn,—melancholy link—not so much the planetary as the mythological Saturn, thrown down to 'hell' (Sandys' rendering of Ovid's *Met.* 1.) at the end of the Golden Age. Lead, Saturn's metal, then rises to gold. Chapman's *Hymnus in Noctem,* Burton's & Milton's pensive or creative melancholy, go on to Keats' melancholy Hyperion themes & the *poète maudit* theme in France" (*LN,* 1:52).[84] Similarly with G. R. S. Mead's study of Hermes Trismegistus, *Thrice-Greatest Hermes:* while conventional academics would judge this massive work (815 pages) to be an example of ersatz scholarship and set it aside, Frye, whose copy of the three-volume study is copiously annotated, thinks it might well be a "spiritual vision" of the hermetic sermons and fragments (*LN,* 2:618).

In *Words with Power* Frye writes that he does "not profess to under-

stand much of what is going on in alchemical literature, but the emphasis on a 'mysterium conjunctionis' seems clear enough, and survives in
various disguised forms" (208). These forms appear in the red and white
union in Shakespeare's "The Phoenix and the Turtle," Carroll's *Through
the Looking Glass,* and Tennyson's *The Princess.* But the more important
context for alchemy in *Words with Power* is a complex of ideas that Frye
associates with creative ascent—the purgatorial, the technological, the
educational, and the utopian. Alchemy relates to the first two of these
strands. As we have seen, the purgatorial archetypes have to do with transformation; the technological ones, with machines, wheels, furnaces, fire,
and the like. The two come together in Frye's reading of Yeats's Byzantium poems, an expansion of his "golden tree" remark in *Anatomy of Criticism:*

> Yeats's "Byzantium" also describes a mysterious technological-
> purgatorial-alchemical world in which "blood-begotten spirits" cross
> water at their death to be processed in "smithies," and go through a pur-
> gatorial operation which involves dance, fire, and transformation into
> "glory of changeless metal." In Yeats, as in Eliot, a descending move-
> ment of the old chain-of-being type complements the purgatorial as-
> cent. Eliot preserves its more traditional Christian features: in Yeats's
> "Sailing to Byzantium," we get a more paradoxical vision of the divine,
> spiritual, human and natural elements in the chain as respectively a
> "drowsy Emperor," sages in "God's holy fire," lords and ladies of Byzan-
> tium, and a toy bird in a golden tree representing nature transfigured
> into the "artifice of eternity." The vision is not one of authority or
> divine grace but of an order raised above time, where the poet sings of
> past, present and future in the final line. Both the Byzantium poems
> may cause us to wonder whether Yeats is talking about life after death
> or about the poet's imaginative transforming of reality. We soon realize
> that this is one of those either-or questions that have to be turned into
> both-and answers before it makes sense. (*WP,* 302)[85]

We have noted Frye's repeated insistence that poetic thinking is
schematic. In *The Critical Path* he observes that poets are attracted to the
kind of pattern making that associates, for example, seven metals and
seven planets. But when science dismisses such associations as superstition, they do not disappear; they go underground and then emerge again
imaginatively, often insistently, as in Yeats. Frye obviously knows that the
probability of the alchemists changing base metals into gold is exactly
zero, but the Enlightenment did not put an end to poetic symbolism. It
simply shifted the value of the alchemical mental outlook, as it did the

mental outlook of the other occult arts, from the scientific to the poetic (30n.1). The principle of recurrence, not the progress of science with its truth of correspondence, is what drives the poetic imagination.

> Whatever science may say, the poet's world continues to be built out of a flat earth with a rising and setting sun, with four elements and an animate nature, the concrete world of emotions and sensations and fancies and transforming memories and dreams. Chemistry, with Boyle, becomes "skeptical" of the schematic constructs of alchemy, and eventually develops an elaborate periodical table of elements. But the four elements are still there in Dylan Thomas and the Eliot Quartets, and are likely to remain in poetry until that remote time in the future when chemistry, or whatever the appropriate science will then be, will have discovered that there are in fact four elements, and that their names are earth, air, fire, and water. (*CP*, 83)

There are fewer than twenty passing references to alchemy in Frye's published work, but in the notebooks this occult art appears in more than seventy entries. A large portion of these focus on alchemical symbolism: the red and white union, gold as the world's inner fire, the male and female conjunction. But there is a larger sense in which the alchemic process symbolizes that transformation and regeneration of humanity noted by Frye in his student essay on Lull. The transmutation of base metals into gold by means of the philosopher's stone and the production of the elixir of life were part not of a scientific quest, as Eliade has shown, but of a spiritual one. For Eliade this was part of the human effort to transform nature and to achieve immortality by mastering time.[86] Frye appears to have been influenced by Eliade's view of alchemy and temporality, but he alters the terms of both goals: in Frye the transformation of nature becomes the transformation of consciousness, and the achievement of immortality becomes the achievement of the resurrection. In terms of the four-part circle of the Great Doodle, alchemy belonged to the quadrant of Promethean revolutionary fire. Here is one somewhat enigmatic notebook formulation from the time Frye was planning his "third book":

> In the big third book the key quadrant is Prometheus, because I start with Eros on the other side of it, and the key to Prometheus is resurrection. Resurrection brings the future into the present. It's the Xn [Christian] (or Jewish-Xn-Moslem) revy. [revolutionary] doctrine corresponding to the Buddhist Eros journey to the unborn world. They both destroy the irreversibility of time, but perhaps the essential Xn work (in the alchemic sense) is to *achieve* the resurrection, presenting it—not expecting it in the future. The resurrection of Christ, we are

told, fulfilled the past. A scientific discovery, made at a certain date, is *of* what always was true; and similarly the event of 28 A.D. or whatever meant that all the Egyptians who wanted to rise with Osiris or Pharaoh were right. Hence it's retrospective, as I've said; but it's the reversing of the future that's important. (Retroactive, really.) (*RT,* 104)

As we see, the alchemic vision is not a matter of some future hope of eternal life. The Christian Great Work is a resurrection that reverses the future and is achieved in the present—what biblical theologians would call realized eschatology.

On the flyleaf of Notebook 11h Frye sketched the diagram shown here in diagram 3. Frye identified the upright triangle (Hermes-Prometheus-Logos) as having an "alchemical structure" and the inverted triangle as having a "Knight's Tale Structure." One cannot be certain what these two phrases mean (the diagram is not directly connected to anything in the notebook), but they appear to be the comic and tragic versions of the Eros cycle. The *mysterium conjunctionis* in alchemy is mirrored in literature in the fusion of two bodies, as in Shakespeare's "The Phoenix and the Turtle" (Frye's favorite example), with its red and white symbolism. In Chaucer's *Knight's Tale,* where Arcite fights in red and Palamon in white under the moon, Eros is realized only through the death of Arcite, who wins the battle but loses the hand of Emily to Palamon. The point is that Frye sees the alchemical structure as an ascending one, moving away from the tragic vision of death toward the Logos vision. As he says in Notebook 12, "transformation & alchemical myths go up" (*TBN,* 157).

The Great Doodle is, among other things, a cycle, and in Frye's mental diagram the religious quest is traced counterclockwise from Adonis through Eros. But the Great Doodle also has its vertical and horizontal axes, and Frye has another version of the alchemic structure that is organized along the Nomos–Nous axis. This is related to a part of his ogdoad project he called "the book on its side," a cryptic phrase he used to describe the book he intended to write following his large "third book." The book on its side has a number of permutations,[87] but essentially Frye associates it with a narrative, linear movement along his Nous–Nomos axis (rather than a cyclical movement), and it is alchemical (rather than astrological) in its schematism. The Nomos–Nous axis is diachronic. If the alchemic process is, as Eliade says, related to temporality, and if it is, as Frye says, a matter of achieving resurrection in the present, then alchemical transformation is a temporal process. In Notebook 11f (1969–70) Frye writes that the mental diagram of his Logos vision is spread out in space. Thus, it belongs to *dianoia* aspect of his dialectic of space and time,

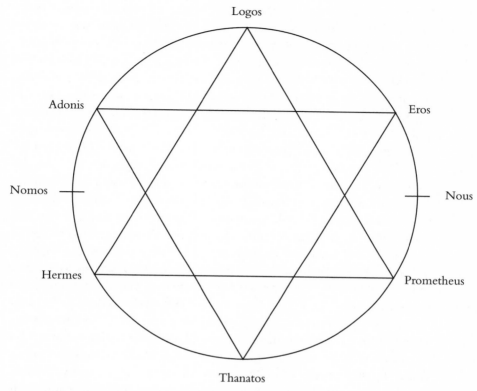

Diagram 3. The Alchemical and Knight's Tale Structures

eye and ear, doodle and babble. But the other half of the mental diagram (the upright triangle) is what he calls an "alchemical" process-arrangement. Thus, it belongs to the *mythos* aspect of the dialectic or the Nomos-Nous axis. When Frye was speculating on the shape of his "third book" in the early 1970s, he comes to realize that there is yet another perspective from which to view the spiritual quest. "I've got Logos on the top & Nous on the east because that's where they traditionally belong; but I'm going to run into trouble towards the end when the terms reverse. That is, the Logos vision is ultimately a Nous; it's not the centre of Christianity but its Greek natural-theology extension, & runs from the Great Pyramid to T. de Chardin's 'noosphere.' Similarly Nous keeps focussing on the real Logos, the resurrection from, and of, the dead. This is, I suppose, where the synchronic [Liberal] perspective turns into the diachronic [Tragicomedy] one, and I have to start a new book" (*TBN,* 220–21).

This new book is the book "turned on it side," the phrase referring to a reorientation of the cyclic Logos mental diagram so that it is now seen as sideways or along the temporal axis. "I want a Prologue in space-time," Frye writes, "to be followed, after I box the compass once, with a second book starting with a Prologue in time-space, where the symbols are diachronic & Los-centered & alchemical, not synchronic & Orc-centered & astrological" (*TBN,* 221); or, in another formulation of the same idea, out of the cycle of Adonis-Eros and Logos-Thanatos there emerges "one gigantic dialectic of resurrection, where the total cycle turns on its side and we get the alchemical great work" (*TBN,* 229).[88] The alchemic great work, then, is "another approach to literary symbolism" (*TBN,* 258).

One wonders if the "alchemic great work" might not be a pun, referring as well to the various transformations of Frye's own Great Doodle. In one of his letters to Henri Cazalis (14 May 1867) Mallarmé speaks of there being only one book that would embody the structure of the universe, "the Great Work, as our ancestors the alchemists used to say"— "our ancestors" being the poets' precursors.[89] Frye picks up the reference in his furnace or "alchemical" chapter of *Words with Power,* in the context of his discussion of Mallarmé as the preeminent poet of "nothingness": "A connection has been suggested between Mallarmé's word 'Igitur' and the Vulgate text of Genesis 2:3 [2:1], *igitur perfecti sunt coeli* ["thus the heavens were finished"]. This has been discredited for lack of evidence, but it is a most penetrating comment none the less. For Mallarmé was also preoccupied by the opposite of his 'Néant' world, speaking of a kind of definitive book that would contain the entire verbal cosmos and would be in literature what the 'Great Work' was to 'our ancestors, the alchemists'" (*WP,* 292). It seems possible to conceive of Frye himself as the alchemist, for the Great Work he produced through a lifetime of effort seeks also to contain the entire verbal universe, even though he was never able to produce the great work of his "third book."

It is perhaps worth noting—and not just incidentally in the context of the alchemical theme of resurrection—that Mallarmé is, following Blake, the poet with whom Frye most closely identified. There are other candidates: Stevens and Yeats and Dickinson, all three of whom were subjects of articles by Frye. But no poet besides Blake is as significant a literary and critical companion as Mallarmé. Although Frye never devoted an essay exclusively to Mallarmé, he is omnipresent in Frye's published writing, first appearing in "Yeats and the Language of Symbolism" (1947) and in almost fifty of his subsequent books and essays. In the notebooks Mallarmé turns up in 118 entries. There are many reasons for Frye's interest in Mallarmé as a *symboliste:* he figures importantly in both of Frye's essays on symbolism.[90] But the principle attraction is that Mallarmé, like Blake, has the imagination of a religious visionary. In his response to a series of papers on the topic "Northrop Frye and Eighteenth-Century Studies," Frye writes,

> I find it difficult to buy the panhistorical visions of so many contemporary literary scholars. They seem to me to operate only within history as such: when you're studying history you're inside a historical cosmos where everything is historical. If you're studying philosophy, you're inside a philosophical cosmos where what you do is climb a philosophical mountain, like Hegel, to find yourself on a pinnacle of absolute knowledge where you know everything except where to get the oxygen for the next breath. Similarly there seems to me to be a total cosmos of literature, within which everything is literary. So far as I can see, only three people have been inspired by that last vision. Two of them were Blake and Mallarmé; the third [Frye himself] has learned what he knows about it from them. But of course these are not differing universes, and they have no boundaries; they are interpenetrating.[91]

Mallarmé is a poet, writes Frye, "who will take me through the third great crisis of the birth of the spirit out of the depth of fallen spirits," who sometimes talks "as though literature was a 'substitute' for religion," who sees the pure poem as a symbol of "something transcendent," who "tries to sink himself in myth & metaphor so completely that the kerygmatic will speak through," and who believes "there really is some kind of resurrection by faith in myth."[92] In Notebook 50 Frye writes, "When Mallarmé speaks of 'glorieux mensonges' (of belief) he doesn't, with respect, know whether they are mensonges or not: he means only that when *he* talks about 'resurrection' he doesn't want it pinned down to the gospel one. But he means resurrection, not just getting up in the morning. I think this is increasingly what *we* have to mean by the Hebrews belief definition [Heb. 11:1], whatever the author meant" (*LN,* 1:309).[93] One of the most revelatory passages about Mallarmé is in Frye's 1984 essay "The Symbol as a Medium of Exchange." Here Frye focuses on Mallarmé's belief in a single, symbolic verbal universe, a universe that is fundamentally spiritual. It's a world containing a symbolic death and resurrection, a world where divinity can be expressed only by the poetic word, a world in which chance (where we've got no choice) and choice (where chance doesn't operate) become the same thing, and a world where rebirth can only occur from the ashes of Nothingness. Mallarmé in fact serves as the backbone of this essay on the symbol, and Frye finds in Mallarmé something very close to a mystical vision and embodying a mythical *gnosis*.

Gnosticism

In one set of typed notes from the 1980s Frye writes, without interpreta-
tive commentary, that Mallarmé and Rilke "talk like Gnostics" (*LN*,
2:603). We can infer what he means from a remark in "The Symbol as a
Medium of Exchange," written about the same time, where he says that
Rilke's angel in the *Duino Elegies* and *Sonnets to Orpheus* represents the
movement from the physical world to a transcendent, symbolic one. Frye
then adds that Rilke "emphasizes that his conception is not Christian, but
it is clearly religious in most senses of the term, an almost Neoplatonic or
Gnostic effort to find through words, and through the symbolic relationships of words, a more intense mode of life and experience" (*MM*, 38).
"Gnostic" here means *gnosis*, in the sense that Frye sometimes uses it;
it refers, as in Hanegraaff's characterization noted at the beginning of this
chapter, to experiential modes of knowing that rely on mythical or symbolic discourse. Frye himself distinguishes between Gnostics and gnostics
(*LN*, 1:348), the former associated generally with certain modes of
thought that arose from the second century, seen by Irenaeus, Tertullian,
and other patristic writers as heretical, and the latter with *gnosis* as both
an intuitive experience of spiritual truths and a form of knowledge, not
lending itself to philosophical propositions and theological doctrines.[94]

Gnosticism was not a religion in an institutional sense and even less
a school. What it was historically and how it is understood today are more
difficult to say. Like many other –isms, Gnosticism's many formulations,
especially since the discovery of the Nag Hammadi Library in 1945,
tempt one to repeat Alice's admonition to Humpty Dumpty: "The question is whether you *can* make words mean so many different things." But
we *can* specify, from the scattered references to both Gnosticism and gnosis in his writings, how Frye understood these terms. His knowledge of
the Gnostic outlook derived from the classic study by Hans Jonas (a student of Heidegger's), the Nag Hammadi Library, Bentley Layton's translation of *The Gnostic Scriptures*, G. R. S. Mead's study of John the Baptist
as a Gnostic, and the translations by Mead of both the *Pistis Sophia* and a
Gnostic translation of the proem to the Gospel of John.[95] There is no evidence that Frye was familiar with the several studies of Gnosticism by
Elaine Pagels, though he would have known about her argument from
Pheme Perkins's *The Gnostic Dialogue*.[96] Among Frye's other sources
would have been a number of works not devoted exclusively to Gnosticism, such as Mead's *Thrice-Greatest Hermes*, the Acts of Thomas, Austin
Farrer's *Rebirth of Images*, and various books by Carl Jung, who, along with

Jonas and Pagels, was influential in bringing Gnosticism to the modern consciousness.

The features of Gnosticism as a religious and philosophical attitude that emerge from Frye's writings include its ethical dualism (nature is evil), its scenario of the numerous stages of spiritual development (the eons and emanations of Valentinus) and other hierarchical constructs, the distance of its vision from New Testament Christianity, its idea of a silent God above Gods often conceived as a hostile Jehovah-like *archon*, its gender inclusiveness, its similarity to other esoteric movements in which special teachings are reserved for a small group of initiates (as in the Sufi form of Islam and the Mahayana form of Buddhism), and its personification of wisdom as female.[97] Mead's translation of the *Pistis Sophia* in the late nineteenth century heightened the interest of the wisdom tradition in Gnosticism: much of this "secret gospel," as Frye calls it in *The Great Code* (67), is devoted to the liberation of heavenly wisdom (Sophia) from bondage in the material world and to her apotheosis in the spiritual one. But for Frye such wisdom has little to do with the biblical variety: "The conception of wisdom in the Bible is never associated with any kind of esoteric knowledge. . . . It is curious but significant that 'gnostic' and 'agnostic' are both dirty words in the Christian tradition: wisdom is not identified either with knowledge or with the denial of knowledge. It is an existential wisdom with its centre in human concern, not in the exploration of nature or other worlds" (*GC,* 67).

These are conventional observations, entirely consistent with what Jonas and other scholars of the Gnostic tradition have noted. Similarly, with the various writers who are said by Frye to contain Gnostic strains: Blake's notion of the Fall, for example, has Gnostic parallels (*FS,* 41), and Hegel's Gnostic commitment to absolute mind leaves no place for a conception of the spiritual body (*LN,* 1:188–89). There is nothing exceptional to be noted about Frye's understanding of Gnosticism as a mode of thought and a body of teachings or about the analogies he sees between Gnosticism and other things. As we might expect, most of the Gnostic ideas are altogether uncongenial to Frye's own assumptions about a unified cosmos. Gnosticism, he writes in one notebook, is "naked mythology, uncorrected & unchecked by a genuinely creative impulse" (10.114)—the same criticism that he levels at a number of esoteric traditions and at Bhakti yoga.

Frye's conception of *gnosis,* on the other hand, does require commentary. His use of this word transposes the context of "gnostic" from knowledge to myth. Twice in *Words with Power* Frye refers to Gnostic teachings as mythopoeia (34–35, 144), an idea that can be traced back to *Fearful Symmetry*, where he writes that Gnosticism as a body of abstract teachings is "dull and puzzling" and that it is therefore more interestingly read as an epic poem (110–11). As we have seen repeatedly, this redirection of modes of thought from historical or doctrinal contexts to poetic or mythological ones is typical of Frye's approach to texts, including the Bible.

The one Gnostic text for which Frye does provide a brief commentary is *The Hymn of the Pearl*, also known as *The Hymn of the Soul*, from the Acts of Thomas. This is a story of a child whose parents take his robe and send him down to Egypt to bring back a pearl guarded by a sea serpent. The child forgets his mission, but after receiving a letter from his parents his memory returns. He then enchants the serpent and returns home. Frye reads this as a quest romance, similar to that of Psyche in Apuleius's *The Golden Ass:*

> At the beginning of his quest [Soul] had been clothed in a garment which is clearly the form of his original identity. He meets this garment again and realizes that it is, in fact, his real self. He sees it "as it had been in a mirror," and it is brought him by twins: "Two, yet one shape was upon both." Putting it on, he makes his way back to his own world. Like Apuleius' story, this is a story of the "Soul"; in other words it is the story of ourselves. Crucial to it is the role of the letter or message, which not only awakens him but is what draws him upward to his self-recognition. It seems that one becomes the ultimate hero of the great quest of man, not so much by virtue of what one does, as by virtue of what and how one reads. (*SeS*, 157)[98]

The *gnosis* of *The Hymn of the Pearl*, read here by Frye in mythical and metaphorical terms, becomes therefore not knowledge in any conceptual sense but knowledge as *anagnorisis*, which is an imaginative category in this context rather than a philosophical or theological one.[99]

Responding to a question about Marcion in a 1971 interview, Frye replied, "Marcion was a Gnostic, and what made the Gnostics heretical was their belief that the order of nature was fundamentally corrupt and that, therefore, the God who would produce this order of nature must be an evil God, whom Jesus fought against. There's something strongly Gnostic about all Romanticism, I think, especially of the Shelleyan kind, because it recurs to this conception that the God who produced the order of nature is somebody to be got rid of. He's a sinister god" (*RW*, 122). Here "Gnostic" refers to a mode of thought—the Shelleyan conception of God as Nobodaddy. But in Shelley's work we also find *gnosis* in the poetic sense, a sense that is outlined in some detail in *A Study of English Romanticism*. In the first chapter of that book Frye examines the differences between Romantic and pre-Romantic mythologies, one feature of which is their dissimilar redemption myths. In traditional mythology, God's grace, descending from *agape* and offered freely, is seen as transforming the human will. But "Romantic redemption myths, especially the revolutionary ones like those of Shelley," Frye writes,

> throw the emphasis on an *eros,* or love rooted in the human sexual instinct. Such an *eros* develops a distinctively human idealism, and for such idealism the redeeming agent is also human-centred. The *agape* or love of God for man creates grace, but what man's love and idealism create is essentially a gnosis, an expanded knowledge or consciousness, and one that is more inclusive and profound than the conscious knowledge of the detached subject. This greater gnosis is identified with the imagination in Wordsworth's *Prelude* and in Coleridge: it is often, as in Coleridge, considered to be a superior kind of reason; it is explicitly identified with love (in the sense of *eros,* of course) in Shelley; in many French and German Romantics it acquires a quasi-occult or theosophical cast; in some, such as Novalis, it could be called a mystical consciousness. In the more conservative and nostalgic it is apt to become simply an overwhelming of the reason with mysteries that only faith, thought of as an intuitive or nonanalytic mode of consciousness, can reach. (20)

Part of Frye's wide-ranging exposition of Shelley's Promethean myth in chapter 3 of *A Study of English Romanticism* is framed by the Pauline virtues: he seeks to discover the Shelleyan version of faith, hope, and love. And it all comes down to this question and answer:

> What is Shelley's equivalent of faith? Clearly it is, as our first chapter has suggested, some form of gnosis. At first this gnosis is a secret, perilous, and forbidden knowledge, like that of Adam in Eden, snatched from under the nose of a jealous Jupiter, and transmitted through the murmuring oracular caverns of the human poetic imagination. Such knowledge, though secretly acquired, is extremely simple in content, being the message of love that comes through hope. According to the argument of *Prometheus Unbound,* Prometheus loves and is loved, and his hope is unbreakable, hence he is bound to triumph in time. But when he withdraws the curse on Jupiter, his knowledge and will to endure are transformed into a vision that fulfils knowledge and makes further endurance needless. This attainment of vision corresponds in Shelley to the miraculous transformation that, in Christianity, grace makes in the human will. (*SER,* 106)

Gnosis therefore comes to be identified with faith. It is, Frye concludes, "an act of vision and consciousness, and . . . therefore not an act in Milton's sense, nor a pseudo-act, nor a parody-act, but a withdrawal from action. It might even be called an achievement of a state of nothingness or void in which reality appears" (*SER,* 109). This sounds quite similar to the spiritual world of heightened consciousness that Frye finds in Mallarmé and Rilke, to the account of Blake's mysticism at the end of *Fearful Symmetry,* and to the various experiences of identity we have examined in previous chapters. When Frye refers to the Egyptian *Book of the Dead* as a "gigantic gnosis" and as having "many affinities" with *samyama,* the last stage of concentration in Patanjali's yoga (*LN,* 1:159), he means that the yogin can acquire the power of the object of concentration.[100] Although it is clear that certain Gnostic ideas have appeal for Frye and no less clear that many more do not, by focusing on *gnosis* he relocates questions of Gnostic belief and doctrine to the circumference and moves those of visionary experience and imaginative power to the center. This procedure is typical, as we will see in our examination of additional esoteric modes in the next chapter.

6 Kook Books and the Occult

[The] lower world, the world of signs, of secrecy, & of oracles, is
also the world of writing—proclaimers have to depend on a writing
secretary or keeper of the secrets. Xy [Christianity], Islam, &
probably Judaism, have the conception of the secret books of life
in which some angel writes down our largely forgotten acts, &
confronts us with them at the Last Judgement. The dark world is
the world of signs, of which the archetype is the sign of Jonah,
the prophet who descended to that world. It stretches from the
paleolithic cave of magic animal pictures to the descent to the cipher
or oracle which we have in Arthur Gordon Pym, in Endymion, in
Rabelais' bottle oracle. This all contrasts with the claim of Jesus &
Mohammed to have said nothing in secret—secret traditions always
have a gnostic, sufi, mahayana sense of heresy about them: the
exoteric tradition is what is primary & holds society together:
the gospel, not the mystery cult.
—*Notebooks and Lectures on the Bible,* 11f.73

For years I have been collecting and reading pop-science &
semi-occult books. . . . Some are very serious books I haven't the
mathematics (or the science) to follow: some are kook-books with
hair-raising insights or suggestions.
—*Late Notebooks,* 2:713

Frye spent sixty years engaging the great tradition. While not everyone
was overly familiar with some of the works mentioned in *Anatomy of
Criticism*—the eccentric fictions of Thomas Amory, say, or the curious
treatises of Urquhart of Cromarty—writers at the fringe of the canon
were the exception rather than the rule; and most of what Frye wrote
about *was* on the syllabus, was in fact on his own syllabi: Blake, the Bible,
Shakespeare, Milton, Spenser, the Victorian prose writers, the Romantic
poets, the modernists from Yeats and Eliot and Joyce to Wallace Stevens.
But as the last chapter sought to show, the notebooks reveal another side
of Frye, one that often moves away from the center toward the esoteric
circumference. Hermeticism is another dimension of his interest in the
esoteric.

Frye uses the word "hermetic" in a variety of contexts. Some relate to the archetype of Hermes—variously the psychopomp, the thief, the cunning one, and the inventor. Others are associated with his reading of a book already mentioned, G. R. S. Mead's *Thrice-Greatest Hermes,* a collection of the hermetic literature with commentary that was available at the beginning of the twentieth century. Frye takes *Thrice-Greatest Hermes* to be not, as is ordinarily assumed, "a deservedly forgotten effort of pseudo-scholarship," but "the spiritual vision" of the *Corpus Hermeticum* (*LN,* 2:618). His views on hermeticism were also substantially influenced, as already noted, by the books of Frances Yates, the other person who was centrally important in the revival of interest in the *Corpus Hermeticum.* For Yates hermeticism was generally a synonym for the various occult "sciences"—alchemy, magic, astrology, and Rosicrucianism.[1] Frye clearly means to include these Renaissance traditions in his own view of hermeticism, but the term often ranges freely beyond them, as in this catalogue of hermetic Romanticism:

> The suggestion of supernatural activity produces the tale form, where there's a series of events suggesting a superpersonal march of action which overmasters the characters or else identifies itself with the heroic will. In here come the myths of hermetic romanticism, as we get them in, for instance, Bulwer Lytton's *Zanoni* & *The Coming Race.* The essential romantic myths are founded, of course, on the mysterious Kantian unknowable noumenon which in rcsm. [romanticism] takes the form of the world as will. From this we get the Akasa-myth: Vril, Od, élan vital, creative evolution (when rescued from the mother-goddess cult of Darwin & Huxley), ether, electricity, magnetism & galvanism (for one *must* be scientific) & other adaptations of anima mundi & astral light theories. (These first turn up in Neo-Platonism: how the hell did they, & the elementals business, ever get stuck on Plato's name?). These of course account for mesmerism & the feats of Indian jugglers, who develop an extensive mythology in the 19th c. Another pattern is the (apparently always allied) theory of elementals or non-physical forms of existence. These merge with spiritualism & Bardo-theories. The neo-Pythagorean heroes, development of Simon Magus & Apollonius of Tyana, appear in Cagliostro, the Wandering Jew, Edmund Dantès (withdrawal & return) & Frankenstein as the portents of a nomadic & anarchic civn. [civilization]. (32.51)[2]

There is not much in the noumenal world, then, that cannot be taken as hermetic. Almost anything associated with Hermes can be hermetic: the Virgin Birth of the Word, themes of ascent and descent, fire symbolism, Boehme's "bitterness" or wrath, the secretly sealed message, recovery and transformation.[3] But if hermeticism is a broadly inclusive category, what Frye called his "kook books" is relatively narrow. These were a group of highly speculative, somewhat zany, and often amusingly eccentric books that attracted his notice. They range from the completely bizarre at one extreme, like Robert Anton Wilson's *Cosmic Trigger: The Final Secret of the Illuminati,* to various movements in New Age religion. They include also the channeling phenomena, as in Bishop Pike's *The Other Side* and Jane Roberts's various Seth books, numerology and synchronicity, astrology, and the Tarot.

Kook Books

Frye uses the phrase "kook book" four times in his notebooks. The first is at the beginning of Notebook 23, written during the early 1980s, where he announces that he has become interested lately in two literary genres. The first is the science fiction trilogy, such as "Asimov's *Foundation,* Herbert's *Dune,* Zelazny's Amber world, Farmer's 'Riverrun' books (not up to the others, in my view), Ursula LeGuin's *Earthsea,* and a number of others. They derive, of course, from the huge success of the Tolkien trilogy, and the blurbs routinely compare them to Tolkien. But the Eddison series was written before Tolkien, to say nothing of the Morris ends-of-the earth series" (*RT,* 366).[4] The second genre

> is the one I call the kook book, the speculative survey of third-force psychology and the like. Those are often a fruitful source of *adagia.* One of them quotes Schroedinger as saying that consciousness is a singular whose plural is unknown, a remark I used in a sermon. Cosmic Trigger: the Final Secret of the Illuminati, by Robert Anton Wilson, is a typical kook book. Powers of Mind, by Adam Smith, is a journalistic write-up of what he calls the "consciousness circuit," and a very lively book it is. The Morning of the Magicians, by Pauwels and Bergier, is another. Such books shade off through Merejkowski's Atlantis and Buckminster Fuller to Jung & Eliade, who of course aren't kooks, but put together some of their patterns. (*RT,* 367)[5]

"Third-force psychology," a phrase made popular by Abraham Maslow, refers to the form of humanistic psychology that focuses on self-awareness and transformation. It is founded on a belief in the conscious evolution of values, the development of inner wisdom through self-actualization, and individual growth beyond ordinary limits. Maslow also wrote about "peak experiences," which Frye refers to twice in the notebooks.[6] Peak experiences encompass a whole range of heightened or mystical states of consciousness, religious and otherwise. One of the speculative surveys Frye mentions, Smith's *Powers of Mind,* is a popular, far-ranging compendium of all sorts of consciousness expanding: EST (Erhard Seminar Training), Zen, Easlen, biofeedback, transcendental meditation, yoga, the *I Ching,* and other such inner-space movements of the 1960s and 1970s that are not accounted for by rational and scientific paradigms.

Louis Pauwels and Jacques Bergier's *The Morning of the Magicians* is a book about "ultra-consciousness," another encyclopedic account of the anomalies of Charles Fort, vanished civilizations, conspiracies, cryptology, Nazism and the Golden Dawn, and tantalizing enigmas of all sorts.[7] The book is a collaboration between Pauwels, an investigator of esoteric phenomena and onetime disciple of Gurdjieff, and Bergier, a physicist. Pauwels is the actual author; Bergier provides much of the theory and documentation. The point of view of *The Morning of the Magicians,* a best seller published in France in 1960 and translated shortly thereafter in both England and the United States, is described by Pauwels as "fantastic realism," meaning that its focus is not on the fantastic as a violation of natural law but on the discovery of the invisible through the visible.[8] It is not "a collection of bizarre facts," writes Pauwels. "It is not a scientific contribution, a vehicle for an exotic teaching, a testament, a document, a fable. It is simply an account—at times figurative, at times factual—of a first excursion into some as yet scarcely explored realms of consciousness."[9] Like Smith's *Powers of Mind, The Morning of the Magicians* is personal, richly anecdotal, often discontinuous, and without a central argument, although it is based on the assumption that events that defy scientific explanation are part of an underlying unity in the cosmos. One can understand why Frye would call both books "lively," but he says nothing else about either in his notebooks. He does, however, write in the margin of his copy of *The Morning of the Magicians,* "This is an important book for me, as it confirms my hunch of a Druid analogy."[10]

Twice above we have used the phrase "Druid analogy" as referring to the myths and rituals of natural religion in its most primitive form. But the phrase is more complex than that. The word "Druid" has its origin (for Frye) in Blake. The Druids, according to the eighteenth-century theory of Blake's sources (largely Edward Davies and William Stukeley), were a race of giants in the mythological past who worshipped trees and serpents, built megalithic temples, and sacrificed human beings in large numbers to a god who hated humanity. Druidism was therefore a sinister and violent mythical complex for Blake, associated with the ominous rumblings of state power and with Deism, and leading ultimately, as Frye says in *The Great Code,* to "annihilation warfare" (95). Because Frye began to write *Fearful Symmetry* when the specter of Nazism was hanging over Europe, the association of Druidism with National Socialism was in the back of his mind.[11]

But the Druid analogy came to represent something broader for Frye than the demonic. The farther from *Fearful Symmetry* he moved in developing his mythological universe, the nearer he came to seeing Druidism not as a demonic parody but as what he would later call a positive analogy. In this sense, the Druid analogy came to represent the "total geography & history of the mythological universe" (*RT,* 348), "the sense of creative cycle running from the Odyssey *nostos* to *Finnegans Wake*" (*RT,* 227), and "the key to all mythologies" (*RT,* 198), including all of the cyclical symbolism charted by Sir James Frazer, Robert Graves, Jessie Weston, and other comparative mythographers. But the mythological universe of the Druid analogy lies outside the biblical one, which is why Frye used the word "analogy" to describe it: it stands for the "secular Bible" (*RT,* 227). When Frye refers to *The Morning of the Magicians* as confirming his intuition about the Druid analogy, he means that it is fundamentally a mythological book, one that contains an imaginative vision of reality. As a verbal construct it is part of the secular Bible—a positive analogy, rather than a demonic parody, and so is part of the universal language of myth and metaphor.

Frye also read Marilyn Ferguson's *The Aquarian Conspiracy,* a kind of American version of *Morning of the Magicians* that chronicles the shift in values said to be emerging in individuals and society in the 1980s.[12] Frye remarks that he got nothing from Ferguson, calling *The Aquarian Conspiracy* a "goo-goo book" (*LN,* 2:713), meaning that it was essentially shapeless—a journalistic account of what Ferguson sees as a silent revolution spurred by a number of religious, psychological, educational, social, and political transformations. There are transformations at the personal level, but Ferguson sees them as leading to a new society. Frye says nothing in his published or unpublished work about "New Age" in this sense, although it is clear from the list of books in section 12 at the beginning of the previous chapter that he was widely acquainted with the great diversity of movements that have been labeled "New Age."

The second instance of the phrase "kook book" is in Notebook 11h, written in the mid-1980s, where in one entry Frye lists five books, followed by this report in the next entry: "For years I have been collecting and reading pop-science & semi-occult books. . . . Some are very serious books I haven't the mathematics (or the science) to follow: some are kook-books with hair-raising insights or suggestions" (*LN,* 2:713). The five books are Wilson's *Cosmic Trigger* (again), Itzhak Bentov's *Stalking the Wild Pendulum,* Rudy Rucker's *Infinity and the Mind,* Ken Wilber's *The Holographic Paradigm,* and Stanislav Grof's *Realms of Human Unconscious,* all published between 1976 and 1982. Of these, the only two real "nut books," as Frye also calls them, are Wilson's and Bentov's.

Rudy Rucker is a polymath (historical novelist, award-winning science fiction writer and founder of the cyberpunk sci-fi movement, painter, computer software expert, mathematician, and professor) whose *Infinity and the Mind* explores the infinite from numerous perspectives, "potential and actual, mathematical and physical, theological and mundane."[13] In the world of the infinite (e.g., set theory, Gödel's incompleteness theorems), where science begins to merge with the fantastic, paradoxes that "tease us out of thought" abound, as Keats says of infinity. Although the book is said to be written for nonspecialists, its arguments depend on a good measure of mathematical sophistication. Frye remarks on the book in the context of his reflections on the actual and the possible: "One function of poetry, or at least of the metaphors in poetry, is to reconstruct the pre-verbalized instant before recognition. When I recognize something to be *that,* it's an object in the s-o [subject–object] universe; before that it could be anything, usually something more humanized. See an excellent book, *Infinity and the Mind,* by Rudy Rucker, p. 146. And why should this world be reconstructed? I suppose to set the actual in its context of infinite possibilities. Rucker is talking about the parallel-worlds problem: I haven't the mathematics to follow him, but the metaphorical side of it interests me" (*LN,* 1:398–99). In the passage Frye refers to, Rucker raises the question about the existence of parallel worlds, although he thinks the argument against multi-universes is stronger than those for. But for Frye this is inconsequential in the context of metaphorical recognition: outside the subject–object paradigm, anything is imaginatively possible.

Ken Wilber, trained as a biochemist, has done much to popularize New Age physics, and according to Hanegraaff, he "is regarded as the foremost theoretician in the transpersonal movement," having the "brilliant ability to combine information from a wide variety of sources into an at times stunningly elegant synthesis."[14] Wilber's *The Spectrum of Consciousness,* written when he was twenty-three, is an effort to synthesize the insights of the psychological, philosophical, and religious traditions into a unified theory of consciousness. Frye read *The Spectrum of Consciousness,* and though he does not remark on it in his notebooks or elsewhere, it would belong to his category of surveys of third-force psychology.[15] Wilber's *The Holographic Paradigm and Other Paradoxes,* a collection of articles, interviews, and responses that originally appeared in the pages of *Re Vision Journal,* was one of Frye's sources, along with the works of David Bohm and Fritjof Capra, for the manifestations in New Age science of the "implicate order" and "Tao of physics" theories discussed in chapter 1. Wilber himself challenges the efficacy of the holographic paradigm of Bohm and others, arguing that its pantheistic assumptions about the whole-part relation are reductionist and dualistic, not permitting finally a view of transcendence. But Wilber is too committed to the idea of levels of insight in the perennial philosophy for him to admit that interpenetration is anything other than "pop mysticism."[16]

Stanislav Grof is a psychiatrist with impressive academic credentials. His early experiments were on nonordinary states of consciousness produced by psychedelic drugs, particularly LSD. When scientific experiments with LSD became illegal, Grof turned to the study of other means of producing what he called "holotropic states," some of which can be described as mystical or spiritual experiences. Frye also read *Beyond Death: The Gates of Consciousness,* coauthored by Grof and his wife Christina, but what he thought of either book is uncertain, since he does not mention Grof elsewhere in the notebooks. With regard to the ontological significance of certain LSD experiences, they do, according to Grof, "represent the same phenomenon that has been described for centuries within such diverse religious, philosophical and mystical frameworks as the cosmologies of certain African and Amerindian cultures, the Orphic cult and Plato's philosophy, early Christian thought, and several major religions of India—in particular, Hinduism, Buddhism and Jainism."[17] How would Frye have judged this claim? He writes that "LSD (when it's a good trip) appears to increase the intensity of the feeling of oneness with the object" (*LN,* 1:17), but he also notes that the intensity of experience advertised by the LSD cults is a parody of ecstatic metaphor (*LN,* 2:504, 506). Frye says that he never took drugs himself (*RT,* 303), but he had read Aldous Huxley's *The Doors of Perception,* an argument for opening up the mind to new perceptions through the use of mescaline. Perhaps the closest he comes to making a judgment about drug-induced states of consciousness is his remark that the "geometrical fancies" of Huxley's LSD "visions are really of an *unborn* world: the speaking of the word is always an incarnation" (*TBN,* 156)—an undeveloped form of the real thing.

Still, it is clear that Frye considers Grof, along with Rucker and Wilber, as engaging in serious inquiry. But what about the two books remaining in the "kook book" list, Wilson's *The Cosmic Trigger* and Bentov's *Stalking the Wild Pendulum*? And what about Dmitry Merezhkovsky's *Atlantis/Europe,* a book that Frye twice describes as a "kook book" (*LN,*

1:17, 2:495)? We would also have to put into this category *Holy Blood, Holy Grail* by Baigent, Leigh, and Lincoln, which reaches the conclusion that the living lineal descendants of Jesus, issuing from his marriage to Mary Magdalene, are alive today. Why would Frye be drawn to Wilson, Bentov, Merezhkovsky, and the authors of the *Holy Blood*? We will begin with Wilson and Bentov, whose books, Frye says in a notebook from the 1980s, are the only two "nut books" that interest him at the moment (*LN*, 2:713).

Robert Anton Wilson's *Cosmic Trigger*, published in 1977, is the most popular of his more than two dozen books: by 1996 it had been reprinted eleven times. Wilson, a New Age guru and former editor at *Playboy*, is an offspring of Timothy Leary and Aleister Crowley. He writes on tantric sex, synchronicities, secret societies, goddess mythology, black magic, and a host of other esoteric topics. *The Cosmic Trigger* is a shapeless book that was itself triggered by Wilson's interest in the Bavarian Illuminati, the alleged conspiracies that are more mysterious than a Borgesian plot. The Illuminati led Wilson on a discontinuous romp through all forms of esoterica: numerology, synchronicities, triple agents, UFOs, presidential assassination plots, the eye of the U.S. dollar bill, Aleister Crowley's escapades, quantum mechanics, and deliberately induced brain changes. The cosmic trigger turns out to be a series of telepathic messages said to have been received from entities on one of the planets of Sirius.[18] Wilson proclaims himself the ultimate skeptic, yet it is clear that he has come to take all this very seriously. Frye is obviously right in calling it a real "nut book," but why would he be drawn to this kind of thing? Here is the single, four-part notebook entry he devotes to Wilson (parts numbered by me for ease of discussion later):

[Part 1] Wilson: epigraph: it's an ill wind that blows nobody's mind

[Part 2] McLuhan's point is that multiple models are the great 20th c. discovery. Like Ulysses. (I'd say it was really the rediscovery of the variation form (ideally 32 or 33).[)]

[Part 3] He makes a lot of 23: 24 & 33 are *closed* cycles, because you say twelve o'clock or north time. 23 and 32 have the open spark gap I mentioned in FS [*Fearful Symmetry*]. Maybe this is the 7–8 relation too. And my 15 (16)—And the climacteric 63 (64 I Ching, chess, etc.). Blake-Jung's 3 & 4. (No: 7 > 8 won't work: it would have to be 8–9 diagrammatically, although 7 > 8 has a lot of tradition going for it. As I've known since Blake, 7 is an *event* number in time, which includes space by turning 8.[)]

[Part 4] Note the close paranoia links: if you get fixated on 23, you develop a "that's for me" feeling about every 23 you see. He'd be nowhere without Jung's "synchronicity." (*LN,* 2:713)

This set of cryptic notes requires deciphering.

Part 1. The epigraph to *Cosmic Trigger*—"it's an ill wind that blows nobody's mind"—is identified by Wilson as coming from *The Principia Discordia* by Malaclypse the Younger, who has made a lame joke from the "ill wind blows" commonplace. Malaclypse the Younger turns out to be Greg Hill, a California libertarian from the 1960s and one of the founders of a wacky "religion" called Discordianism, based on the worship of Eris, the goddess of chaos. *The Principia Discordia* is an iconoclastic and anarchic collage of nonsense, and it is clear that Hill has trouble deciding whether his intent is satiric or not.[19] So why does Frye quote the epigraph? Is "it's an ill wind that blows nobody's mind" one of the *adagia* that he says he often finds in kook books, like the one from Schrödinger? The epigraph is a twist on Pistol's remark in *Henry IV, Part 2:* "Not the ill wind which blows no man to good."[20] Frye would not endorse either kind of ill wind, and mind blowing is central to his project, though he would not use Malaclypse's breezy slang to describe it. Frye's *adagia* for transcending or revolutionizing consciousness are formulated, as we have seen, in spirited prose: The "kerygmatic breakthrough always contains some sense of 'time has stopped.' The sequential movement has become a focus, or fireplace. In intensified consciousness the minute particular shines by its own light (or burns in its own life-fire)" (*LN,* 1:290). Or again, "Apocalypse is the hidden flame lit up, first setting the world on fire, then shining in its own light of awakened consciousness (omnia sunt lumina)" (*LN,* 2:515). These are Frye's own *adagia,* but surely he wouldn't have to turn to a founder of a parody religion—Discordianism, which Wilson calls a "guerilla ontology"[21]—as a source of *adagia.* Nevertheless, while it is impossible to say with any certainty why Frye copied the epigraph, the suggestion lingers that neo-paganism, like Wilson's extraterrestrial visitations, Madame Blavatsky's Theosophy, and Zen koans, can trigger the imagination to move beyond conventional ways of perception. Whatever ill winds keep the mind in a state of inertia and rooted in the commonplace will, Frye would hope, exhaust themselves with all due speed.

Part 2. In explaining the Niels Bohr multimodel approach for fitting data into theories, Wilson writes, "As Marshall McLuhan has pointed out, in *The Mechanical Bride* and other works, the multi-model approach has now influenced all sciences and even appears now in modern art (e.g., cubist paintings show several views at one; Joyce's *Ulysses* describes the same day in various styles—epic, dramatic, journalistic, subjective, naturalistic, etc.). McLuhan has even proclaimed, in his usual apocalyptic style, that the multi-model approach is the most important, and most original, intellectual discovery of the 20th century."[22] In his second entry Frye is merely summarizing this point and then remarking that the multimodel approach is not a discovery but a rediscovery of the musical theme with variations. The parenthetical reference is to the fact that composers sometimes write as many as thirty-two variations on a theme, as in Beethoven's *32 Variations in C Minor* or his *33 Variations in C Major on a Waltz* by Anton Diabelli.

Part 3. Here we come to the heart of the matter—Frye's numerological musings. When Frye says, "He makes a lot of 23," he is referring to Wilson's obsession with the so-called enigma of 23, the belief that the number twenty-three occurs far more frequently in our experience than can be explained by chance. The synchronicities of the number twenty-three, according to Wilson, led him to a "network of adepts that extends far beyond our Earth" and eventuated in his receiving impressions from Sirius.[23] All of this zaniness reminds Frye of one of the numerical schemes he played with tirelessly for his projected third book, which was modeled on Dante's *Commedia,* having three sections of thirty-four, thirty-three, and thirty-three parts—a one hundred–chapter book. The numbers Frye jots down in this paragraph are his musings about various points on the compass of the first cycle, the one that moves counterclockwise from Adonis to Eros, and the second cycle, represented in the "perennial philosophy" diagram (diagram 2, in chap. 5). The point seems to be that Frye feels a certain constraint or inertia imposed by the numbers twenty-four (as in his cycle of phases in *Anatomy of Criticism*) and thirty-three. He calls them "closed," like the myth of the eternal return, and he would prefer to have them open. Thus his remark about the numbers twenty-three and thirty-two having an "open spark gap," which in *Fearful Symmetry* he had described in this way: "The final comprehension of the Bible's meaning is in the spark of illumination between its closing anode and its opening cathode, and if that gap were not there the Bible would not stimulate the imagination to the effort of comprehension which recreates instead of passively following the outline of a vision" (*FS,* 386).

Part 4. Frye's comment on paranoia refers to the relation Wilson sees between conspiracies and Jungian synchronicities. Frye is certainly correct about not being disappointed once "you get fixated" on a number. Such games are easy to play. Frye's own speculations on the variation structure he associates with the number thirty-three appears in paragraph 33 of Notebook 50; his discussion of the Kabbalistic value of the number seven appears in Notebook 7; his fanciful playing with the number twelve is in Notebook 12; in paragraph 328 of Notebook 12 he speaks of the arrangement of the *I Ching* trigrams (3) in a double (2) pattern forming themselves into an ogdoad (8); and so on. Seek and ye shall find.

This deciphering of Frye's abbreviated and obscure comments about *Cosmic Trigger* may help us see why he is interested in Wilson's "nut book." Three issues are relevant: Frye's interest in expanded consciousness (which we have considered in chap. 3), numerology, and synchronicity. We will return to the last two after completing our survey of the kook books.

The second "nut book" is Itzhak Bentov's *Stalking the Wild Pendulum,* which Frye also refers to as a "very good" book (*LN,* 1:357). Bentov, who was killed in a plane crash in 1979, was an inventor who tinkered in his basement laboratory and amassed a considerable knowledge of physics on his own (he had almost no formal education). He began to practice meditation in the 1960s and became particularly interested in yoga, especially "the awakening of Kundalini." Bentov believed that all matter is consciousness and that our bodies mirror the vibrating universe so that we are in constant motion between the finite and the infinite. His central metaphor is the pendulum, which reaches a moment of rest on each side of its arc. These still points are present not only in the physical universe but in ourselves, and these points correspond to "subjective space-time," the locus of altered states of consciousness.[24] *Stalking the Wild Pendulum,* written with wit, humility, and a large measure of learning, and accompanied by a series of naively clever illustrations, is in a category altogether different from that of *Cosmic Trigger.* There is naturally a great deal of charlatanism in the massive literature of consciousness studies, with its self-help gurus, tantric mystics, and cosmic consciousness impostors all peddling their wares. Bentov does not belong to this crowd. In fact, he is a less scientifically sophisticated version of David Bohm. He was able to integrate his vibrating wave theory into the holographic model, received a dust-jacket endorsement from Stanislav Grof, and was a contributor to Wilber's *The Holographic Paradigm.*[25] Still, he was on the outside of the established scientific community, which gets nervous about unjustifiable and facile connections between physics, on the one hand, and mysticism, parapsychology, transpersonal consciousness, and New Age religion, on the other.[26]

Frye will have nothing to do with Bentov's views on reincarnation, which Bentov comes at by way of Carlos Castaneda and the channeling books of Jane Roberts, both of whom Frye read.[27] And he will have nothing to do as well with Bentov's view of "the pyramid-hierarchy of aristocratic levels leading to God the monarch" (*LN,* 1:357). As we know from

Words with Power, the cave is as important for Frye as the mountain. In other words, Bentov has no conception of the world below and no conception of what Frye calls the *culbute,* the revolutionary somersault of which the poets are always aware. But he is attracted to Bentov for the same reason that he turned to some of the New Age scientists—the authors of the Tao of physics and the holographic paradigm books. This is the way he puts it in Notebook 50: "The second essay [of *The Double Vision*] is the reason why this series may come to nothing before my death. It uses books on pop-science about the bootstrap theory, the implicate order, the hologram metaphor, the wild pendulum, & the like, to show how the inner dynamic of science increasingly drives it to describe the physical world as an analogy of the spiritual one" (*LN,* 1:415).

Frye does not actually use these notions anywhere in *The Double Vision,* though he does, as already indicated, make a passing reference to David Bohm's "implicate order" in the closing pages of the book. But consider this passage:

> The physical body is an instrument that allows us to interact best with our physical environment. This body is interpenetrated by "bodies" or "fields" [that] extend beyond the limits of the physical body. . . . The psyche serves as a bridge between the physical level and our real selves—spiritual beings. . . . It's unfortunate that the word "spirit" or "spirits" in the English language is so versatile. . . . We shall use the word "spirit" or "spiritual" to describe the highest level of human evolution, which borders on the absolute. It is very difficult to draw any sharp demarcation lines because the very highest spiritual merges with the absolute, which is the level of the Creators.

Now compare that with this passage:

> Our physical bodies are a part of a world usually described as material, but if matter is simply energy cooled down to the point at which our physical bodies can live with it, perhaps spirit can enter a world of higher energies where the separate things spread around objective heres and theres are no longer things to keep bumping into. In such a spiritual nature, a nature of "implicate order," as it has been called, or interpenetrating energies, and no longer the nature of congealed objects, we should be gods or numinous presences ourselves.

These passages are fairly similar: both seek to relate the material body to the world of spirit, both speak about the higher world of spirit, both call on the idea of interpenetration. The first, perhaps, sounds a bit more like Frye because of its attention to the multiple meanings of the word "spirit" and because it leads up to the idea of creation. But the second passage is Frye's, from the penultimate paragraph of *The Double Vision* (84). The first is from Bentov's *Stalking the Wild Pendulum*.[28] This helps us see, I think, what Frye means when he says that a book like Bentov's shows us how "the inner dynamic of science increasingly drives it to describe the physical world as an analogy of the spiritual one."

About Merezhkovsky's *Atlantic/Europe: The Secret of the West,* Frye writes, "yesterday's kook book is tomorrow's standard text" (*LN,* 1:17). The context of this remark is Frye's reflection in Notebook 27 on the way in which descent themes are connected with the recovery of the past, and he notes that Merezhkovsky's book is a "good guide here." He later expands on this connection:

> There's a lot of semi-occult fascination with Atlantis in the last two centuries: one very fine book (despite its obvious weaknesses and lapses) is Merezhkovsky's *Atlantis/Europe,* which tries to go all out for the historicity of Atlantis and doesn't mention Thera, but is really based on an ascending-ladder diagram in which we go on to the future, unless we get caught in the same cycle again, while Atlantis is our buried or forgotten past. He links the Timaeus and the Book of Enoch is some curious ways, coming close to a lot of the von Daniken mythology, but he's better than that: an example of how yesterday's kook book becomes tomorrow's standard text. (*LN,* 2:495)[29]

On Frye's continuum of the offbeat, Merezhkovsky lies somewhere between the completely bizarre at one extreme and the mythography of Eliade and Jung, to use his examples, at the other. This is why he can call *Atlantis/Europe* both a kook book, the subject of which is "crackpot" (*LN,* 1:172), and a "good guide" and a "fine book," much better than the sensationalist theories of extraterrestrial visitation in Erich von Däniken's *Chariots of the Gods?*

Dmitry Merezhkovsky (1865–1941), a Russian poet and novelist and the founder of the Religious-Philosophical Society, argues that ten millennia ago there existed a powerful and technologically sophisticated people on the island of Atlantis, located in the central Atlantic Ocean. The religion of the Atlanteans was similar to Christianity, founded by a man–god and advocating a message of peace and love. Merezhkovsky's thesis, which is written against a background of what he saw as the impending doom of Europe, is wildly speculative. Like Frazer, Merezhkovsky does not interpret his material in a scientifically rigorous way. His approach is instead symbolic, intuitive, and passionate.

This account of Atlantis is what attracted Frye, who had been interested in the symbolism of Atlantis from the time he had encountered the myth in Plato and in Blake's poetry. In *Fearful Symmetry* he explains Blake's myth of "the Atlantic mountains" in *Jerusalem* and elsewhere: "In the Golden Age before the Fall, humanity or Albion dwelt at peace in its Paradise or Atlantis. The Fall produced a chaotic world and the central symbol of chaos is water. The Platonic story that Atlantis was overwhelmed by a flood gets the meaning of this clearer. The Atlantic Ocean, then, symbolizes the fallen world in Blake; he calls it the 'Sea of Time and Space'" (206). So the myth is associated in Frye's mind with two clusters of imagery, that connected with chaos and the Fall on the one hand and with the recovery of Eden on the other. In the scores of notebook references to Atlantis, the latter images are fundamentally purgatorial, as in the land emerging from the sea in Shelley's *Prometheus Unbound,* or as in this catalogue: "The fire-seed that pushes through the fennel-stalk, the fuse of the flower, the phoenix red bird of fire, Hiranyagarbha, the glowing flame-city Atlantis-Byzantium. Jerusalem rising from the sea" (*LN,* 1:283).[30] The former images relate to the premetaphorical world of identity in Homer and the Bible (*LN,* 1:405), or as Frye puts it in *Words with Power,* the myth of Atlantis symbolizes the "deeper paradisal nature hidden within humanity" (247). The dialectic of chaos and rebirth in Merezhkovsky's explorations of the Atlantis myth had great appeal for Frye, reinforcing his own understanding of the myth.

Frye was also drawn to the discontinuous and at times epigrammatic form of Merezhkovsky's prose, which is arranged in a lengthy series of relative brief numbered paragraphs. Of the several proposals Frye entertains for the writing of the final book of his ogdoad—Twilight—the most intriguing is what he calls his anagogic book, a book of aphorisms. The desire to complete a book of aphorisms emerges from a dozen or so entries in Notebooks 44 and 50. "I wonder, Frye writes, "if I could be permitted to write my Twilight book, not as evidence of my own alleged wisdom but as a 'next time' (Henry James) book, putting my spiritual case more forcefully yet, and addressed to still more readers" (*LN,* 1:417). The reference here is to James's *The Next Time,* the story of a writer whose work is admired by a small coterie but who is frustrated by his failure to reach a large audience. Frye even proposes several models for his anagogic book: Anatole France's *Jardin d'épicure,* a series of learned reflections on sundry topics; Nietzsche's *Gaya Scienza;* Cyril Connolly's *The Unquiet Grave: A Word Cycle by Palinurus;* and Thomas Traherne's *Centuries of Meditations.* "I wouldn't want to plan such a book," Frye writes, "as a dumping ground for things I can't work in elsewhere or as a set of echoes of what I've said elsewhere." "Such a book would feature," he adds, "completely uninhibited writing" and "completely uninhibited metaphor-building," and some of the entries might even be fictional (*LN,* 1:238). A final model for such a book is Merezhkovsky's *Atlantis/Europe* (*LN,* 1:172), the form of which is not all that different from Frye's own notebooks.

The fifth kook book, though Frye does not use the epithet to describe it, is *Holy Blood, Holy Grail* by Michael Baigent, Richard Leigh, and Henry Lincoln, a book that sparked a good deal of controversy after its publication in 1982. The book opens with a mystery in the French village Rennes-Le-Chateau: how did the local priest Berenger Saunière accumulate vast sums of money to refurbish the parish church and build other structures? This mystery is complicated by other puzzles, but after a labyrinthine journey involving the Knights Templar, conspiracy theories, a Poussin painting, the Merovingian monarchs, the grail legend, and Gnosticism, the resolute authors are eventually able to tie all the threads together by the startling hypothesis that Jesus didn't die on the cross but married Mary Magdalene, fathered children, and established a European blood line. While the authors admit that their hypothesis might be open to certain objections over detail, they "are convinced that the essential outlines of [their] hypothesis are accurate."[31]

Frye calls *Holy Blood, Holy Grail* "an extraordinary piece of Romantic Esauism," meaning that it has to do with the theme of the returning rightful heir. But as another example of the quest for the historical Jesus, Frye thinks the book is misguided, as all such quests are, since the Gospels are not interested in the historical Jesus (*LN,* 1:108). Still, what the book helped clarify for Frye was "the prophet-gospel connection. As man, Jesus was of the line of prophets, Moses & Elijah. The gospel is the response to his prophecy in the form of deifying him. A successful Melchizedek priest-king would have been merely another deified Caesar: anything but a spiritual king would have annihilated the prophet. And a purely human prophet, of course, would have had no power to *save:* only myth can do that. And so gospel leads on to objectified apocalypse: the vision of what has been saved" (*LN,* 1:108). *Holy Blood, Holy Grail* makes the point of identifying Jesus with the priest-king figure in the line of David. For Frye this serves only to emphasize his opposing view of Christ as a spiritual rather than a temporal ruler. Jesus, then, is the antitype not of some Melchizedek priest-king but of the prophetic Moses and Elijah.[32]

Another thing that *Holy Blood, Holy Grail* did, Frye later reports, was "start me thinking about the vividness and integrity of mythical history, e.g., the British history that revolves around Arthur. When I picked it up I thought oh God: not *another* book about Cathars and Templars and Grail romances and Freemasons and Rosicrucians. It was, but it was better than most such books because it was hitched onto an Antichrist figure" (*LN*, 1:110), a figure that included all the conspiratorial grand masters of the Prieuré de Sion, one of the most secretive orders behind the Knights Templar, the avowed objective of which was to restore the Merovingian hegemony over all of Europe.[33] Frye seems to mean that the appearance of an Antichrist figure in *Holy Blood, Holy Grail* gives the story a certain mythical quality that moves it toward symbol and away from historical fact. He therefore read the book not as history but as an imaginatively suggestive work of fiction. Thus, *Holy Blood, Holy Grail* triggers for Frye typological themes: "The Virgin Mary is mother: Mary Magdalene is the forgiven harlot, often linked maritally to Jesus by apocryphal writers (D.H. Lawrence and that holy blood squad). Typologically this is correct. Mary of Bethany is the Sophia–daughter, the kernel of the church. It is she who persuades a sorrowful head-shaking Jesus to dig up the corpse of Lazarus and set it going again" (*LN*, 1:248). In Western Christendom Mary Magdalene, Mary of Bethany (sister of Martha and Lazarus), and the unnamed "woman who was a sinner" in Luke 7:36–48 are often assumed to be the same woman—at least since the time of Gregory the Great, who advanced that view. *Holy Blood, Holy Grail,* then, provides a link to one aspect of Frye's understanding of the Mary complex as including mother, forgiven prostitute, and Sophia-daughter. Frye has no concern about the authors' credentials as historians or about the truth of their argument. He is interested only in the imaginative use he can make of their material in his own hypothetical universe. This is the case as well with his numerological musings and his interest in channeling.

Number Schemes, Numerology, and Synchronicity

As we noted in the introduction, Frye had a penchant for number schemes. *Anatomy of Criticism* has its four *mythoi* and four genres, its five modes, its six phases of symbolism, and the like. Elaborate schema developed from these categories, the most elaborate being the phases of the *mythoi*. A similarly elaborate structure—a tripartite one—underlies Frye's analysis of style in *The Well-Tempered Critic*. But in his published work Frye was able to keep a tight rein on anything approaching numerology, the belief that numbers reflect properties of our minds or reveal features of the cosmos, and especially that certain numbers have an occult or mystical significance. The notebooks, however, are filled with number schemes of all kinds that move in that direction.

The phases of the *mythoi* just mentioned seem to border on having some kind of occult significance: "I still should do some thinking about the I Ching: 64 is the number of squares in chess, 32 of pieces. The hexagrams would have to be in sequence, & no doubt I should study the sequence. Of course they have a primary connexion with divination, oracle, knowledge of the future, & hence Thanatos. But my six phases, each three overlapping with another three, indicate some connexion in my own mind" (*TBN,* 261). In the Third Essay of *Anatomy of Criticism,* Frye represents each of the four *mythoi* (romance, comedy, irony, tragedy) as having six different phases. He names each of the twenty-four phases: in comedy, for example, there are the ironic, quixotic, typical, green-world, Arcadian, and gothic phases. And he gives examples of literary works in each category. Frye says that the phases from adjacent *mythoi* tend to merge or blend "insensibly" into one another, and this produces what he calls "a somewhat forbidding piece of symmetry" (*AC,* 177), not unlike the mathematic form of, say, Dante.[34] By "overlapping" Frye means that the first three phases of one *mythos* are always related to the first three of an adjacent *mythos.*[35] Among his unpublished papers is a diagram of the phases and their relations. Later he made some changes to his conception of the phases, but diagram 4 is the diagram he had in mind at the time, which he entitled "Diagram Illustrating the Phases of the Four *Mythoi.*"

Frye does not say—and it is not immediately obvious—what the connection is between this series of sixes and some kind of occult significance. We will thus have to look for clues elsewhere, beginning with some of the number schemes that appear throughout the notebooks. Consider this small sampler:

> 100 sections [for the Third Book] with an occult meaning for every damn one; patterns of repetition connecting them; climactic sequences 27–33, 60–66, 90–99; prime numbers after 50 perhaps philosophical. Odd numbers cyclical, especially 7, 11, 13 & 17; even numbers dialectic, especially 8 & 16; five & decimals mixed, that sort of thing. It isn't *just* childish, either: Dante & Joyce do it. (*RT,* 131)

> I'm back to my alphabet of forms. A fourfold ogdoad would be the full compass of 32. . . . I have a circular vision of 8, a square Eros-Adonis of 12, a triangular katabasis-escape one of 10 (4-3-2-1) and a Thanatos cloven fiction of 2. Incidentally, if the 7's & 12's of Revelation are essentially astrological, then they include the *natural religion* basis of Blake's Europe, & the woman crowned with stars is Enitharmon. (*TBN,* 183)

> Seven is the number of sequence (Stations of the Cross), the *drama* of fall & redemption in history. Eight is the number of thematic stasis. . . .

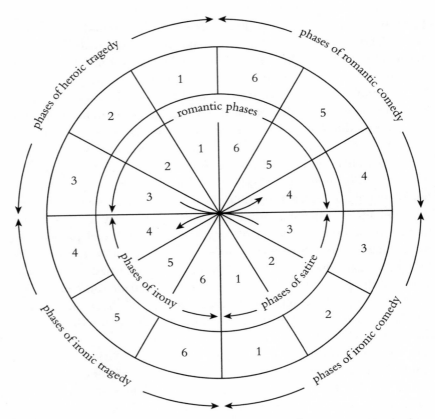

Diagram 4. The Phases of the Four *Mythoi:* Third Essay, *Anatomy of Criticism* (reproduction of Frye's pencil drawing from 1992 accession, box 3, file 7)

Most mandalas & contemplation icons involve an even–number principle of symmetry. But if 8 is the thematic stasis of 7, 13 is the thematic stasis of 12, hence Yeats' 13th cone. Well, anyway: the normal plot sequence is the parabola in seven stages. (*TBN,* 183)

Jung talks about embracing the demonic principle or shadow. In my scheme, to embrace the demonic is to embrace (incorporate or include) the *cycle*. That's why all the "square" (cubic) numbers [1, 8, 27, 64, etc.] have to turn into rolling ones (7, 11, 13, 17). At the Last Supper there is the moral establishment number of twelve: thirteen includes the demonic figure, and eleven is the centrifugal movement of gospel into world. In PT ["The Phoenix and the Turtle"] & its parliament of fowls there are seven birds, one banished. (By the end of the poem there are 5). (*TBN,* 244)

This last passage seems especially cryptic. One can understand Judas as the demonic figure whose disappearance leaves the propagating of the gospel in the hands of the other eleven disciples, so that the conventional number associated with the disciples turns out to be unstable by a factor of plus one and minus one. But twelve is neither a square nor a cubic number (1, 8, 27, 64, etc.), and what Frye means by rolling numbers is unclear: the examples he gives are prime or natural numbers, that is, numbers divisible only by one and by themselves. He perhaps intends to suggest that there is always something shadowy hiding behind the "moral establishment," what he refers to as the concealed, which we will consider shortly. But the connection of number theory to all this, except as some vague analogy, is puzzling. In any event, there are scores of such passages in the notebooks, and they seem to be related to Frye's lifelong desire to "write a book that will be schematic in form as well as in content" (*TBN*, 130).

How seriously did Frye take these speculations about numbers? The first account he gives of number schemes is in *Fearful Symmetry*:

> [T]here is a recurrent desire to believe that some simpler pattern, expressible perhaps in some mathematical formula, underlies the complications of our universe. . . . Pythagoras began with the patterns of simple arithmetic and the cardinal numbers; the *Timaeus* attempted to work out the geometrical shapes considered most fitting . . . from which to deduce all phenomena; and with the elaboration of the Ptolemaic universe the tendency spread in all directions. Many of its manifestations, particularly those that still survive, are occult, or at least highly speculative. But actually the whole tendency to symmetrical pattern-making in thought is very inadequately described as occultism, which is only a specialized department of it. (33)

Frye goes on to say, in an effort to distance Blake from the fold of the occultists, that just as the number seven in the book of Revelation is part of the symbolic unity of the Apocalypse, rather than an indication of the sevenfold nature of reality in general, so "in Blake all recurrent numbers and diagrams must be explained in terms of their context and their relation to the poems, not as indicating in Blake any affinity with mathematical mysticism" (34). This sounds quite similar to what Frye wrote in Notebook 44 almost fifty years later: "Recurrent numbers, seven & twelve & the like, are elements of design only: they represent no hidden mystery or numinousness in things. Not even the trinitarian three or the Jungian four. There are twelve signs in the zodiac, but it would be equally easy to see nine or eleven or fourteen and a half. Only fractions seem so *vulgar*" (*LN*, 1:157–58).

But at other places Frye certainly seems to think that numbers do contain some hidden mystery. He says in another notebook that seven and twelve are in fact "sacred numbers" (*RT,* 258),[36] in which case they would necessarily, it seems, embody some sense of mystery or the numinous. Frye even has a notebook entry on gematria, the Kabbalistic practice of interpreting the Bible by counting the numerical value of the letters of each word and using the result to derive the meaning of a passage; in gematria, each letter of the Hebrew alphabet has a traditional numerical value assigned to it. Frye writes, "In gematria, the numerical value of the Tetragrammaton (or four-letter word) is 26, so that a Trinity would be 78. The word for salt also has that number. Don't know what Rabelais knew or cared about this: I should look at Revelation" (*TBN,* 304). In another notebook he writes, "Re. numbers: one gets 28 either by adding 24 & 4 or by multiplying 4 & 7. For Blake it's important that 24 & 28 make 52. For Chaucer it may be important that 4 humors & 7 planets make 28 temperamental types, along with a 29th narrator who is, so to speak, interlunar. I must track down the moon-on-England reference in Dryden's AA [*Absalom and Achitophel*] & keep in mind Malory's association of 28 & the Round Table. As I've said, there are seven supports or pillars of wisdom, 7 branches of the tree of life, & 7 hills of the unfallen city (2 Esdras) as well as a sevenfold analogy" (7.34).

The number 28 seemed to have special significance for Frye, and like most things for him this can be traced back to Blake:

> The traditional number of cities in Albion, as recorded by Geoffrey, is twenty-eight, a complete list being duly given in [Blake's] *Jerusalem.* The number twenty-eight reminds us of the twenty-eight "Churches" [periods] into which the history of man from Adam to Milton is divided. . . . Now Jerusalem is the emanation of Albion, Albion has twelve sons, and Jerusalem sixteen. Twelve and sixteen make twenty-eight, and in the final apocalypse in which Albion and Jerusalem are united the full complement of twenty-eight will be made up. The Biblical vision of this is again in the Book of Revelation, where God is surrounded by twenty-eight creatures, the four Zoas and twenty-four "elders." (*FS,* 378–79)

Twenty-eight is a crucial number in two of the schemes for the one hundred–chapter book that Frye proposed to write following *Anatomy of Criticism.* He repeatedly labors over its chapter structure, two of his plans taking these forms: 36–28–36 and 28–22–28–22.[37] "Work out the book in chapters," Frye counsels himself, "disregarding the sections. If it's done right, each chapter will automatically fall into four sections, and such significant numbers as 28 and 33 will be right too" (*RT,* 326). Twenty-eight also figured importantly in Frye's "spiral curriculum," as we have seen, and on two occasions he writes of the symbolic significance of the 11.32 number in *Finnegans Wake,* the number that recurs throughout Joyce's epic, representing the length of the cycle of the novel itself and linked with rising and falling, Ireland, the various characters and their associations, among other things. It is the time the Dublin pub opens in the morning, and, Frye speculates, it also represents the time one goes to bed in the evening. But 11:32 is also twenty-eight minutes until twelve, and these two numbers leap out at Frye as "being symbolic both inside and outside the book."[38] The symbolism of the spiritual world is, Frye writes, "[a]strological symbolism, mostly in sevens & twelves (planets & zodiac), along with some 13's & 28's" (*TBN,* 322). The emphasis on sevens and twelves in the book of Revelation, seven relating to the days of the week and the number of planets and twelve to the months of the year and the signs of the Zodiac, might suggest, Frye says in *The Great Code,* "a world where time and space become the same thing" (75). Twenty-eight is of course connected with the lunar cycle, and in focusing on twenty-eight Frye was doubtless influenced by Yeats's exposition of the phases of the moon in *A Vision.* But Frye provides very few clues about what twenty-eight actually represents or symbolizes.

Anatomy of Criticism argues that mathematics, like literature, uses an autonomous hypothetical language, and that the last chapter of Sir James Jeans's mathematical approach to the universe has a "mystical or occult sound," comparable to that of the anagogic phase of symbolism (350–52). But this is not helpful in determining the symbolic meaning of individual numbers. Frye seems to have no interest in numerology as a means of divining the future or uncovering the secret meaning of present events. But beyond using numbers as a tool for his inveterate anatomizing (number schemes), Frye does appear to believe that certain numbers carry a meaning or otherwise have symbolic significance (numerology). Conventional symbolic numbers, such as the twenty-eight character types that Yeats associates with the phases of the moon, might, Frye suggests, have some subconscious basis in representing the complete circle of human temperaments or psychological types (*FI,* 230; 31.35). But we still remain in the dark about the symbolic meaning of twenty-eight. If it is an occult number of some kind, then perhaps its meaning will have to remain hidden. Frye does suggest in several places that his interest in symbolic numbers has to do with concealment itself—that behind any number a Jungian shadow lurks.

Frye writes that when he was reading for his Norton Lectures (*The*

Secular Scripture), he kept encountering the themes of twins and amnesia, and he connects this to the visible and invisible Christ: "In Jesus' descent we have to remember that the real king Jesus is the concealed 'Christ in me'; the outward visible Jesus is his twin, but the twin who suffers the usual tanist fate of martyrdom." This, in turn, Frye associates with

> the concealed extra number, the most familiar one being thirteen. There are thirteen tribes of Israel, because of the division of the Joseph tribe into two, but what is interesting is the number of lists, ranging literally from Genesis to Revelation, that give twelve and leave out one. There are always plausible reasons for the omission—Dan is the tribe of Antichrist, hence left out of Revelation; Levi got cities and is hence left out of the Canaan map; Simeon was absorbed by Judah, so is left out of one list, and I think Gad is omitted in another. The reasons don't matter: what matters is that thirteen visible presences is unlucky: we have to have twelve with a concealed thirteenth who's the essence of all of them. Thirteen presences in the Gospels, as at the Last Supper, mean martyrdom. The concealed presence is the Resurrection one mentioned in the fifth part of Eliot's Waste Land. (*LN*, 2:456)

Frye thinks it is possible to discover more of the curious concealments: "the fourth concealed in threes, such as the Trinity; the eighth concealed in sevens; the concealed number you get by adding all the numbers before the one you're interested in: that is, the sum of the numbers up to seven is twenty-eight and up to twelve seventy-eight, both of which have important overtones in various places." By "the sum of the numbers" Frye means $1 + 2 + 3 + 4 + 5 + 6 + 7 = 28$, and $1 + 2 \ldots + 12 = 78$. He then concludes, "At the transfiguration there are six figures, assuming a separation—no, you don't need to assume anything: there are six. Point? Well, three, seven and twelve appear to be the numbers of order, authority, and descent: hence four, eight and thirteen would be the obvious numbers of ascent. But the latter three could be substituted for by the sum-numbers of the first group, which are six, twenty-eight, and seventy-eight. I noticed a lot of seventy-eights in Rabelais, without getting a clue about why" (*LN*, 2:457).[39]

There is a hint here of symbolic meaning: the concealed numbers behind three, seven, and twelve represent the opposite of the order, authority, and descent that those numbers stand for. But why they should stand for these three things is unexplained, and why the idea of order could not be represented by a number other than a sum number (say, the Pythagorean *tetradactys* or one hundred) remains a mystery. Using numbers to organize material is of course commonplace, though Frye's numerical patterns are more complex and fearfully symmetrical than most. But one looks in vain throughout his notebooks for the meanings, like those of the Pythagorean mystics and Kabbalists, which he seems to believe are inherent in numbers themselves.

When Frye says in his notes on Wilson's *The Cosmic Trigger* that Wilson "would be nowhere without Jung's 'synchronicity,'" he means that Wilson sees the repeated appearance of the number twenty-three as a meaningful coincidence. Frye had read Jung on synchronicity, which means that two events can be meaningfully related by their coincidence in time, rather than by a sequential, causal connection. Jung refers to this meaningful connection as acausal,[40] and he finds evidence for synchronicity not just in his psychotherapeutic practice but in the *I Ching* and astrology as well. Frye is attracted to the principle: "The will to believe applies primarily to magic & divination. If someone reads palms at a party, most are interested, many hope, if they don't actually believe, that there's 'something in it,' & one or two may even say so. The notion of synchronicity, that every object is an event & every event a signature of a total entity, makes a powerful appeal. Belief in a God, when it's a will to believe, is usually a belief in 'providence,' i.e., something that intelligibly explains what happens" (*RT,* 205). This entry comes from one of Frye's notebooks for *The Great Code,* and in that book Frye says:

> Before modern times, there had been a sense of correspondence or affinity between man and nature, of which the most imaginative expression was perhaps the doctrine of the microcosm, the assumption that man contains an epitome of the whole of reality, being half spirit and half physical substance. This conception of correspondence was closely associated with magic, because it provided a basis for divination, for examining natural phenomena in terms of a supposed connection with the patterns of human destiny. The most important form of such divination is astrology, and astrology is based on a conception of coincidence, which is, as Jung says, a synchronic and acausal conception. Even astrologers now could hardly accept astrology on the old causal basis of "influence," assuming that some physical substance emanates from constellations billions of miles away. The assumption is rather that the world is set up in such a way that there is a pattern of coincidence between configurations of stars and human lives that can be systematically studied. (74–75)

In the notebook entry that lies behind this passage, where Frye refers to these acausal connections as "silent écriture," he indicates that he remains suspicious of astrology because it is "too close to the view that creation was made for man." Still, he allows for the possibility that "as long as it's acausal, in the same way that putting a thermometer outside the window doesn't cause but only records a change in temperature, not only astrology but any number of 'mancies' or forms of divination might be alternative ways of recording the phenomena of human (or any other) life; part, as I say, of the silent écriture of a newly intelligible nature" (*RT*, 326).

Synchronicity for Frye is somewhat broader than Jung's definition of "meaningful coincidence." If, as Frye says, synchronicity means that "every object is an event & every event a signature of a total entity" (*RT*, 205), then he is quite close to Boehme's idea of signature. In a book from his middle period, *The Signature of All Things*, Boehme maintains that within and behind things in the external world there was an internal spiritual form that incised its signature in various shapes and forms—in the stars, the elements, living creatures, trees, and herbs.[41] In this sense, everything in the universe becomes what Frye calls "usable design." Awareness of synchronistic patterns depends on a kind of superstition that is close to Coleridge's fancy: "Let's call it creative superstition. It works with analogies[,] disregarding all differences & attending only to similarities. Here nothing is coincidence in the sense of unusable design; or, using the word more correctly, everything is potential coincidence—what Jung calls synchronistic" (*TBN*, 211).

Synchronicity is to time as interpenetration is to space (*RT*, 304). This means that it does not belong to the objective order of the panoramic apocalypse, the order of unusable design, but to the vision of the participating apocalypse where differences give way to analogies, where any design is potentially usable. Frye wonders if the synchronistic order might not be related to the biblical view of the casting of lots to determine one's fortune (*RT*, 326). Such a view assumes the synchronistic relationship between the orders of nature and fortune—the assumption that is the foundation on which soothsayers, magicians, and astrologers practice their occult arts. Fate or fortune is for the astrologer an acausal connection that is found, as the soothsayer says in *Antony and Cleopatra*, in "nature's infinite book of secrecy" (1.2.9).

Astrology

Frye sometimes used the zodiac as a mnemonic or organizing device. One of his outlines for *Anatomy of Criticism* sets up a parallel between its twelve chapters and the four elements, the planets, and the signs of the zodiac (30q.2). And one of his versions of the one hundred–chapter book aligns the signs of the zodiac around the first thirty-three parts of the cycle, as shown in diagram 5. But Frye never incorporated any of these astrological schemes in his published work, and he says little else about them in his notebooks. Notebook 6 (published in *The "Third Book" Notebooks*), which was written in a diary or daybook with a dated page for each day, has separate sections devoted to Frye's archetypal gods. Each is given a heading: Eros, Adonis, Hermes, and Prometheus. The sections for Eros and Hermes begin on the spring and autumn equinox dates (March 21 and September 21), and those for Adonis and Prometheus on the summer and winter solstice dates (June 21 and December 21). Such an arrangement, unique in Frye's notebooks, invites commentary, or at least explanation, especially since the material in three of the four sections does not actually relate to the gods of their titles. There must be some meaning in these celestial mechanics other than the association of the spring and summer gods (Eros and Adonis) with the upper half of the Great Doodle, where they ordinarily reside, and of the autumn and winter gods (Hermes and Prometheus) with the lower half. The answer, if it is one, is tucked away in a remark in Notebook 12, where Frye reveals that a long-standing hunch of his associates the axis of "speculation" on his Great Doodle with the equinox and the Eros-Adonis cycle, and the axis of "concern" with the solstice and the *axis mundi* or Logos-Thanatos dialectic (*TBN*, 143). This appears to be only another mental diagram for organizing the categories of the Great Doodle. If Frye means to suggest something additional, it remains mysteriously hidden.[42]

About 1970 Frye read Franz Cumont's *Astrology and Religion among the Greeks and Romans,* the only book exclusively on astrology mentioned in the notebooks. Frye says he ran across Cumont by the greatest "good luck" because it was precisely the book he wanted at the moment (*RT,* 245)—a synchronistic moment of meaningful coincidence, apparently. At the time, Frye was working through one of his many plans for his book on the Bible, and he found in Cumont's study Stoic incarnations of Chaldean astrology, "founded on the eye & the heavens, the authority of the Emperor, the fated cycle," that parallel the Trinitarian formulations of Christianity. Frye calls the parallels anti-Christian, but he means only that they are analogies of the Judaeo-Christian myth—what he would later call "positive analogies." Cumont, Frye writes, "says that this [Stoic] synthesis had a trinity of heaven, planets & earth. It's clear that he's emphasizing this. So the anti-Father is the world of natural law symbolized by the 'fixed' stars, the anti-Son the world of the eniautos-daimon cycle incarnate in the king, the anti-Spirit the womb-tomb Earth-mother" (*RT,* 245). As Chaldean astrology filtered into the classical tradition, especially

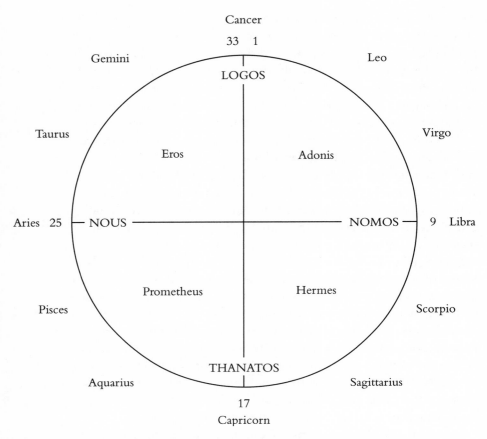

Diagram 5. The Zodiac Schema Parts 1–33 of Frye's 100-chapter book,
Notebook 11f. Reconstructed (not actually drawn by Frye).

among the Romans, it issued in another form of natural religion, quite
similar in its cycles to what Frye had discovered in Sir James Frazer,
Robert Graves, and Jane Ellen Harrison.[43] Chaldean astrology, then, is
another example of how the ideas of an outmoded science that developed
into a theology continue to have a mythological and metaphorical reso-
nance.[44]

In "The Times of the Signs: An Essay on Science and Mythology"
(*SM*, 66–96) Frye traces the separation of astrology and astronomy from
the fifteenth century, when they were more or less the same subject;
through the eighteenth and nineteenth centuries, when "belief and interest in astrology is abandoned by most educated people" and astrology
is finally "consigned to the scrap-heap of exploded superstitions"; to the
twentieth century, when the separation between astrology and astronomy

is still maintained, but the former has become a flourishing industry in the publishing and media worlds, appealing to an audience for horoscopes and the like completely outside the scientific community. The current popularity of astrology, Frye says, "indicates a growing acceptance, by society as a whole, of the schematic and symmetrical type of pattern-thinking which the poets use" (*SM,* 74–75). Astrology, then, is really a subset of mythology, which continues to transform itself, and while it can tell us nothing much about the powers of nature, it can reveal an "otherness of spirit" (*SM,* 96).

Astrology also functions for Frye as a mnemonic device. In one of his detailed outlines of the first four books of the ogdoad he remarks that he can extract from it a "zodiacal agenda," meaning only that Liberal, Tragicomedy, Anticlimax, and Rencontre will each have three parts, which he then proceeds to list (*RT,* 57–58). Here the zodiac serves simply as a small memory theater. Similarly, in one of his outlines for *The Great Code* Frye aligns the eight chapters of that book with the earth and the seven astrological "planets": the moon, Mercury, Venus, the sun, Mars, Jupiter, and Saturn (*RT,* 358). And the zodiac functions as such a memory device in this concentrated *Great Code* outline: "Nous, Aries; Eros, Taurus (low) & Gemini (high); Logos, Cancer; Adonis, Leo (early) & Virgo (late); Nomos, Libra; Hermes, Scorpio (upper) & Sagittarius (lower); Thanatos, Capricornus; Prometheus, Aquarius (lower) & Pisces (higher). L, 1; Nm, 9; Th, 17; Nu, 25; L², 33. I & II are solstitial, III equinoctial" (*RT,* 136).[45] The abbreviations stand for Logos, Nomos, Thanatos, Nous, and Logos 2. The implicit diagram Frye has sketched here is the familiar circle with its four quadrants, the eastern point being Nomos, the western point Nous, the northern point Logos, and the southern point Thanatos.[46] Atop this variation of the Great Doodle Frye has superimposed a reversed zodiac, which here moves west to east beginning with Aries. These three examples are what one commentator refers to as astrological "computer programs," "used to store information in memory by several mnemotechnical systems," such as the zodiacal wheel, the seven planets, and the four elements.[47]

Frye's notebooks contain about two dozen references to astrology besides its use as a memory device, and from these references three different claims emerge. First, astrology as an intellectual holiday from matters of belief is an effort to find analogies of being (*RT,* 356), and so is like any other such metonymic enterprise—philosophical, Thomistic, or poetic. Second, it is a defensible means of grasping typical elements, for example, the analysis of human character that we find in Chaucer's planetary temperaments, the Galenic theory of humors, or the cycle of types in Yeats's

A Vision (31.29, 34.4). And third, as a form of divining the future, astrology "is part of the attempt to evoke a Logos vision, or something akin to it, out of a Thanatos one" (*TBN,* 207). Astrology, therefore, represents a hidden order that belongs to the complex of ideas Frye associates with the *katabasis,* with the message of the oracle, with the *nekyia* or descent to Hades to obtain knowledge of the future, and with what he calls the "point of demonic epiphany." The Tarot cards represent another form of such divination.

The Tarot

In *Fearful Symmetry* Frye writes that "Blake's pictographs are to be interpreted in terms of their sequential relationship to one another, as a progression of signs which, like the alphabet, spell out not a word but the units of all words." Just as Bacon believed that the scientist searched nature to discover a finite series of forms, comparable to what the alphabet is to language, so Blake, Frye conjectures, sought in art a similarly limited "alphabet of forms" that would "box the entire compass of the imagination in an orderly sequence" (*FS,* 417).[48] Blake's *Job,* which has twenty-two plates (the number of letters in the Hebrew alphabet) is an example of an "alphabet of forms," a phrase already used in connection with the Kabbalah and one that recurs throughout Frye's notebooks (he does not use it elsewhere in his published works).[49] It is a shorthand phrase for the mythical and metaphorical conventions used by the imagination, which for Frye can always be represented schematically. The Great Doodle, the HEAP scheme, and all of the other diagrammatic structures that Frye uses to organize the symbolic universe—its cycles and themes and images—belong to the alphabet of forms. Western music is also a "schematic alphabet of forms" (*TBN,* 111). The Greater Trumps of the Tarot pack, with its twenty-two cards, is still another example of this "alphabet."

Frye was aware of several ways that novelists had worked out the Tarot sequence for their own fictional ends. He had read Charles Williams's thriller *The Greater Trumps* in 1949, and in both his diary for that year and in Notebook 32 he sets down the Tarot sequence that Williams used (*D,* 168; 32.99). Later he read the Tarot trilogy of Piers Anthony, who shuffled his deck to produce another pattern for organizing his adventure series.[50] Frye found still other arrangements of the cards in *The Tarot of the Bohemians* by Papus (M. Gérard Encausse) and *The Pictorial Key to the Tarot* by A. E. Waite. Among the numerous schemes Frye developed in Notebook 21 for his book on the Bible, one, as we indicated in the introduction, is related to the Tarot. "This may come to nothing," Frye

writes, "and it mustn't attempt to take over, but there may be a link between the organization of this book & the Tarot sequence. The Greater
Trumps seem to me polarized between the Juggler & the Fool. The Juggler seems to me to be God when seen by Man as the Creator of himself
& Nature; the Fool, or what Waite calls the 'ineffable in zero,' is whatever
in man can be redeemed by God: his archetype is the nothing or abyss out
of which he was created. Hence the two poles of being are the binary of
one and nothing" (*RT,* 172).[51] Between the Juggler (card 1) and the Fool
(card 0 or 22), Frye arranges the remaining twenty cards in five groups of
four, which can be reconstructed from several entries in Notebook 21
(*RT,* 173) as follows:

One. God as creator of man and nature (1)
    1. Juggler (Magician).   Chapter 1. Creation
Figures of spatial and temporal   Chapter 2. Establishment of Order
    activity
    2. Priest (Hierophant) (5)
    3. Priestess (2)
    4. Emperor (4)
    5. Empress (3)
The original establishment of eros   Chapter 3: Eros/Adonis
    6. Fortitude (8)
    7. Temperance (14)
    8. Justice (11)
    9. Lovers (6)
The original establishment of Nature   Chapter 4: Hermes
    10. Sun (19)
    11. Moon (18)
    12. Star (17)
    13. Universe (22)
The group of human death   Chapter 5. Prometheus
    14. Death (13)
    15. Devil (15)
    16. Hanged Man (12)
    17. Hermit (9)
The group of natural death   Chapter 6. Apocalypse
    18. Wheel (10)
    19. Tower (16)
    20. Last Judgment (20)
    21. Chariot (7)
Zero (Nothing); "the ineffable in Zero" (Waite)
    22. Fool (1 or 0)   Chapter 7: Book of the Fool

In this summary Waite's Tarot sequence is indicated in parentheses. The right-hand column represents another version of Frye's obsession, glanced at in the introduction, with a seven-part book. Frye then "boxes the compass," with the quincunx of cards 2 through 21 forming another version of his familiar cycle and quadrant schema, which can be represented by diagram 6. Here the four cards representing power and order (priest, priestess, emperor, and empress) are, Frye says, "the holding centre of the quincunx" (*RT,* 173). But he is not through with his curiously fanciful arranging of the cards. In the seventy-eight cards of the Tarot deck are twenty-two Major Arcana (also called Trumps) and fifty-six Minor Arcana, the latter of which are divided into four suits (pentacles, cups, swords, and wands). Each fourteen-card suit has four court cards (king, queen, knight, and squire) and ten numbered cards. Frye sees in the total deck what he calls "three principles" and three corresponding "systems of writing":

Principles	Corresponding System of Writing

Circular and simultaneous
    Major Arcana or Greater
    Trumps
	Hieroglyphic

Hierarchical
    The "court cards" cards of the
    Minor Arcana (king, queen,
    knight, and squire or page)
	Hieratic

The Demotic
    The forty numbered cards
    of the Minor Arcana
	Alphabetic (demotic–numerical)

To this scheme Frye adds: "The one-to-ten sequence [of the Minor Arcana] is the progressive, numerical, self-hypnotic scientism that's reversed by the one-zero binary" (*RT,* 173).

How are we to explain these cryptic and almost completely unrelated Tarot schemes? They seem to be mnemonic devices Frye can use to organize certain clusters of images, themes, and dialectic oppositions. They also seem to represent a kind of secret symbolic code—an alphabet of forms by which initiates into the symbolism can communicate, so that a simple reference to, say, the Juggler would summon up everything Frye associates with the Logos vision, or a reference to the Fool with everything he associates with the Thanatos abyss. In fact, Frye writes in an early notebook,

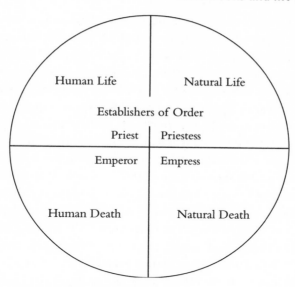

Diagram 6. The Tarot and the Quincunx

> Every once in a while in studying symbolism I feel a surge forward as
> though my unconscious has handed me another cabbalistic symbol
> from a kind of universal Tarot. Freemasonry I understand systematizes
> this into a technique. I think a similar process is the central part of the
> New Testament conception of the gift of tongues: whether actual lan-
> guages in the literal sense were produced by collective excitement I
> don't know: doubtless it's possible, but would it be anything more spir-
> itually valuable than a curiosity if it did happen? Surely the feeling of a
> pattern of universal meaning coming clear piece by piece, so that those
> who understand it could talk to each other in shorthand, would be
> predominant, & would be part of the so-called gift of prophesying.
> (*RT,* 38)

The particular order of the cards is of no importance, for every time the
deck is shuffled another sequence results, and the sequence, whatever it
turns out to be, will suggest a new arrangement of what the cards symbolize. "The reason I'm hung up on the Tarots at the moment," Frye
writes, "is that a pack of cards has a close *technological* resemblance to a
series of pericopes & kernels of concern" (*RT,* 174). Frye's use of "technological" here derives from the original sense of the Greek *tekhnologia,*
meaning the systematic treatment of an art or skill (*techne*).

The Tarot cards, in other words, are thematically analogous to a
large catalogue of concerns, primary and otherwise. Many commentators

see the Major Arcana as representing a spiritual journey, sometimes called "The Fool's Journey." Temporally, for Frye, this journey can take any number of narrative forms, depending on how the cards are shuffled. Spatially, they are all contained in "the total simultaneous pattern [that] always extends from alpha to omega" (*RT,* 174), the alpha–omega aspect of the Word being another shorthand reference for the alphabet of forms.[52] Frye apparently believes that however the cards are shuffled, the Juggler and Fool cards remain constant as a kind of containing form for the other twenty. They form the poles of a dialectic between the point of epiphany and the point of demonic epiphany. In Notebook 38 Frye writes, "According to a set of Chinese pictures Gordon Wood showed me, you have to go into Giotto's O and out again." Wood, a former student of Frye's, had shown him ten ox-herding pictures from D. T. Suzuki's *Essays in Zen Buddhism.* The pictures tell a story of a young ox herd who has lost his ox, eventually finds and tethers it, and then leads it home. The eighth picture, however, is a blank circle, representing the point of demonic epiphany. "That's the Fool," Frye says, "the card numbered zero" (38.17), symbolizing the locus of the katabatic descent. Implicit here is the oracle-wit complex: one has to descend into the nothingness represented by zero before ascending to enlightenment.

In his published work, the Tarot for Frye simply represents a schematic way of thinking that serves as a reference table for poetry. He has a note in *Anatomy of Criticism* that aligns the Tarot and other typological constructs—allegorical alchemy, Rosicrucianism, the Kabbalah, and freemasonry—with the paradigms of his own tables of apocalyptic imagery in the Third Essay of that book (359–60). And in *The Critical Path* he writes that the Tarot is a schematic construct congenial to poetry in the same way that astrology, the *I Ching,* and other forms of patterned thought are—from the less orthodox (Gurdjieff and Velikowski) to the more so (Lévi-Strauss) (145).

Channeling

The kook-book category includes, as we have seen, only a half-dozen or so titles, but Frye might well have included Yeats's *A Vision,* one of the more well-known accounts of twentieth-century channeling. Frye devotes several notebook entries to this esoteric phenomenon, a form of spiritualism in which psychics or mediums are able to channel messages from discarnate spirits of one kind or another. Yeats explains that *A Vision* was dictated by discarnate "instructors" and recorded by his wife, who had the gift of automatic writing. "God knows," Frye writes, "what the spirits of V [*A Vision*] were (spirits of the moon, most likely, of a sort that always seem to be buzzing around Irishmen & Germans)" (31.11)— "dismal pedants," he calls them (31.53); he adds that the "truly orthodox 'scientific' approach to the questions raised in V [*A Vision*] is of course to ignore the evidence & sneer at everyone who offers any. As I have no interest in that, I have no pose of scientific 'disinterestedness' to excuse my ignorance of the subject" (31.15). In his essay on *A Vision* Frye says only that since he has no explanation to offer for Yeats's account of the automatic writing or the spiritual instructors, he is inclined to accept Yeats's explanation "at its face value" (*SM*, 251).

Aside from Yeats, Frye's sources for the channeling phenomenon are three: Jane Roberts, whose "Seth" books have become classics to those familiar with the channeling phenomenon; *The Other Side* by Bishop James Pike, an account of the bishop's speaking to the spirit of his dead son through a London medium; and Edgar Cayce, one of the more famous psychics of the last century.[53] In the early 1970s, almost twenty years before Shirley MacLaine popularized channeling, poet and science-fiction writer Jane Roberts, with the assistance of her husband, began writing what became a series of trance-dictated books. Roberts said that the real author was a discarnate entity Seth (she called Seth an "energy essence personality"), and a substantial literature has grown up around Seth. Apparently, the only Seth book Frye read was the two-volume *The "Unknown" Reality*.[54] Frye has somewhat different responses to each of the three channeling examples.

About Jane Roberts Frye writes only, "I have to alter the self-delusion bit: what I say is true enough, but I shouldn't suggest junking it all. I may yet find myself stealing from the Seth books, and of course there's James Merrill, who extracted an epic from a ouija board" (*LN*, 1:283).[55] The spirit of Seth provided messages through Jane Roberts from 1963 until her death in 1984. The so-called Seth material includes the transcriptions of Roberts's sessions with Seth, first from tapes made by students in her ESP classes and later from written accounts by her husband, Robert Butts. The dictated volumes are known as "Seth Books" (more than 6,000 pages of material), and Roberts also wrote other books about Seth. The two-volume *Unknown Reality* that Frye owned was part of the Seth-book series. The channeled subject matter is wide-ranging: dreams, parallel worlds, out-of-body and space travel, biblical history, subatomic particles, reincarnation, astrology, flying saucers, healing, brain waves, black holes, and countless other topics.

The passage just quoted about "self-delusion" and "stealing from the Seth books" comes from one of Frye's notebooks for *Words with Power*.

There is no prior reference in the notebooks to self-delusion, nor is there any such reference in *Words with Power* itself. What Frye apparently wants to alter is something he had written elsewhere, perhaps in one of the drafts for *Words with Power,* about a paranormal experience involving self-delusion. In any case, it seems clear that the Seth books and James Merrill's Ouija board stand as counterevidence for someone's having been, in Frye's view, self-deluded.

James Pike was a well-known Anglican bishop from California, a prolific author, and a controversial theologian. The story he recounts in *The Other Side* is briefly this: After the suicide of his troubled son Jim in February 1966, Bishop Pike returned to his flat in Cambridge, England, where he and Jim had previously spent several happy months together.[56] Shortly thereafter, he, his chaplain, and his secretary began observing a series of strange phenomena (the mysterious appearance of postcards and books, the disappearance of photographs, objects placed at a 140-degree angle, and so on). On the advice of Canon J. D. Pearce-Higgins of the Church of England, Pike consulted a well-known London medium, Ena Twigg, who was able to summon the dead son. Jim reported that he was responsible for having moved the books and for the other unexplained phenomena. Pike returned to the United States and several weeks later found himself preaching at St. Thomas Episcopal Church in New York City. After the service he encountered a stranger who reported that he had seen two figures standing behind Pike in the pulpit, a tall youth named Jim and a patriarchal figure named Elias; Elias was the name of Jim Pike's maternal grandfather, and the stranger turned out to be Arthur Ford, the famous American medium and the head of an organization called Spiritual Frontiers Fellowship. After returning to California, Pike set up series of sessions with another medium, George Daisley, also connected with Spiritual Frontiers, who told Pike that Jim had contacted him several weeks before. By this time the bishop had become convinced of the reality of the paranormal events, and not long afterward he appeared in a séance on a television program in Toronto, directed by none other than Arthur Ford. A year after *The Other Side* was published, James Pike died in a Judean desert, where he had gone to search for the origins of Christianity. Frye's brief remarks about Bishop Pike are in the context of his notebook entries on Edgar Cayce.

Cayce (1877–1945) was a psychic whose career began with a diagnosis of his own illness and then spread to analyzing the health problems of others, sometimes over great distances, and answering many questions about personal problems. Later, Cayce's "readings" (a stenographer's transcriptions of what emerged from his self-induced trances) turned to the description of past lives, biblical and other events, and mythological places (e.g., Atlantis). Thousands of "readings," catalogued by subject, are in the Cayce archives. Here are Frye's two notebook entries about Cayce:

> A belief is a course of action inspired by a shaping vision. This shaping vision is the opposite of idolatry. In both cases you become what you behold. One is the total "I am" building up inside you; the other is the tabular rasa approach to the objective. The Hebrews, in attacking idolatry, first of all demonized the *oracular* objective, as in the Witch of Endor (note *where* Bishop Pike died). The scapegoat ritual & casting out devils develop from this, I don't know just how. The thing that's wrong is divinizing this world. I've been reading about Edgar Cayce, who's evidence that we may be getting near the point where we can plug into the big phone exchange of *spiritus mundi* without getting silly ideas about *gods*. The Hebrew tradition was not scientific, but by demythologizing nature it helped the growth of science. But of course this too can develop idolatry if it becomes founded in dogma. The doctors who *a priori* attacked Cayce were working on the same principle that W.H. Auden ascribes to Herod. (*TBN,* 322)

> Of course the oracular fallacy operates here too: if Cayce is "right" (tuned in to the spiritus mundi exchange) in one area, say medical diagnosis, I don't see that he must necessarily be right about, say, Atlantis. (Why does Atlantis have to be in the *past*? If it's a myth, of course, it's present, an example or warning.) In Plato Atlantis is only the projected ghost of the *Republic.* (*TBN,* 322)

In the first entry, Frye's point is that Cayce's being in touch with the *spiritus mundi* is a healthy corrective to "the divinizing" of the world, as in the Hebrew tradition, that makes every oracular manifestation a message from the gods. Those who see everything in experience as a divine manifestation will take all oracular pronouncements to be demonic if inconsistent with their shaping vision. Thus the oracular Bishop Pike, who became separated from his wife in the rugged terrain of the Judean desert and was found dead between two rocks in a canyon, is said by his detractors to be as demonic as the Witch of Endor, who lived between Mount Tabor and the Hill of Moreh. But if the source of the vision comes not from gods but from the *spiritus mundi,* then the divinizing and demonizing issue does not arise. And, Frye adds in the second entry, those who attack Cayce in the name of science have, or at least can have, their own idols, like Auden's Herod, who argues that if we grant that Jesus was sinless, then "the human race would be plunged into madness and despair." If you grant one miracle, according to Herod, then you can be hoodwinked into believing anything.[57] Frye then draws a distinction between Cayce's medical diagnoses, which he may be willing to accept, and his "readings" of such past myths as that of Atlantis, which he does not accept. Plato took a mythical view of Atlantis, and so does Frye. As we have seen, Atlantis is for him another version—a positive analogy—of the biblical myth of emergence from the sea of chaos. Whether there was some historical basis for Atlantis is beside the point. Stearn's *Edgar Cayce: The Sleeping Prophet* devotes an entire chapter to Cayce's "readings" of the Atlantis myth, which continued for more than twenty years. The readings correspond in uncanny ways with the accounts of Atlantis in Plato's *Timaeus* and *Critias*.

Just as Plato drops his description of Atlantis in the *Critias*, apparently thinking it necessary to turn to other matters, so we now bring this survey of the esoteric to an end. But before turning to other matters, a recapitulation of at least the reasons that Frye is drawn to the disparate forms of esoterica we have examined can perhaps bring this part of our study into focus.

Recapitulation

We have already mentioned in several contexts A. E. Waite (1857–1947), a student, translator, and popularizer of numerous occult texts and an essentially self-taught scholar of mystical philosophies. Waite grew up under the influence of Eliphas Lévi (Alphonse Louis Constant), whose *History of Magic* he translated. He joined the Order of the Golden Dawn, established several orders of his own, and poured forth a stream of ponderously written books. A friend of Arthur Machen's, he is best remembered today for his Tarot pack, produced in art-nouveau style by his devotee Pamela Colman Smith. Frye read and annotated Waite's *The Holy Grail, The Pictorial Key to the Tarot, The Quest of the Golden Stairs,* and *The Unknown Philosopher: The Life of Louis Claude de Saint-Martin and the Substance of His Transcendental Doctrine*. He also read and annotated Waite's translation of Lévi's *The History of Magic* and Waite's editions of Papus's *The Tarot of the Bohemians* and *The Works of Thomas Vaughan*. Waite's *The Quest of the Golden Stairs* is a faerie-world romance, a less sophisticated version of George Macdonald's prose fantasies. Frye includes it in a catalogue of books that are to be his main sources for his intended essay on faeries and elementals. About *Quest of the Golden Stairs* he says only that it is "superficially off-putting" (*LN*, 1:190). But about Waite's book *The Holy Grail* Frye writes,

I've been reading Loomis and A.E. Waite on the Grail. Loomis often seems to me an erudite ass: he keeps applying standards of coherence and consistency to twelfth-century poets that might apply to Anthony Trollope. Waite seems equally erudite and not an ass. But I imagine Grail scholars would find Loomis useful and Waite expendable, because Waite isn't looking for anything that would interest them. It's quite possible that what Waite is looking for particularly doesn't exist—secret traditions, words of power, an esoteric authority higher than that of the Catholic Church—and yet the *kind* of thing he's looking for is so infinitely more important than Loomis' trivial games of descent from Irish sources where things get buggered up because the poets couldn't distinguish *cors* meaning body from *cors* meaning horn. Things like this show me that I have a real function as a critic, pointing out that what Loomis does has been done and is dead, whereas what Waite does, even when mistaken, has hardly begun and is very much alive. (*LN,* 2:460)

"Loomis" is Roger Sherman Loomis, author of *The Grail: From Celtic Myth to Christian Symbol.* This and several other books by Loomis on Arthurian and other medieval romances established him as an early authority on the subject. As Frye suggests, his work was influential with other Grail scholars, even though his thesis about the development of the Grail legend has now been called into question.

But for Frye the philological and historical matters treated by Loomis are dead, whereas Waite's probing of secret traditions, words of power, and the like is alive.[58] The question why it is alive is part of the larger question of why Frye devoted so much energy to exploring the forms of esoterica we have considered in this and the previous chapter. Several answers suggest themselves.

First, the esoteric tradition comes to us largely in third-phase language, which means that its background is imaginative and symbolic, and thus, like any other imaginative creation, it has a grammar, the rules of which operate in the same way as, say, the grammar of symbolism in Shakespeare or Dante. In his well-known essay "On Value-Judgements," which develops certain ideas from the "Polemical Introduction" to *Anatomy of Criticism,* Frye argues that the critic is not a judge, or at least should not be; the critic, rather, should display an attitude of total acceptance, whatever the textual data in front of her or him.[59] "The dialectic axis of criticism . . . has as one pole the total acceptance of the data of literature, and as the other the total acceptance of the potential values of those data" (*AC,* 25). This principle applies to discursive texts as well, such as works of philosophy or history. A corollary is that genres have a way of changing over time: Frazer may have little standing in the scholarly circles of anthropology or psychology, but he provides us a grammar of the imagination nonetheless. Moreover, to repeat Frye's epigram, "yesterday's kook book is tomorrow's standard text" (*LN*, 1:17). This grammar of the imagination has many common syntactic forms—religious, psychological, literary, philosophical, musical. The circle of fifths in classical music is a "symmetrical grammar" (*SM*, 118). And just as Dante's *Commedia* is an educational treatise that teaches "a grammar of the imagination" (*RT*, 396), so Jung's studies of alchemy provide a grammar of literary symbols (*NFCL*, 129). There is nothing we read, Frye says, "that cannot become a source of imaginative illumination. One would say that few subjects could be duller or less rewarding than the handbooks studied by Miss Frances Yates in *The Art of Memory*, yet her study has all the mental exhilaration of the discovery of a fine new poet" (*StS*, 69–70), meaning that the materials she studies, esoteric texts, yield that exhilaration. In his early essay entitled "Yeats and the Language of Symbolism" Frye indicates that he is a complete skeptic about the objective existence of Yeats's spiritual instructors. But the subjective aspect of *A Vision* is an altogether different matter, because it provides the symbolic structure of Yeats's poetry from 1917 onward, and so it stands as "one of the grammars of romantic symbolism" (*FI*, 231).

Second, for Frye esoteric texts are removed altogether from considerations of belief. This means that they can provide the content for vision. In *Fearful Symmetry* he writes that the

> doctrine of the Word of God explains the interest of so many of the humanists, not only in Biblical scholarship and translation, but in occult sciences. Cabbalism, for instance, was a source of new imaginative interpretations of the Bible. Other branches of occultism, including alchemy, also provided complex and synthetic conceptions which could be employed to understand the central form of Christianity as a vision rather than as a doctrine or ritual, preserving a *tertium quid* which, without detracting from the reality of the religion, would also avoid both the iconic and the iconoclastic pitfalls. (151)

In the *Anatomy* Frye notes that critics often break forth into an "oracular harrumph" when they encounter references to alchemy, the Tarot, Rosicrucianism, and the like (359), and the same attitude persists fifty years later. One encounters readers here and there, having discovered that Frye thought highly of Colin Still's book on *The Tempest* or that he had read some esoteric work, recoiling in amazement, as if it automatically followed that Frye was a card-carrying member of some mystery cult or was engaging in the ritual practices of Freemasonry.[60] Such readers have failed to grasp the elementary principle that there is a difference between the reading of a text and the use to which that reading is put. Frye read widely in a number of fields, and the fact that he read something does not necessarily mean that, using a theory of truth as correspondence, he accepted what he read. He could say, for example, that Lawrence's *Plumed Serpent* provided a good illustration of the recovery of projected gods, even though he thought the novel was "superficially the silliest and most wrong-headed book ever written" (*RT,* 368). To see Lawrence's story as an example of the recovery of projection is to put it in the context of an imaginative construct. To call Lawrence's ideas silly and wrongheaded— an existential rather than a mythological projection—is to remove it from that context.

Similarly, the esoteric requires what we called earlier a "shift in perspective" Frye was naturally willing to grant the powers of pure reason, Cartesian thinking, and the entire Enlightenment agenda, but the fundamental emphasis in all his work is that the imagination provides a critique of pure reason. In fact, it is to the credit of the Enlightenment that we can even speak of a shift in focus from the rational or scientific to the poetic, where the principle of identity means something more than an algebraic equation. Frye says that a remark by A. E. Waite in *The Pictorial Key to the Tarot* suggests something like this: "Christ is the buried {male} individuality in each of us; the rest of our individuality ought to become a unified symbolic female; these two unite, as in the conjunctio symbol of alchemy, and the child they produce is the eternal youth of the resurrection" (*LN,* 2:461). Here alchemical conjunction is no more or less than an example of metaphorical identity. It is no more or less mysterious than an exoteric metaphor, such as the Incarnation.

Third, certain forms of esoterica—alchemy, astrology, the Kabbalah, the *I Ching,* the Tarot pack, numerology—help to confirm Frye's contention that imaginative or poetic thought is schematic. As we have seen, he sometimes calls this the "alphabet of forms," meaning that "they are expressions of the schematic ('all imagination') shape of the mythical apprehension of reality" (*TBN,* 110–11). Mental systems, whatever else they are, are symbolic forms, and once they are conceived symbolically Frye accepts them with a detachment that supersedes all skepticism as to their truth claims (32.66). "All my critical career," he writes, "has been haunted by the possibility of working out a schematology, i.e., a grammar of poetic language . . . the kind of diagrammatic basis of poetry that haunts the occultists & others" (*TBN,* 212). Frye's skeptical sense naturally manifests itself from time to time: Madame Blavatsky is a charlatan, some books are "kook books," Yeats's "spiritual instructors" produce a flood of nonsense, and so on. But for Frye the Cartesian mode of thinking cannot gainsay what is revealing in, say, Yeats's *A Vision,* where the imagination rather than the reason is taken as the primary perceptive and creative faculty. And what is revealing are the mental diagrams that always seem to arise from our subconscious, or whatever source, when we begin to think poetically.

There were other reasons Frye turned to the esoteric tradition. Astrology provided him mnemonic devices, and he mined at least some of the occult arts for *adagia.* But the sources of such things are not uniquely occult. The esoteric tradition for Frye was finally a visionary tradition, analogous to other creative traditions, and analogies were the architectural blueprint for Frye's spiritual world.

> People think they're being iconoclastic & realistic when they ask me if there aren't differences as well as similarities in the patterns I put together. Of course there are, but that again is confusing imaginative & conceptual processes. In imaginative thought there is no real knowledge of anything but similarities (ultimately identities): knowledge of differences is merely a transition to a new knowledge of similarities. In conceptual thought analogy is tricky & misleading beyond the heuristic stage: in imaginative thought it's the *telos* of knowledge. The great ocean into which all analogy empties is the *via negativa* approach to God, which the Incarnation reverses into spring rain, the identity of God & Man. (*RT,* 215)

III Word and Spirit

7 The Dialogue and Its *Aufhebung*

[The] trouble with religions is they spread, like dandelions, & don't give you time or energy for anything else.

—Marginal annotation to *The Book of the Dead*

The end of the journey is interpenetration, or perhaps the hologram model. It's the recognition scene of proclaiming word & responding spirit.

—*Late Notebooks,* 1:395

Mythos and *dianoia,* as we have seen, are central terms in Frye's critical universe—two of the many temporal and spatial pairs he calls on to describe, explain, and interpret texts. As a way of summing up, the terms provide a framework for characterizing Frye's own career. The *mythos* of his lifelong project takes the shape of a quest romance, and our argument has been that Frye's quest is a religious one. "The path is before me," Frye writes, "& it is always there: no God puts my application on file & makes me wait until I hear from him. Nor is there any magical spell on it: I may start out & turn back innumerable times, but the path is unaffected by that, though I'm not" (30r.12). Similarly, from the perspective of *dianoia* or thematic stasis, the architecture of Frye's universe is that of a religious visionary, and one of the spatial projections of that vision is the dialogue of Word and Spirit. Before turning to this dialogue, let us explore briefly these two roles—Frye as a pilgrim on a journey and Frye as a spiritual architect.

The Journey and Its Gate

Frye describes the shape of the journey in different ways. It is, first of all, a horizontal pilgrimage in pursuit of an object of desire. Frye begins with the literary universe of William Blake, and he seeks with unremitting energy the verbal formulations that will carry him to a double vision lying beyond the poetic. This is Frye's own horizontal quest. As we have seen in chapter 2, he calls it a purgatorial journey, and its goal is apocalyptic vision: an interpenetrating, kerygmatic universe in which all subject–object distinctions have been erased and lifted to another level. Two other familiar formulations of the goal are the Logos vision and the gospel of love. The goal, as Frye says, always retreats until the last page, which means that the journey itself, always in process, does not embody or express a goal (*LN,* 1:217). But one primary goal, as we have also seen in chapter 2, is love. The journey, we might say, permits one to see the vision of love panoramically. But love is realized only when the journey has concluded in the thematic stasis of the participating apocalypse.

The shape of the journey is often, in the second place, projected cyclically, and the contour of Frye's career could be described as a cycle, beginning with *Fearful Symmetry* and coming full circle in *The Double Vision.* The cycle had considerable imaginative appeal for Frye, immersed as he was in the historical patterns in Spengler and Vico, the sequence of natural disappearance and renewal in Frazer, the seven cycles of Orc in Blake,[1] and the visionary cycles of Joyce and Yeats. "Cycle" is a word, like "phase" and "mode," that he uses in a number of ways, but when "cycle" is associated with the repeated sequences of nature, sheer routine, endless recurrence, or closed form (as in the spiral into nothingness of the ouroboros), Frye, as we have already noted, abandons it as a comprehensive, containing metaphor because it leaves no space for the resurrected life: "The way or journey is a series of cycles (journey of course is from *journée*) where we get 'up' in the morning and 'fall' asleep at night. At a certain point the cycle stops for us—there's finally a winter-night-old age-sea point with no spring-dawn-birth-rain following. We all take that road; the question is whether (or when) an upward spiral moves against it. It does, of course, but there must be a point at which rebirth must give place to resurrection" (*LN,* 1:289). Without that point we are "trapped in a squirrel cage" of endless repetition (*MM,* 213).

The journey assumes still a third shape in the last half of *Words with Power,* where the horizontal and cyclic quests are displaced by descending and ascending movements along the *axis mundi:* "ascent & descent are a verticalized journey" (*LN,* 1:315), the way down and the way up in the Heraclitean formula. Or in another formulation, the path or way of the journey becomes metaphorically a "reconstructed ladder" (*LN,* 1:23). "A journey," Frye writes, "is a directed movement in time through space, and in the idea of a journey there are always two elements involved. One is the person making the journey; the other is the road, path, or direction taken, the simplest word for this being *way.* In all metaphorical uses of the journey these two elements appear. In pure metaphor the emphasis normally falls on the person; in proportion as we approach religious and other existential aspects of metaphorical journeys the emphasis shifts to *way*" (*MM,* 212). The movement from point to point along the vertical axis of life itself, Frye writes, "is either a journey to death or a purgatorial journey (vale of soul-making), and . . . the presence of God is what makes purgatorial sense of life" (*LN*, 1:358).

We see in these passages, as well as in *Words with Power* and "The Journey as Metaphor" (Frye's most extensive treatment of the topic, *MM*, 212–26), that the distinction between literary and personal odysseys tends to dissolve in Frye's late work. We move, as it were, from the anatomy of the 1950s to the confession of the 1980s. In the essay just mentioned, Frye writes, apropos of the metaphors of the journey he has been examining, that

> the journey is seldom regarded as a good thing in itself. It is undertaken because it must be: if the journey is a metaphor for life, life has to be followed to the end, but the end is the point of the journey, or at least the quality of the end is. It is conceivable, however, that a journey might have a value in itself. If so, obviously there would have to be something inside the traveller to resonate against the experience, so the theme of journeying for the sake of the experience of journeying would often be at the same time a journey into oneself. Such a journey implies not a progress along a straight path leading to a destination, as in Bunyan, but a meandering journey. Instead of going from point A to point B, the journey might have a moving series of point B's, a further B appearing in the distance as soon as one reaches the nearest one. (*MM*, 221)

Frye, as we saw in the introduction, associates the meandering narrative pattern with the Hermes descent or katabasis. The meandering journey, then, belongs to the *axis mundi* variation, and the entire enterprise of Frye's personal journey is a part of this complex—"a maze trod indeed / Through forthrights and meanders," as Gonzalo says in *The Tempest* (3.3.2–3), Shakespeare's most powerful play in Frye's view. "Meanders" is a word that aptly describes the labyrinthine journey of the notebooks; "forthrights," the straighter path from *Fearful Symmetry* to *The Double Vision*.

At the conclusion of his analysis of the four modes of language in *Words with Power*, Frye indicates that the end of the journey toward some higher level of consciousness may end up being speechless, language having finally reached the limit of what it can express:

> In our day the intensifying of consciousness, in the form of techniques of meditation and the like, has become a heavy industry. I have been somewhat puzzled by the extent to which this activity overlooks or evades the fact that all intensified language sooner or later turns metaphorical, and that literature, is not only the obvious but the in-

escapable guide to higher journeys of consciousness. Once again a pur-
loined letter is staring us quizzically in the face. When Dante wanted
to experience states of being beyond life in thirteenth-century Italy the
poet Virgil appeared as his guide. Virgil represents literature in its
Arnoldian function as a "criticism of life," the vision of existence, detached but not withdrawn from it, that is at its most inclusive in the
imaginative mode. Beyond Virgil there is Beatrice, who represents
among other things a criticism or higher awareness of the limits of the
Virgilian vision. It looks as though criticism is both the controlling and
directing force within each verbal mode and the power that enables us
to travel between the modes in both directions, until we reach the limit
of what words can do for us. But what looks like a limit from a distance
often turns out to be an open gate to something else when we reach it.
(*WP,* 28–29)

This is the point at which the metaphor of the journey confronts that of
the gate, an architectural image. The process of arriving at the gate recalls
Jacob's dream journey up the ladder, where all the metaphors are architectural: Jacob arrives at the "house of God," which is also the "gate of
heaven," and once he has had his vision, he transforms his stone pillow into
a "pillar" and changes the name of the place from Luz to Bethel ("house of
God"). He then vows that he will come again to his "father's house" if God
will keep him "in this way that I go" (Gen. 28:10–22). Just as in the Old
Testament Jacob's journey is halted at the gate, so in the New Testament
the pilgrimage or way eventually comes to a halt with Jesus' declaration, "I
am the way" (John 14:6).[2] As we saw in chapter 3, the metaphor of Jacob's
ladder issues in the interpenetration of belief and vision.

When the *mythos* comes to an end, the gestalt vision or the thematic
stasis of narrative, which is the other half of the dialectic, takes over.
Structure, design, or (to return to a phrase used in the introduction) "the
spread-out performance of the eye," now displaces narrative movement.
Just as Frye is the protagonist of a quest romance, so he is a designer of
an imaginative universe. "I'm an architect of the spiritual world," he declares (*LN,* 1:414), and, as we saw in the introduction, he refers to building "palaces of criticism" and "temples" to the gods. The materials of
these palaces are conventional: the myths, metaphors, cosmologies, and
concepts he has assimilated are the same as those of anyone else who has
made things from words. We all read the same texts, or at least they are all
available to us, and so we depend on the same verbal stones, bricks, mor-
tar, glass, tile, beams, and roof trusses in what we create. But the formal
cause of Frye's architecture—its design—is far from conventional. It is as
bold, sweeping, and idiosyncratic as a Frank Gehry building. Frye says of

the structure of the last four chapters of *Words with Power* that he has "no evidence whatever that anyone saw the Bible in this shape: it's a pure construct of my own" (*LN*, 1:51).[3] The fundamental thrust of the present study has been to examine the features of this visionary construct, the architectural features of which include interpenetration, identity, kerygma, expanded consciousness, vision, and the imagination.

The way (quest, journey) and the building (product of the architect's design) represent, therefore, two metaphorical perspectives from which to view Frye's achievement. In his paradoxical universe, however, where at the apocalyptic level all metaphors are identified, the separation between *mythos* and *dianoia* eventually collapses. Jacob reaches the end of his journey at the top of the ladder, and although he may be halted, he still speculates about the "way" that he will continue to travel if God proves to be his companion. And Jesus identifies himself with the "door" (John 10:19), an architectural metaphor, as well as with the "way," a narrative one. This looks like another example of Coleridge's distinction without division. We can distinguish between *mythos* and *dianoia,* time and space, traveler and architect, journey and gate, and the like, but such oppositions in Frye's dialectical world are not finally divisible. They are rather united while remaining distinct, which is another example of interpenetration and *Aufhebung*—like the lifting up to another level of the Hegelian *for itself* and *in itself* that we noted in chapter 3 and elsewhere. We encounter a similar instance of distinction without division in the dialectic of Word and Spirit, a shorthand representation of the ends and means of Frye's grand project.

In *Words with Power* Frye says that the metaphorical journey of the primitive shaman applies to us as readers as well. He quotes the last stanza of the eighteenth-century ballad "Tom o' Bedlam," which we mentioned in passing in chapter 3:

> By a knight of ghosts and shadows
> I summoned am to tourney
> Ten leagues beyond the wide world's end,
> Methinks it is no journey.

This is another example of the journey coming to a halt, at which point, Frye says, we confront what we have seen from the perspective of its *dianoia* or thematic stasis. Then he interjects a now-familiar *Aufhebung:* "There is a further stage of response . . . however, where something like a journeying movement is resumed, a movement that may well take us far beyond the world's end, and yet is still no journey" (96). In Notebook 50 Frye associates this movement "beyond" with prophecy, or at least as passing through the "stock phrases associated with prophecy": "'the Word of the Lord came to' and 'I will pour out my spirit . . . and they shall prophesy.' In prophecy Word and Spirit are no longer proclaimer and listener, but the same thing" (*LN*, 1:286). Tom o' Bedlam is a shaman, and the shaman's world, as Frye suggests in one notebook entry, is an interpenetrating one of Word and Spirit (*LN*, 1:290).

Word and Spirit

Word and Spirit serve as a great code to Frye's words of power. These words in their capitalized forms appear, as one would expect, throughout his work, and in numerous contexts. In *The "Third Book" Notebooks,* "Word" is often associated with what Frye calls the Logos vision and "Spirit" with the traditional Holy Spirit. But "Word" and "Spirit" do not appear in Frye's writing as a dialectical pair until the late 1970s, and only three times before the writing of *Words with Power.* In one of the notebooks for *The Great Code* he refers in passing to "pericopes of Word & Spirit" (*RT,* 268), and when he is trying to work out the relation between the cycle, which he eventually abandoned, and the *axis mundi,* which became his primary spatial metaphor, he speculates in an intriguing entry that "the up and down mythological universes form a wheel, and the wheel is the cycle of recurrence. In the cyclical vision *everything* becomes historical, and there is no Other except the social mass. The impulse to plunge into that is strong but premature. Something here eludes me. The answers are in interpenetration and Thou art That, but the real individual is not the illusory series of phantasmal egos in time: it's the total body of charitable articulation. The assumptions underlying this articulation are Word & Spirit. Probably the crux of the whole book" (*RT,* 327). Here Frye appears to have the answer but does not know what the question is. What are the two things that interpenetrate in this passage, a difficult one to gloss? Thou (the individual) and That (the social mass)? The self and the Other? "Charitable articulation" could be seen as Frye's final cause. The material cause would then be Word in its several senses, the formal cause Spirit, and the efficient cause criticism in all its Frygian permutations: its aphorisms, commentary, schema, imaginative free play, investigations of myth and metaphor, analogical linkages, sober speculations, creative flights of fancy. The word "articulation" reminds us that Frye's universe is a linguistic one. "I'm glad I'm not concerned with belief," he says, "but only with trying to understand a language" (*RT,* 303), which is reminiscent of the statement pointed to earlier about Frye's not believing in affirmations but only in the verbal formulas he constructs. These formulas, he goes on to say, "seem to make sense on their own, & seem to me something more objective than merely getting something said the way I want it said. I hope (but again it's not faith) that this is the way the Holy Spirit works in me as a writer" (*LN*, 1:145). All of this seems consistent with the focus of the present study, which has been on the word, the language Frye uses to articulate the substance of his vision (spirit), which in turn leads to the end of that vision (charity).

The third instance of "Word and Spirit" occurs in *The Great Code* itself, where Frye writes that creative doubt of the Nietzschean variety can carry us "beyond the limits of dialectic itself, into the infinite identity of word and spirit that, we are told, rises from the body of death" (227). *Words with Power* is likewise relatively silent about the pairing of Word and Spirit. In that book Frye does write that "the unity of Word and Spirit in which all consciousness begins and ends" is what constitutes the spiritual self, and he speaks of the "intercommunication" of Word and Spirit (*WP*, 251).[4] In the *Late Notebooks,* however, the phrase "Word and Spirit" occurs some fifty-two times, often as "Word and Spirit dialogue" or "Word-Spirit dialogue." Frye uses "dialogue" here in the sense of dialectic.[5] And what we have been examining in this study is a dialectic of the two major modes in Frye's thought, the literary mode of the word writ large, or *logos* as Word, and the religious mode of spiritual vision, or *pneuma* as Spirit. But dialogue is also a metaphor for the relation between Word and Spirit, or an "intercommunication," as in the passage just cited. The Word, Frye says in Notebook 27, gives substance to the Spirit. Each sets free the other, and they are united in one substance with the "Other." That is, Word and Substance interpenetrate (*LN*, 1:9). "Infiltrate" is another word Frye uses to define the relation (*LN*, 1:271), a relation that because of its omnipresence in the notebooks merits further analysis.

Frye originally intended to use the title "Dialogues of Word and Spirit" for the last half of *Words with Power*—what he eventually called "Variations on a Theme," the four themes being the four archetypes in chapters 5–8: the mountain, the garden, the cave, and the furnace. Word in this context means the Bible, and Spirit refers to the extrabiblical response to the Bible (*LN*, 1:275, 278–79). In another early formulation, developed in Notes 52, Frye relates the Word and Spirit dialogue, described as a series of four responses to four epiphanies (*LN*, 2:427) and to the seven phases of revelation developed in chapter 5 of *The Great Code* (*LN*, 2:462, 471). Four does not divide neatly into seven, but Frye, forever ingenious, simply divides the apocalyptic phase into its panoramic and participating forms to create a proper divisor. This is an outline of the way Frye sets out the relation in Notes 52:

Creation	First epiphany of the Word
Exodus	First response of the Spirit
Law	Second epiphany of the Word
Wisdom	Second response of the Spirit
Prophecy	Third epiphany of the Word
Gospel	Third response of the Spirit
Panoramic Apocalypse	Final epiphany of the Word
Participating Apocalypse	Final response of the Spirit[6]

In another notebook Frye sees this dialectic as the particular revelation of the Bible (Word) and the universal revelation of literature (Spirit), saying that this dialectic is the "essence of the book" (*LN*, 1:100). This organizing pattern was eventually discarded in favor of "Variations on a Theme" (the four archetypes), but not before Frye had sought to connect the four archetypes to what he called the HEAP scheme, noted in passing in my introduction. We need make a brief detour through that quaternion in order to see its connection to Word and Spirit.

Frye is devoted almost to the point of obsession to exploring the metaphorical and thematic implications of the four gods he collectively called HEAP: Hermes, Eros, Adonis, and Prometheus. They are, he says following Blake, "the spectres of the dead" because they have no concentering vision,[7] and Frye sets out like a questing knight to discover such a vision for them, the four quadrants of which will be, when the code is finally deciphered, Hermes Unsealed (the liberation of wisdom), Eros Regained (the liberation of love), Adonis Revived (the liberation of life from death), and Prometheus Unbound (the liberation of power). Each of the four gods represents a cluster of numerous thematic associations: the number of entries dedicated to the HEAP cycle in all the notebooks exceeds eight hundred, and in the late notebooks Frye devotes almost three hundred separate paragraphs to one or more of these "spectres of the dead." The four gods are also called "emblems" and "informing presences," and they eventually become, as just mentioned, the "variations on a theme" in the last half of *Words with Power*.

The four gods had been a part of Frye's consciousness from an early age. His interest in the Adonis archetype can be traced all the way back to his undergraduate reading of Frazer, Prometheus to his reading of Shelley, Eros and Hermes to his reading of Plato. Adonis, Prometheus, and Eros figure importantly in his account of the Orc cycle in *Fearful Symmetry*, and these three also make their way into *Anatomy of Criticism*. Hermes is the odd god out, so to speak, during the years Frye was writing the *Anatomy*. He speaks of Hermes' role as the angel messenger or Covering

Cherub in a notebook entry from the late 1940s (7.39), but this role is not connected with the archetypes of the other three gods. In the same notebook we first encounter a spatial representation of the gods as a cycle of archetypes, with Orpheus now joining Eros, Adonis, and Prometheus as the fourth god, Frye locating them as cardinal points on a circular diagram with horizontal and vertical axes. As noted in the introduction, this diagram was one of the many components of what Frye called the Great Doodle. In his diagrammatic way of representing the HEAP cycle, the gods eventually took their places within the quadrants, rather than at the cardinal points (Eros at the northeast, Prometheus at the southeast, Adonis at the southwest, and Hermes at the northwest), the vertical axis being an ascending and descending stair or ladder and the horizontal axis a temporal movement from the past (wisdom) to the future (prophecy).[8]

The HEAP scheme remained in a state of flux for a number of years: it "keeps reforming & dissolving," as Frye says in Notebook 44 (*LN*, 1:126). He experiments with six additional sequences before finally settling on the order Hermes, Eros, Adonis, and Prometheus. These archetypes—what the four gods represent apocalyptically as well as demonically—gradually define themselves over the years by their different cosmological principles, Blakean and biblical analogues, primary elements, associated images, typical themes, feminine aspects, narrative directions, and the like.[9] But the four gods vanish from *Words with Power*, or at least appear to do so. The reason for their apparent absence, intimated above, is that Frye decided in one of his late revisions of the book to abandon the cycle as his fundamental organizing image and to replace it with the *axis mundi*.[10] Ascent and descent along a vertical axis then became the primary structural metaphor of Frye's "variations on a theme."

Still, the four gods remain hidden in the wings in Frye's published work, coming on stage only for a cameo appearance in the final chapter of *Words with Power*. In one brief passage (277) he explains that each of the four gods, whose symbolism he has so persistently explored for forty years, has been a "presiding deity" over the four metaphors (mountain, garden, cave, and furnace) and the respective ascent/descent themes, their presence serving to configure the last half of the book as follows.

Archetype	God	Ascent/Descent Theme	Dialogical Focus
Mountain	Hermes	Higher Wisdom	Clarifying Word
Garden	Eros	Higher Love	Unifying Spirit
Cave	Adonis	Lower Love	Unifying Spirit
Furnace	Prometheus	Lower Wisdom	Clarifying Word

Here, epiphany and response have been replaced by clarity and unity. "Clarification" is a word that for Frye connotes intelligibility, discrimination, and division, associations it has in 2 Timothy 2:15, where God's workman is enjoined to "rightly divide the word of truth."[11] Such charts as this, however, suggest a much more systematic effort to relate Word and Spirit to the four archetypes than Frye consciously undertakes in *Words with Power.* In the *Late Notebooks* he appears to be aiming for a more or less definitive organizing pattern to replace the discarded epiphany-response dialectic described above. Of the numerous Word-Spirit formulas that emerge, here is a baker's dozen:

1. The images of the Word-Spirit dialogue are a metaphorical counterpart to what Hegel creates conceptually in *The Phenomenology of Spirit* (*LN*, 1:19).

2. Word and Spirit are more or less synonyms for metaphor image (juxtaposed images) and symbol (spiritual meaning) (*LN*, 1:185–86).

3. The interpenetration of word and spirit is higher kerygma, not the proclamation of God associated with lower kerygma (*LN*, 1:209).

4. The "ultimate fusion" of Word and Spirit is, like the fourth awareness, beyond the poetic. This fusion might have been evident in Stevens's great poem of earth and Mallarmé's alchemical Great Work, had they been able to write them (*LN*, 1:214). In like manner, "Spirit is the initiative excluded from literature"; for vision to be total, the Spirit must animate the Word (*LN*, 1:271–72).

5. Word and Spirit have nothing to do with doctrine and everything to do with experience (*LN*, 2:704).

6. The total identity of Word and Spirit results when the hierarchy of Plato's three-storied universe is left behind by an *Aufhebung* that does not cancel myth and metaphor but lifts them to a spiritual level where all ideology is dissolved (*LN*, 1:391). An oracular version of the same point: "[T]he mountain [that is, the image of authority and hierarchy], after passing the metamorphosis of the Word (Transfiguration) moves into the stars and the great cosmic dance begins" (*LN*, 1:279).

7. If we think of the story of Jesus not as history but as a myth occurring in the eternal present, then the doctrine of the Resurrection can be humanized and along with it the often uncharitable idea of salvation (no one is "saved" outside of or before Jesus). "The Word and Spirit in man then coincide into something that has its being in God" (*LN*, 2:671).

8. In the Word and Spirit dialogue, proclaimer and listener, signifier and signified are identified: words become spiritual realities (*LN*, 1:286).

9. In the apocalypse of the Word and Spirit dialogue, the Creation

is transformed and renewed and "the U-shaped comic ending reverses the cycles of history, where resurrection abolishes rebirth and revolution-culbute abolishes revolution-turning wheel" (*LN*, 1:329).

10. Without an interaction of Word and Spirit, the Word dies, as the first generation of Israelites did in the wilderness (*LN*, 1:32).

11. The Word and Spirit dialogue is a dialectic of revelation (*LN*, 1:116).

12. Word and Spirit are a part of the katabatic movement. In the Romantic cosmos, they meet at the bottom of the descent into nothingness; they are different aspects of the same substance (*LN*, 1:294–95).

13. Because the dialogue of Word and Spirit is about human awareness, it moves "in the direction of obliterating all the nonsense of either-or and God plus man." It therefore does not involve any suggestion of the supernatural, though "it doesn't eliminate such suggestions either" (*LN*, 1:368).

If there is a common thread running through these discontinuous speculations, it is the effort to specify the goal of the dialogue, and the language used to formulate that goal is familiar: the unity that comes from the *Aufhebung* (as in no. 1), the interpretation in higher kerygma and resurrection (as in nos. 3 and 9), the fusion achieved in the fourth awareness (as in no. 4), total identity (as in nos. 6 and 8), the dialectic of revelation (as in no. 11), and the erasing of either-or distinctions (as in no. 13). The monologue is always surrounded by the anxieties of the self-alienating ego, but the dialogue is a social form of dialectic. As a communal form, the dialogue of Word and Spirit should issue in, to quote again a passage from *Words with Power*, "the only genuine form of human society, the spiritual kingdom of Jesus, founded on the *caritas* or love which for Paul is not one virtue among others but the only virtue there is" (89). This is the conclusion that Frye draws from what the clarifying Word and the unifying spirit can *create together*, in his words, and thus we come back again to love as the product of the unifying vision.

Imaginative Literalism

In chapter 4 I referred to Frye's "cultural envelope," a metaphor he often uses to represent the way all of us are separated from nature.[12] The envelope contains the laws, customs, rituals, and stories that we ourselves have made that seal us off from the natural world—the culture or civilization that insulates us from nature. Frye calls these constructions primary and secondary concerns. The secondary ones, or ideologies, are derived from the primary ones, which develop out of a mythology. Frye's own cultural envelope was Caucasian, middle-class, Canadian, and of course Christian. If T. S. Eliot's cultural envelope was royalist, classical, and Anglo-Catholic, Frye's was the opposite: he was a liberal democrat and member of the Co-operative Commonwealth Federation, Canada's socialist party (later the New Democratic Party), a Blakean Romantic, and a Low Church Protestant. More particularly, Frye's Christian background was Methodist, which, with its emphasis on experience, was an important influence, although the pietism of Methodism was something he rebelled against early. Part of Frye's cultural envelope was also of course the Bible, which, along with that well-traveled old chestnut *Hurlbut's Story of the Bible,* he read at an early age. But the bibliolatry of Canadian Methodism was something Frye resisted all his life, as he resisted any system that demanded he deduce everything from some verbal system—whether it be the Bible or Catholic dogma or the Marxian gospel or the thoughts of Chairman Mao.[13] Quite why he developed such an antipathy for religious fundamentalism at such an early age, given his mother's conventional piety, is uncertain. But at twelve or thirteen, he reports, the "bundle of threats, contradictions and muddled arguments" of religious fundamentalism "just fell off"[14] as he was walking along St. George Street to high school, relieving him of a great "burden of anxiety."[15] But if Frye escaped from the clutches of fundamentalism, he never escaped from his Christian roots, nor did he want to.

In one of his notebooks for *The Great Code* Frye wonders whether the book might turn out to be a Christian apologetics, and after asking himself whether that would make the book dishonest, he writes,

> The best answer I can give now is to say that if I can show that Christianity is imaginatively possible today, I can show that any other belief is a choice distinct from that, there being no state without belief, & no one belief inevitable for everybody, much less a necessary alternative belief to Christianity. It's that last I should hold on to. I'm a Christian partly *faute de mieux:* I see no better faith, & certainly couldn't invent one of my own except out of Christian assumptions. But some of my other principles are: a) the less we believe the better b) nothing should be believed that has to be believed in. (*RT,* 232)

When Frye says, "My Christian position is that of Blake reinforced by Emily Dickinson" (*LN,* 2:714), he means that he, like she, has managed to escape from the clutches of priestly authority. Such an escape for Dickinson meant that she was free to make her business circumference, as she says in a letter to Thomas Higginson, and able at least to hope that the

Nobodaddy-Jehovah of the Old Testament, whom she strongly distrusted, might "refund us finally / Our confiscated gods," as she says in
one of her poems.[16] The confiscated gods, in Frye's scheme, were the four
gods of his HEAP cycle (Hermes, Eros, Adonis, and Prometheus), who,
as we have seen, were refunded in the last four chapters of *Words with
Power* as the liberation of wisdom, the liberation of love, the liberation of
life from death, and the liberation of power.

If Frye's "Christian position" is partly *faute de mieux,* it is partly not,
and it would be possible to give an account of Frye's theology, which is
often quite explicit. In the film *Northrop Frye: The Great Teacher,* the di-
rector Harry Rasky asks Frye, "I wonder if I would be prying if I say, Does
Northrop Frye talk to God?" After a long pause, Frye answers, "Yes," leaving the puzzled Rasky to wonder whether Frye means, Yes, I do talk to
God, or Yes, it would be prying. If Rasky had had access to or had known
about Frye's prayers, the question would have not been necessary. One
could, in fact, infer an entire theological position from these eloquent
prayers.[17] Some of the terms in his critical universe have, of course, theological overtones (e.g., apocalypse, kerygma, purgatory), some do not
(e.g., identity, vision, interpenetration), and some may (e.g., Word, Spirit,
revelation, love). This is a topic that is worth further exploration. Moreover, some theological doctrines (e.g., the real presence of God, the Incarnation, the Trinity) can be understood only metaphorically, as Frye
himself points out (*NFR,* 7), and this also merits further investigation.
But those are questions for another study, one of the revelations of which
would be that whatever one might say about Frye's "theology," it does not
advance by the Thomistic logic or aggressive reason of second-phase language. "The Bible," Frye writes,

> begins by showing on its first page that the reality of God manifests it-
> self in creation, and on its last page that the same reality is manifested
> in a new creation in which man is a participant. He becomes a partic-
> ipant by being redeemed, or separated from the predatory and destruc-
> tive elements acquired from his origin in nature. In between these
> visions of creation comes the Incarnation, which presents God and man
> as indissolubly locked together in a common enterprise. This is Chris-
> tian, but the answering and supporting "Thou" of Buber, which grows
> out of the Jewish tradition, is not imaginatively very different. Faith,
> then, is not developed by clogging the air with questions of the "Does
> a God really exist?" type and answering them with equal nonsense, but
> in working, in words and other media, toward a peace that passes
> understanding, not by contradicting understanding, but by disclosing,

behind the human peace that is merely a temporary cessation of a war, the proclaimed or mythological model of a peace infinite in both its source and its goal. (*WP,* 135)

Frye wrote a great deal about the Christian religion ("Christian" and "Christianity" appear more than 3,400 times in his work), and a part of the Christian religion is Christian theology. He would doubtless not have much interest in having his "theology" discussed, even if it were seen only as an existential projection, because the word for him always moved in the direction of creeds and doctrines and therefore away from the myths and metaphors he was so passionate about.

In *The Double Vision* Frye says that from the "appalling historical record of Christianity" with its long list of heresy hunts, militancy, intolerance, and demonic perversions, there is a genuine element that has survived. This genuine element is based on charity, "and charity is invariably linked to an imaginative conception of language, whether consciously or unconsciously. Paul makes it clear that the language of charity is spiritual language, and that spiritual language is metaphorical, founded on the metaphorical paradox that we live in Christ and that Christ lives in us" (17). Frye is referring here to Paul's use of the word *pneumatikos* (spiritually), and whatever else the word means, as Frye says elsewhere (*RT,* 435), it means "metaphorically."[18] He then goes on to say,

> I am not trying to deny or belittle the validity of a credal, even a dogmatic, approach to Christianity: I am saying that the literal basis of faith in Christianity is a mythical and metaphorical basis, not one founded on historical facts or logical propositions. Once we accept an imaginative literalism, everything else falls into place: without that, creeds and dogmas quickly turn malignant. The literary language of the New Testament is not intended, like literature itself, simply to suspend judgment, but to convey a vision of spiritual life that continues to transform and expand our own. That is, its myths become, as purely literary myths cannot, myths to live by; its metaphors become, as purely literary metaphors cannot, metaphors to live in. This transforming power is sometimes called kerygma or proclamation. Kerygma in this sense is again a rhetoric, but a rhetoric coming the other way and coming from the other side of mythical and metaphorical language. (*DV,* 17–18)

Some might call this a theological statement. If it is, it represents a theology founded not on history or argument but on the language of myth and metaphor, and it is that language this study has aimed to illuminate. And it has sought to illuminate it by drawing attention not simply to those texts of Frye that are well known and readily available but to those that have just begun to surface. The portrait of Frye is not a revisionary one but, it is hoped, an expanded one.

The passage reproduced above about the human passage in the biblical *mythos* from an original state of nature through the incarnation to the peace of the apocalypse is a condensed version of the romance quest come full circle.

Aufhebungen

It comes full circle as well in his final two books. In chapter 3, we spoke of the *Aufhebung* with which Frye ends the first four chapters of *Words with Power*, a process that moves beyond the oppositions of time (myth) and space (metaphor) to the level of intense consciousness or the identity represented by the Incarnation—to refer again to two of Frye's examples. We see the same process at work at the conclusions of the last four chapters of that book. The context of the conclusion of chapter 5 (the mountain archetype) is the primary concern of free movement, which is expressed in the images of dance, music, and play. But the ultimate source of exuberant, unfettered movement is spiritual freedom, located at the top of the ladder of wisdom (in the *axis mundi* complex of images) and in the collapsing distinction between center and circumference (in the circle complex of images). The paradox is captured for Frye in Paul's "all in all" phrase (1 Cor. 15:28), which takes us beyond the predication of metaphor. Frye calls this *Aufhebung* both interpenetration and the higher unity of spiritual vision, the point at which "the dance of liberated movement begins" (*WP,* 187).[19] The unity that emerges from the *Aufhebung* cancels while preserving the bottom and top of the ladder, the center and the circumference, the two halves of metaphor joined by the copula.

Similarly, at the end of chapter 6 (the garden archetype) the oppositions art and nature, Bridegroom (love) and Bride (beauty) are resolved into Kant's "purposiveness without purpose," in which "the union symbolized by the one flesh of the married state (Genesis 2:24) has expanded into the interpenetration of spirit" (*WP,* 224). Chapter 7 (the cave archetype) concludes with the theme of the double, for which Frye, in a breathless catalogue, provides more than thirty examples. The last of these is the mirror reflection in the Narcissus myth, the reflection of the "I" which is really a reflecting image of an imprisoning natural and social world that Martin Buber calls the "It." The *Aufhebung* that releases us "into the world of sunlight and freedom" is, as noted in chapter 3, Buber's "Thou," who is "both another person and the identity of ourselves" (*WP,* 271). At the end of chapter 8 (the furnace archetype) Frye comes around again to what is for him the epitome of the Bible, the book of Job. In the Job story, the "Biblical perspective of divine initiative and human response passes into its opposite, where the initiative is human, and where a divine response, symbolized by the answer to Job, is guaranteed" (*WP,* 312–13). The *Aufhebung* then lifts this initiative-and-response dialectic to a decentered and interpenetrating union, at which point "the terrifying and welcome voice may begin, annihilating everything we thought we knew, and restoring everything we have never lost" (*WP,* 313).

We need four more examples of the *Aufhebung* of interpenetration to complete the Frygian ogdoad, and these are provided, as we might expect from a book entitled *The Double Vision,* at the conclusions of the four chapters of Frye's final and posthumously published book. Frye uses the phrase "double vision" in several senses. In the Blake quatrain quoted in chapter 3, the double vision refers to the natural versus the spiritual ways of viewing the world. But Blake's vision was really a fourfold one (material, intellectual, emotional, and spiritual), and the *aufgehoben* thrust at the end of each chapter of *The Double Vision* moves to a fourth level of vision. In "The Double Vision of Language" the *Aufhebung* moves beyond the dialectic of the plausible and credible, belief and agnosticism, history and logic, and the language of faith and hope, reaching toward the *agape* vision with its language of love.

The dialectical pairs at the end of chapter 2, "The Double Vision of Nature," are making and creating, the fine and the useful arts, beauty and truth. These oppositions are then lifted to the next level by a sabbatical vision that becomes "the model for an expanding human consciousness" (*DV,* 39). The *Aufhebung* of chapter 3, "The Double Vision of Time," leads to the Spirit, the power that emerges from the dialectic of the Father (or the source of being) and the Son (the Word who has overcome the world). This represents the last act in Frye's version of the three ages of Joachim of Floris, who prophesied that the age of Spirit would follow the age of the Old Testament Father and the age of the New Testament Logos.[20] It is the "Spirit who speaks with all the tongues of men and angels and still speaks with charity." Frye adds that the "Spirit of creation who brought life out of chaos brought death out of it too, for death is all that makes sense of life in time. The Spirit that broods on the chaos of our psyches brings to birth a body that is in time and history but not enclosed by them, and is in death only because it is in the midst of life as well" (*DV,* 58). This purely spiritual vision of Christianity was for Frye the Everlasting Gospel (*LN,* 1:202).

Finally, to complete the ogdoad, the *Aufhebung* of "The Double Vision of God" preserves the purgatorial virtues of faith and hope and lifts them to "the paradisal vision of love" (*DV,* 81). This is the world of "interpenetrating energies," where "the spirit of man and the spirit of God inhabit the same world" (*DV,* 84).

In *Words with Power* Frye notes that the Word–Spirit dialogue takes the form of a double ascent and descent movement along the *axis mundi*. In the New Testament account of the Incarnation the Word descends and the Spirit ascends. But in the first two chapters of Acts the movement is reversed: the Spirit descends at Pentecost and the Word ascends. The withdrawal of the Word (the Ascension) is, as Frye points out, the antitype of the withdrawal of God on the seventh day in Genesis 1. This is the Sabbath vision, provided, Frye says, by a creating God so that we can "escape . . . from natural into spiritual vision" (*DV,* 39). It is a matter of pure coincidence—but perhaps one of Jung's meaningful coincidences nevertheless—that Frye's *Late Notebooks* begin with an entry on original sin and 3,684 entries later end with one on the Sabbath vision, suggesting that Frye's quest as it is played out in that extraordinary record of his imaginative life had come full circle. It is also a matter of pure coincidence that this study of Frye has organized itself into eight parts. As the Sabbath vision provides the occasion for withdrawal and rest as well, it is time now for us to withdraw from our own ogdoad.

Appendix

Chart 1. Phases of language in *The Great Code*, chapter 1

Vico's Three Ages	Poetic	Heroic or Noble	Vulgar
Frye's Three Ages	Hieroglyphic	Hieratic	Demotic
Uses of Language	Poetic	Allegorical-Analogical-Dialectical	Descriptive
Phases of Language	Metaphorical ("This is that"): used by everyone; no cultural ascendancy	Metonymic ("This is put for that"): culturally ascendant language	Similic ("This is like that"): ordinary language that does not become culturally ascendant
Locus of the Phases	Greek literature before Plato; Homer; prebiblical Near East; much of Old Testament	Plato; the intellectual elite; the ascendant language is given authority by society	Sixteenth century and following; Bacon and Locke
Subject/Object Relations	Not clearly separated; linked by common power or energy (*mana*); magic, charm, and spell play central role	More consistently separated; ideas of "reflection" and mirror are foregrounded	Clearly separated; subject exposes itself, in sense experience, to impact of objective world
Use of Words	Words of power releasing magical energy or control	Words = outward expression of inner thoughts and ideas; importance of linear ordering	Words are servomechanisms of reflection
Concrete > Abstract	Concrete: no verbal abstractions	Intellectual and emotional operations of mind become distinguishable; development of abstraction and logic	Concrete "things" in nature are prior

Form of Prose	Discontinuous: epigrammatic; oracular (e.g., aphorisms of Heraclitus and Pythagoras). Truth: hypothetical	Continuous; deductive. Truth: consistent argument. Analogical language = verbal imitation of reality beyond itself. Dialectic and commentary foregrounded	Continuous prose; deduction subordinated to induction. Truth: correspondence to objective world
"God" Language	Plurality of gods; embodiments of personality = nature; unifying element of verbal expression = "god" or personal nature-spirit	Monotheistic God = transcendent reality all analogy points to; Aristotle's Unmoved Mover, Plato's Good; metonymic thinking translates metaphor into hieroglyphic language	Reaction against transcendent perspective; religious questions are "unmeaningful"; "gods" no longer believed in
Metonymic Parallels of the Three Phases of Language	One image is "put for" another image	Verbal expression is "put for" something that transcends actual verbal expression; analogical thinking	Word is "put for" object it describes
Logos	Logos = creative power (Hebrews, Heraclitus)	Logos = rational order in mathematical and verbal forms	Logos = event or reality that words describe secondhand
Humanity (human entity using language or consciousness)	Spirit = unifying principle of life that gives people a participating energy with nature	Soul returns to transcendent world; body returns to nature. Vertical imagery	Mind/brain. Horizontal imagery
Powers	Language is immediate and vital	Language is released from tyranny of nature	Language reveals richness in objective world
Limitations	Language restricted by an identity with nature	Language of deductive reason leads to nothing new	Language precludes imaginative experience

Chart 2. Modes of language in *Words with Power*, chapter 1

Aspect of Verbal Communication	Perceptual	Conceptual	Ideological	Poetic
Mode of Language	Descriptive	Dialectical	Rhetorical	Poetic
Initiative	Ordering of words	Impersonal argument	Ideology	Myth
Excluded Initiative (what remains in the background as an unexamined assumption)	Syntactical or grammatical ordering of words assumed but not the focus of attention	Personal (subjective) desire or energy	Myth, along with the numinous or nonhuman personal	Spiritual vision of faith, opening the way to kerygma
Narrative Types	Textbooks, histories, reference works	Philosophical argument, metaphysical systems. Coordination is central	Dialectic: incorporated by rhetoric into a personal mode	Poetry
Tropes	Avoided or minimized	Ambiguity: positive and constructive force	Metaphor, allegory, rhythm, etc., strongly emphasized	Myth and metaphor: indispensable defining characteristics

Criterion	Truth outside language	Truth inside language: integrity of the verbal structure	Moral truth through dialectic; rationalizing of social authority through rhetoric	The conceivable, hypothetical, or assumed
Art/Nature Relation	Nature (content) imitated by art (form)	Nature (content) contained by art (form)	Nature as hierarchy; human beings dominate nature	Gods identified with nature
"Political" Principle	Open and democratic	Argumentative, impersonal, objective, logical	Existential	Individual: intensifying of consciousness. Social: focus of community
Language as "Mirror"	Data of sense perception reflected through language	"Being" mirrored through speculative language (*speculum* = mirror)	Speaker/writer mirrors speech and audience: identification of speaker and audience	Language of poetry as double mirror
Corresponding Medieval Level	Literal	Allegorical	Tropological	Anagogic
Corresponding Hegelian Level	Consciousness	Reason	Spirit	Religion

Chart 3. Body-mind-soul relations, from *Notebook 32* (early 1950s)

	Body	Mind	Soul
"World"	Natural form	Mental form	Mystical form
State	Unawareness; body is active; mind is passive; autonomous will and desire	Perception of symbolic forms; mind is active; body is passive	Awareness of imperishable soul; natural perspective inverted; soul is motionless; perception and sense experience are arrested
Bodily Activity	Ritual	Myth	Execution of created art
Mental Activity	Repose, relaxation. Power; resistance to mind, as in hypnotism and occult phenomena	Leisure. Will; mind determined to seize and control the body	Contemplation. Total unification; soul and its object or creature of contemplation are universal, and identical with each other
Distancing Techniques	None	Introversion: body quiets mind	Deep introversion of contemplation; spirit quiets mind
Engaging Techniques	None	Extraversion: mind uses body	Deep introversion or charity: soul or spirit uses mind
Control and Its Telos	Natural state of unawareness; nothing to be controlled	Control of body leads to civilization	Control of mind leads to miraculous powers, the mystical experience, Samadhi

Chart 4. The three stages of religion, from *Notebook 11f* (1969–70)

Stages	Body	Mind	Soul
Origin	Bodily response to religion: rituals, dances, *dromena*, hallucinations; polytheistic; magical	Mind withdraws from creation into the death-consciousness of contemplation and observation	Revolutionary monotheism; founded on communication–community–communion triad
Development	From psychophysic energy toward order	God becomes less personal; hidden-divinity tradition	Growing sense of human presence of God
End	Imperial monotheism	"Thou Art That" mysticism; perennial philosophy	Word and its revelation
Gods	Spiritual beings outrank nature spirits; gradually, one God	God as First Cause, Essence, Being	The Word

Chart 5. The three awarenesses, from *Notebook 19* (mid–1960s)

	First Awareness	Second Awareness	Third Awareness
Body–Mind–Spirit	Body-centered perception; mind as *tabula rasa*; reality to be perceived, not manipulated; spontaneous and paradisal	Mind-centered; creates imaginative structure of religious faith, philosophical concept, or poetic imagery as a transformation of the world; anxieties about pastoral myth	Critique of reason releases one from the Cartesian antithesis of subject-object thinking; understanding that the created world is the real one; recapturing of spontaneity
Educational Ladder	Genuine child-nature	Social and cultural environment	Axis of speculation and concern
Status of Individual	No true individuality; attachment to group is unconscious	Restraint of individual	No cleavage between social and individual aspects of personality
Movement of the Awakening	Unconsciousness	Consciousness: epiphany of law and loss of identity	Mirror of awareness: destruction of "simple location," as in Whitehead, Heidegger, the Avatamsaka Sutra; return to "here" and *Sein*
Relation to *Mythoi* of the *Anatomy*	Romance discovery of quest: the imaginative key	Tragic fall and contract	Recovery after ironic vision
Blakean Forms	Luvah	Tharmas	Urthona, Urizen, Los

Chart 6. The three awarenesses, from *Notebook 21* (1969–71)

	First Awareness	Second Awareness	Third Awareness
Mystery of Creation in Revelation	Creation as beginning of things; prominence of natural religion	Creation of the archetype at a moment in history (burning bush or baptism)	Apocalyptic creation at the end of the Bible
Nature of God	Egypt: iconic religion; polytheistic and imperialistic; focus on powers outside the human and on the ruler	Israel: iconoclastic religion; God as unseen; focus on Word or voice	Imaginative approach; antinatural religion; antimperialistic; antireconciliatory; antidialectical; antirevolutionary
Christian Phase	Effort to reconcile everything; Church becomes imperialistic	Emphasis on Word with Luther; revolution and reformation	Interpenetration
Religious Form	Ritual	Doctrine	Myth
First Phase: Ancient and Classical	Religions of Egypt, Mesopotamia, Greece and Rome; Homer; Greek dramatists	The Bible and its poets; late Plato	Ovid and Virgil
Second Phase: Christian	St. Thomas and Dante	Luther and Milton	Shakespeare (Protestant poet in a country shaped by Reformation)
Third Phase: Romantic and Post-romantic	Hegel and his prophet, Goethe	Marx and Kierkegaard, and their prophets, Dostoevsky and Beethoven	Blake and the mythopoeic tradition

continued on next page

Chart 6 continued

	First Awareness	Second Awareness	Third Awareness
Highest Developments of Awareness	Hinduism	Buddhism	Zen
Revelation	*Descendit de coelis* conception of Christ; wine-treader God of fury	Proof-texts as axioms for conduct; manic response of Pentecostal sects; prophesying and gift of tongues	Interpenetration; numinous quality of imaginative power; the definitive experience in modern literature
Focus	Space; centripetal; "here" is where you belong; "there" is the ruler	Time; "this is the revelation: follow it"	History and doctrine broken down and replaced by the deeper underthought of myth
View of Myth	Resemblances among myths are subordinated to an overriding doctrine	Myths split into a true-false dialectic of revelation and demonic parody	All resemblances among myths are positive
Narrative Cycle	*Eniautos*-hero and female will	*Nostos* (return to home)	Kierkegaard–Joyce repetition
The Spirits	Subjected (Prospero)	Projected spirits become flunkeys of the one true God	Recalled to the human mind; recovery of projection

Chart 7. The three awarenesses, from *Notebook 24* (1970–72)

	First Awareness	Second Awareness	Third Awareness
Form of Expression	Philosophical reconciliation	Revolutionary action	Imaginative interpenetration
Traditional Framework: Pre-romantic	Thomas Aquinas: the *Summae* reconcile everything reconcilable within the real universal	Revolutionary authoritarian tradition of Luther, flanked by Machiavelli and Calvin	Shakespeare
Commentator	Dante	Milton	Shakespeare
Second Framework: Romantic and Post-romantic	Hegel, with his idea of Absolute Spirit	Breakup of Hegel by Marx, flanked by Kierkegaard and Nietzsche	Blake and his informing presence through modernism
Commentator or Spokesman	Goethe	Dostoevsky	Not yet born
General Perspective	Conceptual, "catholic" and working by reconciliation and inclusion	Existential, "protestant" and revolutionary	Imaginative, based on interpenetration
Mythological Form	Monotheism, as world-state unifying	Future-directed and Saturnalia-*culbute* version of monotheism	The great wheel of the Logos and Thanatos visions

continued on next page

Chart 7 continued

	First Awareness	Second Awareness	Third Awareness
Key Elements: From Myth to Dialectic to the Recovery of Myth	Focus on the visible; sun = symbol of social order; mental tendency toward the conceptual; myth consolidates by reconciliation and cannibalism: local myths are absorbed into the general cult; monotheism develops as a rationalization of a world-state; no fixed belief, only a prescription of ritual habit	Dialectical: seizes on the *new* conception of "false god": true god has specific name and social context and is potentially incarnate; revolutionary, leading to a future *culbute*; existential because of the partisan incarnation of god; iconoclastic: *internalizes* imagery, and shifts from visible to audible symbols, from the sun to the thunder, and eventually the Word; heavy emphasis on literal belief, with little toleration of variety unknown to the first awareness	Imaginary recovery of projection; recaptures sense of tolerance of first awareness; humanity sees itself as only source of creation and communication
Historical Locus	Ancient world: from Sumeria and Egypt to Rome	Judeo–Christian tradition	

First Stage	Homer and Greek poets	Bible and late Plato	No genuine example, though in later ages Ovid was a source for some
Second Stage	Greek philosophy	Medieval Christendom and Reformation	Shakespeare only, though always potential in creative process
Third Stage	Hegel: established a conceptual imperialism stretching from alienation to identity, where the light of the sun is replaced by the light of the mind	Revolutionary-existential reactions against Hegel: both Marx and Kierkegaard, where the idea is internalized into social or individual action	"The third awareness of the third phase is Frye, of course, but I'll have to locate it in the mythopoeic poets from Blake on."
Focus	Spatial; leans toward Logos vision; demonizes Thanatos vision	Temporal; begins in revolutionary Thanatos movement and finds something alienating about the great imperial "systems"	Time decentralized. Blake's "who Present, Past, and Future sees" and Yeats's "Of what is past, or passing, or to come"
Cycle	Egypt cycle	Exodus cycle	Cycle of the same

Notes

Preface

1. Jonathan Z. Smith, "Religion, Religions, Religious," in *Critical Terms for Religious Studies,* ed. Mark C. Taylor (Chicago: Univ. of Chicago Press, 1998), 281–82.

Introduction

1. Margaret Burgess, "The Resistance to Religion: Anxieties Surrounding the Spiritual Dimensions of Frye's Thought; OR, Investigations into the Fear of Enlightenment," in *The Legacy of Northrop Frye,* ed. Alvin A. Lee and Robert D. Denham (Toronto: Univ. of Toronto Press, 1994), 59–75. Craig Stewart Walker, "Religious Experience in the Work of Frye," in *The Legacy of Northrop Frye,* 41.

2. The conference "Frye and the Word: Religious Contexts in the Criticism of Northrop Frye" was held at McMaster University, Hamilton, Ontario, 17–19 May 2000. The proceedings were published in two volumes: *Northrop Frye and the Afterlife of the Word,* ed. James M. Kee, Semeia 89 (Atlanta: Society of Biblical Literature, 2002); and *Northrop Frye and the Word: Religious Contexts in the Writings of Northrop Frye,* ed. Jeffery Donaldson and Alan Mendelson (Toronto: Univ. of Toronto Press, 2003).

3. In the late 1970s Eugene Garfield and his staff combed through the more than 900,000 items in the *Arts & Humanities Citation Index* for 1977 and 1978 to arrive at a list of the one hundred most-cited authors in periodical literature. The list, published in *Current Contents* 32 (6 August 1979): 5–10, revealed that only Marx, Aristotle, Shakespeare, Lenin, Plato, Freud, and Barthes were more frequently cited than Frye. A second list published by Garfield in the same article shows that for 1978 and 1979 *Anatomy of Criticism* was the most frequently cited book written by an author born in the twentieth century. This article is reprinted in Garfield, *Essays of an Information Scientist* (Philadelphia: ISI Press, 1981), 4:238–43. See also Garfield's "Is Information Retrieval in the Arts and Humanities Inherently Different from That of Science? The Effect that ISI's Citation Index for the Arts and Humanities Is Expected to Have on Future Scholarship," *Library Quarterly* 50 (1980): 40–57. Eight years after his initial survey Garfield updated and expanded the list, publishing the results in "The 250 Most-Cited Authors in the *Arts & Humanities Citation Index, 1976–1983,*" *Current Contents* 48 (1 December 1986): 3–10. Marx remained in first place, followed by Aristotle, Shakespeare, Lenin, Plato, Freud, Barthes, Kant, Cicero,

Chomsky, Hegel, and Frye. At the time, then, Frye was the third most-cited author born in the twentieth century. Such surveys, of course, reveal nothing qualitatively, but they do indicate how widespread Frye's presence was only two decades after the publication of the *Anatomy*.

4. Frye's previously unpublished writings have, since 1996, been appearing as part of the Collected Works of Northrop Frye, under the general editorship of Alvin A. Lee and published by the University of Toronto Press. Of the thirteen volumes of manuscript material, ten have now been published. Lee projects the completion of the edition in 2008. For the list of published and forthcoming volumes, see www.utppublishing.com/series/frye.html.

5. *Selected Letters of Edith Sitwell,* ed. Richard Greene (London: Virago Books, 1997), 294.

6. "The Present Condition of the World," in *LS,* 207–20; "The Church: Its Relation to Society," in *NFR,* 253–67.

7. Letter to Robert K. Leland, 30 October 1984. For a study of Frye's relation to the church, see Jean O'Grady, "Frye and the Church," in *Northrop Frye and the Word,* 175–86.

8. Cf. "[I]n my view of the Bible as a model of kerygmatic criticism, which I think of as getting past the imaginative creation for its own sake without going back to the old ideological dialectics, I think I'm passing beyond 'deconstruction' into a reconstruction no longer structural" (*LN,* 1:338).

9. The books devoted wholly to Frye are Murray Krieger, ed., *Northrop Frye in Modern Criticism* (New York: Columbia Univ. Press, 1966); Ronald Bates, *Northrop Frye* (Toronto: McClelland and Stewart, 1971); Jan Ulrik Dyrkjøb, *Northrop Frye's litteraturteori* (Copenhagen: Berlinske Verlag, 1979); Robert D. Denham, *Northrop Frye and Critical Method* (University Park: Pennsylvania State Univ. Press, 1978); David Cook, *Northrop Frye: A Vision of the New World* (New York: St. Martin's, 1985); Eleanor Cook, et al., eds., *Centre and Labyrinth: Essays in Honour of Northrop Frye* (Toronto: Univ. of Toronto Press, in association with Victoria University, 1985); John Ayre, *Northrop Frye: A Biography* (Toronto: Random House of Canada, 1989); Agostino Lombardo, ed., *Ritratto de Northrop Frye* (Rome: Bulzoni Editore, 1989); A. C. Hamilton, *Northrop Frye: Anatomy of His Criticism* (Toronto: Univ. of Toronto Press, 1990); Robert D. Denham and Thomas Willard, eds., *Visionary Poetics: Essays on Northrop Frye's Criticism* (New York: Peter Lang, 1991); David Cayley, *Northrop Frye in Conversation* (Concord, Ont.: Anansi, 1992); Caterina Ricciardi, *Northrop Frye, o, delle finzioni supreme* (Rome: Empirìa, 1992); Joseph Adamson, *Northrop Frye: A Visionary Life* (Toronto: ECW Press, 1993); S. Krishnamoorthy Aithal, ed., *The Importance of Northrop Frye* (Kanpur, India: Humanities Research Centre, 1993); Jonathan Hart, *Northrop Frye: The Theoretical Imagination* (London: Routledge, 1994); Alvin Lee and Robert D. Denham, eds., *The Legacy of Northrop Frye* (Toronto: Univ. of Toronto Press, 1994); Ning Wang and Yen-hung Hsü, eds., *Fu-lai yen chiu: Chung-kuo yü hsi fang* [Frye Studies: China and the West] (Beijing: Social Sciences Press of China, 1996); Ford Russell, *Northrop Frye on Myth: An Intro-*

duction (New York: Garland, 1998); David Boyd and Imre Salusinszky, eds., *Rereading Frye: The Published and Unpublished Works* (Toronto: Univ. of Toronto Press, 1999); Monique Anne Gyalokay, *Rousseau, Northrop Frye et la Bible: Essai de mythocritique* (Paris: Honoré Champion, 1999); Caterina Nella Cotrupi, *Northrop Frye and the Poetics of Process* (Toronto: Univ. of Toronto Press, 2000); Jean O'Grady and Wang Ning, eds., *Northrop Frye: Eastern and Western Perspectives* (Toronto: Univ. of Toronto Press, 2003); James M. Kee, ed., *Northrop Frye and the Afterlife of the Word*, Semeia 89 (Atlanta: Society of Biblical Literature, 2002); Jeffery Donaldson and Alan Mendelson, eds., *Frye and the Word: Religious Contexts in the Criticism of Northrop Frye* (Toronto: Univ. of Toronto Press, 2003); and Janos Kenyeres, *Revolving around the Bible: A Study of Northrop Frye* (Budapest: Anonymus, 2003). A separately published monograph, a Maoist diatribe by the pseudonymous Pauline Kogan, is *Northrop Frye: The High Priest of Clerical Obscurantism* (Montreal: Progressive Books and Periodicals, 1969). The bibliographies are my *Northrop Frye: An Enumerative Bibliography* (Metuchen, N.J.: Scarecrow Press, 1974), *Northrop Frye: An Annotated Bibliography of Primary and Secondary Sources* (Toronto: Univ. of Toronto Press, 1987), and *Northrop Frye: A Bibliography of His Published Writings*, 1931–2004 (Emory, Va.: Iron Mountain Press, 2004), updated from time to time in the *Northrop Frye Newsletter.*

10. At present there are one hundred one translations of Frye's books: Arabic (1), Bulgarian (1), Chinese (9), Czech (2), Danish (1), Dutch (1), Farsi (1), French (11), German (3), Greek (1), Hebrew (1), Hungarian (4), Italian (18), Japanese (16), Korean (11), Polish (1), Portuguese (4), Romanian (3), Serbo-Croatian (4), and Spanish (8). Another index of Frye's reputation is the attention his work has received at fifteen conferences and symposia, held on four continents, since 1965: "Northrop Frye and Contemporary Criticism," session at the annual meeting of the English Institute, September 1965; *Great Code* Symposia at Dalhousie University, 1982; "Northrop Frye and the Bible: A Symposium," University of Toronto, 1982; "Northrop Frye's *The Great Code*," session at the annual meeting of the South Atlantic Modern Language Association, Atlanta, 10 November 1984; "Ritratto di Northrop Frye," Rome, May 1987; "Northrop Frye and the Contexts of Criticism" and "*Anatomy of Criticism* in Retrospect," sessions at the annual meeting of the Modern Language Association, San Francisco, December 1987; "Northrop Frye and Eighteenth-Century Studies," 1990 Minnesota Conference of the American Society for Eighteenth-Century Studies, University of Minnesota, April 1990; "Northrop Frye and English Studies," University of Toronto, 25 February 1991; "The Legacy of Northrop Frye in the East and West," Sookmyung Women's University, Seoul, 22 May 1992; "The Legacy of Northrop Frye," Toronto, 29–31 October 1992; "Northrop Frye Research Seminar," University of Newcastle, Australia, 4–9 July 1994; "Northrop Frye and China," Peking University, 12–17 July 1994; "The International Symposium on Northrop Frye Studies," Inner Mongolia University in Hoh-Hot, China, 15–17 July 1999; "Frye and the Word," McMaster University, Hamilton, Ontario, 17–19 May 2000; "Frye and the United Church Ministry,"

Toronto, February 2001. In addition there is the annual "Northrop Frye Festival" in Moncton, N.B., which devotes a part of its program to Frye studies.

11. Preface to the Beacon Press edition of *Fearful Symmetry* (Boston, 1962), [ii]. The study of Blake was, Frye says, "a step, a necessary step in learning to read poetry, and to write criticism. . . . no one can read Blake seriously and sympathetically without feeling that the keys to poetic thought are in him" (*StS*, 176, 178).

12. A. C. Hamilton, *Northrop Frye: Anatomy of His Criticism* (Toronto: Univ. of Toronto Press, 1990), 38–39.

13. William Blake, *The Complete Poetry and Prose of William Blake,* ed. David Erdman, rev. ed. (Berkeley: Univ. of California Press, 1982), 273.

14. Ibid., 664.

15. Ibid., 13.

16. Among the annotated books in Frye's library by Barth are *Church Dogmatics,* 2 vols. (1975) and *The Word of God and the Word of Man* (1957); by Tillich, *Systematic Theology,* 3 vols. (1951–63), *Biblical Religion and the Search for Ultimate Reality* (1964), *Theology of Culture* (1964), and *Christianity and the Encounter of the World Religions* (1964); and by Bultmann, *Kerygma and Myth* (1961). Frye owned other books by each of these theologians, but as they are not annotated it is likely he did not read them; he seems to have always read with a pencil (or occasionally a pen) in hand. The scattered remarks about Luther in Frye's work, published and unpublished, seldom get beyond commonplace generalizations.

17. The royal metaphor—"all one body we"—comes from the hymn "Onward Christian Soldiers" (st. 2, line 2), though it derives ultimately from Paul. See Rom. 12:4 and 1 Cor. 12:12–13.

18. "Credible est, qui ineptum est; certum est, quia impossible." Tertullian, *De carne Christi,* 5, in *Patrologia Latina,* ed. Jacques-Paul Migne (Paris, 1844–64), vol. 2, col. 751. Frye's source for the paradox is Sir Thomas Browne, who quotes the last half of the Latin epigram in *Religio Medici,* in *Sir Thomas Browne: The Major Works,* ed. C. A. Patrides (London: Penguin, 1977), 70 (pt. 1, sec. 9). Frye would also have encountered the paradox in Jung's expanded translation: "And the Son of God is dead, which is worthy of belief because it is absurd. And when buried He rose again, which is certain because it is impossible." *Psychology and Alchemy,* trans. R. F. C. Hull, 2nd ed. (Princeton, N.J.: Princeton Univ. Press, 1968), 15. For Frye's other references to the Tertullian paradox, see *NFR,* 21, 162; *MM,* 97–98; *LN* 1:313, 2:596, 695; and *RT,* 74.

19. See the index of *SE* for the references to Schleiermacher. Alvin Lee has noted that Frye doubtless encountered Schleiermacher in the classes of John Line, who taught systematic theology, philosophy, history of religion, and philosophy of religion at Victoria and Emmanuel Colleges during Frye's student years. See *NFR,* xxv–xxvi.

20. *SE,* 325.

21. See Rudolf Otto, "The Mysticism of the 'Two Ways' in Schleier-

macher," appendix 2 in *Mysticism East and West* (New York: Macmillan, 1932), 233–43. Frye's annotated copy of this book is in the Northrop Frye Library.

22. Unpublished typescript in the Northrop Frye Fonds, 1991 accession, box 37, file 4, par. 2.

23. Friedrich Schleiermacher, *On Religion: Speeches to Its Cultured Despisers,* trans. John Oman (New York: Harper, 1958), 282–83. This passage, from the first edition of *On Religion,* was recast in the third edition. Frye owned a copy of *On Religion,* but there is no direct evidence he read it.

24. René Wellek, "Romanticism Re-examined," in *Concepts of Criticism,* ed. Stephen G. Nichols (New Haven, Conn.: Yale Univ. Press, 1963), 221.

25. Jaroslav Pelikan, *The Melody of Theology: A Philosophical Dictionary* (Cambridge, Mass.: Harvard Univ. Press, 1988), 220.

26. Glen R. Gill, "Northrop Frye and the Phenomenology of Myth," Ph.D. thesis, McMaster University, 2003.

27. Frank Kermode, *The Sense of an Ending: Studies in the Theory of Fiction* (New York: Oxford Univ. Press, 1967), 7.

28. Michael Kosok, "The Formalization of Hegel's Dialectical Logic," in *Hegel: A Collection of Critical Essays,* ed. Alastair MacIntyre (Garden City, N.Y.: Doubleday, 1972), 255.

29. Alvin Lee, introduction to *NFR,* xxx.

30. See, e.g., *LN,* 2:595, and *MM,* 122.

31. "Essentially contested concepts" are ideas that are open to interpretation and so involve disagreements about their meaning and use. See W. B. Gallie, "Essentially Contested Concepts," *Proceedings of the Aristotelian Society* 56 (1955–56): 167–98, and *Philosophy and Historical Understanding* (New York: Schocken, 1984).

32. Cf. "I've never known an instant of *real* quiet in my mind" (*LN,* 1:161).

33. See also *LN,* 1:200 and 267.

34. Cf. "I talk very well; it would be nice to know what I was talking about, but if I did I might stop writing, as St. Thomas Aquinas did when he died" (*LN,* 1:270).

35. *LN,* 1:188, 259, 409, and 2:482.

36. Marginalia in Samuel Taylor Coleridge, *The Inquiring Spirit: A New Presentation of Coleridge from His Published and Unpublished Prose Writings,* ed. Kathleen Coburn (London: Routledge & Kegan Paul, 1951), 41. The book is in the Northrop Frye Library. Frye's annotation comes at the end of a selection of Coleridge's notes for "An Essay on Passions."

37. See, e.g., the sequence of entries devoted to Brontë's *Shirley* in *LN,* 1:140–42.

38. It is not clear whether Frye always typed his first draft from a holograph manuscript. The notebooks do contain drafts for a small portion of his books and essays. But if such drafts were typical, only those that were written in the notebooks have, with two or three exceptions, survived. The best guess is that Frye most often used his notebooks in composing his first typed versions.

Knowledge about the process of Frye's revising comes from personal correspondence and conversations with Jane Widdicombe.

39. *LN,* 1:346, 2:427, 1:331.

40. "Response," *Eighteenth-Century Studies* 24 (Winter 1990–91): 249.

41. For the high school, Edmonton, and *Fearful Symmetry* epiphanies, see the holograph notes in the Northrop Frye Fonds, 1991 accession, box 50, file 1, where Frye describes the experience at the Edmonton YMCA as "one of the great nights of my life"; John Ayre, *Northrop Frye: A Biography* (Toronto: Random House, 1989), 44, 69; and *NFC,* 47–48. For the Blake intuition, see *NFC,* 47–48, *WGS,* 275–76, and Frye's letter to Pelham Edgar in Edgar's *Across My Path* (Toronto: Ryerson Press, 1952), 85–86. There was actually a second, less well known Blake epiphany, mentioned in *TBN,* 60, and described sketchily in *NFC,* 48. For the Seattle illumination, see 20.1; *RT,* 227, 371; *LN,* 1:399, 405, 2:491, 621; *TBN,* 162, 178, 194; 33.65. For the St. Clair illumination, see *TBN,* 47, 90, 124, 148, 178–79, 332, 333, 336; 55-4.3; *LN,* 2:621; 33.65; and *RT,* 133, 202, 227. There was perhaps a seventh epiphany that occurred when Frye was walking to Victoria College along Bathurst St. in 1944. See "Work in Progress," in *TBN,* 338, and what may be a commentary on that experience in a series of autobiographical notes where Frye says that "the vast abstraction had finally become transparent" by 1944 (holograph manuscript in the 1991 accession, box 50, file 1, par. 2). Still another epiphany may have occurred in Yugoslavia only four months before Frye's death: in Notebook 50 he speaks of "that loud flash I got in Zagreb: the ideal of spontaneity, where the moment of composition and the moment of performance are the same" (*LN,* 1:415).

42. A. V. Miller, in his gloss on par. 14 of the "Preface" to Hegel's *Phenomenology of Spirit,* trans. A. V. Miller; analysis by J. N. Findlay (Oxford: Oxford Univ. Press, 1977), writes, "When Science first emerges, it has on the one hand a tendency to stress simple intuitive rationality and a relation to what is divine, but also on the other hand to develop this insight into an organized wealth of detail" (496). In the margin of his copy of the *Phenomenology* Frye wrote, "my position on sc. crit. [scientific criticism]." Intuitive rationality produced the deductive schema for Frye, which he then filled in with inductive detail.

43. In a less-complex fourteen-chapter sketch Frye says that he would prefer a 3-7-4 to a 4-6-4 pattern for the arrangement of *The Great Code* (*RT,* 186); the only reason for the preference apparently is that the former preserves the double-seven pattern.

44. It does not escape Frye's notice that the sum of the numbers up to seven equals twenty-eight and the sum up to twelve equals seventy-eight. One version of *The Great Code* was projected to have twenty-eight chapters (*RT,* 171). For his musings about the number seventy-eight, see *RT,* 173.

45. See Dolzani's introduction to *TBN.*

46. See Henry Wadsworth Longfellow, *Poems and Other Writings* (New York: Library of America, 2000), 228–30.

47. See *TBN,* 147–48, 159, 177, 198, 200, 204, 249, and 254.

48. The chart is reproduced in *RT,* 591–94.

49. Michael Dolzani, "The Book of the Dead: A Skeleton Key to Northrop Frye's Notebooks," in *Rereading Frye,* 19–38. See also Dolzani's introductions to *TBN* and to his forthcoming edition of Frye's notebooks on romance.

50. "Expanding Eyes," in *SM,* 100–101.

51. See also the prefaces to *SM,* vii, and *StS,* viii.

52. This is true despite the following claim in Notebook 11f: "A quest book is a better type of book to write & more fun to read than a Pisgah-view book, where one sees everything all the time & no road ever turns a corner. I think that's the real reason why this compass scheme bores me. I've never started a book, even an essay, knowing exactly where it was going & how it would end" (*RT,* 130). The two approaches here (the quest versus the Pisgah-vision) turn out to represent not an "either-or" alternative but a "both-and" dialectic—the quest as *mythos* and the Pisgah-vision as *dianoia.*

53. Vera was Frye's older sister. *The Sleepy King* by Aubrey Hopwood and Seymour Hicks (Philadelphia: Henry Altemus, 1900) is a fairy tale in which a young girl descends to the bottom of a magic oak to awaken a miserly king who has been sleeping for two hundred years.

54. Letter to Benjamin Bailey, 22 November 1917.

1. Interpenetration

The aphorism given in the second epigraph to this chapter received elaboration in Frye's response to papers by Eric Rothstein and J. Paul Hunter at a special session entitled "Northrop Frye and Eighteenth-Century Studies" at a meeting of the American Society for Eighteenth-Century Studies in Minneapolis and published in *Eighteenth-Century Studies* 24 (Winter 1990–91): 243–49.

> I find it difficult to buy the panhistorical visions of so many contemporary literary scholars. They seem to me to operate only within history as such: when you're studying history you're inside a historical cosmos where everything is historical. If you're studying philosophy, you're inside a philosophical cosmos where what you do is climb a philosophical mountain, like Hegel, to find yourself on a pinnacle of absolute knowledge where you know everything except where to get the oxygen for the next breath. Similarly there seems to me to be a total cosmos of literature, within which everything is literary. So far as I can see, only three people have been inspired by that last vision. Two of them were Blake and Mallarmé; the third has learned what he knows about it from them. But of course these are not differing universes, and they have no boundaries; they are interpenetrating. (245)

My friend Michael Dolzani's gloss on the original notebook aphorism: "pan-Fryed."

1. One can discover more than thirty polar categories in the First Essay of *AC* alone.

2. Dialectic has several meanings in Frye: debate, dialogue, the Hegelian process. Here the word means simply what Frye calls in *AC* "the principle of opposition in thought" (333).

3. Cf. the following passage from "Letter to the English Institute: 1965," in *Northrop Frye in Modern Criticism,* ed. Murray Krieger (New York: Columbia Univ. Press, 1966):

> One of the most accurately drawn characters in drama is Reuben the Reconciler, who is listed in the dramatis personae of Ben Jonson's *Sad Shepherd,* and whose role was apparently to set everybody right at the end. Jonson never finished the play, so he never appeared. I wish we could throw away the notion of "reconciling," and use instead some such conception as "interpenetration." Literature itself is not a field of conflicting arguments but of interpenetrating visions. I suspect that this is true even of philosophy, where the place of argument seems more functional. The irrefutable philosopher is not the one who cannot be refuted, but the one who is still there after he has been refuted. (28–29)

One might say the same thing about irrefutable critics.

4. The motto that Frye had in mind for *WP*—"And those who have loved now love the more"—is the last half of a couplet from the *Vigil of Venus,* "Cras amet qui numquam amavit, quique amavit cras amet." As it turned out, he did not use the motto in the book.

5. Frye presented the Birks Lectures, entitled "Revelation and Response," at McGill University, 4–7 October 1971. If he spoke from a manuscript, it has not survived.

6. "Oswald Spengler," in *RW,* 321. For Frye's other major essay on Spengler, see "Spengler Revisited," in *SM,* 179–98.

7. In his two essays on Spengler, Frye makes essentially the same point, though not in terms of interpenetration: Spengler "sees everything a culture produces as characteristic of that culture: in other words as a symbol of it. History consequently becomes a collection of symbols representing something that can hardly be expressed in words at all, because the existence of a culture can't really be proved; it can only be pointed out, and felt or intuited by the reader, through the arrangements of the symbols" ("Oswald Spengler," 321). "[C]ultures differ profoundly from one another, so profoundly that no mind in a Western culture can really understand what is going on in a Classical or Egyptian or Chinese mind. The differences can only be expressed by some kind of central symbol" ("Spengler Revisited," 182–83). Frye is drawing on ideas Spengler sets forth throughout the first volume of *The Decline of the West,* but especially in chap. 5, on symbolism and space. See also Frye's "The Shapes of History," in *NFCL,* 78.

8. See also *NFC,* 61, where Frye further reports that he "later found" the idea in Whitehead.

9. Alfred North Whitehead, *Science and the Modern World* (New York: Macmillan, 1929), 133. Frye quotes this passage in 34.62; the only place it appears in his published work is *DV,* 41. Wallace Stevens quotes the same passage in "A Collect of Philosophy," *Opus Posthumous,* ed. Milton J. Bates, rev. ed. (New York: Knopf, 1989), 273, and Frye, citing the reference in Stevens, refers to Whitehead's "great passage" in "Wallace Stevens and the Variation Form" (*SM,* 292). Cf. the gloss on the passage from Whitehead in the notebook Frye devoted to his "double vision" lectures: "in an interpenetrating world everywhere is the one particular spot" (*LN,* 2:431).

10. Editor's preface to Peter Fisher, *The Valley of Vision: Blake as Prophet and Revolutionary,* ed. Northrop Frye (Toronto: Univ. of Toronto Press, 1961), v.

11. *The Lankavatara Sutra: A Mahayana Text,* trans. Daisetz Teitaro Suzuki (London: George Routledge and Sons, 1932). An annotated copy is in the Northrop Frye Library.

12. D. T. Suzuki, *Studies in the Lankavatara Sutra* (London: Routledge and Kegan Paul, 1930), 95–96. There is no direct evidence that Frye read this book. He may have learned about the Avatamsaka Sutra from Suzuki's introduction to the Lankavatara Sutra, which has a brief overview of the Avatamsaka (xxxvi–xxxvii).

13. *Lankavatara Sutra,* 192.

14. "The Double Vision" is the three-lecture typescript that Frye later expanded into the four-chapter book *The Double Vision.*

15. *Lankavatara Sutra,* xxxvi.

16. D. T. Suzuki devotes about half of his *Essays in Zen Buddhism, Third Series* (London: Rider, 1958), to the Avatamsaka Sutra. This is the book by Suzuki that Frye quotes from in *GC,* 168, referring to the Buddhist view of interpenetration as a gloss on Blake's seeing the world in a grain of sand. Frye's knowledge of the Avatamsaka Sutra appears to have come largely from Suzuki's work, although in the mid-1980s he did acquire and annotate vol. 1 of *The Flower Ornament Scripture: A Translation of the Avatamsaka Sutra,* trans. Thomas Cleary (Boulder, Colo.: Shambhala, 1984). Cleary's English translation of the complete sutra did not appear until 1993. The interpenetration of the whole and its parts is also central to the Lotus Sutra, which forms the basis of the T'ien-t'ai school of Mahayana Buddhism, but Frye does not refer to this sutra in his published or unpublished writings. An annotated copy of *Essays in Zen Buddhism, Third Series* is in the Northrop Frye Library. On the relationship of Hua-yen interpenetration to Whitehead, see Steve Odin, *Process Metaphysics and Hua-yen Buddhism: A Critical Study of Penetration vs. Interpenetration* (Albany: State Univ. Press of New York, 1983).

17. It is not possible to date the material in Notes 54-3 with certainty; it appears to be from the mid-1970s. Frye's remarks on Lewis in *SM,* which elaborate the somewhat cryptic references in the notebook, were written at about the same time, the essay "Spengler Revisited" having first appeared in *Daedalus* in 1974.

18. Cf. this entry from Notebook 44: "Malraux says Spengler's book started out as a meditation on the destiny of art-forms, then expanded. What it expanded into, I think, was a vision of history as interpenetration, every historical phenomenon being a symbol of the totality of historical phenomena contemporary with it. That's what fascinated me, though of course I didn't know it for many years" (*LN*, 1:245). Frye makes a similar remark in *NFC*, 61. Malraux's comment on Spengler is from *The Voices of Silence*, trans. Stuart Gilbert (Princeton, N.J.: Princeton Univ. Press, 1978), 619.

19. Notebook 11e is difficult to date with certainty, but since Frye says that he bought the notebook when he was in New Zealand (*RT*, 322), it was written after his 1978 lecture tour there. "Thou Art That" or "That Thou Art" (*tat tvam asi*), one of the principal precepts of Vedanta contained in the Hindu Upanishads, means that the Absolute is essentially one with oneself.

20. Whitehead, *Science and the Modern World*, 128.

21. Ibid., 133.

22. Ibid., 74.

23. Ibid., 133–34.

24. Whitehead, *Religion in the Making* (New York: Macmillan, 1959), 91. There is no evidence that Frye read this book. But Frye saw in Mircea Eliade's account of the concept of the religious space—i.e., wherever one is, one is at the center of the cosmos—an example of the principle that "everything is at the center." See his marginal annotations to that effect in his copy of Eliade's *The Sacred and the Profane: The Nature of Religion*, trans. Willard R. Trask (New York: Harcourt, Brace, 1959), 45, 57.

25. Jorge Luis Borges, *The Aleph and Other Stories*, trans. Norman Thomas di Giovanni (New York: Bantam Books, 1971), 10, 12.

26. G. W. F. Hegel, *Phenomenology of Spirit*, trans. A. V. Miller; analysis by J. N. Findlay (Oxford: Oxford Univ. Press, 1977), 517. In his own copy of Hegel's *Phenomenology* Frye wrote "interpenetration" in the margin beside Findlay's commentary.

27. See 34.61, which contains both passages. Frye quotes the Plotinus passage from *The Fifth Ennead*, 8th tractate, sec. 4, trans. Stephen MacKenna. The Plotinus passage is also cited by Aldous Huxley in *The Perennial Philosophy* (New York: Harper, 1945), 5, which Frye read at about the same time (*RT*, 23). He appears not to have read the MacKenna translation until the late 1950s (see 18.100).

28. See p. 114 of Frye's annotated copy of *Science and the Modern World*, in the Northrop Frye Library.

29. See 34.61–62, which indicates almost certainly that Frye copied the Plotinus passage from Otto.

30. Rudolf Otto, *Mysticism East and West* (New York: Macmillan, 1932), 41, 53.

31. Owen Barfield, *What Coleridge Thought* (Middletown, Conn.: Wesleyan Univ. Press, 1971). See esp. chap. 3, "Two Forces of One Power." Barfield's

interest in interpenetration is recorded in another of Frye's notebooks as well (*LN*, 2:435).

32. Samuel Taylor Coleridge, *Theory of Life*, qtd. in Barfield, *What Coleridge Thought*, 52–53. In a letter Coleridge also speaks of the interpenetration of "opposite energies," and he uses the word as well in *The Friend* (qtd. by Barfield, 34, 220). For other senses of interpenetration in Coleridge, see Barfield, 93, 97, 145, 155, and 220. "Intussusception," the reception of one part within another, is a medical and a physiological term.

33. Qtd. in Barfield, *What Coleridge Thought*, 36.

34. For Frye's extensive commentary on Lull's contemplative mysticism, see "The Life and Thought of Ramon Lull," an essay written during Frye's final year at Emmanuel College, in *SE*, 217–34. References to Bruno appear throughout his published and unpublished work.

35. Cf. Shelley's idea that the elevating delight of poetry "is as it were the interpenetration of a diviner nature through our Own." *A Defence of Poetry*, in *Shelley's Critical Prose*, ed. Bruce R. McElderry (Lincoln: Univ. of Nebraska Press, 1967), 31.

36. On Bohm and Krishnamurti, see Walter J. Hanegraaff, *New Age Religion and Western Culture: Esotericism in the Mirror of Western Thought* (Albany: State Univ. of New York Press, 1998), 70–71; J. Krishnamurti and David Bohm, *The Ending of Time* (London: Krishnamurti Foundation Trust, 1984); Krishnamurti and Bohm, *The Future of Humanity* (The Hague: Mirananda, 1986); and Renée Weber, "Field Consciousness and Field Ethics," in *The Holographic Paradigm and Other Paradoxes*, ed. Ken Wilber (Boston: Shambhala, 1985), 35–43.

37. In Notebook 11h Frye quotes from an interview with Bohm, "The Physicist and the Mystic—Is a Dialogue between Them Possible?" in *The Holographic Paradigm*, 205. The passage quoted is from a discussion about the phenomenology of thought. Bohm says, "Thought is already implicitly beyond any limit it sets up: that's the way it's built," which, Frye supposes, is the reason that "every conception I set up as a goal to be reached turns out to be the principle I have to start with" (*LN*, 2:714–15). Frye's copy of *The Holographic Paradigm* has 163 marginal markings and annotations. Frye is less impressed with Capra, saying that Capra has a "commonplace mind" and that he did not learn much from his "two books on the Tao of Physics" (*LN*, 2:713). Annotated copies of Wilber's book and Capra's *The Turning Point: Science, Society, and the Rising Culture* (New York: Simon and Schuster, 1982) are in the Northrop Frye Library. Frye apparently did not own a copy of Capra's *The Tao of Physics* (Boulder, Colo.: Shambhala, 1975), but the notebook entry just cited indicates that he had read at least parts of it. Frye may also have known about Bohm from Marilyn Ferguson's several references to his work in *The Aquarian Conspiracy: Personal and Social Transformation in Our Time* (Los Angeles: J. P. Tarcher, 1987), another popular account that Frye annotated. A relatively nontechnical account of the holographic paradigm, published after Frye's death, is Michael Talbot, *The Holographic Universe* (New York: HarperCollins, 1991).

38. David Bohm, *Wholeness and the Implicate Order* (London: Routledge and Kegan Paul, 1981), 172. An annotated copy of Bohm's book is in the Northrop Frye Library.

39. See *Wholeness and the Implicate Order,* esp. chaps. 6–7.

40. Bohm appears to hold that the hologram is not an analogy of the implicate order, as Capra claims (*The Turning Point,* 95–96), but an example of such order. See Bohm, *Wholeness and the Implicate Order,* 145–47, 177–78.

41. From the laser experiments, Bohm concludes that "there is no one-to-one correspondence between parts of an 'illuminated object' and parts of an 'image of an object on a plate'" (*Wholeness and the Implicate Order,* 146)—which of course runs counter to the "explicate" assumptions of traditional physics.

42. Frye adds, "David Bohm's book, *Wholeness and the Implicate Order,* has something on this."

43. Bohm, *Wholeness and the Implicate Order,* 149.

44. See also *LN,* 1:108 (par. 36), 109 (par. 39), and 110 (pars. 45–46).

45. Capra, *The Turning Point,* 94. Frye's annotation is in the 1982 Simon and Schuster edition, but the pagination is the same as that of the Bantam edition.

46. Frye owned none of Schrödinger's books, and there is no evidence that Frye had read him. On two occasions he quotes Schrödinger's remark that "consciousness is a singular of which the plural is unknown" (*MM,* 122; *LN,* 1:291), and he refers to Schrödinger's idea of common consciousness in *LN,* 2:545. The source of the references is almost certainly Kenneth Walker, *A Study of Gurdjieff's Teaching* (London: Jonathan Cape, 1965), 86. An annotated copy is in the Northrop Frye Library.

47. See Bohm's *Wholeness and the Implicate Order,* 203; and "The Enfolding-Unfolding Universe: A Conversation with David Bohm," conducted by Renée Weber, in *The Holographic Paradigm,* 47, where Bohm also uses the word "interpenetrate" to describe the relationship between the *unfolded* order and the *enfolded* order. Frye underlined this instance of the word in his copy of *The Holographic Paradigm.* In Wilber's "Physics, Mysticism, and the New Holographic Paradigm: A Critical Appraisal," Frye also marked Wilber's use of the word to describe the relationship of various levels of consciousness (*The Holographic Paradigm,* 160).

48. Bohm appears to have been encouraged to think about wholeness in nature from his conversations with Krishnamurti, beginning in 1961. See "David Bohm," *New Scientist* 96 (11 November 1982): 363.

49. David Bohm, "The Physicist and the Mystic," in *The Holographic Paradigm,* 187–88.

50. Bohm refers to Pribram's studies in passing (*Wholeness and the Implicate Order,* 198). In Wilber's book, see esp. his "A New Perspective on Reality," 5–14; Marilyn Ferguson, "Karl Pribram's Changing Reality," 15–25; and Pribram's own brief account of his work, "What the Fuss Is All About," 27–34. Frye

could also have learned of Pribram's work from Marilyn Ferguson's *The Aquarian Conspiracy.*

51. See Karl Pribram, "Towards a Holonomic Theory of Perception," in *Gestalttheorie in der modernen Psychologie,* ed. S. Ertel, L. Kemmler, and M. Stadler (Darmstadt: Steinkopff, 1975). See also F. David Peat's account of Pribram's work, based in part on correspondence he had with Pribram, in *Infinite Potential: The Life and Times of David Bohm* (Reading, Mass.: Addison-Wesley, 1997), 261. Chapter 14 of Peat's biography provides a nontechnical account of how Bohm arrived at his idea of the implicate order.

52. See Geoffrey F. Chew, *The Analytic S Matrix: A Basis for Nuclear Democracy* (New York: W. A. Benjamin, 1966); *Lectures on Modelling the Bootstrap* (Bombay: Tata Institute of Fundamental Research, 1970); "Bootstrap: A Scientific Idea," *Science* 161 (23 May 1968): 762–65.

53. Capra, *The Turning Point,* 93. On the bootstrap theory, see also Capra, *The Tao of Physics,* 276–90.

54. *Hegel's Science of Logic,* trans. W. H. Johnston and L. G. Struthers (London: George Allen & Unwin, 1929), 1:119–20. Cf. Walter Kaufmann's translation: "*Aufheben* and *das Aufgehobene (das Ideele)* is one of the most important concepts in philosophy. *Aufheben* has in the [German] language a double meaning in that it signifies conserving, *preserving,* and at the same time also making cease, *making an end.* Even conserving includes the negative aspect that something is taken out of its immediacy, and thus out of an existence that is open to external influences, to be preserved." Kaufmann, *Hegel: Reinterpretation, Texts, and Commentary* (Garden City, N.Y.: Doubleday, 1965), 191–92. Still another version of the passage from Hegel's *Logic:* "To sublate (*aufheben*) has a two-fold meaning in the language: on the one hand, it means to preserve, to maintain, and equally it means to cause to cease, to put an end to. . . . Thus what is sublated is at the same time preserved, it has lost its immediacy only but it is not on that account annihilated." Quoted in Raymond Plant, *Hegel* (Bloomington: Indiana Univ. Press, 1973), 143.

55. Hegel, *Phenomenology of Spirit,* 114–15.

56. Ibid., 12. Kaufmann translates the passage as "sublimating this opposition to its becoming" (392).

57. Ibid., 68.

58. Ibid.

59. Ibid., 493. Mark Taylor comments on Hegel's final paragraph: "As 'Absolute Spirit' is embodied in nature and history, truth is gradually revealed first in religious symbols and artistic images and then is translated into philosophical concepts. Speculative philosophy brings this incarnational process to closure by comprehending the modern secular world as the realization of divine life." Introduction to *Critical Terms for Religious Studies,* 3–4.

60. Blake's reference to "the smile of a fool" is in his attack on Sir Joshua Reynolds's ideas of harmony: "Such Harmony of Colouring is destructive of Art

One species of General Hue over all is the Cursed Thing calld Harmony it is like the Smile of a Fool." "Annotations to the Works of Sir Joshua Reynolds," in Blake, *Complete Poetry and Prose*, 662. Frye's suggestion that Hegel did not use the word "synthesis" in connection with *Aufhebung* turns out to be correct. In fact, the well-known thesis-antithesis-synthesis progression is not a movement Hegel himself put forward; his use of the three words together occurs only once and that in a disparaging remark about Kant. See Kaufmann, *Hegel: Reinterpretation, Texts, and Commentary*, 433–34. Kaufmann cites an article that refers to the thesis-antithesis-synthesis sequence as a "legend."

61. In the decentered Bible every verse is a microcosm of the entire structure, which is the opposite of the whole formed by the parts.

62. See *LN*, 1:195, 258, 259, 363, 2:683, 686; *RT*, 296, 298, 313.

63. In a notebook entry about the conclusion to his first Emmanuel College lecture on "the double vision" Frye says: "[S]piritual language is interpenetrative, going much farther than any damn 'dialogue.' Discursive language, being militant, aims at agreement or reconciliation" (*LN*, 2:660).

64. Here, e.g., are two entries from *The Double Vision* notebook: "The movement I'm talking about is away from classbound ideologies toward a primary concern to which the keys are interpenetration and decentralization" (*LN*, 2:437). "Interpenetration and decentralized myth [are] the goal I'm heading for" (*LN*, 2:439).

65. The CCF was a democratic socialist party, organized by farm and labor groups in Calgary in 1932, which sought "a commonwealth in which the basic principle regulating production, distribution, and exchange [would] be the supplying of human needs instead of the making of profits." Qtd. in Desmond Morton, *The New Democrats, 1961–1986* (Toronto: Copp Clark Pitman, 1986), 12. It was the forerunner of the New Democratic Party. Frye always maintained that his own identity was rooted in his association with Victoria University, the United Church of Canada, and the CCF.

66. "Dialogism" is the term used by Mikhail Bakhtin to designate the ways that different "voices" in a literary text disrupt the authority of a single voice (monologism). See his *Problems of Dostoevsky's Poetics*, trans. Caryl Emerson (Minneapolis: Univ. of Minnesota Press, 1984), and *The Dialogic Imagination*, trans. Caryl Emerson and Michael Holquist (Austin: Univ. of Texas Press, 1981). "Montaigne's 'consubstantial' remark" refers to a passage in "On Giving the Lie": "I have no more made my book than my book has made me; a book consubstantial with its author, concerned only with me, a vital part of my life; not having an outside and alien concern like all other books." In *The Essays of Montaigne*, trans. Charles Cotton, bk. 2, chap. 18, par. 5.

67. On the uses of *interpenetration* in the social sciences, see Elías Sevilla Casas, "Metaphor, Interpenetration and Ethnography: A Review Essay with Reflections on Northrop Frye's Ideas," *CIDSE* (*Cenrto de Investigaciones y Documentación Socioeconómica*), Documento de Trabajo, No. 58 (February 2002).

68. For a fuller exposition of the Logos-Thanatos dialectic, see Dolzani's introduction to *TBN,* xxvii–xxxii.

69. Frye often called on Coleridge's principle of distinguishing without dividing. See, e.g., *WP,* 26; *LN,* 1:235, 2:701; and *TBN,* 109. Coleridge had written in *Aids to Reflection,* "It is a dull and obtuse mind, that must divide in order to distinguish; but it is still worse, that distinguishes in order to divide" (London: Pickering, 1849), 17; and in the *Biographia Literaria* he wrote, "The office of philosophical *disquisition* consists in just *distinction;* while it is the privilege of the philosopher to preserve himself constantly aware, that distinction is not division" (181).

70. In *WP,* 126, Frye actually makes a third reference to interpenetration in connection with metaphor, but it is only to cite his earlier use of the word in *GC.* Cf. Blake's aphorism with that of the masters of the T'ien-t'ai school of Mahayana Buddhism, "The whole world is contained in a mustard seed."

71. Nicholas Halmi addresses the whole-part, synecdochic principle in Frye, tracing its philosophical roots and arguing that Frye's monology issues from the fear that without the assumption of some whole at the centre of things we would be left in our search for meaning with a chaotic "process of signification." See his "The Metaphysical Foundation of Frye's Monadology," in *Frye and the Word,* ed. Donaldson and Mendelson, 97–104. For Halmi, parts and whole can, in the monology of the synecdoche, substitute for each other. In interpenetration they are identified with and so become each other.

72. Frye, "Letter to the English Institute," 29.

73. "The Anatomy in Prose Fiction," *Manitoba Arts Review* 3, no. 1 (Spring 1942): 40.

74. These examples of the uses of the word come from *StS,* 116; *MM,* 163; *SM,* 107; *TBN,* 75; *LN,* 1:132, 134, 193, 209; *TBN,* 319; and "Response," *Eighteenth-Century Studies* 24 (Winter 1990–91): 249.

75. Frye marked the word or made marginal annotations about interpenetration in his own copies of Edward F. Edinger's *Ego and Archetype,* Mircea Eliade's *Immortality and Freedom,* José Ortega y Gassett's *What Is Philosophy?,* P. D. Ouspensky's *The Psychology of Man's Possible Evolution,* Gopi Krishna's *Kundalini: The Evolutionary Energy in Man,* Joseph Campbell's *The Hero with a Thousand Faces,* G. R. Levy's *The Phoenix Nest: A Study of Religious Transformation,* Alphonse Louis Constant's *The History of Magic,* C. F. Rolt's *Dionysius the Areopagite,* Francis Huxley's *The Way of the Sacred,* Martin Heidegger's *Poetry, Language, Thought,* Jung's *Mysterium Coniunctionis,* and Hegel's *Phenomenology of Spirit.* See Robert D. Denham, "Annotations in Frye's Books," *Northrop Frye Newsletter* 9, no. 2 (Summer 2002): 20–35, which is based on a survey of approximately one-fourth of Frye's annotated books. There are doubtless a number of other such annotations relating to interpenetration.

76. Frye has a typescript commentary on Eddison in the 1991 accession, box 36, file 13, pars. 4–5.

77. E. R. Eddison, *The Worm Ouroboros* (New York: Ballantine Books, 1967), 371.

78. Had Frye been interested in pursuing the theological analogue, he could have found one in Martin Luther's *Confession on the Lord's Supper* (1528), where the doctrine of Christ's omnipresence in the largest and smallest of objects is another version of the "everywhere at once" formulation.

79. In another notebook, Frye remarks, "I find these sutras a lot of blithering crap, but I suppose they made sense as vade mecums of practical meditation" (for Frye when he read them) (*LN,* 2:713–14).

80. Suzuki, *Essays in Zen Buddhism, Third Series,* 84. Francis H. Cook agrees that *shi shi wu-ai,* the interpenetration of all things, is the distinctive contribution of the Chinese Hua-yen—that is, without antecedents in Indian Buddhism. Hua-yen sees "the universe as the infinitely repeated identity and interdependence of all phenomena. . . . depending on point of view, any object is simultaneously both *chu* [primary] and part of *chan* [secondary]." "Interpenetration results from a situation in which the cause includes the conditions within itself while at the same time, being a result of other causes, its qualities are being absorbed into the other." *Hua-yen Buddhism: The Jewel Net of Indra* (University Park: Pennsylvania State Univ. Press, 1977), 35–36, 68.

81. Suzuki, *Essays in Zen Buddhism, Third Series,* 84–85. Frye's remark about two poems by Wallace Stevens is an example of interpenetration in this sense: "Wallace Stevens speaks of a 'central mind' or 'major man,' which or who includes all other minds without destroying their individuality. He also has a poem in which a fisherman, his river and his fish and the doves cooing around him consolidate into one form, though, again, the individual forms remain" (*MM,* 122).

82. Suzuki, *Essays in Zen Buddhism, Third Series,* 96. Dharmadhatu (realm of dharma) refers, in Mahayana Buddhism, to the unchanging totality in which all phenomena are born, live, and die. Li Tongxuan, the eighth-century Chinese Buddhist layman, begins his commentary on the Gandavyuha by saying, "The inherent baselessness of physical and mental objects is called reality. The interpenetration of one and many, the disappearance of the boundaries of the real and artificial, of affirmation and negation, is called the realm." Appendix 3, *The Flower Ornament Scripture,* trans. Cleary, 1565. Cleary translated Li Tongxuan's guide in its entirety (1565–1627).

83. Suzukii, *Essays in Zen Buddhism, Third Series,* 140–41.

84. Interpenetration is described as an experience in *LN,* 2:525, 581–82, 616; *RT,* 326; and 54-4.112.

85. Translation from Thomas Cleary's *Entry into the Inconceivable: An Introduction to Hua-yen Buddhism* (Honolulu: Univ. of Hawaii Press, 1983), 66.

86. Cleary, *Entry into the Inconceivable,* 9, 6–7.

87. The iron bar is a reference to the discipline and effort required for enlightenment in Zen Buddhism: the candidate who has been assigned a koan must work at his task "like a mosquito biting on an iron bar."

88. If interpenetration is finally beyond space and time, Frye nonetheless

makes repeated efforts to represent the idea diagrammatically. What he calls the "interpenetration of the cyclical & dialectical" (*RT,* 139) appears, of course, as a tacit diagram at several places in *AC,* most visibly, so to speak, in his account of the phases of the *mythoi.* In the notebooks Frye makes dozens of actual sketches of what he calls the Great Doodle, a schematic way of representing a temporal pattern imposed on a spatial one, or vice versa.

89. Borges, "The Aleph," in *The Aleph and Other Stories,* 12–13.

90. In *WP,* Frye remarks that Paul's phrase "all in all," forming a vision in which human beings are the center and God the circumference of an expanding sphere, "suggests both interpenetration, where circumference is interchangeable with center, and a unity which is no longer thought of either as an absorbing of identity into a larger uniformity or as a mosaic of metaphors" (186).

91. Bill Moyers, *A World of Ideas,* ed. Betty Sue Flowers (New York: Doubleday, 1989), 503.

92. Cf. "Buddhism . . . gets past the aural-visual time-space antithesis: Revelation gets to the panoramic apocalypse, invites us, like Rabelais, to have a drink, and that's it. Buddhism understands that the next step, or participating apocalypse, is interpenetration, which destroys the antithesis of the inclusive and exclusive. Hence being a Xn [Christian] is one way of being a Buddhist" (*LN,* 1:262–63).

93. See Suzuki, *Studies in the Lankavatara Sutra,* 308–14.

94. For the use of interpenetration in the eighth-century debate about the two natures of Christ, see John of Damascus, *On the Orthodox Faith,* bk. 3, chaps. 3–4. The interpenetration of God and man is also found in Sufism. See, e.g., Ibn al-Arabi's *The Wisdom of the Prophets.* It is found as well in the word *sappir* (a form of the word *sefiroth*) of the Kabbalah, the glimmering jewel with its many facets of light all reflecting each other—a kind of reversal of the image of *multum in parvo* in the jeweled net of Indra.

95. The allusions here are to William Blake's *All Religions Are One* (1788) and Aldous Huxley's *The Perennial Philosophy.*

96. Francis Huxley, *The Way of the Sacred: The Rites and Symbols, Beliefs and Tabus, That Men Have Held in Awe and Wonder* (New York: Dell, 1974), 311, 323–25.

97. Charles Poncé, *Kabbalah: An Introduction and Illumination for the World Today* (San Francisco: Straight Arrow Books, 1973), 116, 98–99. Frye's two-and-a-half-page typescript is in 1991 accession, box 36, file 11. Both passages quoted are from p. 2.

98. Interpenetration is a common term in a number of other quite diverse fields—the physics of liquids and contemporary architecture, for example, and in Jewish mystical doctrine (e.g., each *Sefirah,* one of the seven celestial levels, contains within itself an element of each of the others). And in Sufism the idea of the mutual interpenetration of God and man is found in *The Wisdom of the Prophets* by Ibn al-Arabi (1165–1240). Among philosophers, Dewey uses the term in his discussion of habits and character (*Human Nature and Conduct,* in

The Middle Works of John Dewey, 1899–1924, ed. Jo Ann Boydston [Carbondale: Southern Illinois Univ. Press, 1988], 14:29–30), and William James uses the word in his account of precepts and concepts (*Some Problems of Philosophy,* in *Writings 1902–1910,* ed. Bruce Kuklick [New York: Literary Classics of the United States, 1987], 1009–10). As we might expect, the idea, if not the word, appears in theological discussions of the Trinity, as when Augustine writes that "in that highest Trinity one is as much as the Three together, nor are two anything more than one. And They are infinite in themselves. So both each are in each, and all in each, and each in all, and all in all, and all are one." *On The Trinity,* bk. 6, sec. 10, par. 12.

2. Identity

1. The few expositions of Frye's views on metaphor that do exist are cursory or based on highly selective statements. Earl R. Mac Cormac, for example, maintains that "Frye tended to look at all metaphors as confined to literature," and he thinks Frye's view of metaphor fails because he confines "poetic metaphors to the literary context in which they occur." *A Cognitive Theory of Metaphor* (Cambridge, Mass.: MIT Press, 1985), 41, 194. But for Frye metaphor is a function of *language,* and metaphors occur in all linguistic contexts.

2. Although Aristotle says that "metaphor is the transference of a name from the object to which it has a natural application" (*Poetics,* chap. 21), his theory of metaphor has affinities with both the substitution view (one term can stand for another, as in metonymy) and the comparison or analogical view ("the ability to construct good metaphors implies the ability to see essential similarities" [chap. 22]). Max Black's theory of interaction, which argues that metaphors create new meanings, rather than simply comparing or transferring meaning from one context to another, is actually an extension of I. A. Richards's theory of the interanimation that occurs between the "tenor" (the underlying subject) and the "vehicle" (the figure that presents the subject). For Black's views, see "Metaphor," *Proceedings of the Aristotelian Society* 55 (May 1955): 273–94, and "Models and Archetypes," in his *Models and Metaphors: Studies in Language and Philosophy* (Ithaca, N.Y.: Cornell Univ. Press, 1962), 219–43. For Richards's theory, developed in a number of his books and essays, see esp. *The Philosophy of Rhetoric* (New York: Oxford Univ. Press, 1936), *Interpretation in Teaching* (New York: Harcourt, Brace, 1938), and "Science and Poetry," in *Criticism: The Foundations of Modern Literary Judgment,* ed. Mark Schorer, et al. (New York: Harcourt, Brace, 1948), 505–23.

3. Blake, *Complete Poetry and Prose,* 81.

4. See, e.g., the definitions of metaphor in Hugh Holman and William Harmon, *A Handbook to Literature,* 6th ed. (New York: Macmillan, 1992); M. M. Liberman and Edward Foster, *A Modern Lexicon of Literary Terms* (Glenview, Ill.: Scott, Foresman, 1968); and J. A. Cuddon, *A Dictionary of Literary Terms and Literary Theory,* 3rd ed. (Cambridge, Mass.: Basil Blackwell, 1991). The definitions

in these handbooks rely on analogy and comparison. The word "analogy" means different things for Frye, depending on the context. He sometimes uses "analogy" or "similarity" as a synonym for the identity of metaphor, as in this passage from Notebook 21, where he is distinguishing imaginative similarity or identity from conceptual difference:

> People think they're being iconoclastic & realistic when they ask me if there aren't differences as well as similarities in the patterns I put together. Of course there are, but that again is confusing imaginative & conceptual processes. In imaginative thought there is no real knowledge of anything but similarities (ultimately identities): knowledge of differences is merely a transition to a new knowledge of similarities. In conceptual thought analogy is tricky & misleading beyond the heuristic stage: in imaginative thought it's the *telos* of knowledge. The great ocean into which all analogy empties is the *via negativa* approach to God, which the Incarnation reverses into spring rain, the identity of God & Man. (*RT,* 215)

5. In *Centuries of Meditations* Thomas Traherne wrote, "The image of God, implanted in us, guided me to the manner wherein we were to enjoy. For since we are made in the similitude of God, we were made to enjoy after his similitude." *Centuries of Meditations,* ed. Bertram Dobell (London: P. J. & A. E. Dobell, 1908), 195. Frye's marginal annotation: "Traherne interprets image as similitude, Blake as identity. Traherne's view is the core of what is wrong with Arianism," which was said to be heretical because it denied that Jesus was of the same substance as God.

6. *Concern* is another important word in the Frye lexicon. It refers here not to existential angst but to those affairs or interests that define human consciousness. The existentially concerned person is the experientially engaged.

7. Rudolf Bultmann, "New Testament and Mythology," in Bultmann, et al., *Kerygma and Myth: A Theological Debate,* ed. Hans Werner Bartsch (1953; New York: Harper & Row, 1961), 9. Frye's views about Bultmann's position on demythologizing derive primarily from this collection.

8. Frye is using the word "tropological" here in a different sense from its use in *The Great Code,* where it is synonymous with "moral," and in *Words with Power,* 16. Here it means "figurative," from which sense Frye derives "ornamental."

9. For these expansions of kerygma, see *WP,* 111–14.

10. See a similar formulation in *LN,* 1:306.

11. In the same entry Frye says that Nietzsche's *Thus Spake Zarathustra* would be excluded from the anthology "for trying too hard."

12. See, e.g., *LN,* 1:259, 260, 303, 306, 334, 337–38, 365, 369, 394, 415, 2:660, 663, 673, 696, 702, 704, and 715.

13. Frye sees Kierkegaard as a genuinely prophetic figure but thinks he could never prevent conceptual rhetoric from usurping the kerygmatic. See *LN,* 1:202, 342, and 365–66.

14. See *FS*, 114; *AC*, 73–82; *WP*, 59–61; *MM*, 97, 232–33; and *GC*, 59–61.

15. For Frye's gloss on Luke 17:21, see *GC*, 54–55, 130.

16. Frye, "Notes for a Commentary on *Milton*," in *The Divine Vision: Studies in the Poetry and Art of William Blake*, ed. Vivian de Sola Pinto (London: Gollancz, 1957), 107.

17. Although Frye does not say so, identity *as* is decentered metaphor.

18. These examples are apocalyptic identifications. Demonically, the individual images of the waste land, the leviathan, the Great Whore, and so on (each identified *as* itself) are also identified *with* Satan or Antichrist.

19. Frye's conception of spirit is indebted to Paul's idea of the spiritual body (*soma pneumatikon*), as well as to Hegel. See *DV*, 14, 45.

20. Here is a highly selective list of meanings that Frye attaches to "identity" in his *Late Notebooks:* the opposite of difference; a link to a lost human nature; the differentiation of one's individuality from another; a synonym for identification, in the sense of a character's being recognized by some token or feature; the reverse of the carrying-out-of-death ritual; union with the powers of nature, as in primitive magic and Paleolithic cave drawings, or the recovery of these lost powers; the both-and perspective, as in the Jesus of Nazareth–Messiah Christ opposition; the continuity of existence over time; renewal at another level of existence (resurrection); Martin Buber's world of "relation"; the premetaphorical world in Homer and the Bible; our pluralistic culture; mystical union; the result of the juxtaposition of images; one's social function; characteristics derived from experience in time; what is characterized by otherness; the state "in which something other than man was yet something that he was"; and Lévy-Bruhl's *participation mystique*. As for the fluidity of his ideas, Frye remarks in Notebook 50, "In my younger days a senior colleague, disconcerted by my leaps in metaphorical identifications, said, 'Well, you can just do anything, then.' You cannot, if you are speaking with some fluency, 'do anything,' but you can express anything" (*LN*, 1:295–96).

21. See, e.g., "The Survival of Eros in Poetry," in *MM*, 44–59; and *WP*, chap. 6.

22. The identification of the Word and the reader is the end of a progression: "With the fourth or Word phase . . . two things become the same thing. So we have the Thunderer-Father stage, the Son-Mother stage, the Spirit-Bride stage, & the Word-Reader stage" (*RT*, 333).

23. *LN*, 1:88, 193, 196, 204, 2:555.

24. See also *RT*, 78, 158, 159, 174, 210, 218, 247, 344, 589. In *RT*, 600, Frye cites Milton's *Christian Doctrine* as the source of the phrase "word of God in the heart." He is referring apparently to the following passage: "Under the gospel we possess, as it were, a two-fold Scripture: one external, which is the written word, and the other internal, which is the Holy Spirit, written in the hearts of believers" (chap. 30, par. 14). Frye distinguishes between art that takes

possession, as in "the mob frenzies of the Bacchanals, the self-hypnotism of the shaman, the hysteria of the sorcerer," and the human possession of art. In the latter, the ironic distancing of the poetic metaphor is at work (*LN*, 1:16).

25. "The spiritual world is the order of being in which what is in this world expressible only by metaphor becomes existential. To reach this we have to go beyond the unities of myth and metaphor to a completely decentered and interpenetrating universe: the stage represented by the decentered Bible" (*LN*, 1:188).

26. Cf. "I've often said that a man's religion is defined by what he wants to identify himself with" (*TBN*, 293).

27. For "myth(s) to live by," see *LN*, 1:240, 242, 306; *WP*, 117, 144; *DV*, 17, 76; *RT*, 378. Although Frye was obviously familiar with Campbell's work, there is no evidence that he had read *Myths to Live By: How We Re-Create Ancient Legends in Our Daily Lives to Release Human Potential* (New York: Viking, 1972). Frye reviewed Campbell's *The Masks of God: Occidental Mythology* in *Book Week* 22 (March 1964): 6, 19, and his library included annotated copies of Campbell's *Hero with a Thousand Faces, The Masks of God: Occidental Mythology,* and *A Skeleton Key to Finnegans Wake,* as well as Campbell's editions of Heinrich Zimmer's *The King and the Corpse* and *Philosophies of India.* For the references to Campbell in Frye's work, see *AC*, 361; "Letter to the Editor," *Parabola* 1 (Winter 1976): 4; "Jungian Criticism," in *Harper Handbook to Literature* (New York: Harper & Row, 1985), 255; *LN*, 1:154, 308, 2:444, 562; *TBN*, 134, 285; *RT*, 136; *WP*, xiii. Although Frye refers to Campbell's *Hero with a Thousand Faces* as early as 1957, we know from *RT*, 136, that he did not actually read the book until sometime after 1969 or 1970.

28. Frye calls his four levels of vision a "seven-storey mountain" because it has three transitional stages. The essential features of this series of speculations can be represented diagrammatically as follows:

Chart 8. Four levels of vision: Seven-storey mountain, Notebook 15 (late 1960s?)

Level 1
Simple perception of time and space; polytheism

Level 1½
Dialectical negation of perception via Gestalt or centripetal grasp of verbal structure; *Aufhebung* of time and space

Level 2
Level of knowledge; perception of divine creator; *quid credas;* monotheism; continuity of all-encompassing circumferential mind. Hegel's *Phenomenology* tries to reach level 4, but as "System"; it is 2nd-level mirage; Creator-Father vision

Level 2½
Annihilation of creation by *kenosis;* transfer of creative power to humanity; dialectical negating of god

Level 3
Existential and normally godless level; existence negated into nothingness. *Aufhebung* is immortality; *quid agas;* continuity expressed by metaphors of dance, exuberance, gaiety; re-creates level 1; clarity of perception transformed into spontaneity; Son of god is born in human beings; creating Son vision

Level 3½
Level of physical death; faith burned up, drowned, buried; point at which historical cycle ends and begins again; spirit as otherness; continuity not possible because of negation of death; resembles 2nd level but is beyond experience. Moses dies on Mt. Pisgah; Nietzsche's vision of superman; Marx's vision of transcendence of history; embryos or neo-golems

Level 4
Level of Pure Spirit; Jesus ascends and Spirit descends; Joshua leads conquest of New Canaan

---

29. Frye uses the cryptic phrase "book on its side" several times in the notebooks as a shorthand reference for the book he intended to write following his large "third book." In *RT,* 182, he identifies the book turned-on-its-side with Ignoramus, the seventh volume in the projected ogdoad, and in *TBN,* 324, with Anticlimax, the third projected volume. We look more closely at this enigmatic shorthand in chap. 5.

30. The invitation to present the Birks Lectures came to Frye on 16 December 1969. Eric G. Jay, dean of the faculty of divinity at McGill University, invited him to lecture in the fall of 1971. Frye accepted the invitation, saying that he would speak on the typology of the Bible, but he was unusually circumspect in his reply to Jay, insisting that he not be required to produce a manuscript for publication and that the lectures not be taped or otherwise recorded. Frye presented three lectures in October 1971 under the general title "Revelation and Response." The two lectures he gave on 5 October were "The City of the Sun" and "The Burning Bush"; the lecture on 6 October was entitled "The Postponed Vision." In Notebook 24 Frye thinks that the Birks Lectures might follow a three-awareness pattern—"the light-dark dialectic of the Father, of the journey of the Logos through the seven creative stages, and of the decentralized interpenetration of the Spirit" (*TBN,* 282). John Ayre says that the lectures were linked with the book on the Bible (336), which would be another ten years in the making. In accepting the invitation Frye indicated that he might be "speaking from notes, and that consequently there is not likely to be a manuscript" (letter to Eric G. Jay, 23 December 1969). Frye apparently did speak only from notes, as no manuscript for the lectures is among his papers.

31. Dolzani, introduction to *TBN,* lii.

32. Frye was attracted to certain features of Julian Jaynes's argument in *The Origin of Consciousness and the Breakdown of the Bicameral Mind* (Boston: Houghton Mifflin, 1976), particularly his idea that consciousness is based on the human ability to think metaphorically and analogically. See *LN,* 1:147, 148–50, 366; *WP,* 50. What Frye distrusted in Jaynes's thesis was the notion that anything beyond consciousness can be seen as a "breakdown" or "hallucination."

33. See above, chap. 2, n. 69.

34. "Hear the voice of the Bard" is from Blake's *Introduction* to *Songs of Experience,* line 1.

35. Daniel 2:25 (NRSV); "like the son of God" in the AV. The phrase "form of the fourth," what Frye calls the "elusive final breakthrough" in *TBN,* 199, does not appear in Frye's published works, except in his quotation from the book of Daniel in *FS,* 272, but in the notebooks and diaries the phrase is used repeatedly to refer to a mysterious presence of some kind, often spiritual, or excluded initiative. See, e.g., *LN,* 1:413; *TBN,* 283, 302; 7.2, 39, 191, 231; 36.149; 8.35, 191; 9.147; and *D,* 77, 78, 284, 285, 338.

36. On projection and its recovery, see *GC,* 24; *MM,* 111–12, 138–39; 54-3.11, 12; 54-4.106, 118, 157; *LN,* 1:86, 299; 2:448, 569–70.

37. While both words are slippery, "awareness" in Frye ordinarily applies to external perception, and "consciousness" to one's internal feelings or intuitions. One can understand the reason for Frye's substitution of the latter for the former.

38. On *participation mystique,* see *AC,* 295–96; *LN,* 1:16, 2:503; and *MM,* 113. There is no evidence that Frye had read Lévy-Bruhl. His source for *participation mystique* was doubtless Jung, a considerable portion of whose work Frye knew well.

39. The Blake reference is from his "Annotations to Swedenborg," in *Complete Poetry and Prose,* 604.

40. "[I]n the New Testament love is regarded not as one virtue among others but as the only virtue there is, and one which is possible only to God and to the spirit of man, a virtue which, in Paul's language, believes and hopes everything [1 Cor. 13:7], and thereby includes all the other virtues because, outside the order of love, faith and hope are not necessarily virtues at all" ("On the Bible," in *NFR,* 164). "Charity is not only the greatest of virtues, but the only virtue there is" ("Northrop Frye," an interview with Bill Moyers, in *A World of Ideas,* 504). See also the commissioning in "Baccalaureate Service (IV)," in *NFR,* 373.

41. Regarding the association of nature and love, Frye thinks it is no accident that ecology and feminism have come to the forefront of consciousness at about the same time (*WP,* 225). Cf. "The only thing that gives him [N]ietzsche away—and I haven't got the clue to that yet—is the unvarying contempt of women in his writing. Blake is disturbing enough on this, but at least his poetry is concerned with nameless shadowy females that are not women. The

spirit *and the bride* say come, and Nietzsche's self-transcending man is a male. Sublimating love through violence (will to *power*) won't work" (*LN,* 1:389).

42. The observation gets repeated, though without the personal reference, in *Words with Power:*

> [I]n Blake we have the conception of the "Emanation" or "concentering vision," the feminine principle that expands into the totality of what is loved. . . . In our day Jungian psychology has developed the conception of the anima, or feminine element in a male psyche, with symbolic affinities with nature. Before Jung had clarified his conception, however, Rilke had produced a poem called "Wendung" (turning), where he says that he has internalized a large body of images in his earlier work, and that these images now form a single creature or "maiden within." We also referred earlier to one of Pound's final fragments, beginning:
>
> > M'amour, m'amour,
> > what do I love and
> >   where are you?
>
> Part of the answer, at least, is the "paradiso terrestre" which, he says, the *Cantos* were an attempt to construct. (*WP,* 199–200)

In his notebook Frye writes a bit later, "I have discovered something of the reality of love in losing Helen" (*LN,* 1:156).

43. At one point Frye even considered the ascending movement in Hegel's *Phenomenology of Spirit* to be a climb up the ladder of love. See *LN,* 2:499.

44. Frye picks up the phrase from Keats's letters, first uses it in *SR,* 161, and returns to it in his notebooks for *The Great Code* (*RT,* 255) and *Words with Power* (*LN,* 1:148, 308, 358, 371). In the first two of these passages from *LN* Frye says that he prefers "spirit-making" to "soul-making," a preference he often expresses in other contexts in his late work.

45. Of all the other things that make Frye nervous about doctrine, the idea of reincarnation, part of the Roman Catholic doctrine of purgatory, gives him pause: "Purgatory in Catholic doctrine is a concession to reincarnation. But it's hard to see how reincarnation, with its total loss of memory at each return, can lead to spiritual regeneration" (*LN,* 2:672).

46. Notebook 45, in *RT,* 380–412. Frye identified the last half-dozen cantos of the *Purgatorio* through the ninth canto of the *Paradiso* with his Eros vision, thus conceiving the structure of the *Commedia* as having four rather than three parts: "I've always felt that Dante's trinitarian obsessions made him fail to see the real fourfold form of his poem, Purgatorio 27 to Paradiso 9 being the missing fourth world and scherzo movement" (*TBN,* 339). The Eros vision may begin for Frye at *Purgatorio* 26 (see 10.11) or at *Purgatorio* 28 (see *TBN,* 130), but in any case Frye sees these sixteen or so cantos as belonging to the pastoral world of Eden, Blake's Beulah, and other comic complexes. See Dolzani's note in *TBN,* 380, n. 5.

47. "The essential progress of man upward to his own original home is thus a purgatorial progress, whether an actual doctrine of purgatory is involved or not." Frye, "Vision and Cosmos," in *Biblical Patterns in Modern Literature,* ed. David H. Hirsch and Nehama Aschkensay (Chico, Calif.: Scholars Press, 1984), 9. See a very similar formulation in "The Survival of Eros in Poetry," in *MM,* 45.

48. On the purgatorial vision of Spenser's faerie world in Frye's books, see *WP,* 300; *MD,* 82; *SR,* 129; and *SeS,* 99; in the notebooks, see *RT,* 371; and *LN,* 1:190, 371.

49. See *CR,* 46–47.

50. "Vision and Cosmos," 10. Frye's rather startling identification of God with purgatory, following the suggestion in Hans Küng's *Eternal Life? Life after Death as a Medical, Philosophical, and Theological Problem* (Garden City, N.Y.: Image Books, 1985), is an example of *identity-with,* at the same time revealing Frye's radical view of divine immanence. See *LN,* 1:308.

51. "Vision and Cosmos," 8–9; *MD,* 82.

52. Cf. "The language that lifts us clear of the merely plausible and the merely credible is the language of the spirit; the language of the spirit is, Paul tells us, the language of love, and the language of love is the only language that we can be sure is spoken and understood by God" (*DV,* 20–21).

3. Vision

1. See, e.g., "Romanticism," pt. 3, in *SE,* 53–65; "The Relation of Religion to the Art Forms of Music and Drama," *SE,* 313–43; "Bach Recital," *Saturday Night,* 30 November 1935, 8; "Hart House Quartet," *Saturday Night,* 7 December 1935, 23; "Music and the Savage Breast," *Canadian Forum* 18 (April 1938): 451–53 (rpt. in *RW,* 14–18); "Music in Poetry," *University of Toronto Quarterly* 11 (January 1942): 167–79; "Music in the Movies," *Canadian Forum* 22 (December 1942): 275–76 (rpt. in *RW,* 24–28); "The World as Music and Idea in Wagner's *Parsifal,*" *Carleton Germanic Papers* 12 (1984): 37–49 (rpt. in *MM,* 340–55); "Introduction: Lexis and Melos," in *Sound and Poetry: English Institute Essays, 1956,* ed. Northrop Frye (New York: Columbia Univ. Press, 1957), ix–xxvii. Notebook 5 is devoted to Mendelssohn, Schumann, Haydn, Mozart, et al.; as early as 1934 Frye was planning to write an Emmanuel College thesis on "the development of the Christian tradition in music," and Notebook 5 appears to date from that period. Notebook 17 is devoted to William Byrd, and Notebook 20 also contains notes on music. Frye's letters to Helen Kemp and his diaries are filled with references to music. See also Frye's interview with Ian Alexander, "Music in My Life," in *WGS,* 269–79.

2. The other two categories in Aristotle's list of the qualitative parts of dramatic tragedy, *ethos* and *lexis,* figure importantly in the way Frye's organizes *Anatomy of Criticism,* but they generally have less significance in his other work as critical *terms.* In his later work, *ethos* expands into existential and social concern, and *lexis* expands into his general theory of language.

3. For the references to these various epiphanies, in the notebooks and elsewhere, see chap. 1, n. 41.

4. For Frye's notebook accounts of the kernels, see *RT,* 80, 117, 189–90, 194, 195, 196; 18.60; 32.102; 35.46, 52, 70; 36.84, 85; 7.213; *TBN,* 194, 239–40. See also *D,* 330. In Frye's published writing, the first reference to kernels as seeds of longer forms—in this case scriptural forms—is in *AC,* 324. See also "Literature, History, and Language," in *Bulletin of the Midwest Modern Language Association* 12 (Fall 1979): 3; and *CP,* 41–42. Charm and riddle are said to be "generic" kernels in *SM,* 123.

5. "When I get time to read anything I read Rabelais," Frye wrote in 1935. Fifty years later he says in one set of his typed notes, "I've picked up my copies of Rabelais again, as I always do when I get to thinking about a book on the verbal universe. Rabelais is probably the writer who most clearly grasped all the dimensions of language and verbal communication" (*LN,* 2:458).

6. For these associations, see *TBN,* 162, 178, 231, 254; 10.21; 30k.3.

7. In the interview with Ian Alexander (n. 1, above), Frye proposed the playing of five compositions during the course of the interview: Schubert's *Impromptu,* opus 90, no. 1, in C minor; "I am a courtier brave and serious," from Gilbert and Sullivan's *The Gondoliers;* "O Isis and Osiris," from act 2 of Mozart's *The Magic Flute;* Sir Hubert Parry's arrangement of Blake's *Jerusalem;* Clementi's sonata *Didone Abbandonata,* opus 50, no. 3, in G minor; and the fugue at the end of Verdi's *Falstaff.* When Alexander asked Frye whether he agreed with the sentiments of the Verdi finale—that the world is all jest—Frye replied, "[I]t was a very profound devotional, religious poet, George Herbert, who said, 'All things are big with jest; nothing's that plain / But may be witty, if thou has the vein.' I've always had a strong interest in the nature of comedy and the way in which even tragedy seems to fit inside as a kind of episode in a total story which is comic. While I'm not sure that everything in the world is simply a jest, there is a point at which the witty and the oracular come together" (*WGS,* 278–79).

8. Pausanias, *Description of Greece:*

> After his ascent from *Trophonius* the inquirer is again taken in hand by the priests, who set him upon a chair called the chair of Memory, which stands not far from the shrine, and they ask of him, when seated there, all he has seen or learned. After gaining this information they then entrust him to his relatives. These lift him, paralyzed with terror and unconscious both of himself and of his surroundings, and carry him to the building where he lodged before with Good Fortune and the Good Spirit. Afterwards, however, he will recover all his faculties, and the power to laugh will return to him. (Bk. 9, chap. 39, par. 13, trans. W. H. S. Jones)

Frye makes this point in *SeS,* where he cites both Plutarch and Pausanias. In Plutarch's account, in his *On the Divine Sign of Socrates* (sec. 22), Timarchus, a friend of Socrates', is said to have emerged with a radiant countenance after two nights and one day in the cave. See also Robert Graves, *The Greek Myths* (New York: George Braziller, 1959), 180. Sara Toth suggests that there is perhaps a Christian analogue of all this in the *risus paschalis,* the loud laughter that rang out in medieval churches from funny stories provided by medieval priests at the end of their sober Lenten sermons (personal correspondence).

9. François Rabelais, *The Histories of Gargantua and Pantagruel,* trans. J. M. Cohen (Harmondsworth, Eng.: Penguin, 1955), 711 (bk. 5, last par.).

10. Suzuki's introduction to *The Lankavatara Sutra,* xvii.

11. *The Lankavatara Sutra,* 13–14; marginal comment (on 14) in Frye's copy, in the Northrop Frye Library. Frye also remarks on the Buddha's laugh in 33.34.

12. In one of his many "doodles" where he outlines sets of opposing pairs (e.g., metaphorical/metonymic, centripetal/centrifugal) Frye includes the pair "oracular magic/witty recognition" (*LN,* 1:400).

13. Benjamin Walker, *Beyond the Body: The Human Double and the Astral Planes* (London: Routledge & Kegan Paul, 1977), 194. Frye's annotated copy is in the Northrop Frye Library.

14. Nicol Macnichol, ed., *Hindu Scriptures: Hymns from the Rigveda, Five Upanishads, the Bhagavadgita* (London: Dent, 1938), 32; annotated copy in the Northrop Frye Library.

15. William Blake, *The Mental Traveller,* line 6.

16. For the displacement-condensation distinction, see *WP,* 148–49; *LN,* 1:308, 399–400; *MM,* 30, 359; and "Response," *Eighteenth-Century Studies* 24 (Winter 1990–91): 245–46.

17. One of his outlines for *The Secular Scripture* reveals that Frye planned to entitle chap. 10 "From the Dice Throw to the Recovery of Laughter" (54-9, holograph notes at the bottom of p. 1 of the typescript).

18. Frye, "Rencontre," in *LS,* 103. Cf. his remark in Notebook 19: "All the things in literature that haunt me most have to do with katabasis" (*TBN,* 76).

19. In Notebook 53 Frye says that the St. Clair revelation occurred on New Year's Day a few years after the 1951 Seattle epiphany. But from his account of an experience on St. Clair Ave. on 1 January 1950, it appears that the St. Clair experience happened six or so months before the Seattle one. See *LN,* 2:621, and *D,* 215.

20. In Notebook 21, however, Frye does link the Edmonton "vision," as he calls it, with the Seattle and St. Clair epiphanies. The Edmonton vision had to do with the movement from alienation to identity. See *RT,* 226–27.

21. Letter to John Paul Fullerton, 27 June 1984, in the Northrop Frye Fonds, 1988 accession, box 38, file 14. "I'm a Blakean, a visionary disciple," Frye writes in one of his diaries (*D,* 12).

22. William Blake, *Milton,* bk. 1, pl. 15, lines 21–25, in *Complete Poetry and Prose,* 109.

23. Expanding on infinity and eternity in a letter to a friend, Frye writes,

Revelation encourages us to think in terms of infinity and eternity, not in the mathematical sense, but in the religious sense. As we experience time, the present, the only part of it we do experience, never quite exists. As we experience space, the centre or the "here," never quite exists either— everything we experience in space is "there." Under the impact of revelation the whole fallen world turns inside out, into an eternal now and an infinite here. In terms of the Kantian distinction between the thing perceived and the thing in itself, we never see the thing in itself because we are the thing in itself. Reality is the immediate data of ordinary experience universalized—that it why it is revealed to the childlike rather than the sophisticated in us. The beginning of the vision of eternity is the child's realization that his own home is the circumference of the universe as far as he is concerned. The end of it is the regenerate Christian's realization that the universe is a city of God, the home of the soul, and the body of Jesus.

Letter to Hugh E. Moorhouse, dated only "14 November." Moorhouse believes the letter was written before 1950 (personal communication, 22 September 1994).

24. The reference is to *aitherios Dinos,* the "ethereal vortex" or "heavenly whirl" in Aristophanes, *The Clouds,* in *Eleven Comedies* (New York: Horace Liveright, 1930), 320 (line 380 in the Greek text). The satire comes from Socrates' pulling Strepsiades' leg about the cause of thunder. He is doubtless also punning on *Dinos* and *Dios* (Zeus).

25. The reversal in *Oedipus the King* is, of course, closely connected with the ironic reversal of the central metaphors: Teiresias (the seer) is literally blind but can figuratively see; Oedipus can literally see and is renowned for his knowledge and insight but is figuratively blind to his own situation; then at the reversal Oedipus is able to figuratively see only after he has literally blinded himself.

26. For the notebook entries having to do with the vortex, see 8.4, 65, 140, 170, 177, 191, 196; *RT,* 47, 96, 217, 227, 332; *LN,* 1:46, 2:436, 437, 462, 690; 31.31, 53; 33.34; 34.23, 78, 99; *TBN,* 72, 77, 107, 179, 191, 197, 260; 7.6, 32, 33, 46, 51, 66, 70, 71, 79, 81, 82, 86, 140, 149; 18.16.

27. The paper was published four years later in *Shenandoah* 39, no. 3 (1989): 47–64, and then reprinted in *MM,* 93–107.

28. The word appears more than 90 times in *The Great Code* and *Words with Power,* 159 times in the notebooks for these two volumes, and 119 times in *The "Third Book" Notebooks.*

29. In the 1991 accession, box 24, file 8.ee, pars. 4 and 9. Frye picked up the "Hans Denck principle" from E. J. Furcha, ed., *Spirit within Structure: Essays in Honor of George Johnston,* (Allison Park, Pa.: Pickwick, 1983), 112. See *LN,* 1:6, 2:732 n. 13.

30. Cf. this passage from Notebook 50:

[T]rying to reduce belief to the credible is a waste of time and desolation of spirit. One doesn't bother to believe the credible: the credible is believed already, by definition. There's no adventure of the mind there. (Didn't Coleridge say that Donne was a Christian because it would have been so much easier to be an atheist?) Belief is the Wright brothers getting a heavier-than-air-machine off the ground after the most distinguished scientists had "proved" that it was impossible. In short, belief is the creation that turns the illusory into the real. Being kerygmatic, it emerges on the further side of the imaginative. (*LN,* 1:313)

Frye is remembering one of Coleridge's marginalia: "Themes that rule, while they create, the moral will—this is Donne! He was an orthodox Christian, only because he could have been an Infidel more easily, & therefore willed to be a Christian: & he was a Protestant, because it enabled him to lash about to the Right & the Left—and without a motive to say better things for the Papists than they could say for themselves." Samuel Taylor Coleridge, *Marginalia,* ed. George Whalley (Princeton, N.J.: Princeton Univ. Press, 1984), 2:220.

31. In his typed notes for this essay Frye does say that he "can't honestly distinguish the two words" (1991, box 28, file 3.ee, par. 1).

32. See *DV,* 19; for the interview, see *NFC,* 186–87; for "Symbols," see *RW,* 252. The early formulation in *Fearful Symmetry* is in Frye's commentary "All Religions are One" (28).

33. Cf. "One essential link is the identification of vision with hope. 'Fear and Hope are—Vision,' said Blake. Hope is the basis for the model-thinking so closely associated with mythical concern." From Frye's typescript notes for "The Dialectic of Belief and Vision," in 1991 accession, box 28, file 3ee, par. 27. For Frye's other commentaries on Heb. 11:1, see *RT,* 239; *DV,* 19–20; *NFC,* 186–87; *LN,* 1:69, 71, 73, 74, 195, 309, 2:431, 432, 597, 613; *WP,* 128–29; *MM,* 226; and *NFR,* 8, 131, 160–61. In Notebook 44 Frye writes, "The hypostasis of the hoped-for, the elenchos of the unseen. If I could articulate that in my own words, I could burn the straw and pass on (I'm thinking of St. Thomas Aquinas on his deathbed)" (*LN,* 1:188–89). Earlier Frye *had* tried to articulate it in his sermon on Heb. 11:1, "Substance and Evidence" (*NFR,* 321–27).

34. Hegel, *Phenomenology of Spirit,* 294–97. See also p. 15.

35. Cf. "I have no interest or belief in absolute knowledge: I may be climbing the same spiral mountain, but by a different path" (*LN,* 1:188). In Notebook 50, Frye refers to Hegel's *Phenomenology of Spirit* as an *Odyssey:* "the Begriff starts at the hidden centre & ends *as* the circumference" (*LN,* 1:362), and in Notebook 11e he writes, "My original hunch about Hegel was that if his absolute knowledge were thought of imaginatively, it would take in the existential" (*RT,* 337).

36. In "Reconsidering Levels of Meaning" Frye says that "for the last century or so, I suppose most of our philosophy has really been founded on Hegel and Hegel's *Phenomenology of Spirit,* which is a great voyage of intellectual discovery ending with the principle that spirit can be understood only by spirit" (unpublished typescript, p. 8).

37. In one of his notebooks Frye does say, "The closing passages of Hegel's Phenomenology include my distinction in GC [*The Great Code*] between the panoramic and the participating apocalypse" (*LN*, 2:650).

38. Frye uses the same expression throughout the 1980s. See, e.g., *CR*, 68; *WP*, 73; *GC*, 23; "The Survival of Eros in Poetry," in *Romanticism and Contemporary Criticism*, ed. Morris Eaves and Michael Fischer (Ithaca, N.Y.: Cornell Univ. Press, 1986), 31; "The Koine of Myth," *MM*, 16; "The Expanding World of Metaphor," *MM*, 113; and *LN*, 2:504.

39. "Ladder" is one of the few concrete words Hegel uses in the Preface to the *Phenomenology*, a word that Frye marked in his own copy of the book (14).

40. See *LN*, 1:19, 258–59, 338; 2:436, 452, 468, 499, 683, 686. In *WP* Frye calls attention to the similarity between his four modes of language and the medieval four levels of meaning, though he adds that his theory of language is, "with many qualifications," closer to Hegel than to Dante (4). Frye's most expansive use of Dante's theory of polysemous meaning is the Second Essay of *AC*. In one of his pre-*Anatomy* notebooks Frye claims that dreams can be interpreted in the same four-level context: "The therapeutic role of dreams must ultimately be that of enlarging vision, & dreams should be interpreted on the same principles as works of art: observe faithfully (literal), note all references to external events (allegorical), place in relation to your own libidinous urges (moral) & then aim for anagogic completeness" (*RT*, 60).

41. "Reconsidering Levels of Meaning," typescript of an unpublished lecture, p. 9.

42. "Litera gesta docet, / Quid credas allegoria, / Moralis quid agas, / Quo tendas anagogia" (The letter teaches what was done, allegory what to believe, morals teach how to act, anagogy where you will go), attributed to Augustine of Denmark (354–430).

43. I am indebted to the verso of Richard Outram's broadsheet *Word at Midwinter* for reminding me of Frye's use of *quo tendas* in *WTC*.

44. In the 1991 accession, box 28, file 4ee, par. 2.

45. For Frye's connection with the Longinian tradition, see Caterina Nella Cotrupi, *Northrop Frye and the Poetics of Process* (Toronto: Univ. of Toronto Press, 2000).

46. Percy Bysshe Shelley, "A Defence of Poetry," in *Criticism: The Major Statements*, ed. Charles Kaplan, 2nd ed. (New York: St. Martin's, 1986), 332.

47. Cf. this passage from *Myth and Metaphor*:

But as soon as we enter the world of design, beauty, play, and the assimilating of nature and art, we begin to wonder whether creation itself, rather than the exercising of consciousness within it, is not the primary human activity. The Romantics who followed Kant developed a conception of "imagination," designed to express this. Imagination is a constructive, unifying, and fully conscious faculty that excludes no aspect of consciousness, whether rational or emotional. As such, it is for many Romantics the primary activity of human consciousness. In Blake, for example, the word "reason" usually has an unfavourable sense, because for him it means the Cartesian split between subject and object that all creation begins by trying to overcome. But the words "mental" and "intellectual" in Blake are consistently synonyms for imaginative. For Shelley, the language of imagination is the key to human freedom and equality, because it is purely constructive, in contrast to the language of assertions that carry their own negations along with them, and are consequently aggressive and hostile. For Coleridge, there is a "primary" imagination, an existential consciousness very close, it seems to me, to Kant's practical reason, and a "secondary" one which embodies itself in its artifacts. (179–80)

48. See "Long, Sequacious Notes," in *NFCL*, 170–77, a review essay of Kathleen Coburn's edition of Coleridge's selected prose, *Inquiring Spirit* (1951). Frye's copy of the book is extensively annotated, containing 484 markings and marginal comments. In "Literature as a Critique of Pure Reason" he says that Coleridge's primary imagination is very close to Kant's practical reason (*MM*, 180).

49. See, e.g., Barfield, *What Coleridge Thought,* chaps. 6 and 7.

50. In 1951, ten years before his essay on Coleridge, Frye had written that the imagination for Coleridge was not so much a constructive power as a reproductive one (*FI*, 29–30). Since it is not possible to say whether the great chapter that Coleridge planned to write on the imagination would have confirmed this, it is perhaps better to take Coleridge at his word in chaps. 13 and 14 of the *Biographia Literaria.*

51. Cf., from Notebook 3: "Do I want a new religion? No, not in doctrine, anyway: I don't find at any level of my mind an ideal of belief. One dead, one powerless to be born: there must be some other way of formulating the whole problem. Seeing is believing, must be the answer: if I want to believe more than I see I'd better improve my seeing apparatus" (*RT,* 70).

52. Blake, *Complete Poetry and Prose,* 664, 273.

53. Samuel Alexander, *Space, Time, and Deity: The Gifford Lectures at Glasgow, 1916–1918* (London: Macmillan, 1966), 23, top margin; copy in Northrop Frye Library.

54. Coleridge, *Biographia Literaria,* chap. 14.

55. Sidney, "An Apology for Poetry," in *The Critical Tradition,* ed. David H. Richter (New York: St. Martin's, 1989), 139.

56. Cf. "Nearly every time we use a preposition we are using a spatial myth or an unconscious diagram" ("Myth as Information," in *NFCL,* 70). A similar statement appears in "The Transferability of Literary Concepts," *The Association of the Princeton Graduate Alumni* (Report of the Fifth Conference held at the Graduate College, Princeton University, 30–31 December 1955), 59. In his

1949 diary Frye says that someday he may write a book "on the geometry of vision, which will analyze the diagrammatic patterns present in thought which emerge unconsciously in the metaphors of speech, particularly prepositions (up, down, beside & the like)" (D, 78).

57. Cf. this passage in Paul Tillich's *Systematic Theology* (Chicago: Univ. of Chicago Press, 1956), which Frye read and annotated: "Ecstasy is not a negation of reason; it is a state of mind in which reason is beyond itself, that is, beyond its subject-object structure. In being beyond itself reason does not deny itself. 'Ecstatic reason' remains reason; it does not receive anything irrational or antirational—which it could not do without self-destruction—but it transcends the basic conditions of finite rationality, the subject-object structure" (1:112). I am indebted to Richard Outram for pointing me to this passage.

58. For the mystics "no word, such as 'Being,' is strictly applicable to God, because words are finite and God is not: the real God is 'hidden,' beyond all thought, and *a fortiori* beyond words" (GC, 12). Deut. 30:19 presents the life-death dilemma "from a perspective that only God is assumed to be able to attain: a concern for the continuation of human life in time that goes far beyond the purely imaginative, together with a view of the human situation that goes equally far beyond the purely historical" (GC, 52). Such metaphors for the "eternal" as peace, rest, and repose "are metaphors drawn from death, and seem hardly definitive for a conception of something genuinely beyond life" (GC, 73). "The real world is beyond time" (GC, 76). "[T]o call the Bible and the person of Christ by the same name . . . is a conception of identity that goes far beyond 'juxtaposition,' because there are no longer two things, but one thing in two aspects" (GC, 77). "[I]t is only through the study of works of human imagination that we can make any real contact with the level of vision beyond faith" (GC, 231–32).

59. The references are from *WP,* 116–17, 130, 62, 71, and 76.

60. Susanne Langer, *The Practice of Philosophy* (New York: Henry Holt, 1930), 190. Frye records his debt to Langer's idea of "naïve induction" in *AC,* 357.

61. For Spirit knowing itself as Spirit, see Hegel, *Phenomenology of Spirit,* 483.

62. Although Cicero connected *religio* with *relegere,* "to read over again," later writers have preferred the etymology of *religare,* "to bind again" (*OED*).

63. Frye often uses these phrases synonymously. Projection refers to the tendency in mythological times for men and woman to attribute their fears and desires to the gods. It is a manifestation of the will to identify, as we see in the example Frye frequently calls on, the Paleolithic cave paintings, where this will becomes ecstatic metaphor. Later, projection is kidnapped by ideology. Frye believes that we recover what we have lost—the original sense of projection in myth. Re-creation, he says in one set of notes, is part of the recovery process (54-3.12). Recovery is possible because the kernels of myth have been retained as the excluded initiative of ideology.

64. Terence Cave, "Northrop Frye: Recognition at the Center," in *Recog-*

nitions: A Study in Poetics (Oxford: Clarendon Press, 1988), 190–99. Even though Cave notes a great deal of "semantic slippage" in Frye's various accounts of *anagnorisis,* he nevertheless believes that Frye "gives the lover of recognition scenes better value for money than almost anything else in the history of poetics" (199). See also David Gay's study of recognition as a central focus in Frye's late work, "'The Humanized God': Biblical Paradigms of Recognition in Frye's Final Three Books," in *Northrop Frye and the Afterlife of the Word,* ed. James M. Kee, Semeia 89 (Atlanta: Society of Biblical Literature, 2002), 39–57.

65. See Aristotle's *Poetics,* chaps. 10, 11, and 16.

66. Northrop Frye, "Plot," in *The Harper Handbook to Literature* (New York: Harper & Row, 1985), 353. Frye wrote the entry on plot and seventeen other entries in the *Handbook.* The hundreds of other entries were written by his co-authors, Sheridan Baker and George Perkins.

67. Cave also notes how the focus of Frye's view of *anagnorisis* slides back and forth between plot and reader. See *Recognitions,* 194–95. For Frye's additional comments on the two meanings of *anagnorisis,* see 11b.37; "The Road of Excess," in *Myth and Symbol: Critical Approaches to Literature,* ed. Bernice Slote (Lincoln: Univ. of Nebraska Press, 1963), 7–8; *MD,* 4; and *DV,* 43.

68. In both Plato and Aristotle *anagnosis* means reading, as it does in Acts 13:15, 2 Cor. 3:14, and 1 Tim. 4:13. There is no warrant for Frye's thinking that *anagnorisis* can also mean "reading." The only form of *anagnorisis* in the New Testament is *anagnorizomai* (Acts 7:13), which derives from *ana-* (in the midst) and *anagnorzio* (to know, to make known, to recognize), and translated as "made known" in the AV; the Liddell-Scott-Jones *Greek-English Lexicon* records only "recognition" for *anagnorisis.*

69. The word *anagnorisis* appears in the notebooks some sixty times; "recognition," as a literary category, hundreds and hundreds of times.

70. Frye records this response after hearing the performance by the Toronto Symphony Orchestra and the Mendelssohn Choir at the annual Bach Festival, 19 April 1950. Cf. the judgment in an earlier notebook: "I think Bach is the great Protestant poet of the Pathos: not only two Passions, but even the B minor centres on the Kyrie and the Crucifixion. Milton and Bunyan are the Protestant poets of the Agon: Blake of the Anagnorisis. I wonder, if the Mass were analyzed from this point of view, what would happen" (5.22).

71. Unpublished typescript in the 1991 accession, box 28, file 4oo, par. 129.

72. See also "Conversation about Canadian Fundamentals," black notebook binder no. 2 (PN85.C353 1971) in the CRTC Archives, p. 82; this notebook contains a typed transcript of a taped conversation among Frye, André Martin, and Rodrigue Chiasson, when Frye served as a consultant for the Canadian Radio-Television Commission in the late 1960s.

73. Unpublished typescript in 1991 accession, box 28, file 4ss, par. 23.

74. Cf. 36.89: "You can't have humanism without the idea of Renaissance or rebirth: a gigantic anagnorisis or Kierkegaardian *repetition* of past culture."

75. Cf. "Epiphany is not a new experience: it is the knowledge that one has the experience: it's recognition or anagnorisis" (*TBN,* 34).

76. Notebook 5 cannot be dated with certainty, but it appears to have been written in the mid-1930s.

77. On the importance of this conclusion, see David Gay, "'Waiting to Be Recognized': Reading as Process in Northrop Frye's *The Double Vision,*" *Christianity and Literature* 44 (Spring–Summer 1995): 327–43.

78. William Blake, letter to Thomas Butts, 22 November 1802, in *Complete Poetry and Prose,* 721. The lines were composed more than a year earlier while Blake was walking from Felpham to Lavant to see his sister.

79. The fullest account of the conventional understanding of literal meaning as it applies to the Bible is in Frye's lectures "Symbolism of the Bible," lecture 24 ("The Language of Love"), in *RT,* 601–7.

80. "A Literalist of the Imagination" is the title of chap. 4 of *FS.* For the literal as opposed to the symbolic meaning, see *FS,* 9, 142, 151, 340, 342–44, 371–72. "Literalist of the imagination" is a phrase from Marianne Moore's *Poetry,* which she adapted from Yeats's "William Blake's Illustrations to the *Divine Comedy,*" where he writes about Blake: "The limitation of his view was from the very intensity of his vision; he was a too literal realist of imagination, as others are of nature; and because he believed that the figures seen by the mind's eye, when exalted by inspiration were 'eternal existences,' symbols of divine essences, he hated every grace of style that might obscure their lineaments." William Butler Yeats, *Ideas of Good and Evil* (London: A. H. Bullen, 1903), 182. Moore provides this information in her *Collected Poems* (New York: Macmillan, 1981), 267.

81. The date of this notebook entry is uncertain, but it appears to have been written in the mid-1970s. Frye later refers to completely cutting off the word "literal" from all connections with referentiality (*RT,* 361).

82. See esp. *GC,* 56–64, 224–28. "The primary and literal meaning of the Bible, then, is its centripetal or poetic meaning" (61).

83. See *DV,* 69, and *LN,* 2:721. Frye's source for the commentary by Dante's son was William Anderson, *Dante the Maker* (London: Routledge and Kegan Paul, 1980), 347. The annotated copy in the Northrop Frye Library is the 1983 edition (London: Hutchinson).

4. The East

1. Jonathan Culler, "A Critic against the Christians," *TLS,* 23 November 1984, 1327; Terry Eagleton, *Literary Theory: An Introduction* (Minneapolis: Univ. of Minnesota Press, 1983), 199–200.

2. See *AC,* 56, 143, 156, 283, 288, 297, 317, and 324.

3. These quotations come from *D,* 322; *RT,* 227, 155; 7.53; and *MD,* 13. See also *RT,* 23, 48, and 228. D. T Suzuki translates *paravritti* as "revulsion" (*Studies in the Lankavatara Sutra,* 72, 105), and he remarks that it "somewhat cor-

responds to what is known as 'conversion' among the psychological students of religion" (xvii).

4. The Avatamsaka (Sanskrit for "garland") is known in Chinese as the Hua-yen (or "flower ornament") scripture. See chap. 1.

5. Frye struggled with these dense texts. "[T]he initial impression the [Lankavatara] Sutra makes on the candid reader [is] of an almost intolerable prolixity & obscurantism" (*RT,* 46).

6. This, in any case seems to be Frye's position, which is consistent with that of the commentator he was most familiar with, D. T. Suzuki. For a different perspective, which Frye could not have known, see Florin Giripescu Sutton, *Existence and Enlightenment in the "Lankavarata-sutra": A Study in the Ontology and Epistemology of the Yogacara School of Mahayana Buddhism* (Albany: State Univ. Press of New York, 1991).

7. Frye appears to draw his account of the similarities and differences between *cittamatra* and *vijnaptimatra* from Suzuki's introduction to *The Lankavatara Sutra,* xxi–xxviii. It is possible that he might have been familiar as well with Suzuki's distinctions in *Studies in the Lankavatara Sutra,* 278–82, though there is no direct evidence that Frye read the latter book. While Suzuki constantly reminds us that translating Eastern into Western categories necessarily violates the Eastern text, he nevertheless frames his commentary on *cittamatra* in *Studies* in both psychological (165–82) and philosophical (241–63) terms.

8. See Suzuki, introduction to *The Lankavatara Sutra,* xxi–xxviii.

9. Ibid., xl.

10. *The Lankavatara Sutra,* 58. The insertion is square brackets is Suzuki's.

11. The "unnumbered fool" is the zero or cipher card of the Tarot pack, the twenty-first card in most forms of the Greater Trumps. Frye's eighth book, about which he says very little in his notebooks, was Twilight. He conceived of it as a form that would combine the creative and the critical—something aphoristic, anagogic, erudite, imaginative, even fictional—and he proposed several models for Twilight: Anatole France's *Jardin d'épicure,* a series of learned reflections on sundry topics; Dmitry Merezhkovsky's *Atlantis/Europe;* Nietzsche's *Gaya Scienza;* Cyril Connolly's *The Unquiet Grave: A Word Cycle by Palinurus;* and Thomas Traherne's *Centuries of Meditations.* "I wouldn't want to plan such a book," Frye wrote, "as a dumping ground for things I can't work in elsewhere or as a set of echoes of what I've said elsewhere." "Such a book would feature," he added, "completely uninhibited writing" and "completely uninhibited metaphor-building" (*LN,* 1:238). Blake's "eighth eye" is the elusive vision of the unity of God and man for which we are still searching. See *FS,* 401.

12. The 108 questions are those posed by Mahamati to the Buddha in the Lankavatara Sutra, chap. 2.

13. See *TBN,* 30, 231; 13.92; and 18.123. Of the nineteen references to the Avatamsaka in the notebooks, practically all of them relate to interpenetration.

14. Frye is quoting from Suzuki's *Essays in Zen Buddhism, Third Series,* 77. No complete version of the Avatamsaka in Sanskrit is extant. The most comprehensive translation into Chinese by Siksananda at the end of the seventh century is referred to as the eighty-scroll version, distinguishing it from the first full translation by Buddhabhadra (359–429) in sixty scrolls. The Gandavyuha, sometimes identified with the Avatamsaka or the Hua-yen scripture, though complete in itself, is actually the final section of the eighty-scroll version, constituting about one-fourth of the entire Avatamsaka. Suzuki devotes most of his attention in *Essays in Zen Buddhism, Third Series,* to the Gandavyuha.

15. Cleary, *Entry into the Inconceivable,* 1–2.

16. Bodiharma, the first Chinese patriarch of Zen, "regarded the Lankavatara Sutra as the only book worth studying," and "his followers used only this sutra as their text." William A. Briggs, *Anthology of Zen* (New York: Grove Press, 1961), 17; Frye marked this passage in his copy of the book.

17. Cf. a similar statement in the seventh of Frye's lectures on the Bible, "The World of Angels," *RT,* 468.

18. See 18.74; *RT,* 322, where Frye says, "Zen is the gabbiest encourager of silence I know"; and *TBN,* 29, 73.

19. "The Koine of Myth," *MM,* 7; "The Dialectic of Belief and Vision," *MM,* 96; "Literature and the Visual Arts," *MM,* 188; and "The Mythical Approach to Creation," *MM,* 244.

20. Frye's edition of the *Bardol Thödol* was *The Tibetan Book of the Dead, or, The After-death Experiences on the Bardo Plane,* ed. W. Y. Evans-Wentz, trans. Kazi Dawa-Samdup, 2nd ed. (London: Oxford Univ. Press, 1949). The source of his comments on bardo in Notebook 3, which predates the publication of this edition by a few years, is unknown, outside of his discussions with Peter Fisher.

21. As Frye's marginal annotations reveal, he loathed all the manifestations of priestcraft in *The Tibetan Book of the Dead,* although he did enjoy a certain sardonic humor in the priest's "reading the mysteries of liberation into a dead man's ear," which reminded him of Joyce's Finnegan and the earwig symbolism. Marginal annotation in *The Tibetan Book of the Dead,* 81.

22. See *The Tibetan Book of the Dead,* 102. Frye's marginal annotation to the three states identifies them with birth, dream, and trance, respectively.

23. "There is a Moment in each Day that Satan cannot find / Nor can his Watch Fiends find it, but the Industrious find / This Moment & it multiply. & when it once is found / It renovates every Moment of the Day if rightly placed." William Blake, *Milton,* pl. 35, lines 42–45. Frye uses the phrase "timeless moment" to describe Chikhai bardo in 14.31.

24. In addition to the references in *The Great Code* and "The Journey as Metaphor," Frye refers to bardo only twice elsewhere in his published work: *SER,* 63–64, and *FI,* 229, 233. Bardo appears in eighteen entries in the diaries and sixty-five in the notebooks.

25. *The Tibetan Book of the Dead,* xl.

26. Cf. "The Tibetan conception of Bardo, an archetypal dream achieved

by the soul (or whatever it is) between death & rebirth, is something I have now to struggle with. It's Blake's Beulah, of course" (8.47).

27. *The Tibetan Book of the Dead*, 38. The dialectic of heaven and hell "looked at as a picture," Frye notes in the margin, is what makes the *Bardo Thödol* "both wise and humane."

28. See *SR*, 64 (Yeats); 33.20 (Joyce); 33.63–64 (Gogol); 31.72 (Morris).

29. Also 20.5, 10, and 30o, six paragraphs beginning "The cosmic voyage. . . ."

30. On Frye's bardo-novel fantasies, see 2.13–19, and *D*, 129–34.

31. See *D*, 131, 132, 134, 142, and the following notebook entries: 2.15, 16; *RT*, 54; 31.8, 52, 97; and 35.118.

32. The context for this point is Yeats's view of purgatory—what Yeats "dimly felt" about Protestantism. But it appears to be Frye's view as well. In one of his marginal annotations, however, Frye writes that "the Purgatorio is like this book [the *Bardo Thödol*], *our* life seen from the other side of the world" (*The Tibetan Book of the Dead*, 81).

33. In the notebooks and diaries there are more than fifty references to chess, most of which speculate on the game as an archetype.

34. Michael Dolzani's reading of the chess-in-bardo problem focuses on its associations with the *agon* and the recognition. See his introduction to *TBN*, liv–lv.

35. The last phrase is from a marginal annotation in *The Tibetan Book of the Dead*, 96.

36. Little is known of Patanjali. Whether or not he is the same Patanjali who wrote a celebrated commentary on Panini's grammar is uncertain. He appears not to have authored the sutras but to have compiled them. The date of the Yoga-Sutras is also unknown; scholars date the compilation to sometime between the second century B.C. and the fourth century A.D.

37. At the end of section 3 of his copy of the Yoga-Sutras, Frye wrote in the bottom margin, "how to become God in six easy lessons. Wonder how far anyone actually got." *The Yoga-Sutras of Patanjali*, ed. Manilal Nabhubjai Dvivedi and Pandit S. Subrahmanya, 4th ed. (Adyar, Madras: Theosophical Publishing House, 1947), 110.

38. See, e.g., Frye's annotations in Shunryu Suzuki, *Zen Mind, Beginner's Mind*, ed. Trudy Dixon (New York: Weatherhill, 1970). Frye read this book sometime during or after 1978, the year Willard McCarthy gave him the book. In a notebook from the late 1940s, when Frye seems especially distressed about his physical state, he enjoins himself to consult books on yoga for advice. He also urges himself to center his life more on "the human act, the act of kindliness, of Chih-kai [Chik-hai] Bardo" (30r.11). Even as late as the mid-1980s, Frye is still writing about yoga as a discipline that would free the mind from a "frozen," material consciousness: "Yoga is the involuntary suppression of the voluntary actions of the mind. We're all born with a natural yoga: we're freed by objective energy and our consciousness freezes it into matter. Matter is mater, the mother.

Materialism, dogmatism, the authority of elders and impotent kings, all assist the freezing process. A higher discipline that would freeze the mind could liberate the spirit" (LN, 2:716).

39. Tathagata = "the thus-gone one," i.e., the one who has attained supreme enlightenment.

40. The annotated books on yoga in Frye's library are Tibetan Yoga and Secret Doctrines, or, Seven Books of Wisdom of the Great Path; Chao Pi Ch'en, Taoist Yoga: Alchemy and Immortality; Mircea Eliade, Yoga: Immortality and Freedom; Paramhansa Yogananda, Autobiography of a Yogi; Gopi Krishna, Kundalini: The Evolutionary Energy in Man; Ernest Wood, Yoga; and Patanjali, The Yoga-Sutras.

41. Frye almost certainly remembered the "head-going" etymology from a remark by Jung in The Secret of the Golden Flower: A Chinese Book of Life, trans. Richard Wilhelm, with a commentary by C. G. Jung, rev. ed. (New York: Harcourt, Brace, 1962), 97. An early version of this note is in 30m.15.

42. The Yoga-Sutras, 31 (sec. 1, sutra 41). D. T. Suzuki says that in Buddhism "no distinction is made between knowledge and knower." Studies in the Lankavatara Sutra, 141.

43. Frye refers to Tantra only once in his notebooks, comparing the guru-chela relationship to that in Plato's dialogues (33.21). His knowledge of Tantra as an ecstatic cult derived, at least in part, from Philip Rawson's Tantra (London: Thames & Hudson, 1973), which he annotated throughout, noting especially Blakean analogues. For Frye's notebook entries on Kundalini, see LN, 1:173–74, 313, 353, 357, 2:704, 713, 718; RT, 368; 7.14, 56.

44. Frye refers to the serpent or ouroboros symbolism in his review of Jung's book. See "Forming Fours," in NFCL, 126. There is no evidence that Frye later read the lectures from Jung's seminar on Kundalini, though he would have been familiar with some of their content through James Hillman's commentaries in Gopi Krishna's Kundalini: The Evolutionary Energy in Man (Boulder, Colo.: Shambhala, 1971), 38–45, 68–73, 94–102, 131–33, 153–58, 176–80, 202–5, 235–39, and 250–52.

45. Frye had read The Secret of the Golden Flower in 1949 (see D, 184–85, 189); in Wilhelm's discussion of the text and Jung's commentary he encountered a number of Chinese philosophical and religious ideas that he kept returning to. Frye's copy is fairly heavily marked and annotated.

46. See, e.g., RT, 368; 7.14; and LN, 1:313, 2:718.

47. See Frye's brief essay "The Ouroboros," Ethos 1 (Summer 1983): 12–13. He would have been familiar with Jung's remark that in Kundalini we have an analogy to the alchemical symbolism of the golden flower—light from darkness, gold from lead, consciousness from unconsciousness. See The Secret of the Golden Flower, 101–2.

48. Frederic Spiegelberg, introduction to Krishna, Kundalini, 8–9.

49. Lao-tzu, The Wisdom of Laotse, trans. Lin Yutang (New York: Modern Library, 1948). This edition combines selections from Lao-tzu's texts with related passages from Chuang-tzu.

50. The following annotated editions are in Frye's library: Chuang-tzu, *Chuang Tzu: Genius of the Absurd,* arranged from the work of James Legge by Clae Waltham (New York: Ace Books, 1971); *The I Ching,* trans. James Legge, 2nd ed. (New York: Dover, 1963); *The I Ching, or, Book of Changes,* trans. Richard Wilhelm and Cary F. Baynes, 3rd ed. (Princeton, N.J.: Princeton Univ. Press, 1967).

51. See Frye's annotated copies of Philip Rawson and Laszlo Legeza, *Tao, the Chinese Philosophy of Time and Change* (London: Thames & Hudson, 1973); Holmes Welch, *Taoism: The Parting of the Way,* rev. ed. (Boston: Beacon Press, 1966); and Chao Pi Ch'en, *Taoist Yoga: Alchemy and Immortality,* trans. Lu K'uan Yu (London: Rider, 1972). Frye was also familiar with the parallels between Heidegger's *Da-sein* and the *Tao-te Ching* recorded in Werner Brock's notes to *What Is Metaphysics?* in *Existence and Being* (Chicago: Regnery, 1949), 369; Frye marked the passage in his own copy of the book.

52. Frye's library contains annotated copies of Eliade's *Birth and Rebirth: The Religious Meanings of Initiation in Human Culture* (1958), *Cosmos and History: The Myth of the Eternal Return* (1959), *Patterns in Comparative Religion* (1958), *The Sacred and the Profane: The Nature of Religion* (1959), *Yoga: Immortality and Freedom* (1958), *Shamanism: Archaic Techniques of Ecstasy* (1972), *The Two and the One* (1965), *Myths, Dreams and Mysteries: The Encounter between Contemporary Faiths and Archaic Reality* (1968), *The Forge and the Crucible* (1971), *Zalmoxis, The Vanishing God: Comparative Studies in the Religions and Folklore of Dacia and Eastern Europe* (1972). Frye reviewed the first five of these books in the late 1950s. See "World without Time," in *NFCL,* 95–106. Additionally, he owned copies of Eliade's *Gods, Goddesses, and Myths of Creation: A Thematic Source Book of the History of Religions,* pt. 1 of *From Primitives to Zen* (1974), *Myth and Reality* (1963), *Myths, Rites, Symbols: A Mircea Eliade Reader,* vol. 2 (1976), and *The Old Man and Bureaucrats* (1979).

53. The finger and moon illustration is found in *The Lankavatara Sutra,* 193. On "head-going," see n. 40, above. Waley did not originate the translation of "Tao" as "the way," but his *The Way and Its Power* (1934) was influential in its view of the *Tao-te Ching* as a manual for cultivating a way of life based on individual morality. See Julia M. Hardy, "Influential Western Interpretations of the *Tai-de-Ching,*" in *"Lao-tzu" and the "Tao-te-Ching,"* ed. Livia Kohn and Michael Lafargue (Albany: State Univ. Press of New York, 1998), 170.

54. Lao Tzu, *Tao te Ching,* trans. D. C. Lau (London: Penguin, 1963), 102 (chap. 41, st. 92).

55. *Tao te Ching,* 132 (chap. 70, st. 170).

56. *The Wisdom of Laotse,* 297.

57. See, e.g., *LN,* 1:5, 10, 117, 227, 2:468, 679.

58. "Out of Tao, and the *T'ai-chi,* there develop the principles of reality, the one pole being the light (yang) and the other the dark, or the shadowy (yin). . . . Less abstract than yin and yang are the concepts of the Creative and the Receptive (*Ch'ien* and *K'un*) that originate in the *Book of Changes* . . . and

are symbolized by heaven and earth, and through the efficacy of the dual primal forces within this field of activity (governed by the one primal law, the Tao), there develop the 'ten thousand things,' that is, the outer world." Richard Wilhelm, "A Discussion of the Text," in *The Secret of the Golden Flower,* 12. See also the marginal marks opposite the heaven and earth commentary in Frye's copies of *Chuang Tzu,* ed. Waltham, 5; Welch, *Taoism,* 22; and Rawson and Legeza, *Tao,* 6.

59. *Tao te Ching,* 101 (chap. 40, sts. 88, 89).

60. *The Wisdom of Laotse,* 150.

61. *Tao te Ching,* 103 (chap. 42, st. 94).

62. Frye writes little about Confucianism outside of the *I Ching.* But he would have found the *Analects* congenial to his thinking about interpenetration. See Charles Muller, "*Tiyong* and Interpenetration in the *Analects* of Confucius: The Sacred as Secular," *Bulletin of Toyo Gakuen University* 8 (March 2000): 93–106.

63. From a typescript in 1991 accession, box 35, file 2:

> The remaining 49 stalks [of the 50 that one begins with] are first divided into two heaps at random. Thereupon one stalk is taken from the right-hand heap and put between the ring finger and the little finger of the left hand. Then the left-hand heap is placed in the left hand, and the right hand takes from it bundles of 4, until there are 4 or fewer stalks remaining. This remainder is placed between the ring finger and the middle finger of the left hand. Next the right-hand heap is counted off by fours, and the remainder is placed between the middle finger and the forefinger of the left hand. The sum of the stalks now between the fingers of the left hand is either 9 or 5. . . . These stalks are now laid aside for the time being. Then the remaining stalks are gathered together again and divided anew. Once more one takes a stalk from the pile on the right and places it between the ring finger and the little finger of the left hand; then one counts off the stalks as before. This time the sum of the remainder is either 8 or 4. . . . The procedure is carried out a third time with the remaining stalks, and again the sum of the remainder is 8 or 4.

Frye copied these instructions from an appendix, "The Yarrow-Stalk Oracle," in the Wilhelm-Baynes translation of the *I Ching* (see next note).

64. In his edition of the Wilhelm-Baynes translation of the *I Ching* Frye wrote what appears to be a summary of the results of his experiment with the toothpicks—a table with seven rows of numbers that end in either six or three. The divining operation requires that the process of manipulating the stalks or coins be repeated six times. But Frye's fifth step, if that is what the numbers represent, issued in zero, so he apparently abandoned that step and went on to the next, yielding six complete repetitions. See Frye's copy of the *I Ching, or Book of Changes,* trans. Richard Wilhelm and Cary F. Baynes (Princeton, N.J.: Princeton Univ. Press, 1950), 253.

65. See my introduction to *D*, xxx–xxv.

66. It is not without interest to note some of the passages in Wilhelm's commentary on the K'un hexagram that Frye marked in his copy of the *I Ching*: "The movement of the Receptive is an opening out, and in its resting state it is closed. In the resting, closed state, it embraces things as though in a vast womb. In the state of movement, of opening, it allows the divine light to enter, and by means of this light illuminates everything" (387). "Everything becomes spontaneously what it should rightly be, for in the law of heaven life has an inner light that it must involuntarily obey" (390). "The reference [to winter and spring] is to the solitary union with the Creative, the receiving of the seed and its quiet ripening to birth" (392). "Therefore in all matters the individual hits upon the right course instinctively and without reflection, because he is free of all those scruples and doubts which induce a timid vacillation and lame the power of decision" (394). "It is the way of the earth to make no display of completed work but rather to bring everything to completion vicariously" (ibid.). "[He] is near the ruler but does not receive *recognition* [Frye's underlining] from him. In such a case the only right thing to do is shut oneself off from the world" (ibid.). "He seeks the right place for himself and dwells in the essential. His beauty is within, but gives freedom to his limbs and expresses itself in its works. This is the perfection of beauty" (395). "Reserved grace, unseen yet present in all movements and deeds, is the perfection of beauty" (ibid.). "THE CREATIVE [the Ch'ien hexagram] represents time, producing sequence; THE RECEPTIVE represents space, which indicates juxtaposition" (396). A biographer would have little difficulty in finding these abstractions illustrated in Frye's life. In his copy of the Legge translation of the *I Ching*, Frye wrote "Docility" opposite the K'un hexagram (or Khwan, as Legge transliterates it); and in his commentary on the hexagram, Legge says that "it is not to be wondered at, if some men of active and ill-regulated imaginations should see Noah and his wife in those two primary trigrams," at which point Frye inserts the marginal note, "including me." *The I Ching*, trans. James Legge, 2nd ed. (New York: Dover, 1963), 49.

67. Frye's marginal annotations in his copy of the *I Ching* make the following parallels between the trigrams and Blake's Four Zoas and their Emanations: Ch'ien = Tharmas, Sun = Vala, K'an = Los, Ken = Urizen, K'un = Enion, Chen = Orc, Li = Enitharmon, and Tui = Ahania. See Frye's copy of the *I Ching*, trans. Wilhelm and Baynes, l–li, 266.

68. For Frye's *I Ching* speculations, see *TBN*, 183, 209–13, 217, 229, 260, 261, 301, 309, and 328.

69. For the results of Dolzani's detective work, see *TBN*, 402–3, nn. 258 and 261, and the diagrams on 403 and 404.

70. *I Ching: Books of Changes*, trans. James Legge, ed. Ch'u Chai and Winberg Chai (New York: Bantam, 1964), 382–83.

71. Frye refers to his anticlockwise arrangement in *TBN*, 211. In a marginal note on p. 32 of his edition of the Legge translation of the *I Ching* Frye writes beside a chart of the Fu-hsi trigrams, "this one is closest to my own Great

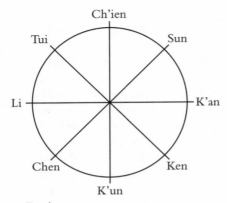

Frye's note:
"Chinese primordial
arrangement, S [South] at top"

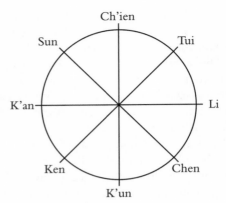

Frye's note:
"My arrangement, N [North] at
top*

*identical with Fu-hsi's except
that it's anti-clockwise. I should
remember that I'm placing
myself within the mirror."

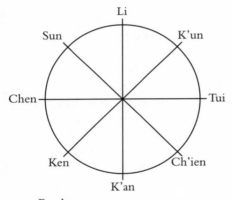

Frye's note:
"Chinese inner world
arrangement"

Frye's note:
"mine would have to be this"

Diagram 7. *I Ching* Arrangements

Doodle." Diagram 7 shows reproductions of his sketches, drawn on p. 254 of his
copy of the Wilhelm–Baynes edition of the *I Ching.*

72. Typescript in 1991 accession, box 28, file 4ll, par. 7.

73. The phrase comes from William Blake's annotations to Berkeley's
Siris, in *Complete Poetry and Prose,* 664.

74. There are even three editions of his work in English that have been
published especially for Eastern readers: one of *Anatomy of Criticism* for Korean

and Taiwanese students, and one of *The Modern Century* for Japanese readers. Professor Wu Chizhe of the University of Inner Mongolia in Hoh-Hot has been an especially energetic translator of Frye into Chinese.

75. See *Fu-lai yen chiu: Chung-kuo yü hsi fang* [Northrop Frye Studies: China and the West], ed. Ning Wang and Yen-hung Hsü (Beijing: Social Sciences Press of China, 1996). These essays, in Chinese, are the proceedings from the conference "Northrop Frye and China" held at Peking University, 12–17 July 1994. For the proceedings from the International Symposium on Northrop Frye Studies at Inner Mongolia University in Hoh-Hot, China, 15–17 July 1999, see *New Directions in Northrop Frye Studies,* ed. Wang Ning and Jean O'Grady (Shanghai: Shanghai Foreign Language Education Press, 2001), and *Northrop Frye: Eastern and Western Perspectives,* ed. Jean O'Grady and Wang Ning (Toronto: Univ. of Toronto Press, 2003). The last two volumes differ slightly. The Korean conference was held 22 May 1992 at Sookmyung Women's University, Seoul, and its proceedings were published as *The Legacy of Northrop Frye in the East and West: Proceedings of the Third Annual International Conference of Canadian Studies* (1992).

5. The Traditions

1. Antoine Faivre, *Access to Western Esotericism* (Albany: State Univ. of New York Press, 1994), 34.

2. Wouter J. Hanegraaff, "Some Remarks on the Study of Western Esotericism," *Esoterica* 1 (1999): 3–19.

3. Faivre's introduction to *Modern Esoteric Spirituality,* ed. Antoine Faivre and Jacob Needleman (New York: Crossroad, 1992), xi–xix. For a similar account of the same four features, see Faivre, "Preface: Esotericism and Academic Research," in his *Theosophy, Imagination, Tradition: Studies in Western Esotericism,* trans. Christine Rhone (Albany: State Univ. of New York Press, 2000), xxi–xxiv.

4. Faivre holds a chair in the History of Esoteric and Mystical Currents in Modern and Contemporary Europe at the École Pratique des Hautes Études, Religious Studies Section, Sorbonne. See the extensive bibliographical guide to research in his *Access to Western Esotericism,* 297–348, brought up to date in *Theosophy, Imagination, and Tradition,* 249–59. Faivre lists more than two dozen journals devoted to esotericism. In addition, see the peer-reviewed online journal *Esoterica,* edited by Arthur Versluis, at www.esoteric.msu.edu. To date, the State University of New York Press has published thirty-nine titles in its Western Esoteric Traditions series.

5. Hanegraaf, *New Age Religion and Western Culture: Esotericism in the Mirror of Secular Thought* (Albany: State Univ. of New York Press, 1998).

6. Faivre, "Ancient and Medieval Sources of Modern Esoteric Movements," in *Modern Esoteric Spirituality,* 1–70.

7. Sections 2–11 of the list are arranged alphabetically. There is no significance to the arrangement of items within each section.

8. "The *akasa* is a Sanscrit word which means sky, but it also designates the imponderable and intangible life-principle—the astral and celestial lights combined together, and which two form the *anima mundi,* and constitute the soul and spirit of man; the celestial light forming his *nous, pneuma,* or divine spirit, and the other his soul or *astral* spirit. The grosser particles of the latter enter into the fabrication of his outward form—the body. *Akasa* is the mysterious fluid termed by scholastic science, 'the all-pervading ether'; it enters into all the magical operations of nature, and produces mesmeric, magnetic, and spiritual phenomena." Footnote in Helena Petrovna Blavatsky, *Isis Unveiled* (New York: J. W. Bouton, 1877), 1:139–40.

9. On the elemental spirits in Milton, see "The Revelation to Eve," *StS,* 145, 147, 151. Elementary spirits were traditionally seen as inhabiting the four elements: sylphs in air, gnomes in earth, salamanders in fire, and nymphs or undines in water.

10. "Yeats and the Language of Symbolism," *FI,* 227.

11. See *LN,* 1:189–90, 195; *RT,* 54; 32.51, 53; 7.97; 25.7–14. Frye never wrote the projected article.

12. *LN,* 1:190. Frye's desire to write such an article might well have also been spurred by Frances Yates's *The Occult Philosophy in the Elizabethan Age* (London: Routledge & Kegan Paul, 1983), chap. 14 of which is devoted to Shakespeare's faery world. Her book was published about the time that Frye began writing his late notebooks.

13. "Yeats and the Language of Symbolism," *FI,* 218–37. On Blavatsky and other late nineteenth-century occult systems, see 220–21.

14. "Yeats quotes legends indicating that the seasons of this world are the reverse of ours, like the southern hemisphere, and, in the *Autobiographies,* a remark of Madame Blavatsky that we live in a dumbbell-shaped cosmos, with an antipodal world at our North Pole. This conception is most readily visualised as an hour-glass, the emblem of time and the basis of Yeats's 'double gyre' diagrams, and in the play that is explicitly called *The Hour-Glass* we are told that 'There are two living countries, the one visible and the other invisible; and when it is winter with us it is summer in that country.'" From "The Rising of the Moon," *SM,* 267.

15. Frye read both *An Abridgement of The Secret Doctrine,* ed. Elizabeth Preston and Christmas Humphreys (Wheaton, Ill.: Theosophical Publishing House, 1966); and *The Secret Doctrine: The Synthesis of Science, Religion and Philosophy,* 2 vols. (Pasadena, Calif.: Theosophical Univ. Press, 1970). His copies of the three volumes contain more than 300 marginal annotations and hundreds of marked passages, though there are none following p. 174 of vol. 2 of *The Secret Doctrine.* Frye's marginalia are occasionally judgments, but most are what he calls "links"—parallels he finds to other things in his reading. For Frye's notebook entries on Blavatsky, see *TBN,* 70, 71; *RT,* 207; 7.10, 36, 85; 31.5, 9, 19, 33, 40, 42–43, 48; 32.28, 49, 52, 54, 66; 34.69; 35.19; 37.11; 42.41; 54-13.24; 9.98; and 1991 accession, box 28, file 4j.5. In the published work there are only occasional

passing remarks to Blavatsky: see "Yeats and the Language of Symbolism," *FI*, 221, 222, 228, 231; *FS*, 344; "The Pursuit of Form," *Canadian Art* 6 (Christmas 1948): 57; "Cycle and Apocalypse in *Finnegans Wake*," *MM*, 373; "The Rising of the Moon," *SM*, 246, 267.

16. See Frye's copy of *An Abridgement of The Secret Doctrine*, xxiii.

17. On *Zanoni*, see *TBN*, 339, 342; 10.110; 32.51, 57, 58; 54-4.56; 1991 accession, box 28, file 6.108, 171, 292, 476; 1991 accession, box 28, file 4k.11; *NFCL*, 214; *LS*, 69; *SeS*, 113.

18. In one of his marginalia to Madame Blavatsky, Frye writes that for her the "essence of religion [is] not the Poetic Genius but a doctrine, not the constructing power but something it constructs." See his copy of *An Abridgement of The Secret Doctrine*, xxiv. Although the Theosophical Society, founded by Blavatsky (1831–91), H. S. Alcott (1832–1907), and W. Q. Judge (1851–96) did not propose an official doctrine for its members, Faivre agrees that for Blavatsky, "theosophy" did designate a doctrine. See Faivre, *Theosophy, Imagination, Tradition*, 27–28.

19. Frye's library included only nineteen books with "mysticism," "mystic," or "mystical" in the title. Fourteen of these are annotated. In his library were also two editions of *The Cloud of Unknowing* (both annotated), four collections of Boehme's works (all annotated), two of Eckhart (both annotated), five of St. John of the Cross (four annotated), and six books on the Kabbalah (all annotated). Frye would doubtless have included William Law, Thomas Taylor, John Woolman, and perhaps Immanuel Swedenborg among his "mystics." But even if he considered such books as Aldous Huxley's *The Perennial Philosophy* and Alan Upward's *The Divine Mystery* as belonging to his library of mysticism, still the total number of books in that category would amount to hardly more than three dozen titles.

20. Whether Frye knew that Lull, who read Arabic, had been influenced by Al-Ghazzali and other Sufis is uncertain.

21. Published as William Ralph Inge, *Christian Mysticism* (London: Methuen, 1899), 335–48 (appendix A). The appendix was omitted from the 1966 Meridian Books edition. Frye's annotated copy is the 1956 Living Age edition.

22. Bernard McGinn, *The Foundations of Mysticism: Origins to the Fifth Century* (New York: Crossroad, 1991), xv–xvi. This is the first volume of McGinn's projected five-volume study, *The Presence of God: A History of Western Christian Mysticism*. Vol. 3 appeared in 1998; vols. 4 and 5 are forthcoming.

23. Cf. this marginalia from Frye's copy of Boehme's *The Signature of Things* (London: Dent, 1934): "Blake was a mystic, perhaps, but so revolutionary a mystic I suspect he smashed the mystic tradition as Swift smashed the anatomy" (7). For Frye's review of the criticism on Blake as a mystic, see "William Blake," in *English Romantic Poets and Essayists: A Review of Research and Criticism*, ed. Carol W. Houtchens and Lawrence H. Houtchens (New York: New York University Press for the Modern Language Association, 1966), 16–

328 Notes to Pages 173–174

18. Frye's essay originally appeared in the 1957 edition of this book and was revised by Martin K. Nurmi for the 1966 edition.

24. William James, *The Varieties of Religious Experience* (New York: New American Library, 1958), 292–94.

25. See *WP,* 112: "A famous passage in William James' *Varieties of Religious Experience* [p. 298] tells us that the author came out of a trance induced by nitrous oxide with the feeling that 'our normal waking consciousness, rational consciousness as we call it, is but one special type of consciousness, whilst all about it, parted from it by the filmiest of screens, there lie potential forms of consciousness entirely different.'" In *The Origin of Consciousness in the Breakdown of the Bicameral Mind,* Jaynes argues that human brains from about the tenth to the second centuries B.C. were bicameral: the hallucinatory area in the right temporal lobe of the brain worked intuitively, sending auditory commands to the brain's left hemisphere, where the message was spoken or enacted. That is, the brain was split in a way similar to the functioning of schizophrenia. Consciousness, according to Jaynes, arose about 1000 B.C., only after the right-left brain synthesis. Frye does not endorse the reference to the voices and visions of the preconscious state as mental disturbances or hallucinations, but he does feel, given the widespread psychoses engendered by the ego consciousness of the contemporary world, that a return to the intensified consciousness of the bicameral state has much to recommend it. On Jaynes, see *WP,* 50–51; *MM,* 73–74; and *LN,* 1:161, 162. Annotated copies of James's and Jaynes's books are in the Northrop Frye Library.

26. See also "William Blake," in *English Romantic Poets and Essayists* (1957), where Frye writes,

> [I]t is still possible to rehabilitate the term [mystic] for Blake if some . . . conception of it, less ethical and more speculative and aesthetic, is taken as a norm. For instance, if one begins by reading the *Bhagavadgita,* preferably in the Wilkins translation that Blake used, then learns from such traditions as those of Zen Buddhism how mysticism and art may be associated, then cautiously makes his way to the Western world by way of the Christianized Platonism of the Renaissance, he will come much closer to the kind of associations with the term which fit Blake. Suggestions about the affinities between Blake and Oriental thought are made from time to time: the affinities are remarkable, but probably few would care to follow them up in a field where almost nothing but pure analogy can be established. A more solid link is afforded by Blake's very probable knowledge of some of Thomas Taylor's translations from Plato and the Neoplatonists. (17)

27. Jacob Boehme, *Six Theosophic Points and Other Writings,* trans. John Rolleston Earle (Ann Arbor: Univ. of Michigan Press, 1958), Frye's note in bottom margin on p. xxiii of Nicholas Berdyaev's introductory essay, "Unground and Freedom."

28. On Eckhart's "God behind God," see *RT,* 100, 130. On Boehme's Unground and the shadowy or hidden Father-God, who is discovered only after a titanic struggle, see *TBN,* 213, 214, 215, 257; *LN,* 1:182–83, 2:480. The "hidden divinity" version of the *via negativa* derives from a translation of the *Mystical Theologica* of Pseudo-Dionysius, who is given the name St. Denis in the anonymous *Cloud of Unknowing.* See his *Dionise Hid Divinity* in *The Cloud of Unknowing and Other Works,* trans. Clifton Wolters (Harmondsworth, Eng.: Penguin, 1978), 205–18. Boehme also speaks of a hidden divinity—an "eternal hiddenness," he calls it (*Six Theosophic Points,* 41). Frye's marginal annotation: "I suppose this hidden divinity is what is specifically occult about occultism" (bottom margin, p. 41). Frye refers to Blavatsky as a "deifier of the void" in *RT,* 207 and 31.32; and similarly to Carlyle in 31.32.

29. For the "deification of the void," see also *RT,* 103, 129, 248; *TBN,* 214; 31.33; and 10.112.

30. Boehme was influenced not only by Paracelsus but by the esoteric traditions of the Kabbalah, alchemy, astrology, and hermeticism.

31. Jacob Boehme, *The Signature of All Things, with other Writings* (London: Dent, 1934), 12. An annotated copy is in the Northrop Frye Library.

32. Cf. "'God' is certainly a word that belongs to metonymy: as Eckhart and others say, no word can possibly express all you mean by the word. The thought is infinite; the word which in the secondary stage of language expresses the thought is finite. As soon as you name God, you've finitized him; you have to believe that the universal is what's real even to keep the notion going. Hence the mystical 'hid divinity' conception" (*RT,* 290). See also *WP,* 109. My exposition of *The Cloud of Unknowing* and other forms of the "hid divinity" derives in addition from scattered passages in the notebooks: *LN,* 1:161, 2:531–32; *RT,* 100, 207, 371; *TBN,* 110–11, 214.

33. Aldous Huxley, *The Perennial Philosophy,* 25.

34. Eckhart makes this point in two sermons, "Sermon Five" and "Sermon Twenty-Three," in *Breakthrough: Meister Eckhart's Creation Spirituality in New Translation,* ed. Matthew Fox (New York: Doubleday, 1980), 91–94, 325–30. Frye refers to this metaphor of Eckhart's in *WP,* 193, and in about half of his notebook references to him: *LN,* 1:152, 153, 328, 329, 339. In *WP,* 318, Frye cites as his source the Colledge and McGinn translation of *The Essential Sermons,* an annotated copy of which is in the Northrop Frye Library. Frye marked passages relating to *Gottheit* in his copy of Nicholas Berdyaev, *The Beginning and the End* (New York: Harper & Brothers, 1957).

35. "Siger of Brabant, William of Ockham, Nicholas of Autrecourt, Peter Abelard, Meister Eckhart, Roger Bacon, Scotus Erigena: in all repressive societies most of the really first rate people are either accused or suspected of heresy" (*LN,* 1:252). See a similar statement in *LN,* 2:720.

36. Huxley, *The Perennial Philosophy,* 2–3.

37. In one of his notebooks from the early 1970s, Frye quotes without commentary Huxley's justification for the anthology approach: "The construc-

tion of an all-embracing system of metaphysics, ethics & psychology is a task that can never be accomplished by any single individual, for the sufficient reason that he *is* an individual with one particular kind of constitution & temperament & therefore capable of knowing only according to the mode of his own being. Hence the advantages inherent in what may be called the anthological approach to truth" (33.27). The passage is from *The Perennial Philosophy,* 153.

38. "Huxley turned out better than I expected: he's often stupid, but he does know what the perennial philosophy is, up to a point" (*RT,* 26). "Huxley's Perennial Philosophy is a book I must keep in touch with" (*RT,* 360). This last remark is triggered by Huxley's quoting Eckhart and Dame Gertrude More on the soul as female and the spirit male (*The Perennial Philosophy,* 12, 98); Frye remembers having written a note about this five or so years later. See *LN,* 1:10.

39. "[Stage] I is what I used to call the Druid analogy; II is my version of the perennial philosophy; III is Biblical" (*RT,* 136). See also *RT,* 156.

40. Frye's annotated edition of *The Principal Upanishads,* ed. S. Radhakrishnan (London: Allen & Unwin, 1953), was published after he had read Huxley. The *tat tvam asi* passage is on p. 458 of Radhakrishnan's edition.

41. Huxley, *The Perennial Philosophy,* 4.

42. Frye would have been aware of Rudolf Otto's equation of *tat tvam asi* with Eckhart's "God is the same One that I am." Qtd. in Otto's *Mysticism East and West,* 12.

43. Another one of Frye's unpublished notes that identifies "Thou Art That" with ecstatic metaphor is in the 1991 accession, box 28, file 4ee, par. 32. Here Frye writes that although there is always a certain vagueness associated with pure vision, "Nevertheless pure vision, the Bible as myth, nothing happened in past time; it's all happening now, is one of my landing places. I think I have to expand it by way of my three stages of metaphor. Or rather, the lunatic and lover are behind the poet, the 'I am' metaphors of Christ and the 'Thou art that' of Hinduism are ahead of him."

44. The Rimbaud remark comes from a letter to Georges Izambard (13 May 1871), in *Lettres de la vie littéraire d'Arthur Rimbaud,* ed. Jean-Marie Carré (Paris: Gallimard, 1990), 39.

45. Frye's notes on Herbert Silberer's *Problems of Mysticism and Its Symbolism* focus on its symbols. See 7.15–16.

46. Frye's brief critique of Zaehner is similar to that of Bernard McGinn, in *Foundations of Mysticism,* 338–39.

47. Frye remarks that Underhill is "dismally unrewarding," but later says, "I apologize to the Underhill: she improves as she goes on, & it's only her opening chapters that are feeble" (*RT,* 15, 21–22). Still, Underhill's more or less orthodox version of Christian mysticism allows no place for art. To her comment that for the artist "the senses have somewhat hindered the perfect inebriation of the soul," Frye remarks sardonically, "You have to learn to do without pretzels" (*RT,* 20).

48. See also Notebook 27, where Frye instructs himself, "See Jean Dan-

ielou in the *Man and Transformation* Eranos book, or Gregory of Nyssa, a mystic who uses flight instead of climbing" (*LN*, 1:62). The first reference is to Daniélou's "The Dove and Darkness in Ancient Byzantine Mysticism," in *Man and Transformation: Papers from the Eranos Yearbooks* (New York: Pantheon, 1964), 270–96. Gregory uses the image of flight in his *The Life of Moses*, where he says that the human being's "very stability becomes as a wing in his flight towards heaven; his heart becomes winged because of his stability in good." Or again: "The soul moves in the opposite direction [from heavy bodies], light and swiftly moving upwards once it is released from sensuous and earthly attachments, soaring from the world below up towards the heavens." *From Glory to Glory: Texts from Gregory of Nyssa's Mystical Writings,* trans. and ed. Herbert Musurillo (Crestwood, N.Y.: St. Vladimir's Seminary Press, 1979), 150, 144. Daniélou's article cites a number of passages of flight in Gregory.

49. *Religio Medici,* in *Sir Thomas Browne: The Major Works,* ed. C. A. Patrides (London: Penguin, 1977), 70.

50. *All and Everything* consists of ten books in three series: *Beelzebub's Tales to His Grandson, Meetings with Remarkable Men,* and *Life Is Real Only Then, When "I Am."* Frye read the first series, *All and Everything: Ten Books, in Three Series, of Which This Is the First Series* (London: Routledge & Kegan Paul, 1967). A third edition of the book was issued by Penguin/Arkana in 1999 with the title *Beelzebub's Tales to His Grandson: All and Everything: First Series.* There is no evidence that Frye read the other two parts of the trilogy.

51. In addition, Frye mentions Gurdjieff in passing in *CP,* 145, and *SM,* 177.

52. For Gurdjieff's distinction between essence and persona, see P. D. Ouspensky, *In Search of the Miraculous: Fragments of an Unknown Teaching* (New York: Harcourt, Brace and World, 1949), 248; and Kenneth Walker, *A Study of Gurdjieff's Teaching* (New York: Award Books, 1969), 88–100.

53. For a useful account of Gurdjieff's life and influence, see Jacob Needleman, "G. I. Gurdjieff and His School," in *Modern Esoteric Spirituality,* 359–80.

54. In *GC,* 244, Frye's cites Walker, *A Study of Gurdjieff's Teaching,* chap. 7. Frye's annotated edition is the 1967 (Jonathan Cape) reprint. The primary source for Gurdjieff's examples of objective art come from Ouspensky's *In Search of the Miraculous,* 27, 297. Cf. *RT,* 187–88: "[W]hile the shape & unity of the whole canon is important, we shouldn't *reduce* the variety to unity, but see them both as interpenetrating. The unity of originality, the unity of *Paradise Lost* or *Hamlet,* is a different kind of unity, a function of universality *through* individuality. I think this raises the whole question of objective art ("code of art"), Gurdjieff, (as usual, he gives the impression that he doesn't know what he's talking about but has derived the notion from someone who did). Beethoven's music beyond music, etc. It also raises the question of inspiration as belonging to the *reader.*"

55. Needleman, "Gurdjieff and His School," 372.

56. "What we call Statics, Chemistry, and Dynamics—words that as used in modern science are merely traditional distinctions without deeper meaning—are really the *respective systems of the Apollonian, Magian and Faustian souls,* each of which grew up in its own Culture and was limited as to validity to the same." Oswald Spengler, *The Decline of the West: Form and Actuality,* trans. Charles Francis Atkinson (New York: Knopf, 1926–28), 1:384.

57. Frye's spellings of the Hebrew *qabbala* are more numerous than the *sefiroth* in the Tree of Life: Kabbalah, Cabbala, Cabala, Kabbala, kabbalism, Kabbalism, kabalism, cabbalism, cabalism, Cabbalism, Cabalistic, cabalistic, Kabbalistic, Cabbalists, and cabbalists. I have used Kabbalah simply because it is listed first in *Merriam-Webster's Collegiate Dictionary,* 11th ed.

58. For the books on Kabbalism in Frye's library, see section 8 in the list at the beginning of this chapter. Frye naturally read about Kabbalism in sources not devoted solely to this tradition of Jewish mysticism, such as Israel Regardie's *The Golden Dawn* (1937–40), and in *Words with Power* his quotation from the *Sepher Yetzirah,* a key Kabbalistic text, comes from *Origins: Creation Texts from the Ancient Mediterranean,* trans. Charles Doria and Harris Lenowitz (Garden City, N.Y.: Anchor, 1976).

59. "This can't be as puerile as it sounds," Frye writes in the margin of p. 142 of *The Kabbalah Unveiled,* "but my first attempt to read it flakes out here." Or again, "all this stuff is just the afterbirth of literature"—one of the marginalia in Poncé's *Kabbalah,* 209. The context of the comment is Poncé's account of the separation of man and woman in the *Zohar.*

60. Frye read and annotated Frances Yates's *The Rosicrucian Enlightenment* (Frogmore, St. Albans, Herts: Paladin, 1975), *The Art of Memory* (London: Routledge & Kegan Paul, 1966), and *Giordano Bruno and the Hermetic Tradition* (London: Routledge & Kegan Paul, 1964). In *The Occult Philosophy in the Elizabethan Age,* which Frye also annotated, Yates devotes separate chapters to Pico, Reuchlin, and Agrippa.

61. Qtd. by Daniel C. Matt in *The Essential Kabbalah: The Heart of Jewish Mysticism* (New York: HarperCollins, 1995), 16.

62. Positive analogies exist in other religions as well. When Buddhism came to Japan it treated the Shinto *kami* (lit. "the superior ones," i.e., all that is humanly incomprehensible for human beings, such as the celestial bodies, seas, mountains, animals, plants, and even ancestral spirits) as emanations of Buddha (*RT,* 350).

63. See, e.g., Poncé, *Kabbalah,* 145–57. The *Sefiroth* were the ten primordial numbers, conceived of as divine emanations, the "speech" of God, the foundation of existence, unity in multiplicity, among other things. The passages that Frye marked in his copy of Z'ev Ben Shimon Halevi's *Kabbalah* have to do with the world-tree and ladder images in the Kabbalah.

64. For the tree analogies, see *LN,* 1:262, 2:655; for the numerical one, *RT,* 404; for the respect-for-the-letter analogy, *FS,* 416; for the withdrawing God analogy, *LN,* 2:425; and for the androgyny one, *LN,* 1:104, 2:453; *NFR,*

122; and *WP,* 189. In addition to the treatment of positive analogies in *WP,* see *LN,* 1:45, 153, 2:439, 453, 459, 486, 532–33, 541, 582. Frye's first use of the phrase "positive analogy," in a 1980 notebook, is in connection with the Buddhist *kami* (see n. 62, above). The idea that Creation involved the withdrawal of God (*tsimtsum*) derives from the father of modern Kabbalism, Isaac Luria (1533–72). See Poncé, *Kabbalah,* 80–81.

65. Frye, however, does say in Notebook 27 that the biblical Adam is probably an Adam Kadmon or a version of Milton's *archetypus gigas* (*LN,* 1:26).

66. Frye quotes from 1:4 (or 2:1 in some translations) of the *Sepher Yetzirah,* in *Origins: Creation Texts from the Ancient Mediterranean,* 58, an annotated copy of which is in the Northrop Frye Library.

67. Gershom Scholem's translation substitutes "thing" for "word": "make a thing stand on its essence, and make the Creator sit on his base." Wm. Wynn Wescott's translation: "Search out concerning it, restore the Word to its creator, and replace Him who formed it upon his throne." Scott Thompson and Dominique Marson's translation: "Place the word above its creator and reinstate a Creator upon His foundation."

68. On the Faustian fallacy ("In the beginning was the act," *Faust,* pt. 1, line 1237), see *GC,* 18; *MM,* 240; *WP,* 34; *LN,* 1:34, 171, 172, 270, 2:520, 521, 589; *RT,* 323, 333.

69. The *homoousios* vs. *homoiousios* debate was about whether Christ was of the same substance as the Father, the position argued by Athanasius, or of similar substance, the position of Arius. About the controversy, Frye writes that "intensity of speculative thought is in direct proportion to its verbalism. This is symbolized by the fact that the crisis in the world's mental history, the Athanasian-Arian struggle over the definition of the Trinity, was focussed on literally a single iota of difference" (42.45). The Council of Nicea ruled in favor of Arius's iota, rejecting identity in favor of similarity. In the passage quoted, I have italicized Frye's "1."

70. These plans are inferred from what Frye says in Notebook 30n, a relatively early notebook devoted to the study of language, and from one of his early outlines for a book on the Bible and its imaginative contexts, which was to have an eighth chapter devoted to occult traditions, including those of the Renaissance Kabbalists Pico della Mirandola (1463–94) and Johannes Reuchlin (1455–1522). See 42.28 and 34.86.

71. Frye himself notes the connection in *RT,* 302.

72. In the holograph notebook the words I have put in square brackets, Frye's answers to his own quiz, were written above the line. In Notebook 34 we have another Kabbalistic riot of free association, which Frye laughingly suggests is not unlike a hashish-induced vision:

> Adam & atom are the same word, the invulnerable or adamant subject contemplating the undividable unit of the object. The root F-R is common to Africa & to Pharaoh, & is linked (by me) with αφρος, foam, as the similar

M-R root of America means sea. The similarity in form between Africa & America is due partly to a tri-consonantal root, F-R-K or F-R-H (I suppose the h in Pharaoh is a guttural) in one case and M-R-K or M-L-K in the other. The M-R-K root of America is also found in Mexico, which with its guttural Spanish x is the same word as America. Its variant is the Hebrew malek, king, & in such reminiscent names as Amalek. The A-T-L root of Atlas & Atlantis is found, as I think Blavatsky says, in the 'atl' ending so frequent in Aztec, & in the vanished root $\star\tau\lambda\alpha\omega$ from which Atlas is supposed to be derived, and which must have a foreign appearance in Greek, as the $\tau\lambda$ combination is nowhere found in Greek except in derivatives of this hypothetical root. I think very early an opposition between L & R similar to the one suggested by the initial letters of the modern left & right must have existed in the Atlantean language. One form gives us Atlas, the other Atreus, the eponymous ancestor of Greek tragedy. Note alma [kind] & arma [weapons] in Latin, & the connotations of altus [great] & atra [black]. I imagine Arthur derives from this, as do Tartarus & tellus [earth]. Note English lamb & ram. The A-M-N combination seems to be common to the Egyptian chief god Amon, the Hebrew amen, & the Indian om mani. An M-R root, part of America, is common to Mary, maris (sea), mariah (bitter) & so on; perhaps Hamlet continues an allied tradition. Italy, also called Hesperia, preserves the $\tau\lambda$ root of Atlantis; the Hesperidean kingdom. The critical part of me makes no comment except that none of it is any sillier than the derivation of American from the Christian name of Vespucci, which is unquestioned everywhere. *Finnegans Wake,* with its Mark & Armorica patterns coinciding, has some of it; Blavatsky may have some more. Note Madoc in the M-R-K pattern. Well, in Latin (notice the l-t in the word, which makes it an analogy of Italy as Roma is of the reversed form preserved in amor: this is in FW [*Finnegans Wake*] & perhaps implied even in Dante, where Maro [Virgil] illustrates a third form) the alt & lat roots express expansion into height, depth & breadth; the art & rat roots express fitting together, articulation (the original sense of *ars*) & reasoning. Maybe I should try hashish. However, I shall publish nothing unless I can hide behind somebody's skirts, & I suspect there are a fair number of skirts. Even the Anglo-Israelites, precisely because they are so wrong, must have a kernel of vision, & the IBR root (cf. Welsh idris) is in Hebrew, Iberian & British. This form is a modulation of the MRK root, as the word Eborecum shows, & hence York is the chief city of America. Wonder if the MRK root is a point about alchemical Mercury. (34.69–70)

One of the skirts to hide behind is made of Kabbalistic cloth.

73. For the other brief references to alchemy, see *SE,* 137, 141, and 402.

74. Spengler had written, "The Arabian Culture owned the arabesque and cavern-vaulting of the mosque, and out of this world-feeling there issued *Alchemy* with its ideas of mysterious efficient substantialities like the 'philosoph-

ical mercury,' which is neither a material nor a property but some thing that underlies the coloured existence of metals and can transmute one metal into another." *The Decline of the West,* 1:382; see also 248, 383, 393.

75. About Percival's book Frye says that it "is a remarkable essay in this field, the main achievement of which is to establish a number of analogous patterns between Blake's symbolism and the symbols of astrology, alchemy, and cabbalism. The disadvantage of the book for the Blake student is that in establishing analogues to such symbols as the 'Seven Eyes' the author frequently fails to lay the primary emphasis on the (usually Biblical) source. But, with this reservation, Percival's book is a study that will become steadily more useful and enlightening as Blake's own argument becomes more clearly understood, and as the morphology of occult systems of thought becomes better established." "William Blake," in *The English Romantic Poets and Essayists* (1957 ed.), 21.

76. Herbert Silberer, *Hidden Symbolism of Alchemy and the Occult Arts,* 216.

77. Robert Fludd (1574–1637) was a Renaissance hermeticist and exponent of Rosicrucianism. He makes a brief appearance in Silberer's *Hidden Symbolism* (175), and Frye had read about him in the four Frances Yates books that he annotated (see n. 60, above). The Fifth Monarchists were a group of seventeenth-century millennialists who for a while followed Oliver Cromwell, believing that his government would usher in the reign of Christ.

78. "Forming Fours," *NFCL,* 117–29. The first part of the review (117–25) is devoted to Jung's *Two Essays on Analytical Psychology.*

79. "Forming Fours," 128. For a perceptive account of the alchemical interpretations of the Bible, see Thomas Willard, "Alchemy and the Bible," in *Centre and Labyrinth: Essays in Honour of Northrop Frye,* ed. Eleanor Cook, et al. (Toronto: Univ. of Toronto Press, 1983), 115–27.

80. "Forming Fours," 129.

81. The others are Maud Bodkin, Jessie Weston, Gertrude Levy, Helen Flanders Dunbar, Madame Blavatsky, Enid Welsford, Jane Harrison, Bertha Phillpotts, and Ruth Benedict (*TBN,* 71).

82. See *LN,* 2:618, 621. Interestingly, in *The Great Code,* one of the four places in his published work where Frye refers to Yates, the issue of dating becomes important: he calls on her knowledge to distinguish between the oral tradition about Hermes Trismegistus, which associated him with the wisdom of ancient Egypt, and the written records, which come from the early Christian era (205).

83. For an excellent account of Frye and memory theaters, see Imre Salusinszky, "Frye and the Art of Memory," in *Rereading Frye,* 39–54.

84. The references to Dürer, Chapman, Burton, and Milton appear to be indebted to Frances Yates's *The Occult Philosophy in the Elizabethan Age,* 156–71.

85. See Frye's more extensive reading of the Byzantium poems in "The Top of the Tower: A Study of the Imagery of Yeats," *StS,* 276–77.

86. Mircea Eliade, *The Forge and the Crucible: The Origins and Structures of Alchemy* (New York: Harper & Row, 1971).

87. In Notebook 21 Frye identifies the book turned-on-its-side with Ignoramus (the seventh part of the ogdoad) and in Notebook 24 with Anticlimax (the third part). See *RT,* 170, 182; *TBN,* 324.

88. In still another version of the same idea Frye says that the third part of his projected third book "doesn't deal with the circle as such, but works alchemically from Nomos & Nous, W to E, the Adonis-Hermes & the Prometheus-Eros quadrants being taken together as unities. It's of course Biblical, historical, & deals with literature as an informing power: the existing world (Nomos) & the world that completes existence (Nous) are finally related" (*TBN,* 241–42).

89. *Selected Letters of Stéphane Mallarmé,* ed. and trans. Rosemary Todd (Chicago: Univ. of Chicago Press, 1988), 76.

90. "Three Meanings of Symbolism," *Yale French Studies* 9 (1952): 11–19; and "The Symbol as a Medium of Exchange," *MM,* 28–43. Frye remarked to Patricia Parker that one of the several things that he and Paul de Man had in common "was the powerful influence on both of them of the poetics of Mallarmé." "What's a Meta Phor?" in *Visionary Poetics: Essays on Northrop Frye's Criticism,* ed. Robert D. Denham and Thomas Willard (New York: Peter Lang, 1991), 113–14.

91. "Response," *Eighteenth-Century Studies* 24 (Winter 1990–91): 245. A condensed version of the remark is in Notebook 44, quoted as an epigraph to chapter 1 in the present volume: "The 'subject' swallows everything objective to it: hence the pan-historical critics of today, the Hegelian pan-philosophical absolute knowledge, the pan-literary universe which only three people understand: Blake, Mallarmé, and myself. The *final* answer, naturally, is interpenetration" (*LN,* 1:247).

92. The quotations come from *LN,* 1:41, 182, 202, 303, and 43, respectively.

93. Mallarmé had flirted with the idea of entitling one volume of his lyrics *The Glorious Lie.* See his letter to Henry Cazalis, 28? April 1866, *Selected Letters,* 60.

94. These two meanings are similar to the conclusions of a 1966 Italian conference intended to characterize Gnosticism in ways that would be useful to scholars. See Ugo Bianchi, ed., *The Origins of Gnosticism/Le origini dello Gnosticismo: Colloquium of Messina, 13–18 April 1966,* Numen Book Series, no. 12 (Leiden: Brill, 1967).

95. Hans Jonas, *The Gnostic Religion: The Message of the Alien God and the Beginnings of Christianity* (Boston: Beacon Press, 1958); *The Nag Hammadi Library: in English,* ed. James McConkey Robinson (San Francisco: Harper & Row, 1981); *The Gnostic Scriptures: A New Translation with Annotations and Introductions by Bentley Layton* (Garden City, N.Y.: Doubleday, 1987); *Pistis Sophia: A Gnostic Miscellany,* trans. G. R. S. Mead, 2nd rev. ed. (London: John M. Watkins, 1963). Annotated copies of all of these books except *The Gnostic Scriptures,* which Frye cites in *WP,* 318, are in the Northrop Frye Library.

96. In *The Gnostic Dialogue: The Early Church and the Crisis of Gnosticism*

(New York: Paulist Press, 1980), Perkins argues against the thesis of Pagels's *The Gnostic Gospels* (New York: Vintage, 1979) that the Gnostics represented the spirit of creative individualism as opposed to the authoritarian orthodoxy of early Christianity.

97. For Frye's treatment of these themes, see *SE,* 150, 162, 183, 198–99; *WP,* 144; *LN,* 1:147, 170, 204, 251, 262, 276, 311, 348, 350, 393–94, 2:445, 451; *RT,* 86, 229, 247, 356; *TBN,* 330; *CP,* 121–22.

98. The tale is reproduced in Jonas, *The Gnostic Religion,* rev. ed (Boston: Beacon Press, 1963), 113–16. Frye is quoting from the *The Apocryphal New Testament: Being the Apocryphal Gospels, Acts, Epistles, and Apocalypses: with Other Narratives and Fragments,* trans. Montague Rhodes James (Oxford: Clarendon Press, 1924), 411ff., an annotated copy of which is in the Northrop Frye Library. On the *Hymn of the Pearl,* see also 10.21; 54-4.63, 125; 56.51; *LN,* 1:35, and 2:460, where Frye says, "Jessie Weston's book [*From Ritual to Romance*] was based, I should think, on the Gnostic fallacy of diving for the pearl at the bottom of the sea. There isn't any pearl at the bottom: it's suffered a sea-change into the sea itself."

99. This distinction between the conceptual and the mythological is present in Jonas, who speaks of the "tenets" of Gnostic thought, but adds that "whatever heights of conceptualization gnostic theory attained to in individual thinkers, there is an indissoluble mythological core to gnostic thought as such. Far remote from the rarefied atmosphere of philosophical reasoning, it moves in the denser medium of imagery and personification" (*The Gnostic Religion,* 46–47). Frye's annotated copy of the 1958 Beacon Press edition is in the Northrop Frye Library.

100. The phrase "gigantic gnosis" also appears as an annotation at the end of the abstract for chap. 99 in *The Book of the Dead,* ed. E. A. Wallis Budge (London: Kegan Paul, Trench, Tubner & Co., 1938), clxxvii. Chap. 99 contains instructions enabling the dead soul to sail a magical boat to Sekhet-hetep, the Egyptian version of the Elysian Fields. The deceased was obliged to name the parts of the boat, each of which was identified with a divine figure. For Frye, the *gnosis* in this ritual apparently has to do with power attached to divine names (words with power) or with the fact that knowledge of names is knowledge of divine identity. Frye was an assiduous reader of *The Book of the Dead:* his copy of the book contains more than 400 marginal annotations and hundreds of other marked passages.

6. Kook Books and the Occult

1. Although Frye read and occasionally refers in his notebooks to hermetic writers of late antiquity (Porphyry, Iamblichus, Proclus) and of the early Christian periods (Clement of Alexandria and Pseudo-Dionysius), his comments are too negligible to infer anything substantial about his attitude toward them.

2. For "Akasa," see above, chap. 5, text at n. 8 and note. "Vril," from Edward Bulwer-Lytton's *The Coming Race,* is a "beneficent and all-purpose force," a "unity in natural energetic agencies." "Od force" or "odyle" is the name Baron von Reichenbach gave to the force or emanations emitted by objects in his various experiments with clairvoyants and mediums. "Elan vital" is the life force that Henri Bergson says differentiates human beings from other forms of life. Philostratus's biography of Apollonius of Tyana, which Frye read, shows this neo-Pythagorean to be a miracle worker and magician. Count Alessandro Cagliostro (1743–95) was an Italian adventurer and magician who performed his various occult arts (psychic healing, alchemy) throughout the courts of Europe. Edmund Dantès is the hero of Alexander Dumas's *The Count of Monte Cristo.*

3. For these associations, see *TBN,* 188, 231, 241, 283, 285; *LN,* 1:57, 2:569–70, 618, 622; *RT,* 371; and 18.51.

4. Asimov's series begins with the trilogy *Foundation, Foundation and Empire,* and *Second Foundation* (1942–50) and now includes more than a dozen titles. An annotated copy of *Foundation* is in the Northrop Frye Library. Frank Herbert's Dune Chronicles include *Dune* (1968), *Dune Messiah* (1969), *Children of Dune* (1976), and *God Emperor of Dune* (1981). An annotated copy of *Dune* is in the Northrop Frye Library. Roger Zelazny's Amber novels include *Nine Princes of Amber* (1970), *The Guns of Avalon* (1972), *Sign of the Unicorn* (1975), *The Hand of Oberon* (1976), and *The Courts of Chaos* (1978). Annotated copies of the first three are in the Northrop Frye Library. Philip José Farmer's Riverworld series includes *To Your Scattered Bodies Go* (1971), *Riverboat* (1971), *The Dark Design* (1977), and *The Magic Labyrinth* (1981). LeGuin's trilogy is *A Wizard of Earthsea* (1968), *The Tombs of Atuan* (1971), and *The Farthest Shore* (1972). An annotated copy of *A Wizard of Earthsea* is in the Northrop Frye Library. Eric Eddison's Zimiamvia trilogy is *Mistress of Mistresses* (1935), *A Fish Dinner in Memison* (1941), and *The Mezentian Gate* (1958). Annotated copies of all three are in the Northrop Frye Library. William Morris's series includes *The Wood beyond the World* (1894), *The Well at the World's End* (1896), and *The Sundering Flood* (1897), annotated copies of which are in the Northrop Frye Library.

5. Annotated copies of all these titles and of Fuller's *The Critical Path* and *Intuition* are in the Northrop Frye Library. The source of Erwin Schrödinger's remark "Consciousness is a singular of which the plural is unknown" is his *What Is Life? The Physical Aspect of the Living Cell* (Cambridge: Cambridge Univ. Press, 1947), 90. Frye quotes the passage in his sermon "A Breath of Fresh Air," *NFR,* 334, and in *MM,* 122. Frye's spelling of "Merejkowski" follows the spelling on the cover of *Atlantis/Europe.* The title page has the more common "Merezhkovsky."

6. *LN,* 1:58, 2:717.

7. We know from *LN,* 1:290, that Frye read Charles Fort (1874–1932), considered by some to be the father of modern paranormal investigation. Fort wrote four books about extraordinary phenomena inexplicable by conventional means. They were collected into a single volume, *The Books of Charles Fort* (New

York: Holt, 1941), an annotated copy of which is in the Northrop Frye Library. In *AC* Frye writes, "Charles Fort, one of the few who have continued the tradition of intellectual satire in this century, brings the wheel full circle by mocking the scientists for their very freedom from superstition itself, a rational attitude which, like all rational attitudes, still refuses to examine all the evidence" (231).

8. Louis Pauwels and Jacques Bergier, *The Morning of the Magicians,* trans. Rollo Meyers (New York: Avon, 1963), xxvi.

9. Pauwels, *The Morning of the Magicians,* xxix. For a comprehensive summary of the book see R. T. Gault, "The Quixotic Dialectical Metaphysical Manifesto: *Morning of the Magicians,*" www.cafes.net/ditch/motm1.htm.

10. Frye's copy of *The Morning of the Magicians* (St. Albans [England]: Mayflower, 1975), 185, top margin.

11. "[I]f you look carefully at the book [*FS*], and even more at the footnotes, you'll see it's a very anxious, troubled book. It's written with the horror of Nazism just directly in front of it all the time. When I first read Rosenberg's *Myth of the Twentieth Century*—the big Nazi bible, about the Atlantis myths and the Nordic heroes and so forth—it just sent the shudders up my spine. If this kind of thing had prevailed in the world, everybody would not only be reading him, but thinking that Blake thought that way too." "Northrop Frye," an interview in Imre Salusinszky, *Criticism in Society* (New York: Methuen, 1987), 41. "People often don't realize how much the Blake book was haunted by the Nazi movement." "Northrop Frye on Literature and Religion," an interview with Andrew Kaufman, *The Newspaper* (University of Toronto), 27 October 1982, 5.

12. Ferguson expected an imminent transformation. Frye read the 1980 edition of her book *The Aquarian Conspiracy: Personal and Social Transformation in the 1980s* (Los Angeles: J. P. Tarcher). Deciding apparently to extend the time for the "conspiracy" to succeed, Ferguson changed the subtitle of the second edition (1987) to *Personal and Social Transformation in Our Time.*

13. Rudy Rucker, *Infinity and the Mind: The Science and Philosophy of the Infinite* (New York: Bantam, 1983), xi.

14. Hanegraaff, *New Age Religion and Western Culture,* 58.

15. Ken Wilber, *The Spectrum of Consciousness* (Wheaton, Ill.: Theosophical Publishing House, 1977). An annotated copy is in the Northrop Frye Library.

16. See "Reflections on the New-Age Paradigm: An Interview with Ken Wilber," in *The Holograph Paradigm and Other Paradoxes,* ed. Ken Wilber (Boston: Shambhala, 1985), 249–94.

17. Stanislav Grof, *Realms of the Human Unconscious: Observations from LSD Research* (London: Souvenir Press, 1975), 177. Frye's annotated edition (New York: Dutton, 1976) has the same pagination.

18. Robert Anton Wilson, *Cosmic Trigger,* vol. 1: *Final Secret of the Illuminati* (Tempe, Ariz.: New Falcon Publications, 1986). Frye owned the 1978 Simon and Schuster edition.

19. One of the several online editions of *The Principia Discordia* is available at www.illuminatus.net/princ1.html.

20. *Henry IV, Part 2,* 5.3.90. Cf. John Heywood, "An ill winde that bloweth no man to good." *Proverbes,* pt. 2, chap. 9.

21. Wilson, *Cosmic Trigger,* 59.

22. Ibid., 15.

23. Ibid., 111.

24. Itzhak Bentov, *Stalking the Wild Pendulum: On the Mechanics of Consciousness* (Rochester, Vt.: Destiny Books, 1988), chap. 4. Frye read and annotated the 1979 Bantam edition.

25. Bentov is not mentioned in Hanegraaff's *New Age Religion and Western Culture,* and he receives only passing notice in a footnote in Ferguson's *Aquarian Conspiracy.*

26. See, e.g., Ken Wilber, "Physics, Mysticism, and the New Holographic Paradigm," in *The Holographic Paradigm and Other Paradoxes,* 157–86; and Jeremy Bernstein, "A Cosmic Flow," *American Scholar* 48 (Winter 1978–79): 6–9.

27. Bentov, *Stalking the Wild Pendulum,* 101, 108.

28. Ibid., 11–12, 120–21.

29. Some have argued that the lost civilization of Atlantis was the Aegean island Thera.

30. Literally, "the golden egg or embryo," the Hiranyagarbha is a new-birth or purification rite by which the Brahman becomes a cosmic soul. It is first described in the Atharva-Veda Parishishta. The ceremony is explained in Mircea Eliade, *Rites and Symbols of Initiation: The Mysteries of Birth and Rebirth* (New York: Harper, 1958), 56.

31. Michael Baigent, Richard Leigh, and Henry Lincoln, *Holy Blood, Holy Grail* (New York: Dell, 1983), 406.

32. On the Melchizedek figure of Gen. 14 and Pss. 2 and 100, see *GC,* 178–79.

33. Baigent, Leigh, and Lincoln do not refer to an Antichrist, but see *Holy Blood, Holy Grail,* 106–7, 410–11.

34. Frye has an interesting note on the Italian roots of aesthetics based on mathematic form: "The insistence on number as the basis of beauty is almost uniformly Italian, for even Pythagoras came from Magna Graecia; it's in Dante [&] the great Florentines, Michelangelo being Yeats' example; it's in Fascist Marinetti futurism with its roots in Machiavelli; Galileo & Vico; it's in Croce's apotheosis of aesthetics, for the numbered form is part of the aesthetic fallacy, ideal forms being, as I've said, conceptions of propriety & decorum rather than beauty" (31.52).

35. For an explanation of the further intricacies of this pattern, see my *Northrop Frye and Critical Method,* 76–85.

36. In *Infinity and the Mind* Rucker remarks, in an account of the special significance of the number ten, that the "Pythagorean would feel quite at home in a bowling alley, ritually building and destroying the *tetradactys* with a sphere

punctuated by a triad of holes, and recording his progress with a series of numbers inscribed in squares" (59). The *tetradactys* was for the Pythagoreans a triangular symbol composed of ten dots moving upward from a base of four, like the arrangement of pins in a bowling alley. Frye's marginalia beside Rucker's comparison—"quite a flash of insight"—seems to refer only to the clever image Rucker used to describe what for the Pythagoreans was the sacred pattern of the fourth triangular number.

37. See *TBN,* 130, 282, 283, and 325.

38. From 1991 accession, box 28, file 4j. On 11:32, see also *RT,* 228.

39. The number seventy-eight appears throughout books 4 and 5 of *Gargantua and Pantagruel:* seventy-eight hogsheads, seventy-eight pieces of high-warp tapestry, seventy-eight kinds of complaints, seventy-eight thousand parasangs in length and breadth, seventy-eight standards, seventy-eight thousand royal Chitterlings, seventy-eight galleys and frigates, seventy-eight stairs, and so on.

40. See C. G. Jung, *Synchronicity: An Acausal Connecting Principle,* trans. R. F. C. Hull (Princeton, N.J.: Princeton Univ. Press, 1973). Frye's source was the three-essay collection *The Interpretation of Nature and the Psyche; Synchronicity: An Acausal Connecting Principle,* by C. G. Jung; *The Influence of Archetypal Ideas on the Scientific Theories of Kepler,* by W. Pauli (New York: Pantheon Books, 1955).

41. Jacob Boehme, *The Signature of All Things* (Cambridge: James Clarke, 1981), 12. This is a reprinting of the J. M. Dent edition (London, 1934), which is the edition Frye annotated with more than seventy marginalia.

42. Frye does say that the first cycle of his projected one hundred–chapter book is solstitial (*RT,* 136), but that remark is equally mysterious.

43. The *eniautos-daimon* was a projection of the year festivals among the Greeks—a god who died for his people, sometimes a bull-god, a god born of his own sacrifice. The phrase *eniautos-daimon* was not actually used by the Greeks themselves, who called their year *daimones* by a number of different names. Frye's source for the *eniautos-daimon* was Jane Ellen Harrison's *Themis: A Study of the Social Origins of Greek Religion* (London: Merlin Press, 1977), chaps. 6 and 8.

44. Frye also observes that Cumont links Chaldean astrology "with the neo-Pythagoreans (Philostratus *and,* apparently, Heliodorus' *Aethiopica*)" (*RT,* 245). Frye had read Philostratus's *Life of Apollonius* in the late 1960s or early 1970s, Apollonius emerging for him as a magus of the Prospero type (*RT,* 214). In his published and unpublished writings Frye does not associate Heliodorus's romance, which he had read in preparing for his Norton Lectures at Harvard (*SeS*), with anything particularly magical. Two annotated translations of *Aethiopica* are in the Northrop Frye Library.

45. This passage is the basis for diagram 5, in chap. 5.

46. The horizontal axis is a reversal of what is frequently found in Frye's west-to-east schematic for Nomos-Nous. Similarly, he changes the quadrants

ordinarily occupied by Eros, Adonis, Hermes, and Prometheus. Here the order is, moving clockwise from twelve o'clock, Adonis, Hermes, Prometheus, and Eros.

47. Ioan Petru Culianu, "Astrology," *Encyclopedia of Religion,* ed. Mircea Eliade (New York: Macmillan, 1987), 1:472.

48. The analogy of Frye's alphabet of forms to Chomsky's syntactic rules suggests itself. Both rely on a finite set of principles to create an infinite number of sentences (in Chomsky's case) and literary works (in Frye's).

49. The phrase occurs four times in *TBN,* 110–12. See also *LN,* 1:130 and *TBN,* 183. In his 1952 diary Frye speaks of his theory of modes that appeared five years later as the First Essay of *Anatomy of Criticism* as a "conspectus or alphabet of themes" (*D,* 534).

50. Piers Anthony, *God of Tarot* (1979), *Vision of Tarot* (1980), and *Faith of Tarot* (1981), annotated copies of which are in the Northrop Frye Library. Anthony provides an elaborate key to his use of the Tarot in an appendix to each of the volumes. The three books were published in a single volume *Tarot* in 1987.

51. The phrase "ineffable in zero" comes from Waite's preface to Papus, *The Tarot of the Bohemians: The Absolute Key to Occult Science* (North Hollywood, Calif.: Wilshire Book Co., [1970]), xii, an annotated copy of which is in the Northrop Frye Library.

52. On the containing form of what Frye calls the "alpha-omega book," see *TBN,* 110–11; *LN,* 1:79, 130, 2:555.

53. Frye's information about Cayce came primarily from Jess Stearn's *Edgar Cayce—The Sleeping Prophet* (New York: Bantam Books, 1971). An annotated copy is in the Northrop Frye Library. Frye would also have known about Edgar Cayce from Pike's *The Other Side,* where Cayce speaks through one of the bishop's channelers, George Daisley. See James A. Pike, *The Other Side: An Account of My Experience with Psychic Phenomena* (New York: Dell, 1968), 160–66.

54. Jane Roberts, *The "Unknown" Reality: A Seth Book,* 2 vols. (vol. 1, New York: Prentice-Hall, 1977; vol. 2, Englewood Cliffs, N.J.: Prentice-Hall, 1979). An annotated copy is in the Northrop Frye Library.

55. James Merrill, *The Changing Light at Sandover* (New York: Atheneum, 1984). The opening of Merrill's poem, incidentally, includes a reference to Frye:

> Saw my way
> To a plot, or as much of one as still allowed
> For surprise and pleasure in its working-out.
> Knew my setting; and had, from the start, a theme
> Whose steady light shone back, it seemed, from every
> Least detail exposed to it. I came
> To see it as an old, exalted one:
> The incarnation and withdrawal of
> A god. That last phrase is Northrop Frye's. (4)

The phrase comes from *AC,* 158.

56. Although Pike's *The Other Side* is not among the books in Frye's personal library, the eight entries in the notebooks having to do with Pike's disturbing tale indicate that he had almost certainly read the book, although he was surely familiar with Pike as well from the numerous accounts in the media and the popular press: Pike first publicly revealed on a Toronto television program that he had received messages from his son, the program having been arranged by an acquaintance of Pike, the religion editor of the Toronto *Star.*

57. W. H. Auden, *Collected Poems,* ed. Edward Mendelson (New York: Random House, 1976), 304.

58. Although Frye read and annotated Loomis's *The Grail: From Celtic Myth to Christian Symbol* (Cardiff: Univ. of Wales Press, 1963), his critique of Loomis is taken directly from John C. Wilson's introduction to Waite's *The Holy Grail: The Galahad Quest in the Arthurian Literature* (New Hyde Park, N.Y.: University Books, 1961), x–xii. Frye's annotated copies of both books are in the Northrop Frye Library.

59. See "On Value-Judgements," in *StS,* 66–73.

60. See, e.g., Philip Marchand, "Frye's Diaries Confirm McLuhan's Suspicion," *Toronto Star,* 30 November 2002.

7. The Dialogue and Its *Aufhebung*

1. In *Fearful Symmetry* the words "cycle" and "cyclic" form a refrain throughout, occurring 175 times.

2. Frye makes this point about Jesus' declaration in a number of places. See, e.g., *WP,* 94; *LN,* 1:155, 156, 159, 262.

3. And in a similar vein: "I haven't the least objection to having it said that my religion is essentially my own creation" (*LN,* 2:467).

4. The only other instance of Frye's pairing of "Word" and "Spirit" in a dialogical context in *Words with Power* is in the chapter on "Identity and Metaphor": "The ideal harmony of Word and Spirit in the New Testament is often thought of as restoring the kind of awareness that Adam had before the fall. In any case it points to some kind of union between the imaginative and the actual that we have not yet identified" (90). Frye does not use the pairing in his commentary on the Tom o' Bedlam passage, but the prophetic word and spirit are, as we have seen, part of his speculations on the ballad stanza in one of the late notebooks.

5. Frye in fact refers to the "dialectic of Word and Spirit" in *LN,* 1:100.

6. For Frye's exposition of this scheme, see *LN,* 2:471. For briefer expositions, see *LN,* 2:479, 508, 509, 524, 579, 582.

7. "Urthonas Spectre terrified beheld the Spectres of the Dead / Each Male formd without a counterpart without a concentering vision." *The Four Zoas,* in Blake, *Complete Poetry and Prose,* 369.

8. The cyclical and dialectical principles were for Frye the "two great structural principles of literature" (54-8.70).

9. For a fuller discussion of the HEAP scheme, see my introduction to *LN*, xxx–xxxi, and Dolzani's introduction to *TBN*, xxvii–xxxii.

10. See Dolzani's cogent account of this transformation in his introduction to *TBN*, xxx, and his discussion of the importance of "the vertical axis," xxxiv–xxxvi.

11. See *WP*, 89 and 133. Cf. "[T]he unifying sense comes particularly from the Spirit of love and community, and the individualizing one from the Word, the two-edged sword that divides and discriminates, in the mental, spiritual and physical life" (*LN*, 1:301). See also *LN*, 1:281, where Frye wonders if Word does not represent "all distinction & separation" and Spirit "all union and reconciliation." He also tried to work out, not altogether successfully, the relation of the four gods to Blake's Four Zoas. There are two notebook efforts to illustrate the archetype-Zoa correspondence (*LN*, 1:57 and 272). For a less expansive effort, one that deals with Urizen and Orc, see *WP*, 244–45.

12. See, e.g., *WP*, 247; *MM*, 87; "Vision and Cosmos," in *Biblical Patterns in Modern Literature*, ed. David H. Hirsch and Nehama Aschkenasy (Chico, Calif.: Scholars Press, 1984), 5.

13. See *TBN*, 75.

14. Untitled autobiographical notes, typescript in the Northrop Frye Fonds, 1991 accession, box 49, file 3; cf. "Around twelve or thirteen I suddenly realized that I didn't believe in the dogmas of Biblical religion, and started breathing mental oxygen" (unpublished typescript, 1991 accession, box 50, file 1).

15. John Ayre, *Northrop Frye: A Biography*, 44.

16. Letter 268, to T. W. Higginson, in *The Letters of Emily Dickinson* (Cambridge, Mass.: Harvard Univ. Press, 1958), 2:412. For the "confiscated gods," see Poem 1260 ("Because that you are going"), in *The Poems of Emily Dickinson*, ed. Thomas H. Johnson (Cambridge, Mass.: Belknap Press, 1958), 3:875–76. Frye elsewhere refers to the phrase in *WP*, 134; *NFR*, 132; *RT*, 150, 321; and in *LN*, 1:181, 351, 2:615.

17. Sixteen of Frye's prayers are in *NFR*, 373–85. Among the Frye papers at Victoria College are typescripts of five prayers that are as yet unpublished.

18. Paul's distinction between the *soma psychikon* and *soma pneumatikon* was an important one for Frye in his later writing. See *GC*, 20, 56; *WP*, 124–25; *DV*, 14; and "Lacan et la parole dans sa plénitude," *Ornicar* 33 (April–June 1985): 12. His fullest exposition of the difference is in one of his Bible lectures:

> Paul, in speaking of how to read the Bible, in 1 Corinthians, 2:14–15, says: "But the natural man receiveth not the things of the Spirit of God: for they are foolishness unto him: neither can he know them, because they are spiritually discerned." Verse 15: "But he that is spiritual judgeth all things, yet he himself is judged of no man." He's discriminating there between the spiritual man, the spiritual body, the *pneumatikos,* and what the King James Version translates as the "natural man." But the King James Version is

struggling with the fact that there is no adjective in English for "soul" corresponding to "spiritual." Because what Paul says is the *soma psychikos* for "natural man," the man with the soul; in other words, Paul is drawing the essential line not between the physical body and the soul, but between the soul and the spirit. And the *soma psychikos,* the soul-body complex, seems to be a part of what he means elsewhere by "flesh and blood" as distinct from "spirit," which is of course a metaphor from "breath" and expresses the sense of a life which includes the bodily life. (*RT,* 502).

Frye had little patience with conceptions of the soul, whatever their source, and even less if the soul were divorced from the body. The word *spirit* for him did not imply such a disjunction. Spirit is incarnational: it transforms the body.

19. Cf. "The Bible turns on a *social* consciousness moving from centre to circumference & back again, a paradox resolved by interpenetration" (*RT,* 216). Also: "That God may be all in one: that's the text for interpenetration. I notice that Jung misquotes it as *one* in all, because he thinks of unity and reconciliation as the end" (*RT,* 339). The reference is to C. G. Jung, *Mysterium Coniunctionis,* trans. R. F. C. Hull, 2nd ed. (New York: Pantheon, 1970), 471.

20. Joachim of Fiore's doctrine of the three ages—of the Father, the Son, and the Holy Spirit—was developed in his *Liber Figurarum* and *Expositio in Apocalypism.* See Delno C. West and Sandra Zindars-Swartz, *Joachim of Fiore* (Bloomington: Indiana Univ. Press, 1983), 10–29. References to Joachim are scattered through Frye's work: *LN,* 1:47, 63, 202, 223, 2:630, 640, 651, 714, 720; *TBN,* 101, 198, 202; *RT,* 17, 276, 323, 404; 32.102; *D,* 86, 234, 250–51, 276; *GC,* 85; *DV,* 66; *NFR,* 262; *SE,* 210, 211, 223. An earlier holograph version of the passage about Joachim in *The Double Vision* (58) is on a small card in the 1991 accession, box 28, file 3.

Index

Italicized page numbers refer to diagrams and charts.